SEPARATED BY THEIR SEX

SEPARATED BY THEIR SEX

WOMEN IN PUBLIC AND PRIVATE IN THE COLONIAL ATLANTIC WORLD

MARY BETH NORTON

CORNELL UNIVERSITY PRESS
Ithaca and London

First published 2011 by Cornell University Press

Printed in the United States of America

Library of Congress Cataloging-in-Publication Data

Norton, Mary Beth.
    Separated by their sex : women in public and private in the colonial Atlantic world / Mary Beth Norton.
        p. cm.
    Includes bibliographical references and index.
    ISBN 978-0-8014-4949-9 (cloth : alk. paper)
    1. Women—United States—History.   2. Women—Great Britain—History.   3. Women in public life—United States—History.   4. Women in public life—Great Britain—History.   5. United States—History—Colonial period, ca. 1600–1775. I. Title.
    HQ1416.N67   2011
    305.40973'09032—dc22   2010044492

Cornell University Press strives to use environmentally responsible suppliers and materials to the fullest extent possible in the publishing of its books. Such materials include vegetable-based, low-VOC inks and acid-free papers that are recycled, totally chlorine-free, or partly composed of nonwood fibers. For further information, visit our website at www.cornellpress.cornell.edu.

Cloth printing   10 9 8 7 6 5 4 3 2 1

For John (J. B.) Heiser

❧ Contents

❧ ILLUSTRATIONS

❧ PREFACE

Separated by Their Sex: Women in Public and Private in the Colonial Atlantic World is, in effect, a "prequel" to my 1980 book, *Liberty's Daughters: The Revolutionary Experience of American Women, 1750–1800*.[1] When I researched and wrote that volume in the mid- to late 1970s, it never occurred to me that many of the cultural patterns I was explicating might have developed only in the early and middle years of the eighteenth century. Yet my research for this book has demonstrated that such was the case. In 1980, I pointed out that many revolutionary-era Anglo-American women were intensely aware of their feminine identity, and that they regarded themselves as inferior to men. I observed that they constantly used words such as "little" and "narrow" to describe their concerns; that they conceived of their role as a confining *private sphere;* and that they believed that the political realm lay outside that sphere.[2] As this book shows, those ideas had developed since 1700, reaching fruition only in the decades of the 1730s and 1740s.

As I worked on *Liberty's Daughters,* I also focused exclusively on colonial manifestations of those ideas and did not explore their transatlantic origins. In the 1970s, early American historians like myself tended to examine the colonies more in isolation than we do now, when the Atlantic-world paradigm has had greater influence on our approaches to colonial history. My research for this book, especially my extensive readings in colonial newspapers, has revealed how much published material in eighteenth-century America originated in the home country. Even when essays were not reprinted from English sources, colonial authors attempted to imitate English models, in both form and content—and in particular they sought to fashion themselves after Joseph Addison and Richard Steele, the influential writers of *The Spectator* and *The Tatler.*[3]

Further, I did not fully realize how much the lives of the women and men I was studying depended on the prosperity of the mid- to late-eighteenth-century colonies. Many, though by no means all, of my female correspondents and diarists lived in towns or on southern plantations; their husbands were primarily merchants, planters, or professional men such as lawyers or clerics. Many were highly literate, had household servants, and enjoyed some leisure time in which they could read and write. That literacy and leisure time, indeed, allowed them to create the very documentary sources I was using and to reflect in their letters and diaries on the circumstances of their lives. Women's leisure and literacy both were recent products of the new prosperity and a culture valuing gentility, which have been the subject of much recent scholarship.[4]

The chronological predecessor of this book—*Founding Mothers and Fathers: Gendered Power and the Forming of American Society,* which covers the period from settlement to approximately 1670—reveals that a century earlier, when the American colonies were considerably less prosperous, cultural assumptions about women's roles differed greatly from those of revolutionary America. First, notions of rigid, gendered divisions between the terms *public* (male) and *private* (female) did not exist, for although there were many widely accepted public/private distinctions, none of them had a gendered dimension. Second, high-ranking women were widely viewed as having appropriate public roles. Indeed, such women's position in society at large resulted more from their high status than from their gender identity. Third, cultural arbiters drew few distinctions between appropriate behaviors for men and women; instead, prescriptive directions for the two sexes resembled each other more than they differed. These observations are elaborated in the pages that follow.[5]

The disjuncture between the ideas about women that prevailed in Anglo-America before 1670 and the notions that dominated thinking and writing about women in 1750 and thereafter prompted the research that has resulted in this book, which places developments of the years 1640–1760 in transatlantic perspective. *Separated by Their Sex* focuses on changing ideas, primarily as related to developing gendered definitions of *public* and *private.* It completes a trilogy examining women and gender in early America, which further includes a fourth volume that considers Salem witchcraft.[6]

The *public* of this book's title encompasses but is not wholly coterminous with the public sphere as outlined by Jürgen Habermas. That Habermasian public sphere could also be referred to as civil society, the context in which citizens discuss and possibly try to influence public policy.[7] For Habermas, the public sphere was separate from the state, but for the purposes of this book the public realm is defined not only as such evaluative discourse but also as political action that took a variety of forms. Here the focus is women's involvement in governmental activities on several levels—as petitioners, observant commentators, and (some men declared) meddlers in matters of policy and partisanship. In assessing women's relationship to the public realm in the decades between 1640 and 1760, I accordingly reconstruct their role as what Margaret Hunt has felicitously termed "state actors."[8]

Separated by Their Sex thus pursues a line of historical inquiry focusing primarily on early modern Anglo-American women's involvement in the realm of public affairs.[9] That subject has been ignored even by historians who have concerned themselves centrally with the development of new ideas about women and gender that originated in England in the first half of the eighteenth century and eventually made their way across the Atlantic to Britain's North American colonies. Those scholars have stressed the contemporary rise of domesticity and the creation of novel notions of feminine and masculine sensibility and polite conduct.[10]

Although examining such developments in depth, researchers have failed to scrutinize the related process through which Anglo-American culture excluded women as a group from the public realm. By neglecting that inquiry, they have in effect assumed that a fundamental characteristic of eighteenth-century gender divisions predated 1700. Yet the insistence that no women should have a public role requires detailed investigation. In fact, the two processes—one confining women to the *private* and domestic, the other barring women from the *public* and political—were intricately intertwined, just as were the definitions of the words *public* and *private*.

The *Oxford English Dictionary* makes the relationship of the two terms clear. The *OED* declares at the outset that as an adjective *public* is "in general, and in most of the senses, the opposite of *private*." Likewise, the initial definition for the adjective *private* states, "restricted to one person or a few persons as opposed to the wider community; largely in opposition to *public*." The words have had many linked meanings in English. Especially relevant to this investigation are a definition of *public* first recorded in the early sixteenth century, "Of, relating to, or designating the business, government, or service of a community or nation"; a now obsolete meaning of *private* as "a person who does not hold any public office or position" (which dates to the late fifteenth century); and the related appearance of the phrases "private family" to refer to "a family in its personal capacity . . . a family household as distinct from an institution" (first noted in 1598) and "private life," defined as "a person's domestic or personal life, as distinct from that relating to his or her employment, official position, public image, etc." (initially used with respect to men only, starting in the sixteenth century). The *OED* includes neither *public sphere* nor *private sphere* in long lists of common phrases created by joining the adjectives with other words, nor does it acknowledge a gender dimension to any of the definitions.[11]

Nevertheless, historians have regularly employed the gendered concepts commonly encompassed in the phrase *separate spheres* as they attempt to comprehend Anglo-American men's and women's lives in the eighteenth and nineteenth centuries. The use of *public* and *private spheres* has aroused considerable commentary.[12] In addition to providing diagnostic tools for current scholars, these categories have been studied to discern whether they prevailed in the past as key cultural precepts. The terms have been subjected to a variety of historical analyses designed to assess whether they accurately depicted reality; frequently, scholars have concluded that they did not. Sometimes the historic and modern categories have been confusingly employed in tandem, as scholars have simultaneously created and applied their own understandings of past and contemporary meanings of the gendered *public* and *private spheres.*[13]

But in spite of the attention accorded the concepts, only a very few scholars have investigated the historic uses of the terms themselves, and no one has studied with precision the ways in which the newly gendered definitions of *public* and *private* and related terminology worked their way into everyday use in Anglo-America. Such an inquiry seems requisite, however, if historians are to understand fully the linguistic and cultural developments which affected people's lives and which have proved historiographically compelling for so many scholars.[14]

That inquiry must start in early- to mid-seventeenth-century Anglo-America, before the gendering of *public* and *private.* At that time, English people believed that high social status rather than gender identified the appropriate wielders of power in both household and state. Aristocratic men and women led society and polity, and ordinary folk of both sexes were expected to defer to them. Such an ungendered axiom calls into question the standard presumption of modern women's historians that sexual difference has determined the nature of every woman's life in all times and places.[15]

Separated by Their Sex identifies the origins and development of gendered notions of the *private,* specifically that meaning which came to be equated with *domestic.* This book examines the process by which masculine and feminine characteristics came to be mapped onto the existing ungendered binary public/private. It seeks to describe with chronological precision the transition from the mid-seventeenth century, when contemporaries did not articulate a belief that women should be confined to a so-called private sphere, to the mid-eighteenth century, when such ideas constituted normative assumptions. How did English people—whether resident in their homeland or in North America—develop their understanding that *no* woman (other than possibly a hereditary monarch) should have a role in public life? How and when did they begin to create an exclusively feminine private sphere and how did that concept develop over time? Such questions inform this book.

Focusing on these concepts necessarily means that *Separated by Their Sex* largely—though not entirely—ignores the reality of women's daily lives in both Britain and the colonies. The gendered meaning of the public/private distinction only peripherally affected many women, especially poorer women, in their quotidian existence. Regional differences further ensured that women's lived experiences diverged in various ways.[16] Yet even so the developing notions of *women's sphere* carried weight; no one could live wholly unaffected by contemporary cultural understandings of how women should behave, or by definitions of appropriate or inappropriate activities for representatives of what came to be termed "the sex." And the fact that in many respects such notions persist to the present day reveals the significance of an investigation of their historical roots in Anglo-American culture.

✍ ACKNOWLEDGMENTS

This book has been a long time in the making. I first realized I would have to write something like it in the late 1980s, when I initially recognized the disjuncture between my research findings about gender definitions in seventeenth-century America and those for the following century, as published in *Liberty's Daughters* (1980). Yet I could not begin to work on it until I finished *Founding Mothers and Fathers* (1996) and *In the Devil's Snare* (2002), although the latter ultimately turned out to be less directly related to the theme of this book than I had anticipated when I started to research Salem witchcraft. Over those many years, I have discussed the project with more people than I can readily recall, so these acknowledgments focus on those who have generously facilitated it more recently and directly.

Separated by Their Sex has taken its transatlantic shape in large part because of the academic year 2005–6, which I spent at the University of Cambridge, as Pitt Professor of American History and Institutions—ironically, researching the English side of the story. Newnham College and the History faculty were welcoming hosts, and Flat 1, 21 Chaucer Road, the Pitt Professor's residence, a remarkable place to live. My special thanks go to Gillian Sutherland and Betty Wood; to colleagues at Newnham, especially Terri Apter, Catherine Seville, and the then-principal, Onora O'Neill; and to Tony Badger, the Paul Mellon Professor of American History. Thanks as well to the helpful staff of the rare book and manuscript room of the University Library, where I spent many hours reading documents and printed materials.

While I was in the United Kingdom, I also worked frequently in London at the British Library, where the reference staff of the rare book room responded helpfully to many inquiries; and I spent a week at the Bodleian Library in Oxford, where my friend Frances Lannon warmly invited me to stay in the Principal's Lodge at Lady Margaret Hall. Ms. Mari Takayanagi of the Parliamentary Archives recently offered valuable assistance.

The bulk of this book was drafted during the 2008–9 academic year, when I was *L.A. Times* Distinguished Fellow at the Huntington Library in

xviii   **ACKNOWLEDGMENTS**

San Marino, California. My friend Roy Ritchie, research director of the Huntington, and the rest of the staff, especially Susi Krasnoo, Carolyn Powell, and the readers' services division, made the year pleasant and productive. Conversations with other long-term fellows over lunch or dinner were both fun and stimulating; thanks for socializing and intellectualizing alike to Barbara Oberg, Joe Roach, Fredrika Teute, Jan Golinski, Julie Kim, LeeAnn Whites, and others, as well as to such local denizens of the Huntington as Terri Snyder, Cynthia Herrup, and Barbara Donagan.

The expansive geographical and chronological scope of this project meant that I received assistance from a number of scholars in a wide variety of historical fields. Warren Billings, Mary Kelley, Joe Roach, and Rachel Weil each commented on a chapter draft. For useful materials, enlightening conversations, or both, I thank Paula Backsheider, Patricia U. Bonomi, Holly Brewer, Sheila Cooper, Dena Goodman, Bernie Herman, Itsie Hull, Barbara Lacey, Mary Ann O'Donnell, Ben Ray, Emma Rothschild, David Shields, Hannah Smith, Randy Sparks, Rachel Weil, Karin Wulf, and especially Margaret Hunt, who helped in several ways. Judy Lucey of the New England Historic Genealogical Society answered a key inquiry. Susan Klepp and Karin Wulf kindly allowed me to consult their edition of the diary of Hannah Callender Sansom before publication, a deed of scholarly generosity for which I am deeply grateful. Bernie Herman graciously located and supplied me with the illustration of house plans in chapter 5.

I presented papers based on different chapters of this book in many venues over the past few years, receiving very constructive comments. Thanks to the History Department colloquia of Cornell University and Ohio State University; to the History and Economics and American History seminars at the University of Cambridge; American Studies groups at the University of London and University of Oxford; and two seminars based at the Huntington Library: USC-Huntington American Origins and UCLA-Huntington Long 18th-Century.

As is always the case, Cornell University and its magnificent libraries served as key supporters of my research throughout the project. The staff of the Interlibrary Loan office was especially helpful in obtaining numerous reels of microfilm for chapter 1. I further thank my research assistants—Lydia Gilbert, Paul Karasick, Jacqueline Kelly, Sara Martinez, and Kim Todt—for vital help in gathering and investigating materials. The Mary Donlon Alger and Return Jonathan Meigs III endowments helped to cover various research costs.

Working with Michael McGandy, my editor at Cornell University Press, has been a genuine pleasure. The comments of two anonymous readers and

Michael's astute editorial assistance have been vital in shaping the final draft of this wide-ranging book.

Finally, this book is dedicated to my dear longtime companion, John (J. B.) Heiser. As a marine biologist, he has scholarly interests very different from my own, yet from the inception of this unusual project he has enthusiastically encouraged it. He has offered his own comments on most of the text as an intelligent, engaged outsider, and he has helped me to understand where concepts and ideas need to be clarified. But most of all and as always, he has simply been his own supportive self. This dedication is but a small return for his many generosities.

Abbreviations

AHN	America's Historical Newspapers online database (Readex)
ANB	John A. Garraty and Mark C. Carnes, eds., *American National Biography* (New York: Oxford University Press, 1999), 24 vols.
BL	British Library, London
EAI	Early American Imprints online database (Readex)
ECCO	Eighteenth-Century Collections Online
EEBO	Early English Books Online
HEHL	Henry E. Huntington Library, San Marino, California
NAM	Edward T. James et al., eds., *Notable American Women* (Cambridge, Mass.: Harvard University Press, 1971), 3 vols.
ODNB	H. C. G. Matthew and Brian Harrison, eds., *Oxford Dictionary of National Biography* (Oxford: Oxford University Press, 2004), 61 vols.
OED	*Oxford English Dictionary*
TNA	The National Archives, London
WMQ	*William and Mary Quarterly*

🍂 SEPARATED BY THEIR SEX

Introduction

> There is no vertue in men so differen wch woemen
> may not hope in some sort to attaine, for e[ven] say-
> ling and warre and goverment of kingdomes have
> been often times well handled by weomen, *Queene
> Dido* may be example for all, or rather *Q Elizabeth* in
> whose tim theis things flourisht.
>
> —Sir Robert Filmer (c. 1588–1653), undated
>
> Poli[ti]cks is what does not become them; the Gov-
> erning Kingdoms and Ruling Provinces are Things
> too difficult and knotty for the fair Sex, it will render
> them grave and serious, and take off those agreeable
> Smiles that should always accompany them.
>
> —*New-York Weekly Journal,* 19 August 1734

The contrasting observations of Sir Robert Filmer, the English political theorist, and an anonymous New Yorker, penned about a century apart, summed up contemporary understandings of women's relationship to politics and governance at the time each author wrote his essay. As was commonplace in the seventeenth century, Filmer, proclaiming women's potential political and military abilities, cited Queen Elizabeth I for evidence of the truth of his assertion. The eighteenth-century American, by contrast, ignored her and all other female monarchs. Moreover, he referred to women in a manner that would have been alien to Filmer, since the term *fair sex* as a synonym for *women* first entered English usage about the time of Filmer's death. That language change alone hints at the significant alteration in the way Anglo-American culture viewed women by the middle decades of the eighteenth century.[1]

Responding to challenges to the authoritarian governmental practices of the Stuart monarchs, Sir Robert Filmer advanced the argument that fathers—metaphorical and actual—ruled, had always ruled, and should always rule. He saw in the family the origins of the polity and analogized between the monarch and the head of the household, conflating the power structures of family and state. For Filmer, authority flowed downward from the top of familial and political hierarchies. To his mind, both fathers and monarchs wielded God-given power.[2]

Yet, ironically, at the same time as Filmer appeared to lodge all power in the hands of fathers, his worldview valued status above gender, as the epigraph demonstrates. He and others interpreted the fifth commandment, "Honor thy father and mother," as the source of authority in state, family, and society alike, viewing its parental terminology as commanding obedience to all superiors. His schema analogizing family and state placed high-ranking women like Queen Elizabeth—who can be termed metaphorical mothers within the meaning of the fifth commandment, whether or not they actually bore children—among the hereditary rulers of society and state as well as household. In so thinking, Filmer was not alone. His contemporaries envisioned society as a hierarchical structure composed of superiors and inferiors; individuals of both sexes owed deference to those above them on the scale and insisted on receiving deference from those below. Although a high-status woman was expected to defer to her husband or father, she rightfully demanded obedience from her social inferiors as well as from her children and servants. The notion that a hierarchy based on rank might give way to one resting on gender—with the consequence that a lower-ranking man would take precedence over a higher-status woman—was literally unthinkable in seventeenth-century England.[3]

Social standing rather than sex thus served as the key determinant of a man's or woman's ability to exercise appropriate authority inside or outside the household. Gender identity did not exclude a woman from the political realm if in other respects she qualified as a wielder of power. Historians of seventeenth-century England have found that high-ranking women (often but not always heiresses and widows) could vote, hold local office, and even occasionally designate members of Parliament for seats their families controlled. So, too, in England's North American colonies the behavior of high-status women revealed their (and others') assumption that they took precedence over ordinary men. In Maryland in early 1648, for instance, the gentlewoman Margaret Brent, while acting in effect as the chief financial officer of the colony for eighteen months, thought it logical to ask the assembly for "vote in the howse for her selfe and voyce allso." Both the assembly's earlier decision to name Brent attorney for the colony's proprietor and her request for the vote and speaking privileges rested firmly on her claim to authority as one of the highest-ranking residents of the colony. Women like herself who wished to do so could pursue political aims without being confronted by the contention that representatives of their sex were categorically excluded from such activity. The notion that *all* women inappropriately entered the public realm, in short, had no place in the thinking of seventeenth-century Anglo-American men and women alike.[4]

The first chapter of this book is designed to demonstrate that proposition. A case study of Lady Frances Berkeley, wife of Virginia's governor during Bacon's Rebellion of 1675–76, it reveals the traditional context within which she maneuvered to achieve her political ends. Lady Frances, an aristocrat by birth and marriage, engaged in behavior recognized and accepted by her contemporaries. Whereas her specific actions sometimes evoked criticism, her political activism in general did not.

By contrast, the subjects of the second chapter, the groups of English-women who petitioned Parliament during the Civil War of the 1640s, lacked such high standing. Thus they encountered very different reactions to their efforts at political organizing. Because most were ordinary women, their claims to political participation constituted radical breaks with the past. Even though they petitioned Parliament three decades before Lady Frances vigorously opposed Bacon and his allies, their actions—and the responses of men to those actions—presaged the future whereas hers represented historic practice. Accordingly, the chapters appear in what might seem to be reverse chronological order.

Conceptually gendering the *public* (political and government affairs) as exclusively male required that gendered manhood, rather than ungendered status, define appropriate wielders of political power. Such a redefinition was developed in England in the wake of the Glorious Revolution of 1688–89. During the ensuing decades, elite eighteenth-century Anglo-American women were instructed that their femininity was more important than their rank in determining their proper public role. And the vehicle for that instruction—both implicit and explicit—was the burgeoning print culture of the Anglo-American world in the 1690s and thereafter. After England abandoned press licensing in 1694, publications of all sorts blossomed, especially in London. The American colonies had few printing presses before the 1730s; thus, most colonials read English publications almost exclusively. Even after such American printers as the Philadelphian Benjamin Franklin began to write and publish their own essays, large quantities of English books and periodicals continued to be imported into North America. The result was that the growing number of literate people on both sides of the Atlantic had regular access to English—or English-imitating—books, magazines, newspapers, and pamphlets. Elite colonists came to pride themselves on their ability to follow genteel cultural norms as explicated by British authors. Such works conveyed consistent prescriptions for men's and women's behavior.[5]

The process of excluding women from the *public* and political—which is traced in chapter 4—was insufficient by itself to create the concomitant gendered category of the *feminine private* as applied to domestic life. Another shift also had to occur: cultural depictions of men's primary identity had to move out of the household context, and men's and women's perceived roles in the household consequently had to change.

Just as the epigraphs contrasted the ideas about women and politics prevalent in the mid-seventeenth and the mid-eighteenth centuries, so two quotations, from 1598 and 1688, respectively, illustrate the related modification of the normative descriptions of men's and women's appropriate functions in the household:

> The governours of families, if (as it is in marriage) there be more then one, upon whom the charge of government lyeth, though unequally, are, first the *Cheefe* governour, which is the *Husband,* secondly *a fellow helper,* which is the *Wife.* [1598]
> The *Government* of your *House, Family,* and Children,... is the Province allotted to your Sex, and... *discharging it well,* will for that reason be expected from you.... When a *Husband,* whose Province is without Doors, and to whom the Oeconomy of the House would be in some degree Indecent, findeth no *Order* nor *Quiet* in his *Family,* ... the *Mistaken Lady,*...will at last be convinced of her *Error.* [1688]

To Richard Cleaver, the earlier author, husband and wife together were "Lords of the house"; to the second, George Savile, Marquis of Halifax, the woman alone bore responsibility for managing the home. Cleaver devoted numerous pages of his tract to the husband's duties to his family. By contrast, Halifax regarded a husband's involvement in household affairs as "in some degree Indecent" and stated unequivocally that a wife had sole charge of her children and house.[6]

Because scholarship on Englishmen of the late seventeenth century and thereafter has stressed other aspects of their lives, it is not clear whether they in fact surrendered control of households to their wives, as Halifax's comments would seem to indicate. But the cultural norm had nevertheless unquestionably shifted, and by the middle of the eighteenth century, when the word *masculinity* was first coined, definitions of manhood primarily stressed the need for a man to display "civility" in sociable company rather than to govern his household successfully, leaving that function instead to his wife.[7]

In close conjunction with the (normative) exclusion of men from the home, a striking development of the approximately seven decades beginning in the late 1680s was the frequent appearance of novel English phrases to describe women and their appropriate roles in and around the household. In the 1690s, John Dunton, the influential editor and publisher of the *Athenian Mercury* and the primary subject of chapter 3, began to explore in his myriad publications some of the implications of these new ideas.[8]

One of Dunton's favorite expressions was to term women the *fair sex,* a usage without a counterpart for men. After its initial appearance in print in 1652, English authors from the 1680s on commonly employed the phrase.[9] When those same authors first began to delineate the special characteristics and responsibilities of that *fair sex,* they, like the Marquis of Halifax, used *province,* utilizing a meaning that the *OED* dates to the early seventeenth century: "the proper function or area of concern of a particular person or group." Indeed, Halifax's reference in 1688 to "the Province allotted to your Sex," as quoted above, seems to be the earliest such usage. Six years later, a man added other functions when translating a French author: "'Tis the Woman's Province to determine concerning the Fashions, to judge of Language, to distinguish the genteel Mein, and the fine and courtly Behaviour." In its initial uses, accordingly, the term conveyed disparate but related meanings, connoting both women's responsibilities to household and family and their purported facility at reaching appropriate cultural assessments.[10]

By 1724, the language was sufficiently well established that a publication adopted such phraseology to outline the concept of *separate spheres,* although not employing that precise terminology:

> born, as we think they [women] are, only to the Domestick Part of Life; we are surprized, when we see them deviate from those duties; as we are, when a Man descends to those Meannesses, which are properly in the Province of women. And indeed, the Distribution of distinct Offices to each Sex, is the Work of Providence, to keep the World in Order; for if Women were to neglect the bringing up of their Children, and Men the Obligations of Social Life, all would be in Confusion.

The unknown author thus asserted that women were born for "the Domestick Part of Life," including childrearing; insisted that women not "deviate" from such responsibilities, which consisted of "Meannesses" ranking below men's duties; designated men's and women's roles as entirely "distinct," with men responsible for "Social Life"; and predicted "Confusion" if the order of the world that maintained such divisions were ever violated.[11]

Although that author did not use the word *sphere,* others did, and that term came to dominate discourse about women's roles on both sides of the Atlantic by the middle of the eighteenth century. *Sphere* originated in works studying astronomy; early in the seventeenth century it took on a meaning the *OED* defines as "a province or domain in which one's activities or faculties find scope or exercise, or within which they are naturally confined; range or compass of action or study." *Sphere,* defined and utilized in that way, had a connotation of limitation and constraint lacking in *province.* At first the term was used primarily with respect to men. For example, the Marquis of Halifax wrote in 1695, "It is best to keep Men within their proper Sphere; few Men have Understanding enough exactly to fill even one narrow Circle; fewer able to fill two." American clergymen seemed particularly drawn to the concept when they sought to detail the proper roles of different sorts of men. In 1710, one declared, "There are Various *Degrees* and *Orders* of men…and Each Degree have their proper Sphere to move and act in." And three years later, another averred self-servingly, "It has always been found that the Laity are a Clog to Clergy-men, when they begin to soar a-loft, or above their proper Sphere."[12]

With respect to women, in the seventeenth century *sphere* most often appeared with a somewhat different meaning, "a place, position, or station in society; an aggregate of persons of a certain rank or standing." As the *OED* explains, in that sense the word applied primarily to "elevated rank." After the untimely and unexpected death of Queen Mary II from smallpox in 1695, many of the memorial tributes incorporated such references, as did a poem: "Blest Princess! How distinguish'd, how ador'd! / How much above ev'n Her own Sphere She soar'd!"[13] Before long, though, English authors began to apply to women the more restrictive definition of *sphere* that had first been used withregard to men. "'Tis woman's sphere to mind / Their Children and their Houses," wrote a poet in 1710. The fact that *sphere* indeed implied restraint and lower status when applied to women emerged subtly from other, later statements such as a reference to one whose "worth is above that of the common sphere of women" or to the belief that "the sphere which *Women* are capable of acting in [is] extremely narrow."[14]

The earliest appearance of a female-gendered reference to *sphere* in American imprints came in two texts of English origin, both published in the colonies in 1746. One referred to "the only natural Sphere of Womankind," and the other used the phrase "a Wife thus *wisely* and *discreetly* filling her Sphere of Action."[15] But that the phraseology was not alien to American usage at the time is suggested by the appearance of related language in a 1747 poem by the Philadelphian Grace Growden. Reacting to a female preacher—presumably a Quaker—whom she criticized for poor performance as a speaker, Growden observed, "Thou mayst Conquer in a nother spear," urging her subject to focus on more conventionally feminine activities. Six years later, the *South Carolina Gazette* published "Advice to a Young Lady lately Married," reprinted from a 1752 London paper. The poem incorporated not only *sphere* but also *province* and *the fair* (often used in the same way as *fair sex*). Such uses of language had by then become firmly established on both sides of the Atlantic.

> Small is the Province of a Wife,
> And narrow is her Sphere in Life,
> Within that Sphere to move aright
> Should be her principal Delight:
> To guide the House with prudent Care,
> And properly to spend and spare; . . .
> To form the tender infant Mind;
> These are the Tasks to Wives assign'd:
> Then never think domestic Care
> Beneath the Notice of the Fair.[16]

By the mid-1750s, therefore, the novel terminology had accordingly prevailed, frequently coupled with related uses of *private*. Such phrases pervaded published and unpublished writings alike, as seen in chapters 4 and 5.

It is easier to describe the new cultural norms and modified uses of language than it is to explain why such changes occurred. Indeed, the major purpose of the investigation reported in this book is to describe *how* and *when* the transformations took place, rather than *why* they happened. Still, the altered gender definitions seem to be just one among several significant shifts in English/European/American culture in the decades surrounding 1700. Scholars in different fields have suggested various reasons for the changes, most of them related in one way or another to the combined impact of political transformation in Britain and some aspects of Enlightenment thought.

The Glorious Revolution of 1688, in which the Catholic James II was forced out by Parliament and replaced by his Protestant daughter Mary II and her husband, William III, is generally seen as having substituted Whiggish political theory and practice (as epitomized in John Locke's *Two Treatises of Government*) for the family-state analogies of Sir Robert Filmer and other supporters of absolute monarchy. Unlike Filmer and his allies, Locke and other Whigs distinguished between the power of fathers and the power of rulers, arguing that the polity originated in agreements among men in a theoretical state of nature rather than in the historical authority of family patriarchs. Such a construct meant that women—seen by Locke solely as *wives* dependent on husbands for any link to political power—could no longer rely on the family analogy to claim authority outside the household context, although within it they had important functions. That division between family and state, with women confined theoretically to the former, served as the foundation for the cultural division that by the mid-eighteenth century manifested itself in the language of the *feminine private* and the *masculine public*.[17]

But more than politics was involved in the creation of gendered notions of separate spheres. Some scholars have stressed the contemporaneous rise of commercial capitalism, with its allied themes of the need for virtue and concern about excessive luxury. Women's exercise of private virtue in the home, away from the depravity of commerce, began to be viewed as the source of morality in society. Therefore, it was crucial for women to be protected from corruption, theoretically if not in actuality. Normative statements about appropriately gendered modes of conduct accordingly emphasized the potential dangers for women venturing outside that realm.[18]

The most far-reaching explanations for the development of new concepts of masculinity and femininity relate the changes in question to general themes of Enlightenment thought, in particular the desire to categorize humans in innovative ways. Thomas Laqueur's contention that around 1700 a two-sex model of humanity replaced the earlier theory that women were imperfect biological men has been particularly influential. Laqueur and others link the novel notions of sexual difference to men's desire to reserve the public sphere for themselves. In order to exclude women from the polity, some historians argue, men sought to identify the ways in which women's nature diverged fundamentally from their own. The two-sex model allowed them to ground such statements of difference in seemingly fixed biological categories. They could therefore conclude that females were "naturally" inferior to males. In some respects, separate-spheres doctrine contradicted such hierarchical notions in that it posited a rough equality of the sexes in distinct bailiwicks, but in practice men were unquestionably more equal than women.[19]

Such explanations need not be seen as mutually exclusive. Indeed, scholars who stress one usually cite at least one of the others as well.[20] Regardless of which analysis is specifically advocated, all point to a congeries of developments in which transformations in gender definitions played a key role. All such changes tended to divide cultural representations of men and women more sharply than before. Instead of men and women being seen as variants of the same biological sexual construct, in the eighteenth century they were viewed as incommensurably different. Rather than both sexes being held to the same essentially ungendered standard of virtuous conduct, their roles in upholding morality came to be seen as separate and distinct. And in place of a system of thought that made rank the crucial influence on one's political role, gender became the dominant determinant of the ability to become an appropriate state actor.

❧ CHAPTER 1

Lady Frances Berkeley and Virginia Politics, 1675–1678

The rebel and councillor Nathaniel Bacon, flanked by his fusiliers, confronted Governor Sir William Berkeley and his council outside the state house in Jamestown during the early afternoon of June 23, 1676. The dramatic events that followed so impressed a witness, Thomas Mathew, that he could still describe the scene vividly almost three decades later. "We Saw from the Window the Governour open his Breast, and Bacon strutting betwixt his Two files of Men with his Left Arm on Kenbow [akimbo] flinging his Right Arm every Way both like men Distracted." What Mathew and others inside the state house could not hear was that Berkeley dared Bacon to shoot him while baring his breast. The governor offered to fight a duel with Bacon then and there, but Bacon declined; and the rebel adopted "outragious Postures of his Head, Arms, Body, and Leggs, often tossing his hand from his Sword to his Hat," as the governor abandoned the field, retreating in disarray toward his private quarters in the state house. Bacon's actions were "impetuos (like Delirious)," Mathew remembered; and all the while the rebel was swearing, "'Dam my Bloud, I'le Kill Governor Councill Assembly and all.'"[1]

Just two weeks earlier, Bacon had behaved very differently. Separated from his armed men and brought before Berkeley and the council, Bacon had humbly asked the governor forgiveness for his "late unlawfull, mutinous, and rebellious practices...without order and commission." Penitently, he kneeled before the governor after "many low bowings of his Body," promising "upon the word and faith of a christian and of a gentleman" that he would after a grant of clemency behave "dutifully, faithfully and peaceably" to the Virginia government. Accepting Bacon's characterization of himself as a "gentleman," Berkeley magnanimously pardoned him and restored him to membership on the council ("to the wonder of all men," observed one later narrative).[2]

By contrast, at the June 23 confrontation, Bacon's body language and words were contemptuous in the extreme. Unlike the supplicant "low bowings" and kneeling Bacon had earlier displayed, he adopted the arms akimbo stance of a superior. But more than that: his unrestrained body movements showed that he had completely lost control of himself. Bacon was "Distracted," displaying "outragious Postures." The elderly Governor Berkeley too had been drawn into such movements. That he would bare his breast and behave in a "Distracted" way was shocking indeed. Bodily restraint and controlled gestures were among the key markers that distinguished high-status men from their low-ranking counterparts, so neither combatant had conducted himself properly.[3]

Both Bacon and Berkeley were deeply concerned with preserving and displaying their own high social standing; accordingly, their violation of the rules of gentlemanly deportment revealed the passionate emotion fueling their confrontation. One crucial element of that passion inhered in their personal relationship: Nathaniel Bacon was distantly related to the governor's cherished wife, Lady Frances Culpeper Stephens Berkeley. The patronage of Lady Berkeley and her husband had enabled Bacon to rise rapidly in the society and polity of the Chesapeake colony. Thus his challenge to the governor's authority had a significant personal dimension overlooked in most accounts of the rebellion.[4]

Although Lady Frances herself did not participate in the June 1676 encounters, she was more deeply involved in the events of Bacon's Rebellion and its aftermath than has commonly been recognized.[5] As a woman of noble birth and one of the two highest-ranking people in the colony, she was an important state actor. Throughout the crisis, she did not hesitate to take the steps she thought necessary to safeguard Virginia's government from the challenge posed by her own kinsman and to protect her and her husband's personal interests.

The Cousins

Frances Culpeper was born in 1634 in Kent, youngest of the five children of Katherine St. Leger and Thomas Culpeper, a cousin of John, Baron Culpeper of Thoresway. Her father, a strong supporter of the monarchy during the English Civil War, was rewarded for his loyalty in 1649 with one of several patents issued by the future King Charles II for huge tracts of land in Virginia's Northern Neck, which lay between the Potomac and Rappahannock rivers. The following year, Thomas Culpeper moved his family to Virginia, where both Frances and her older sister Anne married around the time of his death in 1652. Frances's new husband was Samuel Stephens, who owned land in both Virginia and what would eventually become North Carolina. Named the governor of that Albemarle region in 1667, Stephens served for only two years before his death.[6]

The couple had no children; Frances Stephens thus inherited most of her deceased husband's large estate outright under the terms of their prenuptial agreement. In April 1670, the Virginia General Court, with Governor Sir William Berkeley presiding, ordered that her title to the property be confirmed and that she be named executor. The next month, in a new prenuptial agreement, Governor Berkeley guaranteed Frances Stephens a life estate in England worth £600 annually, and they were wed before the end of June. At the age of thirty-six, Frances Stephens Berkeley had not only acquired the title she would employ for the rest of her life (even during a third marriage), but had also assured herself of a substantial income. In both respects she was exceptional; few seventeenth-century colonial women entered into profitable prenuptial agreements, and fewer still ever gained the honorific "Lady."[7]

Frances Berkeley made the most of her circumstances. Born to a branch of a noble family and guaranteed an independent income, married in succession to two colonial governors, she successfully wielded economic, political, and social authority. Although she had no children of her own, she personified the metaphorical powerful mother of Filmerian theory. Described by a contemporary as "very well bred" and "of very good discourse," she understood how to use her high standing to advance her family's interests. Through her role as hostess, she deployed sociability to gain allies and disseminate her views widely. Surviving correspondence shows that she generously dispensed patronage to younger relatives, expecting deference in return. She played up her connections to prominent men (both kin and non-kin) in order to win influence over key decisions and decision makers. Above all, she employed political and economic clout, even though, as shall be seen, on two occasions her actions caused her husband considerable embarrassment. After her husband's death, she established herself as an important political figure by becoming the focal point of opposition to his successor.[8]

Sir William Berkeley, the widower governor attracted to this vivacious and powerful woman, was sixty-four in 1670, twenty-eight years the senior of

FIGURE 1.1. Lady Frances Culpeper Stephens Berkeley, by an unknown artist, c. 1660, about the time of her marriage to Sir William Berkeley. Both her beauty and her aristocratic birth must have attracted the older governor. Courtesy of the Museum of Early Southern Decorative Arts (MESDA) at Old Salem, North Carolina.

his new bride. Knighted by Charles I in 1639, he had served as governor of Virginia since 1641, though with interruptions caused by the Civil War and Interregnum. Popular and successful for most of his tenure in office, Berkeley organized Virginians to thwart a major Indian offensive in the mid-1640s and to repel several attacks by the Dutch two decades later. He governed Virginia from his house at Green Spring primarily by forging and resolutely maintaining an alliance with a group of wealthy families, but by the time he married Frances Culpeper Stephens that alliance was nearing the end of its usefulness. Newcomers to Virginia, including his wife's distant relative Nathaniel Bacon, began to challenge its hegemony openly. In retrospect, one Maryland observer saw the Berkeley-Stephens marriage as the first step in the governor's decline: "Old Governor Barkley," he wrote, "Altered by marrying a young wyff," had abandoned his "wonted publicq good" and adopted a "covetous todeinge [toadying]" that led to his ruin.[9]

The man who precipitated that ruin, Nathaniel Bacon, arrived in Virginia in the summer of 1674.[10] Born around 1647 in Suffolk to a landed family and termed by his tutor a man of "quick wit" but "impatient of labour," he studied at Cambridge and the Inns of Court. After Bacon was implicated in a fraudulent scheme and his new wife was disinherited by her father for marrying him, Nathaniel's father shipped him off to Virginia with a sizable inheritance. Perhaps the father hoped that the young man's older first cousin once removed, another Nathaniel Bacon (thereafter known locally as "Sr." to distinguish himself from the newcomer), would assist him. The childless Nathaniel Sr. was a member of the colony's council and a close associate of the governor.

Yet in the end the young immigrant's kinship to Lady Frances Berkeley was more important to his rapid advancement than his intellect, his inheritance, or his ties to Nathaniel Sr. She and the immigrant called each other "cousin," a generic seventeenth-century term for distant relationships. Later Nathaniel Jr. was to refer to her "kindness" in her treatment of "her poore and Unworthy kinsman." After the families' connection had begun to crumble, the governor reminded the young man that he had initially offered him "all the services that was in my power," for three reasons: because "gent[lemen] of your quallitie come verey rarely into this Country"; because of "your owne particuler merritts which I always esteemed verey greate"; and especially because of "your relation to my dearest." Bacon at that time acknowledged the governor's "generosity" and "kindnesses," admitting that he owed Berkeley "gratitude and obedience." The newly arrived Bacons in fact lived for a brief period with the Berkeleys at Green Spring before settling on their own plantation, located in Henrico County, forty miles up the river from Jamestown. That landholding also fatefully included a piece of property lying twenty miles further northwest, near the falls of the James River. In March 1675, the governor appointed Bacon to his council, a remarkable sign of favor for one so young and so recently resident in Virginia.[11]

Two contemporaries remarked that the reasons for Bacon's ascent, "all on a suddain," were "best known to the Gouvernour," thereby slyly characterizing the appointment as nearly inexplicable and perhaps corrupt. But Bacon's rise may readily be understood in the context of the known influence of Lady Berkeley on her husband, which he himself acknowledged in the exchange with Bacon quoted in the last paragraph. On numerous occasions, she expressed great solicitude for members of her extended family, no matter how distant the relationship. For example, in the early 1670s she wrote twice to inform Robert Filmer (son of the author of *Patriarcha*) about the Virginia financial affairs of his brother's widow, Mary Horsmanden Filmer, who was Frances's first cousin once removed. Referring to herself as Robert's "Most affectionate Cosin," Lady Frances asked about the reported ill health of Robert's wife, commenting that "her owne Childern canot be more concerned nore more truile wish her recoverie" than she did. Years later, she wrote in the same vein to her nephew, Sir Abstrupus Danby, Virginia-born but living in England, about her concerns for his sister's (her niece's) financial well-being during widowhood and a difficult second marriage. Such evidence suggests that for Lady Frances Berkeley, loyalty to family constituted a paramount value. Those she identified as kin won her favor, and she expected them to reciprocate with similar care and concern for her and her husband. Robert Filmer the younger (whom she thanked profusely for services rendered in England) and "Strupie" (whom she described warmly as the son she never had) met her demanding test. Nathaniel Bacon, a kinsman whose interests she had worked to advance, did not—and he accordingly incurred her wrath.[12]

The Rebellion

In 1674, just as the twenty-seven-year-old Bacon relocated to Virginia, the colony was experiencing difficult economic times. Tobacco prices had fallen, and planters complained of being gouged by English merchants. Parliament had recently laid new duties on colonial products. Virginians, especially the large land speculators who sat in the assembly, were deeply concerned about potential claims to quitrents and other fees from the Northern Neck proprietors, including Lady Berkeley's second cousin, Thomas, Lord Culpeper, and her own natal family. In response, the General Assembly levied special taxes in order to purchase the Northern Neck patents and pay the expenses of agents dispatched to London to negotiate agreements for that purpose. Although few in Virginia favored the proprietors' claims, the heavy burden of those taxes—which largely benefited the colony's grandees—later figured prominently in lists of grievances prepared by ex-rebels.[13] But those problems, separately or together, would not have caused a rebellion. Indian relations ultimately produced the spark that set off the conflagration.

Indian trade was the lesser of two intertwined matters at issue. In a letter to Governor Berkeley in September 1675, Nathaniel Bacon indicated that one of the reasons he had decided to establish himself in the west, "soe remote both from the businesse and best converse of this Country," was to profit from commerce with the Indians. Berkeley himself controlled the issuance of trading licenses, a policy instituted some years earlier to try to forestall fraudulent practices. He granted a lucrative license jointly to Bacon and William Byrd I, the second husband of Mary Horsmanden Filmer. Both men were by Lady Frances's reckoning relatives deserving of her patronage, and their kinship with her surely facilitated her husband's issuance of the trading license to the partnership. The conduct of the Indian trade, like the taxes levied to pay the Northern Neck proprietors, often appeared on the lists of grievances later cited as reasons for the rebellion.[14]

The more important source of friction pertained to the land itself. The territory beyond the rivers' headwaters had been reserved for Indians under a treaty Berkeley negotiated in 1646 to end struggles with the Powhatans that had begun in 1622. Land to the east was fully claimed, so neither newly arrived high-ranking men like Bacon nor recently freed indentured servants could find satisfactory lands on which to settle. Both groups of claimants bumped up against the "friend Indians" on the other side of the treaty line, who were themselves being squeezed from the west and north by powerful Indian nations such as the Susquehannocks and the Senecas. Clashes—and perhaps even an all-out Indian war—were probably inevitable, but the ensuing civil war was not. That developed, on the one hand, because Governor Berkeley was determined to uphold the treaty and to maintain a firm distinction between "friend" and "enemy" Indians; and, on the other, because Nathaniel Bacon, viewing all Indians as hostile, insistently sought the governor's imprimatur for his expeditions against them. Had Berkeley acceded to the frontiersmen's demands, the internal conflict could have been avoided.

The trouble began in July 1675 when Indians from Maryland raided a plantation owned by a Virginian they believed had cheated them. Retaliatory incursions across the Potomac River boundary between the two colonies followed, until during the following January a party of Susquehannocks attacked plantations near the falls of the Potomac and Rappahannock rivers, killing more than thirty settlers. Among those murdered in such raids was Bacon's overseer on his frontier property. Governor Berkeley responded by summoning the militia, but he soon recalled the men who had mustered at his command. For reasons that remain unclear, he decided to postpone military action until after the scheduled March meeting of the assembly. At that session the assembly voted new taxes to pay for the construction of forts at the heads of the rivers, an action much derided by Berkeley's critics. They insisted that the forts would be useless, that "it was merely a Designe of the Grandees to engrosse all their Tobacco into their owne hands," and that the scheme was "a great Grievance, Juggle and cheat." Virginians petitioned Berkeley to appoint a leader for them, asserting that they would "hazard ... their Lives and Fortunes" to fight the Indians (not entirely altruistically, for they anticipated plunder), but he refused to comply.[15]

The governor's actions (or lack thereof) in the winter and early spring of 1676 later drew sharp criticism from commissioners dispatched from England to investigate the causes of the rebellion. Before the war, Virginians had no "just cause of Complaint of his management," the commissioners concluded, but "his dilatory Proceedings for the Security of the People" and the "very ineffectuall" laws adopted by the March assembly together constituted "great, and fatall Errors." The commissioners listed five specific mistakes: the governor's reluctance "to Provide for Public Safety"; "the Great, and heavy Imposition" of taxes for the forts; the continuing financial burden of attempting to purchase the Northern Neck patents; and the "suddaine Disbanding" of the militia just as troops mustered to march against the Indians, along with Berkeley's rejection of the petition requesting a new force under a leader of his choosing. And the fault was not Sir William's alone. Reportedly, Lady Frances "reviled" volunteers from New Kent County when they came to Green Spring in April seeking the governor's approbation. All this, the commissioners declared, "gave occasion to the unquiet impatient Crowd to follow and cry up Bacon; whose forwardnesse to head them encouraged them to choose him their Generall."[16]

The commissioners' account indicated that Bacon attracted support not only because of his "forwardnesse" but also because his rapid rise in the colony "made him the more considerable in the eye of the Vulgar." He was, the commissioners concluded, "very ambitious and arrogant," a man who became "powerful and popular," especially by exercising his acknowledged talent for persuasive rhetoric. Women as well as men found Bacon's arguments compelling. Several women carried messages for the rebel, and Sir William later complained that Mistress Sarah Grendon "spread through the whole country" that "I was a great[er] frend to the Indians than to the English." Buoyed by the widespread support and ignoring repeated warnings from the governor, Bacon led angry frontiersmen in an attack on some neighboring Indians. Infuriated that his authority was being flouted so openly, Berkeley in May 1676 proclaimed Bacon and his men to be "Mutineers and Rebells" for moving against the native peoples without his permission.[17]

Lady Frances Berkeley had no comparable power to outlaw her kinsman formally, so she acted informally against him, wielding a woman's classic weapon: slanderous talk. Men, too, told negative tales about those they disliked or distrusted, but they had additional means of attack, such as filing lawsuits or engaging in physical confrontations—or, as in this case, declaring an opponent to be a rebel. Married women, even powerful ones, could not take that sort of action. So Lady Frances, like many other women in similar circumstances elsewhere in the colonies and England, spread damaging tales about Bacon among her wide network of acquaintances. Word of her verbal assaults reached the rebel himself. On May 25, he informed the governor that he had heard that Frances had "raised severall scandalous & false reports of mee that I was not worth a Groate was a Parliament Captain that my bills were protested." He had, he declared, "too high an estimation" of her to fully believe that she had spread such stories, and he asked that she be more "generous" to him.[18]

While denying that she had ever charged Bacon with favoring Parliament (he was too young to have participated in the Civil War), Lady Frances vigorously defended the accuracy of her other statements in a written response witnessed by her husband and three additional men.[19] She had spoken about Bacon's finances, she revealed, only after she realized that the people "universall[y]" believed that Bacon would not just lead them but also "beare all their charges, releeve and maintaine the wives & children of those that should goe out with him." Because that false impression was causing "infinite mischiefes and Calamities," she had decided "to unravell the thread by giving an account that came to mee without inquireing." She truly wished that her young relative had "as much [property] as the people beleeve," but she had been brought up to tell the truth, and she had been "forst upon the stadge" to defend "my Husbands Honor." In brief, she was insisting that she had not sought the negative information about her kinsman, nor had she spread it indiscriminately, but once she became convinced of its importance to the future of the colony and its residents, she had felt compelled to publicize it.

Lady Frances asserted that impeccable witnesses—in particular, Nathaniel Bacon Sr. and William Byrd I—had informed her that the younger Bacon's financial circumstances were not what they seemed. He owed substantial amounts of money to both those kinsmen. A third man, a ship captain, told her that in England he had witnessed Nathaniel's father's refusal to pay a small promissory note written by his son. Although the elder Bacon later relented, he declared publicly that he would cover no more of Nathaniel's debts. A fourth high-status man, she disclosed, had claimed to hold a lien on much of Bacon's English estate. When questioned on that point, however, she admitted hearing that assertion not directly from the man himself, but rather from thirdhand gossip. Having revealed her sources, she then challenged Bacon: "if they have done him wrong, Hee may disprove them."

Moreover, she accused Bacon of an offense that to her mind was "worse" than his reputed poverty, to which even honorable men could be subject: the crime of "Ingratitude...off a deep dye." He had repaid the governor's "favourable Amitie" by questioning Berkeley's "Courage & conduct" in office, and he had even "rent the Heart off a woman & his Kinswoman whom by all Laws off Honor & Humanity Hee was bound to protect." She cited a particular "affront" to the hospitality and familial honor she valued so highly: he had offered her payment for "the Happinesse I received in haveing his wives Company a week or a ffortnight at my house." Such a move had been "petty," she averred; even worse, his break with the Berkeleys had deprived her of the pleasure of associating with his wife, for whom she still felt "perfect esteem & kindnesse."

Lady Frances's formal response to Nathaniel Bacon's charge that she had slandered him closed with an anguished addendum that conveyed a sense of the distress her words had caused her, him, and possibly the colony at large. I wish "from my heart," she wrote, that all the "things that have been said or done about these matters could be torne out of all Records." Although her kinsman had first breached the familial bonds she so cherished, she thereby indicated that she recognized her own violation of her values. She could explain the reasons for her "just Resentments," but perhaps even she could not wholly excuse her verbal outburst. And possibly her husband could not do so either. On May 31, the Virginia councillors referred to "that unhappy Separation which this wild mans mischeivous doings hath caused between our most Noble Governour and his Incomparable Lady." Although at that moment Lady Frances was preparing to travel to England to plead Virginia's cause in London, the councillors' language, including their expression of "greife...soe great we cannot enlarge upon the subject," suggested that more divisiveness than a mere physical separation lay behind their remarks.[20]

Frances Berkeley's defamatory words about her kinsman obviously aroused considerable interest among her fellow Virginians. Her role in Bacon's rapid advancement would have been widely rumored at the very least; that she had turned on him must have intrigued many gossipers. The story spread so widely it reached Bacon's own ears, although it is unclear how or how quickly he heard the tale, because nothing indicates when (or to how many people) Frances had spoken. As her passing reference to "records" implied, Nathaniel might have been preparing to file suit against her. That would have been embarrassing for the Berkeleys. Still, it was unlikely Bacon could have won, for before damages could be assessed, Virginia slander law required the leveling of a false charge of criminal conduct, and she had not accused him of a crime. Even so, the formal statement describing her words and motives could well have been aimed at deflecting such a lawsuit.[21]

Yet despite the lack of clarity about why she drafted her account—or, for that matter, why her husband and two councillors, along with one of Bacon's allies, signed as witnesses to it—several points are clear. She—not Bacon Sr., Byrd, or either of her other two sources—had deliberately spread the tales of her kinsman's impecunious finances. She had taken information most likely revealed over a hospitable dining table at Green Spring and had shared her knowledge with others outside the closed circle of councillors and prominent Virginians. She had disseminated the slander for what might be termed a *public* purpose. In hopes of diminishing support for Bacon's cause, she intended to disabuse his men and their wives of what she took to be their "universall" belief that he would reward his followers monetarily.

But she also acted for reasons that would later be called *private:* she felt personally betrayed by a kinsman whom she had supported unconditionally and whose wife she considered a friend. Bacon had offended both her and her husband and had rejected her patronage. She believed she correctly resented his open challenge to Sir William's governance of Virginia and his insulting offer to reimburse her for his wife's expenses. Such commingled concerns were all of one piece in Frances Berkeley's mind. She never employed the terms *public* and *private,* nor did she draw any distinction between the various ways in which Nathaniel Bacon had wronged her and her husband. Her worldview, as disclosed by the content of her slanderous remarks and her motives for them, combined rather than separated familial and political matters.

Lady Frances Berkeley thus revealed herself as an archetypal aristocratic woman of her time. Like Sir Robert Filmer—a man she could well have deemed "cousin," had she known him—she knew that high-ranking women could be state actors and could "well handle" the "goverment of kingdomes." She readily, though with admitted anguish, shouldered a responsibility to the people of Virginia: when the kinsman she had aided appeared to be misleading them about his financial condition, she thought it imperative to inform them of their error. In the absence of any newspapers or other printed outlet, the only way she could accomplish that goal was to ensure that knowledge of the stories she had heard and believed became widespread. Although she thus opened herself to a potential slander suit and had to violate norms of family honor, she had felt compelled to act on the people's behalf. That same sense of obligation to the public ensured that she—not a member of

Virginia's council—became her husband's, and her colony's, emissary to London. No one expressed surprise or concern about her journey. Since her husband could not leave in that time of crisis, she (as the second-highest-ranking person in the colony) was clearly the appropriate person to represent him in England.

The Commissioners' Investigation

Around the beginning of June 1676, as her husband and her cousin vied for control of Virginia, Lady Frances Berkeley sailed to England. While she was there, the two men and the forces loyal to them clashed repeatedly at different locations in the province. In September, Bacon and his men seized Jamestown and burned it to the ground, but after Bacon died from dysentery in October, the rebellion collapsed in the absence of his charismatic leadership. By late January 1676/7 (in the Julian calendar then used in England and its colonies), the rebellion was over and Governor Berkeley had restored his authority in Virginia.[22]

Lady Frances was probably in London during the autumn, at the time plans were drawn up to send troops to quash the rebellion and to dispatch a three-member commission to investigate the uprising's origins. Whether she influenced those decisions is unknown, but she did supply a secretary of state with information from Virginia by forwarding at least one letter she received from home. She did not learn until late November, when she was ready to return to America, that Charles II had named Herbert Jeffreys lieutenant governor and had issued an order directing Sir William to return to England at the earliest possible moment. In response, she petitioned the monarch on behalf of her husband, noting his "great weaknes of body" and the "ruine and disorder" of his estate, and asking that he be given "such liberty of Time for his stay there as may be expedient for the Safety of his life and fortune." Such details showed that she had received recent personal news from Virginia; presumably, she had been kept informed of events throughout her sojourn in the mother country.[23]

On January 29, 1676/7, two of the commissioners and fewer than one hundred (out of a total of one thousand) soldiers arrived in Virginia; the other troops landed a few weeks later. Sir John Berry, a naval officer, and Francis Moryson, a Virginian who had been one of the agents negotiating to end the Northern Neck proprietorships, eagerly inquired about recent developments. To their surprise, they learned not only that Bacon was dead and the rebellion ended, but also that Berkeley and his councillors were engaged in judging, convicting, and hanging rebel leaders under martial law. Charles II, though, had ordered that all rebels other than Bacon himself should be pardoned. Accordingly, from the outset of their stay in Virginia the commissioners found themselves at odds with Governor Berkeley.[24]

Nevertheless, the two commissioners' first report, drafted on February 2, sympathized with Sir William, praising his efforts to achieve peace with the Indians.[25] No one, they declared, had been "a more eminent or active Instrument in suppressing this Rebellion and Quieting the divisions and Disorders among the people." Berkeley's house at Green Spring was "very much Ruin'd" by the rebels, and they believed that no colonist had suffered more than the governor. They had been directed to inquire into the Virginians' grievances but thus far had discovered none of any importance other than the high salaries paid to legislators, which could easily be lowered.

Still, two troubling comments marred their otherwise positive missive. Their conversations with the governor showed that he wanted the rebels' confiscated property to be given as restitution to those who had remained loyal to him. Because the commissioners' instructions said nothing about such matters, they neither approved nor disapproved his plans. And when they gave him printed copies of the king's pardon proclamation, he declined to distribute them. Instead, he indicated that he would issue a pardon order of his own, in which "about Eight persons not yett taken" would be exempted, along with others already jailed, "which are the Chiefe of the Rebells." They urged him not to delay informing the "Trembling Countrey" of Charles's "Gracious Pardon," but he declined.

Both initial sources of friction accurately predicted much greater discord to come. As the days and weeks passed, the commissioners—and their third colleague, Herbert Jeffreys, who arrived with most of the rest of the troops and Lady Frances on February 10—grew progressively more angry at what they saw as the governor's unwillingness to comply with the king's instructions. In the end, Sir William explicitly excluded thirty-nine men and one woman (Sarah Grendon, whom he had accused of declaring that he preferred Indians to Virginians) from the royal pardon. His councillors continued to convict and execute leading rebels without jury trials and to order their property confiscated. Men who had offended less openly were offered the opportunity to make "compositions" (in effect, to pay heavy fines) to escape similar punishments or banishment from the colony.[26]

When the commissioners asked Virginians to detail their grievances, the list included not only heavy taxes and other complaints from the pre-war period, but also the greed displayed by Berkeley and his cronies after Bacon's death. The governor and the relatively few men who had remained loyal to him had suffered greatly during the war, but from the commissioners'

perspective they were acting extralegally when they took goods or compositions from men who had not been convicted, or when they appropriated
to themselves property that should have gone to the crown because it had
belonged to men executed for treason. By May, Jeffreys had concluded that
Berkeley's actions after the war caused "as greate commotions and rais'd as
loud Cryes in this Countrey since the Peace, as ever before the rapine &
depredations of the Rebells in tyme of Warr did."[27]

Scattered evidence suggests that after her return Lady Frances Berkeley
played an active role in attempts to recoup the family fortunes through confiscations and compositions. Sir William was so ill with malaria when she
arrived that he was impotent, able to greet her only with "Vocal kindnesse"
despite their many months apart. That his health remained poor throughout
the spring, and that his much younger wife could well have played a major
role in events during those months, can be inferred from his death in June.
In later correspondence, Lady Frances complained bitterly about the dam-
age done to Green Spring and their other properties during the rebellion.
The house cost "almost as much to repair as if it had beene new to build,"
she revealed, implying that the necessary resources had come from property
seized from "the chiefe Rebells." Later complaints and lawsuits disclosed her
involvement in some of those seizures. For example, the same day Henry
Jenkins, a tanner, informed the commissioners that the governor had unjustly
confiscated twenty-two head of his cattle, "he was sent for very late that
night to green Spring, where the Lady Berkeley told he should have his cattle
return'd home to him." And that happened, as promised, the next day. The
episode showed both that Lady Frances had excellent sources of information
about the progress of the commissioners' investigation and that she was making decisions about the disposition of seized property.[28]

Another incident in the early spring of 1677 demonstrated that Lady
Frances was taking an active role in political as well as financial affairs. On
March 25, Francis Moryson wrote to ask her to intervene with her husband
on behalf of "a poore, condemned person," Robert Jones, who years earlier
had been banished to Virginia by Parliament for supporting Charles I in
the Civil War. Jones, Moryson had concluded, was not "a bloody malitious
Rebell, but one merely seduced into that fatall snare, by the artifice of others." Lady Berkeley responded immediately, assuring Moryson that Jones
would be pardoned. She did not indicate that she would consult her husband,
though that had been Moryson's request; instead, she simply observed that, as
Moryson wished, "mercy" would be shown to him. She thus implied that the
decision was hers to make. And, given the governor's illness and her willingness to take actions she deemed necessary, perhaps it was.[29]

By the time of these incidents, Governor Berkeley had stopped communicating directly with the commissioners. In February and March, the relationship among the men grew steadily more acrimonious, a development to which Frances Berkeley surely contributed. The commissioners pressured Berkeley to leave, as the king had directed, and repeatedly chided him for continuing the unauthorized confiscations of rebels' property. The governor defended himself by claiming that he had seized no more than "the Thirtieth part of my lost Estate," insisting that he was merely imitating Charles I's actions during the Civil War. "I was by when the King seised the Estates of many that were in Rebellion against him without Conviction," he declared. The latter argument angered the commissioners, who completely lost patience with Berkeley after March 21, when he failed to respond to their request for a "very strict" accounting of the confiscations. In late March, chagrined in retrospect by their "too easy Credulity" at the beginning of their stay, they admitted to a London official that the facts now appeared "contrary to his first Professions, and our late account." Rather than being a quieter of disturbances, Berkeley was causing them.[30]

The acrimony came to a head on April 22, when the commissioners paid a courtesy call on the governor before he was to depart for England. The day before the visit, Moryson wrote to voice one final concern: the commissioners' belief that they had uncovered a scheme by the governor to thwart Virginia's goal of voiding the Northern Neck patents. As part of the postrebellion settlement, James, Duke of York and heir to his brother, Charles II, had promised to force the patentees to surrender their claims without further cost to the colony. Moryson accused Berkeley of secretly trying to obstruct "this good and Royall Act," warning him, "think how ill [your actions] will be taken both here and in England…especially when two soe neare Relations as yours and your Lady's are concern'd." The threat was not even thinly disguised: the commissioners were threatening to publicize how William Berkeley was favoring his extended family's financial well-being rather than the colony's. Frances Berkeley responded to this piece of blackmail in a way that left the commissioners outraged.[31]

The visit by Berry, Moryson, and Jeffreys to Green Spring on April 22 evidently went smoothly and civilly enough. Then, they later recounted, when they and their entourage set off to walk to their barge to be ferried back to the plantation where they were staying, "my Lady Berkeley with great forwardnesse often press'd the making ready of the coach for us."[32] The commissioners reported that because there were too many people in their party to ride together comfortably, "wee chose rather to walk on foot, to the landing place." Lady Frances nevertheless "urg'd the Courtesey of the coach," ordering it to follow them to their barge, "that when wee would, wee might take turnes [riding]." By "greate and good luck," though, they observed in retrospect, they all walked the entire way.

As they entered the barge, they turned to look behind them and recognized that the postillion riding one of the horses harnessed to the coach was Virginia's executioner. They had seen him regularly at Green Spring place halters on prisoners' necks, "when they were to make (in that posture) their Submission for their Crimes att the Barr of Justice." The commissioners charged that the hangman had been designated their escort specifically to dishonor them. He had "boldly" taken his position on the horse in full view of the governor and several councillors, yet no one acknowledged his identity and the affront to them. Lady Berkeley had retired to her room before their departure "and peep'd through a broken quarrell of the Glasse, to observe how the Show looked." This "trick," the commissioners concluded, "lookes more like a womans, than a mans malice."

Since executioners were universally reviled in seventeenth-century Anglo-American culture, the commissioners were infuriated by the insult. They let the governor know it in no uncertain terms. Whereas they previously addressed Sir William as "Right Honorable," their letter of April 23 began curtly with "Sir." With their visit they had paid him a "Civill complement" that surely deserved better than to send them off as he had. Berkeley had offered a "high Indignitie" to the king, to their official role, and to themselves "in our Private persons as Gentlemen." He *had* to have known that the hangman had been the postillion, "purposely sent for as a Retainer to Performe the Ceremonys of yesterdaye."[33]

This time the governor responded with alacrity, claiming to be "as innocent in this as the blessed Angells themelves" and likening himself to Jesus Christ and Charles I, both of whom had also been falsely accused of heinous offenses.[34] "I never saw the ffellows face but once before, and did not know hee was in my house," Berkeley insisted. "But I have sent the Negro [coachman] to you to bee rackt Tortur'd or whipt, till hee confesse how this Dire misfortune happen'd, and I hope this will give you satisfaction."

His wife replied at greater length. While admitting that she had ordered the coach and thus that any fault was hers, she nevertheless described the identity of the postillion as an "innocent mistake." (How the error might have occurred, she did not say.) All she did was to direct the coachman—surely one of their slaves—to prepare the coach "with all the speed he could to wayt upon you to the Landing." After saying farewell, she had returned to her room while the governor saw them off. She confirmed Sir William's statement that he would not have recognized the hangman. If there was a problem, she insisted, it lay with the coachman. She, like her husband, reiterated that the commissioners should closely question that bondsman to learn the truth of the matter. But if the commissioners did so, they did not report their findings to anyone. Presumably, certain that an enslaved man could not have been responsible for the insult, they refused to make him the scapegoat and took no action against him.

Having defended herself and her spouse, Frances Berkeley then took the offensive. Describing her husband as "persecuted," she declared that he was being treated "more severely with in this censure … then ever man of his quality & Character has been in the world." She too could cite the king: the commissioners' invective would make Charles II "think you have done some indignity to the choice his royall father & he have made of him in this & many imployments." How could they possibly believe that a man of her husband's standing "could be guilty of putting so vild [sic] an affront upon any person that had his Majesties Stamp & character"?

In her missive Lady Frances vehemently denied that her husband bore any responsibility for the "vile" insult to the commissioners. But of course the commissioners suspected that she herself had instigated the demeaning episode. And with respect to her own culpability, her letter was less than an unqualified defense. Although she called the incident an "innocent mistake" and declared that neither she nor her husband had given much thought to the identity of the postillion at the time, nowhere did she state that she had not planned *in advance* to have the hangman serve in that capacity. Instead, she recounted only her orders to her enslaved coachman on the evening in question. While affirming that the governor would not have recognized the hangman (perhaps because of poor eyesight or his illness?), she said nothing about whether or not *she* knew him—and if he had been at the house as often as the commissioners indicated, she certainly would have been well aware of his identity. Berry, Moryson, and Jeffreys were clearly correct to conclude that she had been responsible for the slur.

She had therefore deliberately violated the norms of hospitality far more overtly than had Nathaniel Bacon in offering payment for his wife's stay with her. She did so with such evident malice that one can imagine her glee as she peered out the window at the executioner escorting her husband's enemies away from Green Spring. The extraordinary cultural value she and the commissioners placed on outward shows of civility and courtliness underscored and amplified the character of the insult she had offered them. The commissioners were right to be deeply offended by her contemptuous gesture.

And yet Moryson, behaving like a gentleman, indicated in his answer to the Berkeleys' letters that he believed the governor's "high and solemn protests," and he forbore mentioning Lady Berkeley's guilt. But simultaneously he reminded Berkeley of the contents of his letter of April 21, which preceded and undoubtedly helped to precipitate the hangman affair. He requested "a full and Perticular Reply," threatening to inform the Duke of York about the governor's attempts to undermine the pending arrangements for the Northern Neck patents. In response, Berkeley again apologized for what he called the "late dire misfortune." But he failed to mention the patents.[35]

By the time the commissioners wrote to England in early May to inform their superiors of the embarrassing episode, the story of the hangman postillion had become widely known throughout the colony. The commissioners knew whom to blame for "the publique Odium and disgrace cast upon us": the Berkeleys themselves. Lady Frances in particular had skillfully disseminated the damaging tale. Even Virginians who opposed the Berkeleys must have laughed when they heard of the clever affront—and then quickly passed the news on to others. The resulting "contempt" for Herbert Jeffreys, the commissioners observed, had made it difficult for Moryson and Berry to combat "the little Character Stamp't on him by Sir William Berkeley and his ffavorites." Jeffreys was now "Sunk...downe Soe low in the People's opinion as to believe him but his [Berkeley's] (but not the Kings) Lieutenant Governor." In short, Lady Frances Berkeley, having recently experienced what it was like to have her husband "slighted, Scorn'd and Trampled on by the People," had extracted her revenge by ensuring that his successor faced the same problem.[36]

Berkeley himself did not leave without a parting shot directed at Jeffreys personally. On April 28, he accused Jeffreys of an "unresistable desire to rule this cuntrey," protesting Jeffreys's recent proclamation declaring himself governor even before Berkeley's departure. Adopting the commissioners' own phrasing, Berkeley charged his successor with "a high indignity" and predicted that Jeffreys's term in office would be brief. Either Berkeley would soon return to govern the colony again or Virginia would be placed in the hands of his already designated permanent successor, Thomas, Lord Culpeper, his wife's second cousin. Virginia's residents, Berkeley prophesied darkly, would "quickly find a difference betweene your management and mine," because Jeffreys was ignorant of the "Lawes Customes and nature" of the colony. For once, Lady Frances acted with discretion: she did not convey this letter to Jeffreys until June 7, when her husband's vessel was far out to sea. Jeffreys sputtered with rage after he read it, terming the letter "full of Scurrility, abuse & injury" and expressing his concern that Berkeley's "pernitious artifices" had "Poysoned" the mind of the councillors and the "Credulous." Everyone, he wrote, believed that "I act onely as Sir William Berkeley's

Deputie and that hee shall certainly reassume the Seate of the Government next Shipping."[37]

Thus the Berkeleys' actions shortly before Sir William's departure, especially the cunning slur Lady Frances directed at the commissioners, adroitly reestablished their—now her—preeminent position in the colony. Her aristocratic standing gave her the knowledge and ability to use the devastating symbolism of the hangman postillion to challenge the commissioners' reputations. By making them into public laughingstocks, she shrewdly revenged herself on them. Jeffreys had been put on the defensive and would never recover.

The Green Spring Faction

William Berkeley's parting words to Jeffreys included the comment that "my wife tells me she has armed herselfe with patience to endure all the Ignominies and contumilies that shall be put [on] her." He stressed Lady Frances's need for a "greate stocke of Patiense and Resignation" in the coming months.[38] But Herbert Jeffreys and claimants on Sir William's estate, confronted with his wife's unwavering resistance, turned out to be in greater need of patience than she.

Lady Berkeley revealed the attitudes that would govern her political actions in the coming years in a letter she addressed to her husband on August 9, not realizing that he had already been dead for several weeks.[39] "My Dear Dear Sir," she began, expressing the hope that he would soon return home to Virginia. Yet she also voiced her fear that he would be delayed in England by the complaints which "wretched villains" had submitted to the commissioners and which Moryson and Berry were carrying to London (they had left the previous month). Lt. Governor Jeffreys, she reported, had "sayd publicklie he would lay a 100£ ... [that] you would not be admitted to see his majesties face but would be clapt into the Tower."

Lady Frances made no effort to hide her anger at Francis Moryson, once Berkeley's friend. Although Berry proposed penalizing some men who had behaved badly after being pardoned, she reported, Moryson had rejected the plan. When the commissioners arrived in Virginia, she claimed, "there wase nothing talkt of then but humullitie & sorrow for their faults & protestations never to be guilltie of the like [again]." Now, though, she wrote sarcastically, Moryson "has been ablle through the forse of his great parts & witt... to perswad them they had done nothing amisse."

If matters continued thus, Lady Frances predicted, governmental authority would collapse, and she cited several recent examples. Prominent among the malefactors was Robert Jones, the very man whose pardon she had facilitated. When it was rumored that forty "Rogues" who had escaped capture were going to renew the rebellion, Jones and a large number of others "fell to drinking healths & shooting Guns all night." Jones and the others had then almost killed the sheriff who came to arrest them. Another man "made a riott when the court was setting & told them they had no power to sitt," and a third, in court at Jamestown, publicly declared that Nathaniel Bacon Sr. (a Berkeley supporter) was "a greater traytor then his Cousin Bacon." Such events were occurring "in allmost everie Countie," she observed, praying that God would mercifully deliver Virginia from such troubled times.

The contents of this letter, which she signed, "Your most ffathfull & Most affectionat ff Berkeley," portrayed herself as her husband's staunch ally and vigorous partisan. Her passionately expressed support for him and her derisive comments about his critics in this, her only political letter known to survive today, confirm earlier judgments reached herein about her deliberate maligning of her cousin and her ultimate responsibility for the insult to the commissioners. Lady Frances Berkeley clearly moved with confidence in the political arena. Further, she never wavered in her opposition to Herbert Jeffreys or in her pursuit of what she regarded as her financial rights in the wake of her husband's death.

The latter became especially clear during her prolonged battle with Mistress Sarah Drummond, the widow of one of the men convicted and hanged under martial law in January 1676/7.[40] William Drummond had once served as governor of North Carolina; a major Virginia landowner, he had been one of Bacon's most prominent supporters. His widow traveled to London to present her case directly to the Lords of Trade and Plantations in October 1677. Her petition, designed to win their sympathy, alleged that Sir William Berkeley had a personal grievance against her husband, who had been mistreated, prevented from defending himself properly, and quickly executed within hours of his conviction. She also averred that "he never bore Armes or any Military Office." The governor had "remooved & Imbezziled" goods from her "small Plantation," she charged, leaving her and her children to "wander in the Deserts and Woods, till they were ready to starve." She praised the commissioners, who had allowed her to return home and to maintain control over "a small Remaynder" of Drummond's personal estate until the king made a decision about her case. She asked that the property be fully restored to her.

A committee of the Lords of Trade discussed Sarah Drummond's petition with Berry and Moryson, who concurred that her situation was "very deplorable" and affirmed that many Virginians reported that her husband had been mistreated while in custody. The Lords of Trade recommended to the Privy Council that Jeffreys and the Virginia Council be required to confirm her possession of her current lands and of "the present Crop," and also to aid her in recovering her property "in what hands so ever the same may be found." But they further suggested that these measures be seen as "temporary Reliefe" only, and that she be asked to post bond until a final decision on wartime claims was reached. The Privy Council accepted the recommendation, and that order was drafted for the king's signature.[41]

Yet the contents of Sarah Drummond's petition were disingenuous. True, her husband had not formally served in Bacon's forces, but he had been a key supporter and collaborator of the rebel leader. She had misrepresented how long he had been held before his conviction and what had happened at his trial; evidently, after numerous witnesses had testified against him, he had confessed. The "small Plantation" where the Drummonds lived (although they owned more land elsewhere) had actually been rented from Sir William Berkeley, a possibly relevant fact she omitted. After the Privy Council issued its order, which referred to Berry and Moryson's having confirmed the truth of her petition, Moryson objected to its wording. He and Berry had characterized how Drummond died as "deplorable," but "his guilt...without doubt was enough to condemne him."[42]

Sarah Drummond returned to Virginia with the king's letter and presented it to the Virginia Council (sitting as the General Court) in early June 1678, accompanied by her accounting of the goods she said Governor Berkeley had seized from her plantation fifteen months earlier. The councillors reacted with outrage. Her petition to the king had been "in many particulars highly false and scandalous," they insisted. Her son-in-law argued that the fault lay with the commissioners, a claim that further angered the council members. The council then ducked the whole matter by deciding that because Lt. Governor Jeffreys, to whom the king's letter was addressed, was absent on account of illness, "the matter doth not lye before them." Sarah Drummond reported that the court session was turbulent, filled with "loud and confused" talk by many parties, and that after it ended two attorneys nearly came to blows over some of the insults that had been exchanged.[43]

At the same court session, Mistress Drummond sued Lady Frances Berkeley for the return of her property. The lengthy records of that case were destroyed in the 1860s, but a few surviving documents (and notes by those who saw the records before their destruction) allow at least a skeletal reconstruction of what was alleged on both sides. Mistress Drummond ultimately won the case, possibly in August or September 1678.[44] She filed two separate complaints against Lady Berkeley. The first sought restoration of the property seized from her husband's estate in March 1676/7 by, she claimed, *both* Berkeleys, not just the governor; the second sued Lady Frances for "her own wrong" while acting as her late husband's executrix.

The property taken fifteen months earlier, which Drummond valued at more than £144, included not only tobacco, grain, and livestock, but also 2,600 "Rived" boards and household furnishings. According to the second petition, in June and July 1677 Lady Berkeley had sent "divers of her servants" to the Drummond plantation to seize all the tobacco plants, and then in November had dispatched twenty men to take "all the Indian Corne...then and there growing." Everything seized had been carried to Green Spring and "converted...to [Frances's] own use." As a result of her losses, Sarah averred, she could feed neither her livestock nor her family and servants, and she was "reduced to extreme necessity." She had "fairly and civily" asked Lady Frances to return all these items, but she "hath utterly refused and still doth refuse, for the same, to make any satisfaction." Such resistance to an equitable outcome served as "an open and evil example to other persons to perpetrate and commit the like unlawful attempts," Sarah alleged, requesting both restitution and damages.

Frances Berkeley submitted evidence showing that during Sarah Drummond's absence she had ordered her servants to repair the Drummond plantation's "ruinous state" by preparing the ground for planting. (The Drummonds, after all, had been her husband's tenants; perhaps their rented land was in better condition than Green Spring's in the immediate aftermath of the rebellion.) Even though she had planted neither the tobacco nor the corn she seized, she contended that "she was entitled to the corn [and, presumably, tobacco], in consideration of the labor she bestowed on the plantation."[45]

Just as she did when confronting Nathaniel Bacon and later the commissioners, Lady Frances Berkeley also went on the attack, zealously defending her husband's conduct. She presented extensive documentation to prove that William Drummond had supported "the Grand Rebel Bacon," had been overheard claiming a sword as his "Commission," and had charged that Sir William Berkeley's authority as governor had expired before the rebellion. She also challenged details in Sarah's narrative of her husband's capture and imprisonment. Nor did Lady Frances stop there: she insisted that Sarah Drummond too was "a notorious & wicked rebel." At least three people supplied depositions recounting conversations with Mistress Drummond in which she expressed either support for Bacon or opposition to English authority. According to one witness, Sarah had remarked, "The child that is unborn shall have cause to rejoice for the good that will come yet by *the rising of the country.*" Another revealed that she once took "a straw or small stick, broke it, & said, 'I value the power of England no more than that. . . . We can build ships & trade to any part of the world we pleased as well as N[ew] England.'" In short, Lady Berkeley contended, Sarah Drummond herself had engaged in "inciting & incouraging the people to the late rebellion: persuading the soldiers to persist therein." Surviving materials do not record how Mistress Drummond replied to such charges, but the fact that Frances Berkeley made them confirmed that for her, the best defense remained a good offense.[46]

The same strategy characterized her interactions with the new lieutenant governor, Herbert Jeffreys (and her battles with his widow following his death in November 1678).[47] After her husband's departure, then death, Lady Frances became the focal point of opposition to Jeffreys. No example better illustrates the political power of a high-status seventeenth-century woman than Lady Frances's centrality in the efforts of the so-called Green Spring faction to thwart her husband's successor for the nineteen months he served as lieutenant governor.

Jeffreys filled his reports to his superiors in England with complaints about "the Mallitious Tongues of some ffactious Spirited people in this Country late Creatures of Sir William Berkleys." At first, undoubtedly seeking to be discreet, Jeffreys did not name his predecessor's widow as one of his key rivals, instead focusing much of his ire on Colonel Philip Ludwell, with whom he had an ongoing dispute, and Robert Beverley, the assembly's clerk. But before long he began referring to his antagonists as the "Green Spring Caball" or "the Green Spring Interest," thus linking them inextricably to Lady Frances. He also identified Alexander Culpeper, her brother, as "Their great Sollicitor in all Their Affaires" in England.[48]

Jeffreys first explicitly mentioned Lady Berkeley's pivotal role in the opposition he faced in an account drafted after the court session of early June 1678. Revealing that by then Lady Frances had worked actively against him for over a year, he charged that she had—until the arrival of "Certaine" news of her husband's death—induced "Terrour and fear Amongst the people, Threatning severe punishment at her Husbands returne to the Government." Her rumor mongering "Tended to the Disturbance of the Public Peace and Hindred the good settlement of The Country," Jeffreys observed. After Sir William's death was verified, she met "Often" with her allies at Green Spring "and doe now Endeavour to Possesse the people of the Beleife that my Lord Culpepper is her great freind." She had promised "great favours" to her associates after Culpeper became the colony's governor. Such reports created "a Great Dissattisfaction" among Virginians, Jeffreys remarked, predicting that if it were not soon made clear whether Lord Culpeper would come to America, "They may with their Artifice deceive The People and Keepe Them in

Ignorance." Jeffreys attributed the "Mallice" of the Green Spring group to his own efforts to carry out the king's instructions "in Vindicating the Right of his Subjects, against Those who have Wronged and Oppressed Them."[49]

The beleaguered lieutenant governor cited specific incidents to support his account of confronting inveterate antagonism from Lady Berkeley and her allies. Two stand out. First, when news arrived in early September 1677 that the king had voided Berkeley's flawed pardon proclamation of the previous February and instead wished to assure Virginians of his "free grace & mercy," the council at first refused to publicize the monarch's decision. Councillors protested that Charles II had been given "false Information" and that they wanted time to convince him of his error. Jeffreys alone was not able to win their agreement to publication, but the support of a visiting official (who arrived at the end of October) allowed him to overcome the council's objections. Charles II's proclamation then brought "great Joy" to all "Except Sir William Berkley's partie," the official reported on his return to London.[50]

Second was the dispute between Jeffreys and Philip Ludwell alluded to earlier. Ludwell had sued a former rebel whom he accused of robbing him during the war. The rebel cited a pardon from Jeffreys as the reason he could not be sued, and the infuriated Ludwell, well fueled by "syder," slandered Jeffreys, calling him "A Pittifull little fellow with A Perrewigg" and "A Worse Rebell Then Bacon" because he had broken Virginia law, "which Bacon Never did." Ludwell, too, charged that Jeffreys did not dispense "Equall Right and Justice." Jeffreys then accused Ludwell of contempt of authority, bringing him to trial before the General Court. That court, composed of Ludwell's fellow councillors, agreed with a jury that Ludwell's words were "scandalous," but they could not concur on an appropriate punishment. After appeals filed by both Ludwell and Jeffreys, the whole matter was referred to the Privy Council for its determination. Frustrated, the lieutenant governor could only continue to repeat his complaints about such "Effronts, Insolencyes, and Injuryes."[51]

And at the core of those complaints remained Lady Frances Berkeley. In July 1678, Jeffreys charged that she "acts still in the same maner as if Her Husband were still livinge." She summoned her cohorts on the council "to the frequent Caball at Greenspring," excluding from those sessions the three councillors who supported Jeffreys. His rivals often invoked Lord Culpeper's name, "telling the people what alteration they shall finde at His Lordships arrivall by this means encourageing their owne factious party and driving the rest of the people into despaire." Another Virginian, the attorney William Sherwood (who had supported Sir William Berkeley during the rebellion but opposed the Green Spring faction thereafter), confirmed the accuracy of Jeffreys's account. "Some discontented persons" allied with Lady Frances "endeavour by all the cunning contrivances that by their artifice can be brought about" to create contempt for Jeffreys, Sherwood reported. He warned a secretary of state that "itt's to be justly feared unless these fiery Sperrits are allayed or removed home there will not be that happy peace & unity which otherwise might be, for they are entred into a faction, which is upheld by the expectation of my Lord Culpeper's doeing mighty things for them & their interest."[52]

In the end, though, Lord Culpeper proved to be no Sir William Berkeley. After Jeffreys died in November 1678, Frances Berkeley's role in Virginia politics appears to have receded into the background. Jeffreys's initial replacement was Sir Henry Chicheley, a Virginian who had served as his deputy. Chicheley, a Berkeley supporter during the rebellion, expressed great respect for Lady Frances and appears to have avoided antagonizing her unduly—or at least he did not complain about her in any surviving letters. Perhaps he knew her well enough to circumvent her machinations. Thomas, Lord Culpeper, Frances's second cousin, did not arrive to take up his post until May 1680, having proved even more reluctant to leave England for Virginia than William Berkeley had been to take the same voyage in reverse. Lady Frances greeted her cousin with what seems to have been greater than her usual warmth, understandably given her high expectations for his future favor. He informed his sister that Lady Berkeley had showed him "more kindnesse . . . than I ever expect or desire"—more even than he had received from his brother and other sisters "in my whole Life." When he wrote, he was living "frankly" with her at Green Spring, "without any of your European selvishnesse, or politick coveteousnesse to disturbe us." Yet the pleasant interlude did not last long; late in the summer of 1680, he abandoned Virginia for England. Prodded by his superiors, he reluctantly returned to his duties in late 1682 but again left for England after staying less than a year. As a result, he lost his governorship to Lord Howard of Effingham.[53]

About the time her second cousin arrived in Virginia in 1680, Frances Berkeley took as her third husband Philip Ludwell, the defamer of Jeffreys who was a widower four years her junior. For the rest of her life, she nevertheless continued to style herself "Lady Berkeley," and her contemporaries always referred to her thus, also terming Green Spring "her" home. She and Ludwell lived primarily there even after he became governor of North Carolina in late 1689. The couple traveled to England several times in the 1680s and early 1690s. During her marriage to Ludwell, which lasted for the fifteen years until her death in 1695, her political activities were less notice-able than during her marriage to Berkeley. Yet, even so, she continued to be known for her hospitality, for her excellent contacts in England, and, typically, for her willingness to be "very free in communicating" her opinions about political matters.[54]

Amid all the criticisms voiced by Herbert Jeffreys and others about Lady Frances Berkeley's political activism, one is glaringly absent: she was never said to have stepped outside the boundaries of the "private sphere," "women's proper role," or the like. *No one ever said that she should not have been meddling in politics.* Nor did she ever offer a comment indicating that she believed she was acting inappropriately. When she wrote that exuberantly political letter to her husband in August 1677, she offered no apologies or demurrals.

Lady Berkeley's actions and the reactions (or nonreactions) to them by her contemporaries therefore underscore that expectations for the public roles of seventeenth-century aristocratic women like herself differed greatly from expectations voiced in the eighteenth century and thereafter about *all* women. The world in which she lived was one in which rank trumped gen-der as a determinant of aspects of high-ranking women's roles. In short, she and her contemporaries recognized that she was an appropriate state actor, and she behaved accordingly.

Sarah Grendon's "Indiscrete Tattling"

Almost all the women who took an active role in the events of Bacon's Rebellion were high-ranking, like Lady Frances. Some of them participated unwillingly—for instance, the "white apron" hostages, the wives of some of Berkeley's gentry supporters, who were forced by Bacon to protect his men during his attack on Jamestown in September 1676. Yet most of the women who voluntarily undertook politically charged actions supported Nathaniel Bacon, not Sir William Berkeley; and, like Mistress Sarah Drummond, they had to face the consequences of their actions after the war ended. In one such case appeared the glimmer—but only a glimmer—of a new attitude toward a high-status woman's public role.[55]

That case involved the Bacon partisan Mistress Sarah Grendon, the one woman exempted from Governor Berkeley's pardon proclamation. "By her lying and scandalous Reports," she was "the first great encourager and setter on of the ignorant Vulgar," Berkeley charged; and she was consistently "an active ayder assistor and abettor of the Rebells." So he referred Sarah Gren-don, "the wife and Attorney" of Thomas Grendon, to the commissioners for examination and trial.[56]

But when the commissioners looked into her case in March 1676/7 in response to a petition from her husband, Thomas, they found little to concern them. Mistress Grendon, who was managing her husband's estate during his absence in England on business, had, Thomas indicated, "utter'd some foolish and indiscrete words," which had led Berkeley to order one of his allies to seize property from her. Berry and Moryson decided that the seizure had been wrong, for three reasons. The confiscated property had been her husband's, not hers, and no one claimed that her absent spouse had any involvement in the rebellion. The warrant, though issued in November 1676, had not been executed until the following February, after "the Country was settled in Peace"; and, most important for this analysis, "the speaking of some foolish words by a simple woman (though tending to disturbance in those ill tymes) was not pretence sufficient to seise the Estate of a husband soe far absent especially without due proofe and conviction."[57]

The commissioners thus adopted Thomas Grendon's characterization of his wife's words as "foolish," adding their own term, "simple woman" (in another document they referred to her "indiscrete tattle"). Sarah Grendon used similar phrasing when she submitted her own petition to the commissioners before her formal trial in May 1677. She was "seduced" to give gunpowder to "the late grand Rebell," she averred, because he had insisted that it would be used only against the Indians, "she being altogeather ignorant of his traitorous intentions." For good measure, she then combined her husband's wording with her own: "And your petitioner (being an Ignorant woman) confesseth she did speake some foolish & indiscreete words reflecting upon the sloe prosecution of the Indian warr, yett the same were not uttered with Intention of evill against his Majesties government in this Colony." She was, she insisted, "most heartily Sorrowful" for what she had said, and she hoped that the most "favourable construction" could be given to her words.[58]

The Grendons' pleas were successful. At the trial in May, as in their informal hearing in March, the commissioners found Sarah not guilty. "Wee found nothing done or acted by her, but what any woman in such a case might have well enough done to preserve her absent husband's Estate," they decided, "though in the maine shee shew'd a great deale of ffeare and a great deale of ffolly. Feare of Bacon's fforce, and ffolly in talking too favorably of his proceedings."[59]

So by turning an outspoken high-ranking female supporter of Bacon into a *simple, ignorant woman* who spoke *foolish and indiscreet words,* the Grendons achieved their goals of winning a pardon for Sarah and laying the groundwork for the restitution of their property. Should the Grendons' defense, and the commissioners' acceptance of it, be interpreted as one of the first occasions on which a high-status woman was seen as resembling other women more than she resembled other people (that is, men) of similar high social standing? Yes; but the matter is not quite so simple as that. Such major changes in thinking do not occur quickly or completely, as was demonstrated in a comment on the case by the attorney general of Virginia. Mistress Sarah Grendon, he remarked, had been subject to "the Comon ffeares and ffollyes of many other as well men as women" in the time of Bacon's Rebellion. She was afraid and foolish, but no more than men had been, too.[60]

Mistress Alice Tilly and Her Supporters, 1649–1650

Although Lady Frances Culpeper Stephens Berkeley and some of her high-ranking Virginia contemporaries moved comfortably in the political arena, seventeenth-century Anglo-American women of ordinary rank did not do so with equal assurance. Assumptions that women of high standing could claim political authority did not translate into notions that lower-status wives and mothers were appropriate state actors, even as supplicants.

A set of female-authored petitions submitted to the Massachusetts General Court in 1649–50 exposed most colonial women's uncertainty about venturing into the realm of politics. The 217 signatories to five closely related petitions sought the release of Mistress Alice Tilly, a jailed Bostonian whom the petitioners described as "the ablest midwife that wee knowe in the land." Individual women had long requested favors of one sort or another from governments in England or America, but in the colonies before the 1760s the Tilly petitioners were unique in joining together in a large sex-segregated group. Although they (like individual petitioners) asked the authorities for special consideration for one person and requested no overarching changes in public policy, Mistress Tilly's supporters nevertheless understood that they were breaking new ground. Their confidence in the midwife's skills never wavered, but in the end their criticism of the Massachusetts authorities' actions was muted and hesitant. Significantly, their petitions, which were irregular in form and content, disclosed a striking lack of prior experience as state actors.[1]

At the end of February 1648/9, the midwife Alice Tilly was arrested, jailed, and charged with medical malpractice that had caused the deaths of one or more patients, "yong or ould." Several months later, in early May, the Massachusetts Bay Court of Assistants, the colony's highest judicial body, tried and convicted her.

Two petitions from groups of women predating her trial and one submitted in its immediate aftermath asked the court to allow Mistress Tilly to continue to attend parturient women without posting bond, despite the serious nature of the crime of which she had been accused and then convicted.[2] The petitioners, primarily married women of childbearing age (but including older female relatives as well), attested to Alice Tilly's "skill & ability," asserting that "wee and many more of us can speake by experience" of the midwife's conduct at childbeds. By contrast, the magistrates they addressed—excluded from childbirths, as were all men at that time—"can speake but by hearesay."

Even though it might thus seem that the women were challenging the decision to prosecute Mistress Tilly, they disclaimed any "desyr to put in to interrupt the Corts proceedeing." Rather, their goal was personal: to ensure that Mistress Tilly, whom they trusted despite the accusations of misconduct, could continue to supervise her patients' childbirths regardless of the outcome of the prosecution. And the post-trial 1649 petitioners achieved that limited goal, convincing the judges that "Authority [may] be aswell manteyned, by Clemency in Remitting, as by Constancy in upholding, a Sentence at Court." Accordingly, after her arrest and even after her conviction and during her nominal confinement for many months in the Boston jail, Mistress Tilly continued her active midwifery practice and was not required to post bail to do so.

But Alice Tilly and her husband had a wider aim: they wanted her innocence formally established. After she was found guilty, they began threatening to leave Boston unless she was freed from even minimal supervision. Her patients and their female relatives, frightened at that prospect, submitted two more petitions in May 1650, asking that "the door of free liberty" be opened to the midwife. The Court of Assistants summarily rejected their request. The judges charged that "nothinge but a compleat victory over magistracy" would satisfy Mistress Tilly, declaring that they had already complied as much as they could "w[i]thout betrayinge all authoritie into her hands." So they insisted that they would go no further, and they directed the petitioners to halt their efforts on the midwife's behalf. Even so, Alice Tilly remained in Boston and presumably attended many more childbeds. It is unclear how long her nominal confinement lasted.[3]

The five petitions varied in length and sophistication and in the number of names attached. Many of the "signatures" appeared in lists of names copied by scribal hands; probably many of the subscribers could not write, even though, as Puritans, they most likely could read. (A few names were accompanied by marks.) Two petitions from Dorchester, where Mistress Tilly had lived and practiced midwifery before she moved to Boston, had 23 and 46 signatures, respectively. The Dorchester appeals were probably drafted by Mary Greenaway, whose name appeared first on both, and four of whose daughters signed multiple petitions. The 1649 document revealed an inexperienced author: it confirmed Alice Tilly's skill but asked nothing of the magistrates, merely stating a pious wish for "god to undertake for her in a way of his owne: to cleare her name." It had no formal address and ended without a closing phrase. The 1650 Dorchester petition employed tangled prose, but it was copied by a more expert hand and was directed "to our honored Governour Deputie Governour And to the rest of the magistrates or any other whom it may concerne." It concluded with the clause, "we shall humbly pray for yor worships prosperitie & remaine thankfully obliged unto your worships." Thus in the intervening year Greenaway or one of her allies seemed to have learned to approximate the phrasing that was expected in formal petitions addressed to the General Court.[4]

The authorship of two of the three Boston appeals—one submitted before the trial in 1649 and one in 1650—is uncertain. These petitions contained the largest number of nominal signatures (69, 173); 27 women's names appeared on both, with 7 of those also appending signatures to the third Boston petition, discussed shortly. Like the 1650 Dorchester appeal, the handwriting in both was that of a scribe, but they were seemingly composed by a person or persons unfamiliar with the standard format of such documents. Although formally addressed to the governor and deputy governor by name, they too concluded irregularly: the first ended, "and yor petitioners shal be thereby ffurther oblidged to pray for yor worships"; the second, "yor Petitioners, who shall how ever count themselves bound to pray for you, & all of God sett over us." Both these phrases were garbled versions of the common closing of appeals to superiors, "and your petitioners in duty bound, shall ever pray, etc."[5]

Significantly, the most successful of the five petitions was the Boston appeal drafted shortly after Mistress Tilly's conviction; those submitted before her trial received no recorded response, and the 1650 petitions, as already indicated, were decisively rejected. But the mid-May appeal, although it was just as inexpert in form as the others, elicited the positive reaction from colonial officials quoted above: the recognition of the need for "Clemency" and flexibility in dealing with Alice Tilly despite her conviction for a serious criminal offense.

What distinguished that petition was not its content but the identity of its signers. Although it had the fewest signatures (only 21), its adherents were the wives of Boston's elite, the friends and relatives of the judges. The first name on the list, the probable originator, was Mistress Elizabeth Wilson, wife of Boston's chief pastor, the Reverend John Wilson. The wives of two of the church's elders—Elizabeth Rainsford and Margery Colbron—also signed. In fact, all but two signers were church members (or, in two instances, the wives of church members); at a time when church membership was restricted to those of acknowledged piety and upstanding conduct, such credentials were an important indicator of status. Further, one of the nonmember signers was Ursula, the wife of David Yale, a wealthy merchant and dissenter from strict Puritan doctrines who was however the stepson of the influential governor of the New Haven colony, Theophilus Eaton. The unique success of this petition reaffirms the influence that higher-status seventeenth-century women could wield in political contexts.[6]

Describing themselves as "humble," "poor," or "trembling" representatives of "the weakest sexe," all the petitioners nevertheless asserted their expertise in assessing Mistress Tilly's skills as a midwife. "We doe Judge her able & fitt for that place & Callinge," insisted one group; "none of those whoe are her accusers could Doe [as well as she] but have either sent for her or left the work undone," declared another. Although they questioned men's judgment in this particular instance, the petitioners made it clear that they did not intend to encroach on the realm of formal politics and law. "Wee dare nott assume above our line to direct [you]," they acknowledged, admitting that either "God" or Mistress Tilly's "owne conscience" might possibly condemn the reported "black side of her actions." They originally requested only what they achieved, Alice Tilly's freedom of movement without the requirement of bail, rather than her acquittal. Even the two 1650 petitions, which asked that she be freed from all supervision, placed that appeal in the context of their need for her services instead of disagreement with the guilty verdict.[7]

In all the petitions, only the last line of the 1650 submission from Boston offered a general statement about the polity. That sizable group of women concluded their appeal by terming themselves "(though weake yett) true hearted well wishers, & endeavourers of the publick good of those churches and Comon wealth God hath cast us in."[8] They accordingly aligned themselves with some female contemporaries in England, who were similarly asserting responsibility for preserving the public welfare. But the English women, caught up in the dramatic events of the Civil War, went far beyond their North American counterparts in their claims to civic activism.

❧ CHAPTER 2

English Women in the Public Realm, 1642–1653

"Wee your poore petitioners," the authors explained, were "imbouldned" to address the House of Lords because conditions in the nation were deteriorating rapidly. In early February 1641/2, the economy was in ruins, with trade in "decay"; Irish Catholics had revolted against English rule; and both "Church, and Common wealth" desperately needed reformation. The supplicants warned of the dangers posed by those "disaffected to the publique good" and asked that such people suffer proper punishment. Another petition, submitted to the Commons the same day by the same group and later published, repeated those observations but also vigorously criticized the House of Lords for failing to expel bishops and papists from its ranks. "Your humble and distressed Petitioners, with bended knees, and upright hearts," it concluded, "shall daily pray for the continuance and prosperous successe of this High and Honourable Court of Parliament, to settle and reforme all things that are amisse in this Common-Wealth, both in Church and State, and all other his Majesties Kingdomes."[1]

Although no phrase in the text of either petition acknowledged it, the two documents were extraordinary. The authors identified themselves as "many poore distressed women in & about London" (to the Lords) or "many hundreds of distressed Women, Trades-mens Wives, and Widdowes" (to the Commons). For the first time in English history, a large group of women had come together to petition Parliament on topics of general concern. That the women did not bother to mount an explicit defense of their ability to address Parliament indicates that in such a time of crisis they believed their collective political intervention to be appropriate.[2]

Ever since medieval times groups of men with civic or corporate responsibilities had offered formal opinions to Parliament on matters with public-policy implications. But for a sex-segregated assemblage of ordinary women to express their ideas on such subjects was unprecedented. Only in the context of the dramatic disruption of traditional hierarchies that presaged the onset of civil war could such documents have been contemplated or drafted. The "distressed women" who produced the two petitions were not the female aristocrats whose political activities might have been anticipated—and thus would have elicited little or no criticism. Rather, ordinary women's claims to participate in public affairs violated customary assumptions about the suitable roles of lower-ranking people even in the absence of gendered public/private divisions. Accordingly, men of various political persuasions—both inside and outside Parliament—reacted with surprise and contempt to the women's assertions.[3]

Until the early 1640s in England, political discourse was expected to circulate solely among government officials and the gentry. Although such nominal secrecy was honored more in the breach than in actuality, ordinary people of either sex were thought to have little reason to seek access to political information and even less reason to offer their own opinions on public matters. Yet disputes between Charles I and Parliament, especially after November 1640, led to appeals by both sides to public opinion and to an explosion in political publications fueled by the breakdown of censorship in 1641. In an era of expanding and relatively widespread literacy, especially in London, the ready availability of print as a mechanism for distributing news and comment offered ordinary folk the opportunity to learn about the issues of the day. It also gave many previously silenced people—such as the female petitioners to the House of Commons—the ability to publish their opinions. Newsbooks (weekly newspapers in pamphlet form) representing a variety of political viewpoints interpreted events for their readers. By such means the authority of public opinion (indeed, the Habermasian "public sphere" itself) was created and invoked for the first time in Anglo-America. And female petitioners stood at the very heart of that process.[4]

The First Women's Petitions

The events of late 1641 and early 1642 that elicited petitions from English men and women had their roots in King Charles I's struggles with Parliament over financing the nation's involvement in wars—first in Europe, then later in Scotland. The king's Scots subjects resisted the imposition of a rewritten Book of Common Prayer in the late 1630s, setting off the so-called Bishops' Wars.[5] For eleven years after 1628, Charles had failed to call Parliament into session, knowing that it would be hostile to his requests for money, but he was finally forced to do so in early 1640 because of a pressing need to pay for the war in Scotland.

The Short Parliament, which sat for less than a month from mid-April to early May, refused to provide the king with any additional revenues until he agreed to correct long-standing grievances. Instead, he dissolved that body and headed north to fight the Scots, who beat his raw troops decisively in August. He had no choice but to summon Parliament again.

The men elected in fall 1640, who composed the Puritan-dominated body later known as the Long Parliament, then challenged the king openly on religious and secular affairs alike. Above all, such men feared the onset of popery. Although Charles I was the Protestant head of the Church of England, his wife, Queen Henrietta Maria, was a practicing Catholic who celebrated Mass in a specially built royal chapel. One of the new Parliament's first moves was to arrest and imprison the archbishop of Canterbury, William Laud, the man most responsible for attempts to impose a new, high-church orthodoxy on the Church of England. Rumors of popish plots abounded throughout 1641. In November of that year, Irish Catholics began a bloody rebellion against English rule. The London press reported at length on the slaughter of many Protestants, offering gory details bolstered by eyewitness accounts spread widely by refugees from the Irish conflict. English Protestants panicked, fearing the nation might be overrun by Catholics, foreign and domestic.

In multiple petitions to Parliament in the fall of 1641 and thereafter, reformers agitated for the abolition of all religious hierarchies and the removal of bishops from the House of Lords. In December 1641 and January 1641/2, Parliament and the king sparred over the presence of bishops among the peers and over control of the army in Ireland; and Charles made a major misstep by personally invading the House of Commons in a futile attempt to arrest five of its leaders. Frightened by the intensely negative reaction to his failed effort, Charles moved to his palace at Hampton Court, outside London. With the monarch gone, London fell under the control of Parliament in the first months of 1642. Large throngs of men began appearing at its doors to express their grievances or demonstrate their support for its actions.

At that juncture the group of "distressed women" drew up and submitted their petitions. No surviving source reveals how the women might have come together or organized themselves for the purpose of drafting and presenting their appeals, but they probably met initially through their parish churches. The petitioners referred to "severall" previous missives they had delivered to Parliament "divers times" before, but without achieving their desired goals because of opposition in the House of Lords. None of those earlier appeals has survived, nor did any contemporary comment on them, but they probably resembled the extant petitions.[6]

Newsbooks, official journals, and contemporary observers reported the women's actions on February 1 and the parliamentarians' response. That day, an estimated four or five hundred women pressed Lords and Commons for an answer to their petitions. Reputedly they insisted, "where there is One Woman now here, there would be Five hundred To-morrow; and that it was as good for them to die here, as at home." When Sergeant-Major General Phillip Skippon asked how he should deal with the "great Multitudes" of female petitioners at the door, the Commons directed him to try to persuade them to leave quietly, explaining that the house was considering more important matters and would respond later. Skippon was evidently convincing, for the petitioners dispersed from the doors of the Commons without incident. One observer, indicating that the women represented a group of about five thousand signatories, commented that "noe time, nor historie can shew, that such great numbers of oppressed Subjects of al sorts, ever petitioned with that humilitie, and desolved so quiettly."[7]

At the House of Lords, matters did not go so smoothly, perhaps because the petitioners blamed that body for the rejection of their earlier appeals. While the women were waiting to present their written request, the Duke of Lennox attempted to enter the chamber. They gave him a copy of their missive, but he replied scornfully, "Away with these women, wee were best to have a parliament of Women." A sympathetic newsbook recounted that several supplicants "catched hold of his staffe, humbly desiring him to receive their petition," but that he pulled back so abruptly the staff broke. The women then gave their document to another peer, who read it to the house. The Lords subsequently admitted twelve of the petitioners to explain their grievances in person.[8]

Even though both houses of Parliament thus took notice of the female supplicants, Lennox's retort revealed his—and other men's—disdain for them, as did the Commons's assertion that other matters before them were of greater consequence than the women's petition. For centuries, men had regarded ordinary women's meddling in politics as risible, an attitude (to take an ancient example) evident in Aristophanes' bawdy comedy, *Ecclesiazusae* (sometimes translated as *Parliament of Women*), in which a group of women disguised themselves as men, took control of Athens, and enacted such measures as

one requiring young men to have sex with older, unattractive women before engaging in sexual activity with more desirable partners of either sex.
Whether or not Lennox was familiar with Aristophanes' farce, his retort to
the female petitioners displayed a similar disparagement of their political acumen and foreshadowed assessments by later male observers, who repeatedly
responded to women's political activity not just dismissively but with sexual
innuendo.[9]

Indeed, the first such response had appeared after the initial (no longer
extant) women's petitions had been presented to Parliament but before the
submission of those dated February 1. In December 1641, a male parodist
published *The Petition of the Weamen of Middlesex, Which they intended to have
presented to the High Court of parliament, but shewing of it to some of their friends
they disswaded them from it, untill it should please God to endue them with more wit,
and lesse Non-sence.* The pun of "weamen"/wee men and the innuendo of
"Middlesex," as well as the long subtitle, pointed to the parodic nature of this
purported petition. So did its nonsensical, partly sexual content, in which the
"weamen" complained about cathedral choristers because those "well tuned
boys" reminded "wee women which are the weaker vessels" of a "Bawdi-
house." The conclusion, "that Males may not seeme to be more religious than
females, wee have bin bold to present this Petition," revealed derision for the
female petitioners' sincerity, if not much of the sought-after wit.[10]

Such negative reactions from parliamentarians and others surely influenced the content of the petition submitted to the House of Commons by
"Gentle-women, & Trades-mens wives In, and about the City of London"
on Friday, February 4. Whereas the appeals of February 1 had not explicitly
attempted to justify women's right to petition, that of February 4 addressed
the subject directly. Its published version declared on the title page that it
would provide "their severall reasons, why their Sex ought thus to Petition,
as well as the Men." Moreover, a new assertion that the petitioners were led
by "a Gentlewoman...and many others with her of like ranke and quality"
demonstrated that they were trying to claim the bona fide role in the polity
long accorded to women of noble standing. They identified their leader as
"Mrs [Mistress] Anne Stagg...Brewers wife," who was a resident of Southwark and perhaps came from a family of minor gentry (which would justify
the use of the title *Mistress*).[11]

Before being challenged by male contemporaries, English women had
initially and innovatively included themselves among the appropriately politically active. Like their menfolk, ordinary women had never before been
viewed—or seen themselves—as possible state actors. But now that men of
the "lower sort" were gathering at Parliament's doors and regularly petitioning

that body, women saw no reason that they should continue to be excluded. Confronted by an initial wave of male hostility, they chose to defend their ability to express their political and religious views in two ways. First, they drew on tradition by insisting that their leaders were gentlewomen and by stressing that status in the title of the published version of their petition. And second, they developed new arguments about women's political and religious obligations as state actors.

The substance of the February 4 petition resembled those of February 1, although it lacked any reference to the "decay of trade." It called for the expulsion of papists and bishops from the House of Lords; supported steps to purify religion, including forbidding the celebration of Mass; and lamented the fate of Irish Protestants. Yet its tone differed significantly from that of its two predecessors. The petitioners wrote *"with lowest submission"* and "all thankfull humility," adopting a humble posture largely absent from the earlier texts. Further, the February 4 petition repeatedly referred to the sex of the supplicants. By contrast, had the titles of the other missives not identified the authors as "distressed women," the contents would not have disclosed their gender. The group headed by Mistress Stagg explicitly mentioned their husbands and children and bemoaned the "savage usage and unheard of rapes, exercised upon our Sex in *Ireland*." They also expressed their sympathy for the women who had been "rendred in a manner Widdowes, and the children Fatherlesse" by the imprisonment of their husbands or by the men's solitary flight "into desert places amongst wild Beasts" (North America) to escape Archbishop Laud's persecution of Puritans, laymen and clerics alike.[12]

Significantly, the appeal submitted on February 4 listed several reasons why women should be able to petition Parliament, even though "it may be thought strange, and unbeseeming our sex." Declaring that their interest in the "common and publique cause of the Church" led to duties required of them, they asserted that Christ had died for all people's sins and expected the same obedience from men and women. Then, too, men's and women's "happiness" stemmed from the same "flourishing estate of the Church and common-wealth"; conversely, women would share "the common Calamities that accompany both Church and Common Wealth." Citing the Old Testament heroine Esther, who had risked her life for her religion, the women pronounced themselves "imboldned" to address the Commons, despite those who might "scoffe and deride our good intent." Disclaiming "any selfe conceit, or pride of heart, as seeking to equall our selves with men, either in Authority or wisdome," they nevertheless insisted on their need "to discharge that duty we owe to God, and the cause of the Church, as farre as lyeth in us."[13]

The "Gentle-women & Trades-mens wives" thus based women's right to petition Parliament firmly on ungendered religious duty. Twice they linked "Church and Common Wealth," and they insisted that men and women shared equally in both "happiness" and "Calamities," even if women did not equal men in "Authority or wisdome." Despite explicit and repeated reference to their gender in the text, they did not assign different religious responsibilities to men and women. Instead, their requests for religious and political reform mirrored men's. In their desire to deflect critics who would "scoffe and deride" them, they adopted a more explicitly "feminine" tone than that of the earlier petitions that same week. They also claimed a higher status. But all three petitions had the same aims. The "Gentle-women" simply had been forced to make explicit the presumptions of the right to participate in the commonwealth that were unstated but earlier assumed by the "distressed" women.[14]

Consequently, despite the significant differences in tone and the claim of the "Gentle-women" that they were "new" petitioners, it is most likely true, as a newsbook reported, that the women who presented this petition to the House of Commons on Friday, February 4, were the same as (or at least shared numerous adherents with) the supplicants of February 1. But regardless of authorship, the deliberately altered, more gendered, and status-conscious approach taken on February 4 had the desired effect. Acknowledging an inferior gender identity while simultaneously claiming a higher rank won for the women a gracious and positive response. The journal of the House of Commons recorded that the members of Parliament for Southwark, including the radical John Pym, were dispatched to tell the petitioners that the house had read the petition, recognized the calamitous circumstances they outlined, "and will use all the best Care they can for the preventing and Remedying of them."[15]

Pym informed the women that their petition had been "thankfully" received and that it had arrived at "a seasonable time." He promised them satisfaction, then asked them to return home, where they should offer prayers for the parliamentarians, who were trying "to perform the trust committed unto us, towards God, our King and Countrey, as becometh faithfull Christians and Loyall Subjects." The women evidently complied, and the next day the peers acted on one of the petitioners' major objectives, voting to exclude bishops from their midst. Yet Parliament also ordered Sergeant-Major General Skippon to organize "good and sufficient Guards" to protect the house chambers from incursions and disruptions. It was telling that both houses took that step after a week of petitioning by women, rather than earlier, when the petitioners were exclusively male.[16]

Satires and a Peace Petition

For the next eighteen months, women petitioners abandoned the political scene. That did not silence male satirists, who highlighted sexual themes in their parodies of women's supposed political statements. In August 1642, shortly after parliamentary and royal troops skirmished for the first time, *The Resolution of the Women of London to the Parliament,* illustrated by a crude woodcut of a man wearing a cuckold's horns, insisted that wives sent their husbands off to war with "hot zeale." Their spouses regularly fought with them, the London women asserted, so now they should fight the enemy. The "resolution" engaged in extended playful punning on the word *withdrawal* and indicated that its authors intended to "live as merrily as may be" and to take lovers in their husbands' absence.[17]

A few months later, in October, the armies clashed at Edgehill, northeast of London. The battle was inconclusive but left London open to possible attack by the royalists. Parliament gathered forces to defend the city, and in mid-November 1642 Charles, whose troops were greatly outnumbered, withdrew to Oxford to regroup. Perhaps with a sigh of relief, London wags began publishing broadsides purporting to be women's petitions to Parliament—broadsides that with seeming deliberation echoed the genuine petitions of early 1642.

In *The Mid-wives Just Petition* of late January 1642/3, the "divers good Gentlewomen of that faculty" complained that "our trade is now decayed" because of the dearth of men in London. Without resident husbands, women lacked access to "necessary comfort and benevolence" (sexual intercourse), and midwives had no business. For their own benefit and the general good, the "midwives" contended, wives should no longer send their husbands to battle but should "keep them fast locked within their own loving armes day and night." The same trope inspired three more mock petitions published in quick succession over the next few weeks. "Virgins" complained of the "insupportable burden" of their unmarried status; "many thousands of wives and matrons" decried the absence of both husbands and lovers; and "rich and wealthy widowes" lamented the loss of suitors and their hopes of "obtaining good and lusty young husbands." The satires all asked for peace, insisting that English women needed their menfolk at home.[18]

The parodies sexualized and personalized women's political views while trivializing possible concerns about continuing the war. Women who entered the political arena, the male authors implied, sought only their own limited goals. They could not see beyond their immediate advantage—in this case, access to men to satiate their inexhaustible sexual desires. Further, the lampoons copied the language of the 1642 petitions. The "midwives" who complained about "decayed" trade precisely repeated the complaint of the "distressed women" on February 1, 1641/2. The "many thousands of wives and matrons" both mocked the number of previous petitioners and claimed to represent "divers Gentlewomen of good credit, and Citizens Wives," thus linking their parody to the "Gentle-women" led by Mistress Stagg. The mock missives even satirized the 1642 petitioners' stated concern for church and commonwealth. All four early 1643 publications contended in one way or another that the presence of men was required to "replenish the Commonwealth with Inhabitants." Without men to father children, the midwives declared, London would lack men "fit for employment both for Church and State." Thus the interests of married and unmarried women, midwives, and anyone concerned with the nation's future all neatly coincided in the skillful sexual satires. And the parodists thereby found means to mock female supplicants' stated concern for the general good.[19]

Ironically, the women who next authored a petition to Parliament aligned themselves with the message of the lampoons. After a year of war and in the wake of a major royalist victory at Bristol at the end of July, in early August 1643 the House of Lords discussed sending six propositions for peace to the king at Oxford. A large group of female Londoners responded with an appeal supporting the propositions.

In the words of Lord Clarendon's contemporary history, the Lords' peace proposals prompted a "long and hot debate" in the Commons. On Saturday, August 5, the Commons voted to continue the discussions the following week. But when Parliament reconvened on Monday, its members confronted a huge crowd of male Londoners who supported continuing the war; the Lord Mayor then presented the city council's statement decrying the propositions. Sir Simonds D'Ewes, a pro-peace MP, described the demonstrators in his diary as a "seditious multitude" composed of "the dreggs and rascality of people" who offered "affronts and violence" to those who favored the propositions. He fiercely criticized the parliamentarians who refused to take steps to suppress the "unlawfull tumults" outside their chamber. When, under such pressure, the Commons voted narrowly to reject the peace propositions, D'Ewes observed that it ended "all our hopes of peace and tranquility for the present."[20]

According to Clarendon, the negative Commons vote on August 7 led the "wise and sober part" in the city to wish to speak up, but male Londoners who favored peace were too frightened to appear publicly. Their womenfolk, he declared, displayed more courage. On Tuesday, August 8, D'Ewes recorded, "a multitude of woemen...came to the very doore of the house of Commons, and there cryed as in divers other places Peace, Peace," while threatening violence toward MPs who favored continuing the war. The following day, adorned with white silk ribbons, they returned to present a formal petition to Parliament, relying, Clarendon observed, on "the precedent of a rabble of that sex appearing in the beginning of these distractions with a petition." Therefore, even though the female supplicants for peace in August 1643 sought the opposite goal from that of their predecessors eighteen months earlier and surely represented different constituencies, contemporaries (and perhaps the participants themselves) drew analogies between the two groups because of their unusual single-sex composition.[21]

Clarendon, sympathetic to their cause, described the petitioners as "a great multitude of wives of substantial citizens"; they termed themselves "many civilly disposed Women inhabiting in the Cities of London, Westminster, the Suburbs and parts adjacent." Other less supportive observers saw them quite differently, insisting that they were "dirty and tattered sluts" or "Whores, Bawdes, Oyster-women, Kitchen-stuffe women, Beggar women, and the very scum of the Suburbs, beside abundance of Irish women." The status of female petitioners thus became a matter of debate, and the legitimacy of their perceived claims rested in part on their social standing.[22]

A pro-Parliament newsbook printed their brief appeal, which another newsbook with a similar political bent termed essentially unexceptionable in its content. Referring to themselves as "your poore Petitioners (though the weaker Sex)," the women declared that they foresaw doom unless Parliament took quick action to end the conflict. Disclaiming a preference for a specific plan, they indicated that they would trust the parliamentarians' judgment to preserve "the true reformed Protestant Religion" and the "just Prerogatives and Privileges of King and Parliament" while seeking peace. They also requested the restoration of "the true Liberties and Properties of the Subject" and "the renovation of Trade for the benefit of the Subject."[23]

The women persuaded a member of the Commons to present the petition to that body, which dispatched six MPs to respond that the house wanted peace and would quickly consider their appeal, and that "in the meantime they should repair to their several dwellings." But the women refused to disperse, insisting instead on meeting with John Pym. As the crowd increased—perhaps to as many as five or six thousand—so did the uproar. One newsbook recounted that the demonstrators shouted, "Give us these Traytors that are against peace, that we may teare them to pieces." Parliament's guards appeared unable to maintain order, and the women, who had blocked the entrances to the house chambers, started to attack members of the Commons and Lords who were going in and out. Eventually, a cavalry troop scattered the crowd.

Two or three demonstrators were killed in the ensuing melee, and others were arrested and taken to prison to be questioned about "the prime contrivers of this Designe."[24]

In its aftermath, male observers assessed the disorderly demonstration. Pro-Parliament newsbooks defended the authorities' brutal suppression of the female peace petitioners, insisting that the women had brought the violence on themselves by their "outrageous" acts. Had they behaved "civilly," in line with their self-description, *Mercurius Civicus* observed, the demonstration would not have ended as it did. But since they had acted with "furious zeal" and had engaged in "insolent abusing of divers men of quality," the women bore the primary blame for the tragic outcome. The *Kingdomes Weekly Intelligencer* asserted that if the petitioners had been "reasonable," they would have been satisfied with the Commons' response. It was imperative, that newsbook stressed, to ferret out the "Ring-leaders" who had recruited women from throughout the city and suburbs of London on the night of Monday, August 7. In response to many inquiries, it claimed, the demonstrators had identified members of the nobility as instigating their actions. Asked where they had acquired the hundreds of yards of white silk ribbon they had worn to display their sentiments visually, various demonstrators mentioned obtaining it at the homes of noble ladies in Southwark, Westminster, or other suburbs of the City of London. Having thus exposed the "malignants" behind the demonstration, the *Kingdomes Weekly Intelligencer* concluded that the entire plot had been hatched in Oxford, the royalist headquarters, in order to cause divisions in London. The peace petition was "the Master piece," intended to provide royalists an opening "(by women) to get an opportunity to rise in Armes, and to sacrifice the Parliament." But instead the plan had been thwarted and its supporters in Parliament arrested.[25]

Sir Simonds D'Ewes, who was not molested by the large number of female demonstrators after he explained to them that he favored peace, reacted very differently to the events of August 9. "No man can excuse the indiscreet violence of these woemen," he observed, but even so the force used against them was excessive. The regular guards could have controlled the situation, but instead the cavalry had hunted down the demonstrators, treating them like "bruit beasts." Consequently, he remarked, he and others wondered why—when nothing was done to the large numbers of men who had violently confronted members of the House of Lords on August 7—"such seveare cruelty was used against these woemen who were onely mislead by theire wicked & unlawfull Example."[26]

The answer to that question, as D'Ewes himself surely knew well, lay in the conjunction of two factors: first, the opposing goals expressed by the male demonstrators on August 7 and the women on August 8–9; and second, the gender-differentiated identity of the two sets of petitioners. The combination of the two came to the fore in a newsbook account. Defending the August 7 men as demonstrating "not against peace, but such a peace as might destroy," the *Parliament Scout* characterized their protest as nothing more than directing some "unadvised words" against the peers. It then asserted that large numbers of people could rightfully (though rarely) petition for redress when injustices had been committed, but that such crowds acted illegitimately if they tried to "extort or fright" an official body to achieve their goals. The case in point: the female demonstrators, whom it described as "all of the poorer sort," some of them "whores," and most with husbands in the royalist or parliamentary forces. The account concluded, counterfactually, "thus we see, to permit absurdities, is the way to increase them; Tumults are dangerous, swords in womens hands doe desperate things; this is begotten in the distractions of Civill War."[27]

The swords, of course, were not in the women's hands at all, but rather in the hands of the cavalrymen who struck at them, like "bruit beasts." Yet the *Parliament Scout,* confronted with thousands of women tenaciously supporting peace proposals, reversed the roles of aggressor and victim. Perhaps the "swords" to which the report referred were metaphoric, in effect expressing the shock of male supporters of Parliament at the "absurdities" of organized female activism born "in the distractions of Civill War."

The newsbooks were undoubtedly correct in their perception that the petitioning women had been well organized; as commentators recognized, the widespread display of white silk ribbons suggested forethought and some financial resources. But in spite of the insinuations that many male or female members of the nobility were involved behind the scenes, only two aristocrats were ever identified as possibilities. One was Lady Winifred Brouncker, the wife of a member of King Charles's entourage at Oxford, but whether she had a role in the peace demonstrations is unclear. The second person named was a "great Earle in this Kingdome"—Henry Rich, first Earl of Holland—an early supporter of Parliament who by August 1643 favored a negotiated settlement.[28]

In an appearance before the Commons on Saturday, August 12, a Mistress Jordan accused the earl of backing the female demonstrators. She testified that she had heard a man assert that the earl had met with many of the women and that he had assured them that most of the members of both houses favored peace. If they demonstrated at Parliament for three or four days in a row, he had reportedly told them, the peace party would carry the day. The Commons appointed a committee to investigate her testimony, but that night the

Earl of Holland fled to join the king at Oxford, which suggests that he might indeed have been involved with the petitioners. For her part, Mistress Jordan asked permission to travel to the Netherlands, explaining that she feared for her life because she had refused to join her neighbors in their "tumultuous rising" against Parliament.[29]

In its implication of widespread discontent with the war in her neighborhood, Mistress Jordan's statement tended to contradict her claims that the female demonstrators had acted not on their own accord but rather at the behest of the Earl of Holland. The House of Commons seems not to have uncovered any further information about the origins of the peace petition; by contrast, a committee of the Lords readily identified and questioned the male organizers of the pro-war demonstration on August 7. In spite of the possible involvement of the earl and Lady Winifred Brouncker, the authorities' inability to learn more about the female demonstrators could well indicate that the women's peace petition was at base a genuine statement of concern by the wives of soldiers of one or both sides (as the *Parliament Scout* had suggested). Further, contrary to the parliamentarian newsbook descriptions, at least some could have been well-off women, who could have purchased the identifying white ribbons.[30]

Following these events of the second week of August 1643, the representative of Venice in England reported to the doge and senate that "every effort, not omitting violence, is used to purge this city of the pacific royalists and neutrals. Many of the women who went to implore peace have been imprisoned, as well as their husbands, the mere suspicion of desiring it being considered the last degree of criminality." Parliament moved quickly to impose an oath of allegiance on all men eligible for militia service and to disarm anyone who refused to take it, with the threat of property confiscation for anyone who concealed weapons. Such repressive measures, vigorously pursued, successfully quieted dissenting voices in London for a considerable period of time.[31]

The Parliament of Ladies

A three-year hiatus in real and lampooned political activity by women followed the dramatic confrontations of August 1643, an interval surely influenced by events in the Civil War. After inconclusive battles in 1643 and 1644, the king's forces suffered two decisive defeats during the summer of 1645. In April 1646, Charles I fled to Scotland, ending the so-called first Civil War; in January 1647, the Scots turned him over to parliamentary forces. Parliament thus gained uncontested control of England. Parliament's newly established preeminence called into question English people's traditional beliefs about government. Instead of a monarch, the nation was now ruled (de facto if not de jure) by a large group of men, only some of noble rank.

The experience of the (male) governed becoming the (male) governors was clearly unsettling, judging by the emergence of an innovative genre of satire late in the summer of 1646: a series of pamphlets presenting variations on the theme of a parliament composed exclusively of women. Men had long fantasized about the potential danger of wives ruling their husbands in households. Because of the generally accepted analogy between state and family, such fantasies could also bring to mind the possible perils of women governing the state. Both notions symbolically placed the ruled (women) in the capacity of rulers, whether in household or polity. The new method of parodying female political endeavors so completely captured men's imagination that, after a final three publications, the trope of mock women's petitions to Parliament disappeared, not to reemerge for more than three decades.[32]

The female parliamentarian satires obviously harked back to Aristophanes and to the Duke of Lennox's brief remark in February 1641/2, yet they quickly surpassed those beginnings. The anonymously authored *The Parliament of Women: With the merrie Lawes by them newly Enacted...that they might have superiority and domineere over their husbands* was the first of its type, appearing in August 1646. Set in ancient Rome, the pamphlet recounted the consequences after a woman concluded erroneously that the Senate had determined that all men should have two wives. Calling together the chief Roman matrons, she proposed instead that all women should have two husbands. Numerous "Tradesmens wives" with amusing names (for example, Tabitha Tireman) then chimed in with double entendre–laden statements supporting her proposition. "Every Musket must have a Scouring-stick, and every Gun must have a Rammer, and every pen must be dipped in Ink before it will write," insisted one. Brief echoes of the earlier petitions and reactions to them resonated through the pages of the satire, as in the explicit involvement of "tradesmen's wives," a reference to "the Commonwealths good" being served by a sailor's wife having a sexual partner during her husband's long absences, and a series of pertinent questions: "Where be those magnanimous and Masculine spirited Matrons? Those valiant Viragoes? those lusty Ladies: those daring *Amazonian* Damsels"? The "Ladies Lawes" that concluded the pamphlet not only authorized multiple spouses for each wife but also permitted women to "vex, perplex, and any way torment their husbands," among other similar provisions.[33]

Yet despite the author's use of the term *parliament* to structure his lampoon, the *Parliament of Women* was essentially an apolitical parody set in the distant past. The Roman matrons never formally constituted themselves as a legislative body, although the propositions on which they concurred were called *laws.* Their purported debates focused entirely on household, familial, and sexual matters, primarily their relationship with their husbands or with potential additional lovers. Thus only the framing conceit itself—and the passing references to earlier female demonstrators—positioned women in the political realm. In the end, the matrons presented their resolutions as proposals to their senator-husbands, who both "laught" and "greatly condemned their wives' levity and inconstancie." That placed the nominally legislating women in the usual position of wives: recommending actions with respect to the household to their spouses, who then rejected them.

Eight months later, building on the trope but not limited by it, a young political satirist named Henry Neville published a pamphlet that inspired numerous imitations and additional editions. *The Parliament of Ladies, Or Divers remarkable passages of Ladies in Spring-Garden, in Parliament Assembled,* which probably appeared in April 1647, did what the *Parliament of Women* had not: it placed the women's politico-sexual discussions squarely in the contemporary Civil War context. Instead of giving the participants names like Tabitha Tireman, it identified real women, and it focused not on tradesmen's wives but on women of the nobility and gentry. Although no numbers survive to suggest how many copies it sold, later in 1647 Neville produced both a "second edition corrected" and a sequel.[34]

Moreover, two imitations quickly appeared employing the same theme, along with a pirated version and even a republication of the 1646 *Parliament of Women* under a new title designed to capitalize on the obvious popularity of Neville's volume: *A Parliament of Ladies with their Lawes Newly Enacted.* One author penned a response to Neville, accusing him of having "very grossly and impiously abused the Parliament of England, in particular, divers honourable Lords, worthy Knights, vertuous Ladies, and well descended Gentlemen." Another published a mock petition to the ladies' parliament, describing in ribald language the standard theme of young women lamenting the lack of sexual partners in wartime. Numerous other parodies adopting the "parliament" trope then followed, and *The Parliament of Ladies* itself was repeatedly reprinted until the late eighteenth century, long after anyone would have known the identity of any of the women being satirized. Clearly, the fantasy of a government composed of women struck a resonant chord with English readers of the seventeenth (and eighteenth) century.[35]

An Exact Diurnall

OF THE

PARLIAMENT

OF

LADYES

Ordered by the LADYES in Parliament, That they de-
clare that Prince *Rupert*, Lord *Digby*, Lord *Capell*, Lord *Cottington*,
Dr. *Williams*, Mr. *Walter*, L. *Hopton*, L. *Culpepper*, Dr. *Duppa*, Sir
R. *Greenvil*, L. *Jermine*, and Major Gen. *Urrey*, Have all
their Pardons granted to them by this C o v R t

Clericus.

FIGURE 2.1. The earliest image of a "Parliament of Ladyes," woodcut frontispiece from a royalist pamphlet published at Oxford, 1647. Men in the foreground are being interrogated and judged. This item is reproduced by permission of the Huntington Library, San Marino, California.

Neville was a supporter of Parliament in his late twenties who had spent the early 1640s on the Continent, primarily in Italy, but returned to England in 1645. A dedicated republican who later served in Parliament and opposed Cromwell, he went on to write many other political tracts, some of them satirical; *The Parliament of Ladies* was the first and one of the most successful. Despite his own sympathies, he parodied prominent women without regard to their political positions, thus implying that his motives related more directly to gender than to politics.[36]

In both the first pamphlet and its sequel, *The Ladies, A Second Time, Assembled in Parliament,* Neville's parliamentary ladies nominally dealt with political, economic, military, and religious affairs. They chose a speaker, appointed committees, consulted experts, considered complaints, received a "humble Petition from many thousands of Citizens Wives, in and about the City of London," sent messages to and received others from the House of Commons, arranged for the sale of delinquents' estates, declared a fast day, discussed the leadership of the army, and issued orders concerning the church and its properties—in short, they behaved like the upper house of Parliament. But nearly every action was presented in the suggestive or gossipy language of double entendre. The political information in both pamphlets was accurate and up-to-date, which must have given readers the sense that they had access to knowledge of the well-born previously available only to insiders. Further, the prose was sly, subtle, and clever. No wonder, then, that Neville's productions achieved such popularity and spawned so many imitators.[37]

The Parliament of Ladies began with the women's formal order that their decrees be promptly published to avoid "misreports and scandals" caused by "malice, or want of wit." An abortive initial meeting in Covent Garden was replaced by a gathering at Spring Garden. Those venues themselves set the stage for the sexual themes of the pamphlet, for both were recently developed public spaces with growing reputations for fostering misbehavior, including illicit sexual activity. When the Spring Garden ladies proceeded to choose their speaker, Neville drew on his knowledge of current events. Their first choice, Lady Holland, demurred, "alleadging her Husbands desertion" (as was noted earlier, the Earl of Holland, who favored a negotiated settlement of the conflict, had joined the king in Oxford for some months after August 1643). Two more women were considered, but rejected, before the ladies finally selected Catherine Cecil, Lady Salisbury, whose husband, a moderate peer, had moved over time from support for the monarch to the parliamentary side.[38]

As the ladies started to conduct business, the sexual allusions began. They called before them Sir Henry Blount, a notorious womanizer with royalist leanings, to question his reported "hereticall and dangerous" statement that "it is better to side with, and resort to common Women, then Ladyes of Honour." Lady Foster—wife of a royalist lawyer—complained that if Blount's opinion prevailed, that would lead to "the utter decay of Trade" and a diminution of "the profit of this House." She, Lady Middlesex (widow of a once-powerful courtier), and two others were then named to a "Committee of Tryers" to investigate the proposition that "divers weake persons have crept into places beyond their abilities," in order to ensure that "men of greater parts might be put into their rooms." The appointments of these women were appropriate, the parliament indicated, "by reason of their great experience in Souldery in this Kingdome." The implication would have been clear to any contemporary reader: these noblewomen were interested in conducting illicit affairs with sexually potent men (those with "greater parts") and, indeed, had perhaps already done so with soldiers.[39]

And so in both pamphlets the innuendo continued for page after page. Especially in the sequel, the text referred to specific alleged relationships. Thus, for example, the ladies acknowledged the "former speciall services" of Lord Montague to several of their number. Lady Stamford (wife of an unsuccessful parliamentary commander) attested that "he was a man well gifted, and had a large tallent, and one that had indured many dangerous incounters in the service of the house, and had been in the Chyrugions hands," the latter phrase one of several veiled references to venereal disease in the pamphlets. Yet Neville's jesting was not wholly sexual in nature. Lady Norton, for instance, complained to the other parliamentarians that Sir Robert Harley had attempted to "deface" her. Harley, one of the most avid Puritan iconoclasts, was known for his energetic destruction of stained glass and religious statues. Neville's version of Sir Robert proposed to attack Lady Norton, "having found out that shee was likewise painted." She was, though, defended by her colleagues, who declared that if any person acting under the authority of the Commons should try to prevent a lady "from painting, washing, or adorning herself to the best advantage,... that act is a great breach of the priviledge of the House."[40]

Neville's imitators failed to match the ingenuity of his successful extended linkage of politics and sexual innuendo. *An Exact Diurnall of the Parliament of Ladyes,* published in May, purported to describe the activities of an Oxford ladies' parliament that charged some royalist men with political or sexual offenses. *Hey Hoe, for a Husband, Or, The Parliament of Maides,* appearing in September, reported on the search for husbands by numerous unattractive virgins. Three years later, *Newes from the New Exchange, or the Common-Wealth of Ladies,* after observing that the ladies had "voted themselves the *Supreme*

Authority both at home and abroad," quickly descended into scurrilous gossip about sexual escapades and venereal disease among the nobility. Repeatedly the author named women and men (some of them also singled out by Neville), describing their rumored liaisons. By the end of the pamphlet, the author had abandoned all pretense to prose; the final leaf consisted of nothing more than a listing of pairs of gentlefolk who were supposedly engaged in illicit sex with each other.[41]

What is to be made of such politically themed pornography, of the crude or shrewd variety?[42] In the parodies by Neville and his male contemporaries, regardless of whether the fantasized women were petitioners or parliamentarians, sexual topics came to the fore. Although female sexuality had long comprised a significant component of men's satirical writings about women, in the political crisis caused by the English Civil War that theme predominated, rather than being part of a series of complaints on such topics as women's frivolity and ignorance. The theme appeared in 1641 as one of several jests in the earliest mock appeal, *Petition of the Weamen of Middlesex,* but quickly became the exclusive concern of the male authors of such lampoons as the parody petitions of 1643. That development did not occur by chance or coincidence. In its culmination, the *Parliament of Ladies* pamphlets, a complete political inversion was invoked and men's sexuality became the topic of feminine discourse. Female petitioners, whether real or imaginative parodies, assumed a traditional role when requesting assistance from a group of men. But a parliament composed exclusively of women constituted another matter entirely.[43]

Equally significant was the chronological conjunction among parliamentary forces' dominance in the First Civil War, Parliament's detention of Charles I after January 1647, and the emergence of the ladies' parliament genre. Just months after Parliament had firmly established its authority over the king and thus the nation, Henry Neville and other men began to express their concerns over what *that* particular inversion of power might mean by imagining female rule in the state. The notion that a group of women (not a sole female monarch) might govern the polity was completely new. Its appearance at precisely this moment signaled both men's recognition of women's growing political involvement and men's comprehension of the unsettled state of governance in general as the verities of monarchical rule were called into serious question for the first time, both on the battlefield and in the public prints. Historians know that the following decades brought both the Stuart Restoration and the Glorious Revolution, which resolved many of the political and social uncertainties, but in the late 1640s Neville and his contemporaries did not know the future. And they expressed their anxieties about that unknown future in politico-sexual terms because, for them, politics and sexuality—or what the modern world would today term the separate realms of public and private—were inseparable and inextricably linked. The themes of the pamphlets thus underscore the observation that for them the modern equation of male = public and female = private did not exist.

It is therefore unsurprising that the supremacy of Parliament gave rise to men's speculation about the possible political supremacy of wives and widows drawn from the ranks of the nobility and gentry. If the male members of Parliament were theoretically metaphorical sons of the monarch, the female parliamentarians, as metaphorical mothers and widows, had a greater claim to legitimate power than they. And in wielding that authority they seized control of men's sexuality, ruling men as they themselves were commonly ruled. The vision of such inverted authority was a powerful and threatening one that clearly captured the minds of male authors and readers alike in the late 1640s.

But that the pamphlets abandoned Neville's key trope in *The Parliament of Ladies,* replacing it with gossip of unremitting scurrility in *Newes from the New Exchange,* also indicates men's ability to subvert the potential power inversion. The vision of a women's parliament was intense but nevertheless brief in its defining moment, and men soon gained greater emotional control over their fears and fantasies. In doing so, they pointed the way toward a solution to the conundrum that confronted them with the impending fall of the monarchy and thus of traditional political theory: to remove decisively the potential for female rule, they had to create a clearer, more inclusive division between men and women. High-status women had to be distinguished from men of their own rank, who were appropriate rulers, and tied more firmly to other members of their sex, who were not. An obvious way to accomplish that feat was to subject them to the sort of slanderous treatment found in *Newes,* in which noblewomen became the objects of men's sexual desires rather than making men the objects of theirs. *Newes* defined noblewomen by their gender instead of their status and thus took a key step toward excluding them from the ranks of legitimate state actors.

Leveller Women's Petitions

Following the clashes outside Parliament in early August 1643, women of all political persuasions temporarily halted their petitioning activities. Women did not again draft collective petitions until spring 1649, after the execution of Charles I. That renewed petitioning was associated with the group known to history (if not necessarily to themselves) as the Levellers.

In spring 1647, about the time that Henry Neville published the initial *Parliament of Ladies* pamphlet, the Civil War entered a complex and radical phase as the New Model Army, formed in 1645, split with Parliament's leaders after Parliament began considering disbanding it. Among the sometime opponents and occasional allies of both army and Parliament were the Levellers, who sought to widen the franchise to all men, propertied or not, and who demanded religious toleration for all sects except Catholics. Levellers within the army helped to instigate the so-called Putney Debates in late October–early November 1647, during which army leaders considered, debated, and rejected the core Leveller precepts of toleration and an expanded voting populace. The army commanders, chief among them Henry Ireton (Oliver Cromwell's son-in-law), were wedded to their own religious beliefs and to the notion that voters should be men with a permanent stake in the community (that is, property owners); they accordingly refused to adopt proposals that would cause such a radical reshaping of English polity and society.[44]

On September 11, 1648, thousands of male Londoners sympathetic to the Levellers submitted a lengthy petition to the Commons laying out their expectations for that body.[45] At the time, the signatories feared the prospect of a negotiated settlement with the king. Declaring that they regarded the Commons as "the supream Authority of England, as chosen by, and representing the People," they insisted that the monarch was accountable to the Commons as "the chief publike Officer of this Kingdom." Among other requests, the petition called for annual parliamentary elections; an end to monopolies, compulsory tithes, and "perpetual imprisonment" for debt; equality before the law for all, including the nobility; and the punishment of royalist leaders. "Mercy to the wicked, is cruelty to the innocent," the authors asserted. This petition became the touchstone for many subsequent texts; at least fifteen similar publications over the next year referred in their titles to the "late large petition" of September 11. Among those were two presented by a group of Leveller women in late April and early May 1649.[46]

The women's petitions sought a specific goal: freeing the Leveller leaders John Lilburne, Richard Overton, William Walwyn, and Thomas Prince from the Tower of London. Lilburne, recognized by all as the preeminent Leveller, was a religious separatist and former lieutenant colonel in the parliamentary forces who had been in and out of jail since the late 1630s, charged first by Charles I and later by Parliament with writing seditious pamphlets on political and religious topics. He and the others had been arrested more than a year earlier for authoring and publishing *The Second Part of Englands New-Chaines Discovered,* which the Rump Parliament (the members of the Commons left after presbyterians had been purged) declared to be treasonous. Leading the female Leveller petitioners was Elizabeth Lilburne, John's long-suffering wife, who had several times voluntarily joined him in prison and who had also addressed Parliament during his earlier detentions, on one occasion "with some scores of Gentlewomen her friends."[47]

The women formulated their entreaty after the Rump in mid-April rejected a plea for the Leveller leaders' freedom submitted by a reported ten thousand London men. The House of Commons reproved the male petitioners, warning them that their "scandalous and seditious" statements revealed a possible complicity in the Levellers' crimes. Perhaps the implied threat to arrest more of their menfolk inspired the women to take action; in any event, an official parliamentary newsbook reported that on Sunday, April 22, women's signatures were solicited "at Severall Congregationall Meetings in and about the City of London" for a petition to be presented to the Commons the next day. "In some places many signed it, in other places none at all, and in some places it was disputed," the story noted dispassionately. A royalist newsbook took a more jaundiced view of the women's plans: "the lusty *lasses* of the *levelling* party are drawing to a generall *Rendezvous* at *Westminster,* to present a *Petition* with one hand, and cock their *Petticoats* with the other," it jocularly observed. That second account was to set the tone for most reactions to Leveller women's efforts over the next several years.[48]

A group of three hundred to five hundred women brought a formal appeal to the House of Commons on Monday morning, April 23. By one account, it had ten thousand signatures, thereby matching the men's plea of the previous week.[49] The women declared that their husbands and brothers had regularly petitioned the Commons "while we in silence have sate at home," but they could remain quiet no longer. "We are not able to keep in our compass, to be bounded in the custom of our Sex," they averred, remarking that "it is not our custom to address our selves to this House in the Publick behalf." Yet, like the female petitioners of February 1641/2, they asserted that "we have an equal share and interest with men in the Common-wealth" and that they could not sit idly by while their menfolk's entreaties were rejected and termed "treasonable and seditious."

Reminding their readers that through the ages God had repeatedly relied on "the weake hand of women," they cited three precedents: the actions of Deborah and Jael in the Old Testament, the women who saved Britain from the tyrannical rule of the Danes, and the Scotswomen who had instigated the triumph over "Episcopall tyranny" in their nation. They also reminded the Commons that they had supported the war effort with contributions of "our mony, our plate, rings, bodkins, &c." Victory was at hand, they declared; yet, even so, tyranny was continuing in the case of the imprisoned Leveller leaders.

They pronounced themselves "amazed" that men who had promoted "the peace and prosperity of the Common-wealth" had been so treated. With "poverty, misery, and famine, like a mighty torrent,... breaking in upon us," how were the families of the jailed men to survive under such conditions?

And so, they pleaded, Parliament should "settle this commonwealth upon foundations of true freedom" and not only liberate the Levellers but also award them compensation. If Lilburne and the others had committed the crime of treason, they should be charged in courts of law and not pronounced guilty by Parliament itself. Moreover, the Commons should ensure that the army could not "intermedle in the Civill Authority." Nothing was worse, they concluded, than "the exercise of an arbitrary Power, or continuance of Authoritie Civil or Military, beyond the time limited by Trust or Commission, or the perverting of either to unjust, bloudy, or ambitious ends."

All in all, it was a remarkable document, sweeping in scope and unyieldingly critical of the Commons. At one point, the signatories declared themselves fearful but nevertheless willing to die alongside their menfolk, who had been threatened with prison for nothing more than "upholding the Cause of the people in their native freedom and right." The address adopted an explicitly feminine stance, describing the difficulties facing the families of the imprisoned men, but it also went far beyond a standard entreaty for governmental benevolence. It offered broad political pronouncements on such key subjects as civilian-military relations and the necessity of the rule of law. And it unhesitatingly insisted that women, as well as men, could discuss such subjects publicly.[50]

Unsurprisingly, perhaps, the reactions to the April 23 appeal were equally remarkable. The Commons refused to consider the petition on Monday but offered a formal response after the women returned on Tuesday and Wednesday, although the parliamentarians "did not think fit to enter any thing about it in the Journall Booke." The speaker directed the sergeant-at-arms to tell the women waiting at the door of the chamber that "the matter you petition about is of an higher concernment then you understand, that the House gave an answer to your husbands; and therefore that you are desired to goe home, and looke after your owne businesse, and meddle with your huswifery." That statement was considerably more dismissive than any official reply to earlier female supplicants, whose appeals had been received (if not always acted upon) and whose marital status had not been mentioned. Parliament's own newsbook, seconded by several others, reported that "this Answer being given to them, they very civilly all went away." A royalist newsbook, by contrast, recounted a different outcome: "Now the *storme* began, and their Tongues pelted *hail-shot* against the *Members* as they passed to and fro."[51]

One account recorded that a "Gentlewoman" led the petitioners; that was probably Elizabeth Lilburne herself, a gentlewoman by virtue of her marriage to a former officer, albeit a radical one. Reportedly, she stoutly confronted the sergeant-at-arms, another MP, and even Oliver Cromwell himself. *Mercurius Militaris* described the Commons' response to the women in the following words: "it was not for women to Petition, they might stay at home to wash their dishes." In this report, the spokeswoman responded, "Sir we have scarce any dishes left us to wash." After another MP remarked, "it was strange that women should petition," she retorted: "Sir, that which is strange is not therefore unlawfull, it was strange that you cut of the Kings Head." When Cromwell emerged from the Commons chamber, she informed him that the female petitioners had not been heard. "Time hath been when you would readily have given us the reading of Petitions, but that was when we had mony, plate, rings and bodkins to give you," she charged, sarcastically. The two then sparred over the legality of holding the jailed men, with Cromwell claiming that they were being held lawfully and she insisting that "they were contrary to Law imprisoned, and we desire their Liberty first, and then if there be ought against them, let them be tryed by the due course and forme of law." Whether or not that confrontation actually occurred, the newsbook accurately portrayed one of the petitioners' major arguments.[52]

In contrast to that straightforward report, most of the newsbook commentaries expressed hostility not only to the radical nature of the women's appeal but also to the very fact of their petitioning. A pro-Parliament newsbook commented snidely that the women probably could not fully comprehend the contents of their own petition. Still others introduced sexual innuendo into explanations for why so many women would petition for the freedom of men not their husbands. One royalist newsbook termed the supplicants an "oppressed Sister-hood" who were complaining about the potential lack of customers in "all the Brothells about Town" because their men had been jailed. Another, calling them such names as "sister *Wagtayle,*" claimed that the petitioners had asked the Commons to "spare those *worthys* for *breeders,* for the better *propagation* of the *righteous,*" and warned "*Holofernes Fairfax* look to thy head, for *Judeth* is a comming, the women are up *in armes,* and vow they will tickle your *Members.*"[53]

In one sense, such invective was not new; it had infused the mock petitions composed earlier in the decade and the *Parliament of Ladies* pamphlets alike. Yet it introduced a newly prominent theme into the published reactions to women's actual collective political appeals. Although earlier commentators had occasionally called female petitioners "whores" or "bawds," they did not expand further on those terms and seemed primarily concerned with establishing the supplicants' low status. Editorialists in 1649 had a different goal: expressing derision for the Leveller women's project at its base and in the strongest possible terms. Their disdain explicitly extended to women's political participation, not simply to the content of their argument. At a time when the monarchy had been overthrown and the English polity was being reconstituted, men of all political stripes seemed determined to keep women out—and at least some women were just as determined to be included.

That was especially clear in the commentary offered in the newsbook *Continued Heads of Perfect Passages in Parliament* in its issue dated April 20–27, 1649. Uniquely, the author summarized the major points of the petition, then supplied his own gendered interpretations of each statement. To the women's request that Parliament "settle this Common-wealth upon foundations of true freedom," he responded: "*That is as much to say, let Women wear the Breeches.*" On the demand that the army not "intermeddle in the civill Authority," he remarked, "*It is fitter for you to be washing your dishes, and meddle with the wheele and distaffe.*" He expanded that argument in his observations on the women's questions about whether the Levellers' actions had been treasonous: "*It can never be a good world, when women meddle in States matters....And their Husbands are to blame, that have no fitter imployment for them.*" After citing Saint Paul's comment that "*it is not fit nor civill for Women to prate in Congregations of men,*" he concluded, "*we shall have things brought to a fine passe, if Women come to teach the Parliament how to make Lawes.*"[54]

None of his remarks pertained to the specific contentions in the Leveller women's appeal. Rather, all related to the petitioners' gender identity and to the inappropriate nature of their venture into the political realm. His argument had two sides: on the one hand, women should involve themselves with household affairs; on the other, they should not "meddle in States matters." He supported his position with a biblical reference and with two remarks that echoed Parliament's comment that a response to the women's husbands was sufficient because of wives' subordinate position in the household. Although he did not employ the terms *public* and *private* to denote the division of roles he laid out, his text forecast the future in its willingness to address both roles explicitly and in his grouping all women outside the set of legitimate state actors. For him, clearly, any "gentlewoman" actually or theoretically among the Levellers was categorized primarily as a female rather than as a person of rank. Like all other women, she should have no ability "to teach the Parliament how to make Laws."[55]

In spite of the negative reaction to their first petition both in and out of Parliament, the Leveller women did not give up easily. In early May, they returned with a new plea that advanced a somewhat different argument. In the interim, many of the supplicants must have participated in a ritualized funeral march through London for a Leveller martyr. Robert Lockyer, one of several Levellers involved in a mutiny in the army, was executed on April 28 as an example to the others. The next day, thousands of mourners escorted his body from the City to a Westminster graveyard. A newsbook noted that the marchers "had Sea Green, and black Ribbons in their Hats, or pinned to their black Ribbonds on their Brests"; the men preceded and the women followed Lockyer's corpse. At the grave, they were joined by "some thousands of the higher sort," similarly attired. The account also observed that "not half so many" attended King Charles's funeral, and that the entire event was "most remarkable, considering the person to be in no higher quality than a private Trooper."[56]

The Leveller women who gathered at the doors of the Commons from Saturday, May 5, through Tuesday, May 8, to present their second appeal also wore sea-green ribbons.[57] Like that of February 4, 1641/2, which also followed the rejection of an earlier missive, this petition—believed to have been drafted by the religious and political radical Katherine Chidley—explicitly addressed women's right to engage in political discussion. Since women are equal before God and Christ, the address began, and have an "equal interest with the men of this Nation" in liberty and security, they could only "wonder and grieve that we should appear so despicable in your eyes, as to be thought unworthy to Petition or represent our Grievances to this Honourable House." Again they stressed the importance of the rule of law and their belief that the laws had been violated when the four Leveller leaders were brutally arrested in their own homes. They bitterly criticized Lockyer's conviction and execution under martial law during peacetime as illegal and unwarranted. "Are we Christians," they asked, "and shall we sit still and keep at home, while such men as have born continual testimony against the unjustice of the times, and unrighteousness of men, be pickt out and be delivered up to the slaughter"? Cannot we "bear any testimony against so abominable cruelty and injustice?" In no uncertain terms they asserted their willingness to die with their menfolk for the cause, if they could not prevail and win the men's freedom: "Slay one, slay all," they insisted.

So, they pleaded, review the previous petition. Do not disregard its contents simply because it comes from "the weak hand of Women," for God often employs the weak "to work mighty effects." Declaring themselves "no whit satisfied" by the answer their "Husbands and Friends" had received to the men's initial petition, they once more requested that Leveller leaders be freed or prosecuted according to "due Process of Law." Our houses are "worse then Prisons to us, and our Lives worse then death...until you grant our desires," they concluded, asking Parliament not to "deny us in things so evidently just and reasonable, as you would not be dishonourable to all Posterity."

One newsbook termed the petition "very high," adding a generic slur on women, "they have ever loved to meddle with what they should not from the beginning." Another jocularly observed, "even the women are marching down in Batalia to give the Members of Westminster a second charge, with the artillery of a Petition." In short, the female petitioners were treated as a joke by the male authors and publishers of newsbooks, which was the ultimate sign of their scornful disdain. After terming the new plea "full fraught with many lofty particulars," one editor wrote laughingly that if Parliament refused to comply with their demands, then "down go the supream *Dragons* with *Ladles* and *Dish-clouts,* and they shall know what it is to jeer Woemen with their *Huswifery,* when their businesse is *Liberty.*" His sarcasm was palpable, and the tone of the commentaries generally spoke volumes. Women's collective interventions in the political realm were henceforth to be dismissed as meaningless gestures.[58]

And that is what the Rump did. Although the newsbooks reported that women approached the Commons on May 7 and 8 as well as May 5, they evidently received no formal response to the second petition. "Being frustrated of their expectations," one newsbook recounted, "they ran up and down . . . , and shewed their petitions to everyone." One man they approached was said to have made a ribald joke in return, and another retorted, *"That if they understood themselves they might be better occupied at home."* The only apparent result was a parliamentary order to the guards at the Tower of London to prevent everyone from visiting the prisoners except their wives and servants, thus excluding large numbers of supporters. That Parliament was not antagonistic to all female petitioners was demonstrated by its nearly simultaneous positive reception of a plea presented "in the names of severall Mariners wives" for financial support in the absence of their husbands. When women behaved in an appropriate manner, the Rump appeared to say, they would be relieved. It is unlikely that Elizabeth Lilburne would have won her husband's freedom had she submitted only a limited personal appeal, but the wide-ranging political claims in the Leveller women's addresses made rejection foreordained.[59]

At the end of May, the newsbook *Mercurius Militaris* mocked the recent petitioning campaign. After printing a sneering poem that began "Ye Sisters of the new Edition, / weep, Snivell, Snot, and cackle," it asked, "What's become of all my brave Virago's, the Ladyes-errants of the Seagreen Order . . . why doe ye not again muster up your Pettycoates and white Apporns, and like gallant *Lacedemonians,* or bold Amazons advance your Banners once more in the

Pallace yard, and spit defiance in the teeth of Authority"? Tell the Rump, the author directed, "that it is liberty they fought for, liberty you come for, liberty you long for, and without liberty the spirituall burdens of your bellyes are quite lost." The Parliament has run the country long enough; "'tis high time that *Cate* of the kitchin, and *Tyne* the turnspit should rule the rost; and tell them that you are now grown as skilfull in State Cookery as themselves . . . ; tell them that if they raigne as Kings, it is no more then reason and joynt interest, in nature that you should raigne as Queenes too." He then moved into standard sexual satire, ending with a vision of sexual anarchy if the Levellers triumphed: "O what a holy brood of free-borne Babes should then have possessed our Canaan, when the whole Land had been contracted into one Bawdy-house, and none but an universall community of blessed Lechers, (Levellers I would say) leaping like Rams the holy Ewes, and exercising their spirituall tallents or deare Brethren upon the gifted Sisterhood of the new Babilon."[60]

The newsbook rant is significant for two reasons. First, in its tone and content it aptly summarized the common reaction to the petitioning Leveller women: it combined sexual innuendo with attacks on the notion that *any* woman might appropriately express political opinions or claim authority in the public realm. Refusing to acknowledge that Elizabeth Lilburne and possibly some of her female allies could lay claim to gentle status (recall that high-ranking people participated in Lockyer's funeral), it lumped all women together as kitchen servants and whores. Second, it was the last of its kind—not because men changed their minds about women's political involvement, but because a few months later Parliament moved to suppress all such publications by adopting a new law banning scandalous works and insisting that books and pamphlets be properly licensed before appearing in print. Consequently, few surviving reports describe the reactions when in 1653 Leveller women again petitioned Parliament on behalf of a reimprisoned John Lilburne.[61]

Much to the Rump's consternation, Lilburne was acquitted when tried for treason in October 1649; he and his Leveller colleagues were accordingly freed from the Tower soon thereafter. However, his pamphlets again aroused the authorities' ire, and he was once more deemed guilty of treason and was banished by act of Parliament in early 1652. After the dissolution of the Rump, he returned to England in June 1653 but was quickly jailed. His next trial for treason began in mid-July, so when Leveller women twice appealed to Parliament on his behalf in late July, the trial was in process.[62]

One of the two petitions was attributed to Katherine Chidley by a contemporary source; the religious language of both 1653 addresses, coupled with the similarity of the first to the appeal of May 1649, makes it likely that she had at least some part in drafting all three. The first missive opened with a now-familiar reference to God's ability to employ "the weakest meanes to work the mightiest of effects," including occasionally using "weak woman." Urging the new Barebones Parliament not to follow the same course as its predecessor (which was "deaf to Petitioners and Prisoners" and "neglected" the "Widdow and the Fatherless"), the signatories called the law banishing Lilburne "sordid and groundless." Should the jury find him guilty, the women contended, the new Parliament "ought to repeal that bloody Act, and deliver him out of that snare." Asking that the trial be halted, the petitioners exclaimed, "You see the thing is so gross, that even Women perceive the evil of it." Terming the Rump's rejection of petitions a "mortall disease," they pleaded for a "full inquiry" into the "unjust" treatment Lilburne had received.[63]

Again, Parliament failed to respond to the Leveller women's plea, and so once more they drafted a second appeal, one that devoted far more space to pleading their own cause than Lilburne's, although they briefly alluded to the "unjust and illegal Act" under which he was being tried. Declaring that they had "attended several days at your House-door" without their plea being formally received, they insisted that "it is ours and the Nations undoubted right to petition" and that that right was being "with-held from us." Likening themselves to Esther, who had saved the Jews from Haman by petitioning her husband the king, they asked that Parliament "will not be worse unto us, then that Heathen King was to *Esther.*" They also called to mind (as they had in 1649) the historic role of English women in repelling Danish invaders and their own recent contributions to the war effort. "And therefore we hope, that, upon second thoughts," they concluded, "your Honours will not slight the persons of your humble Petitioners,... since God is ever willing and ready to receive the Petitions of all, making no difference of persons. The ancient Laws of *England* are not contrary to the will of God: so that we claim it as our right to have our Petitions heard."[64]

A manuscript newsletter gave a detailed account of the submission of one of these petitions, but because of some confusion about dates in the sources, it is not entirely clear which one. The petition in question had more than six thousand signatures; twelve women, led by Katherine Chidley, brought it to the Commons chamber and "boldly" knocked on the door. When one MP dispatched by the house failed to persuade them to disperse, a second emerged to tell them, "the House could not take cognizance of their petition, they being women, and many of them wives, so that the Law took no notice of them." The women responded that "they were not all wives, and therefore pressed for the receiving their Petition." Paradoxically, the women then threatened Parliament with direct action by their "husbands and friends" should the Commons not accept their appeal.[65]

With the exception of a 1659 plea to Parliament from thousands of Quaker women against compulsory tithes,[66] the second Leveller women's petition of 1653 marked the end of women's collective political petitioning during the Civil War era. In early 1642, August 1643, April–May 1649, and July 1653, different groups of women presented appeals to Parliament, seeking various goals but all asserting (though in diverse ways) that women should be regarded as full participants in the English state. To the women, unlike the men they addressed, gender identity did not preclude them from being state actors. When challenged by men to defend their claims to full political participation, they did so vigorously and with reference to biblical precedent and their "undoubted rights." All insisted on their right to express their opinions jointly and in public, and they rejected men's attempts to confine them to household duties alone. They developed a vision of a society in which all women, not just aristocrats and gentry, would engage fully in political discourse along with men.

When men contemplated that prospect, they quailed, responding with visions of untrammeled women's control over male sexuality, government by kitchen women, and unalloyed disorder, as symbolized by total female sexual freedom. The tie between order in the state and familial order was so unquestioned that concerns about men's control in one—raised by the Civil War—immediately affected the other. Yet a worldview in which women appropriately wielded power in households, and family and state were linked, gave men no ready justification for excluding them from the polity, precisely because government and family could not be separated. Although initially the parliamentarians were at least willing to consider petitions on policy matters submitted by groups of women, as the full implications of republican governmental forms became clear, men began to develop justifications for rejecting women's intrusions into public affairs. Women should confine their attentions to their households, men contended; and wives should remain politically silent, for their husbands would represent them to the wider world. Although the petitioning women strongly opposed such formulations (whatever other women might have believed), men adamantly refused to accept their central argument that equality before God could carry with it political equality as well.

Ultimately, the interpretations that began to be developed in the 1640s and early 1650s would lay the groundwork for a revision of traditional understandings of government, family, and the relation between them. But because of the collapse of the commonwealth, followed in 1660 by the Stuart Restoration, the full force of that revision would be delayed until after the beginning of the next century.

Mistress Elinor James and Her Broadsides, 1681–1714

Elinor James, a London printer of the late seventeenth century, was of middling background but always called herself *Mrs.*, or mistress, implying higher
than ordinary status. Appropriately dubbed the "She-State-Politician," she
produced more political writing than any other woman of her day. Nearly
one hundred of her broadsides and pamphlets have survived, and more certainly existed. Over a period of more than thirty-five years, from the early
1680s to the mid-1710s, she regularly published her opinions on the monarchy, Parliament, the Church of England, and policies of the mayor and alder-
men of the City of London, where she lived. Lest someone conclude that
she had not written these works, she insisted, "all my Papers and books that
I have published with my Name have been sincerely mine."[1]

Some appeared with such titles as *Mrs. James's Letter of Advice to both Houses
of Parliament;* many had little or none of the standard deferential prefatory
phrasing that would commonly be expected in missives directed to superiors.
Even when the broadsides were headed by such terms as "humble Request"
or "humble Desire," the confident language within belied her words. Like
many of the female petitioners, she displayed no uncertainty about making
her political ideas known to national and municipal leaders. And she did so
starting at a young age and during a long marriage.[2]

Later in life, Elinor James recalled in several broadsides that she had first
engaged with the political world in 1665 or 1666, when she was a young wife
of about twenty. At that time, she wrote, God had directed her "to tell the
King [Charles II] of his faults, which was very amazing to me." Her husband
pronounced it "a foolish fancy," and her mother was even more disparaging,
claiming "they should all be hanged" if Elinor acted, but she went ahead
regardless. She deliberately dressed poorly when she approached the court,
and much to her pleasure and the courtiers' astonishment, the king received
her with "Grace and Favour." Her message was simple: Charles II should "live
a holy Life, and overcome the sins of the Flesh." It was a message she repeated
over many years, but to little effect: "He did often condescend to promise
that he would do those things which would make him truly happy, but he
delayed too long." Despite his failure to follow her advice, she claimed that

the king always greeted her kindly and listened attentively to her concerns, and consequently "I loved him with a Suparlative Love." In future years, she consistently referred to him as "precious" or "gracious" and proudly proclaimed that he had deemed her "City God-mother."[3]

Elinor James's earliest extant broadside, published in early 1681, expressed her political opinions forthrightly. *Mrs. James her New Answer to A Speech said to be lately made by a Noble Peer of this Realm* replied to an address attributed to Anthony Ashley Cooper, first Earl of Shaftesbury. The audacity of such an intervention into national political debates by a woman of middling status was stunning, suggesting either that she had been remarkably emboldened by nearly two decades of association with Charles II or that this was not her first such production. At issue was the succession to the throne: Charles had no legitimate heir; his brother, James, Duke of York, had converted to Catholicism about a decade earlier and had married a Catholic as his second wife. Several times between 1679 and 1681, Protestants in Parliament, including Shaftesbury, tried unsuccessfully to achieve passage of an Exclusion Act, naming James's Protestant daughter Mary and her husband and cousin, William of Orange, as successors to her father. Although Elinor James was a dedicated communicant of the Church of England, her broadside argued forcefully that Charles was "the Lords Annointed" and therefore that it was "a great sin" to oppose him on the matter of the succession of his Catholic brother. God has directed people to "submit to all Authority," she wrote; how dare the earl oppose the king in such language, "which never was spoken by any Peer to a King or in his presence"? That one of Shaftesbury's supporters could have asked, how dare the wife of a London printer respond in public to a nobleman in such terms? seems not to have occurred to her, or at least she did not acknowledge that consideration anywhere in the text of her broadside. Nor, for that matter, does it seem to have occurred to anyone else; her broadside elicited no known published response.[4]

After James II acceded to the throne, Elinor James appears to have anticipated a relationship with him comparable to that she had enjoyed with his brother. Again, her later publications recalled many intimate exchanges with the monarch. "I lov'd him dearly," she commented, and "Manfully fought under his Banner against all Opposers." But, at the same time, she worked unceasingly to persuade him to abandon Catholicism and return to the Church of England. She advised him to "decline Antichristian Worship" and warned him against the priests and other Catholics surrounding him. "I told him he was undone when he first went to Mass," she stated forthrightly, and she recounted numerous occasions on which she had engaged in verbal sparring with the king or had proposed or adopted various tactics (including fasting for extended periods) to try to reconvert him. Several of her publications from the mid-1680s either begged James to reconsider his religious affiliation or urged parliamentarians to continue to accept him as monarch.[5]

In 1687, she ventured to respond to another publication. The Catholic author of *A New Test of the Church of Englands Loyalty* attacked that church for failing to properly appreciate James II's policy of religious toleration. In the longest essay she ever wrote on public affairs, *Mrs. James's Vindication of the Church of England,* Elinor leapt to defend vigorously both her church and her monarch. James II, she insisted, has been "satisfied with our Loyalty, and declared it to the World, and how dare you condemn the King's Judgment, and Scandalize the Church?" She observed that adherents of the Church of England were actually *more* loyal than Catholics because they acknowledged the king to be "Supream Head and Governour" of their church whereas Catholics did not, being subservient to the pope. Her conclusion revealed the close, even possessive relationship she felt to the king: "You stole away my Soveraign," she charged; "are you not Contented? . . . what disturbs you that you should be Angry with us?"[6]

Throughout the reigns of Charles and James, she regarded herself essentially as an ungendered resident of London who had managed to capture the ear of two successive kings, and she seems to have been regarded similarly by others.[7] Communicating with the next monarch, though, proved more difficult, not least because the Glorious Revolution confounded her. A firm supporter of the Stuarts, Elinor James only slowly and reluctantly accepted the ousting of James II. In numerous broadsides issued during 1688 and 1689, she wrestled with the implications of Parliament's decision to offer the throne to William and Mary. After futilely petitioning against that outcome, she suggested that William should regard himself as an interim ruler and should hand the kingdom over to James II if the latter abandoned Catholicism. That conclusion, expressed in print, caused her arrest and conviction for "scandalous" publications. Thereafter she focused her attention primarily on political figures other than the monarch, addressing most of her broadsides to Parliament and to City of London officials. Although she spoke directly to William III more than once, she seems never to have met Mary, Anne, or George I.[8]

Deprived of the direct access to the monarchs she had earlier enjoyed, James frequently reminisced in print about her relationships with Charles II and his brother. She also referred more often both to women in general (whether real or generic) and to herself as a woman. The change in her rhetoric was sudden and dramatic. Before 1700, Elinor rarely mentioned her gender and just as rarely spoke of women in a general sense. But thereafter such references multiplied.[9]

For instance, in early 1706, she speculated that some might remark, "Why does Mrs. *James* trouble her Head about these matters, *She is but a Woman. Why that is true,*" she admitted, "*I am but a Woman:*... you cannot but think I must be something more than ordinary." James was then reporting attitudes she imputed to others, but four years later she used the phrase to refer to herself for the first time: "My Lords and Gentlemen, *Tho' I am but a Woman,*" she began a broadside addressed to Parliament and Queen Anne. The contrasting sensibility persisted; she began to allude to her gender more often, citing it as an explanation for her inability to make the political headway she sought with the nation's leaders: "I being a Woman they could not believe, neither could they do what I desired." On another occasion she wrote of how she had repeatedly urged "Kings, Queens and Princes to break of[f] their Sins... but however they rejected it... and so brought evil upon themselves, which I would a prevented, but I could not, being that I was a Woman."[10]

Elinor James continued to publish broadsides until shortly before her death in 1719. She confidently insisted on the efficacy of her political advice, explaining that God had given her a "Call" for "medling in Publick Matters." So she asserted forcefully in 1706, "King *Charles* could wish he could take my Counsel, and I wish he had, for then he might have been alive to this day: and if King *James* had taken my Counsel, he need not have gone to *France,* and if King *William* had taken my Counsel, he would have been the Darling of *England.*" Even though someone described her in a handwritten note on a surviving copy of one of her broadsides as "A Mad Woman who used to attend at the Doors of the House of Lds & Commons," someone else in 1715 evidently thought she was well enough respected to warrant issuing a counterfeit political broadside under her name favoring the Pretender and challenging George I.[11]

Elinor James's language in her post–1700 publications suggests that as a woman she was feeling growing social and cultural pressure to stop publishing her opinions on political topics. She ignored those pressures, for, as she said, she had been "medling in Public Matters" her entire adult life. Her newly frequent defenses of her ability to offer political commentaries, though, are one indication of the changing attitudes that in the wake of the Glorious Revolution began to reshape how English people thought about government and the identity of proper state actors. In the 1640s, ordinary women had claimed the right to political involvement, and men had produced no ideologically unified response. They had satirized and sexualized women's views or asserted that all politically active women were wives whose status as *feme covert* should exclude them from the public arena. Englishmen believed that lower-ranking women should play no role in the polity, but with the exception of Henry Neville they linked that exclusion primarily to status rather than gender. As late as the final decades of the century, Elinor James, deeming herself *mistress,* appropriated gentry status and was not initially attacked for inappropriate political activity, even though her ideas drew criticism.

The rethinking of government's origins and structure after the Glorious Revolution, however, had significant long-term consequences for women's involvement in the public realm. John Locke and other Whig theorists redefined government as an institution created and run by *men*—not generic human beings, but specifically *males.* As a consequence, women found themselves not only excluded from the *public* but also increasingly nominally confined to a new, parallel realm termed the *private.* That such ideas affected even Elinor James reveals their powerful impact on women of all ranks.[12]

❦ CHAPTER 3

John Dunton and the Invention of the Feminine Private

John Dunton had his finger on the pulse of late-seventeenth-century English culture. A printer and bookseller, Dunton in 1691 founded the most successful periodical of his day, the *Athenian Gazette, or Casuistical Mercury,* commonly known as the *Athenian Mercury.*[1] A little-known predecessor of the more famous *Tatler* and *Spectator,* the *Athenian Mercury* catered to the male denizens of London's coffeehouses and to a growing number of women who, whether or not they patronized such establishments, nevertheless participated in the same intellectual world. Dunton's periodical invited its readers to enter into dialogue with the editors, and in so doing it opened a remarkable window for historians seeking to discover the cultural currents of his times. The *Mercury's* reach even extended to England's North American colonies: some evidence reveals a colonial audience for the publication, and because Dunton spent time in Boston in the late 1680s, the periodical could well have attracted readers there.[2]

The *Athenian Mercury* filled a unique niche in the late seventeenth century, a time of political turmoil and cultural transition. In the previous fifty years, the nation had endured the trauma and austerity of the Civil War and Commonwealth period, followed by the excesses of the Stuart Restoration and the political uncertainty that led to the Glorious Revolution. And the uncertainty did not end there: like Elinor James, many English people were unsure of their allegiance in the 1690s, regardless of their attitude toward the Catholic James II. The decade was filled with accusations of treason, rumored Stuart plots to regain the throne, and fierce struggles over oath taking to the new monarchs. Queen Mary II came in for particular criticism because she had helped depose her own father. One poet in 1690 sympathized with James II, "a Monarch...brought so low" as "his own Children Strike the fatall Blow." The anonymous author warned Mary of heaven's vengeance on "unrepenting Paracides" and concluded:

> For one usurpers Tytle being good
> The Right of Princes lyes not in the Blood,
> Nor is Confin'd to any certain Line,
> Possession makes all Governments Divine,
> Good Pagan doctrine broach'd to Serve all tymes,
> Success will Sanctify the worst of Crimes.[3]

Probably because of the unrest revealed by such sentiments and the continuing linkage of familial and political matters, the new monarchs stressed the need for altering English people's personal behavior. Their moral concerns were expressed in the widespread founding of Societies for the Reformation of Manners, which sought to monitor and prevent dissipation. Just as during the Civil War, the dethroning of a king raised questions about the political and familial authority of men in general. The emphasis on the importance of reason and learning in the work of philosophers such as John Locke affected thinking about women as well, and the writings of such advocates as Poulain de la Barre, Nahum Tate, Judith Drake, and Mary Astell challenged older views of women's intellectual inferiority. Traditional notions of gendered identities were in flux; the time was ripe for a reconceptualization of male and female roles.[4]

After the turn of the century, John Dunton was to supply that reconceptualization explicitly. Whether he was significantly influenced by exchanges with the readers of the *Athenian Mercury* or whether his thinking evolved more independently is uncertain. Yet it is hard to imagine that he was unaffected by the responses of his readers and contributors to the contents of his periodical. The ideas initially crystallized in the *Mercury* and some of Dunton's other publications served as one of the key foundations for what were to become pervasive eighteenth-century understandings of the appropriate activities of men and women.[5]

Dunton and the *Athenian Mercury*

John Dunton, the descendant of three generations of Anglican clergymen, was born in Huntingdonshire in 1659. Although his father hoped that he would continue the family tradition of a religious vocation, Dunton instead opted for the trade of publishing and bookselling. After serving an apprenticeship, he opened his own shop in 1681 and the following year married Elizabeth Annesley, daughter of a nonconformist minister. During and after their marriage, which ended with her death in 1697, Dunton lauded Elizabeth as the ideal wife, and she seems to have played a major role in managing the family's finances. Indeed, her business acumen clearly exceeded his, for after she died his financial situation worsened considerably. That led him to contract a disastrous second marriage with Sarah Nicholas, the daughter of a wealthy widow, a union that collapsed after it became evident to Sarah and her mother that Dunton primarily sought access to the mother's money. Although Dunton subsequently published numerous works and lived until 1732, he was never able to recapture the success he had gained in the 1690s with his unusual periodical.[6]

In his 1705 autobiography, *Life and Errors,* Dunton recounted the circumstances that led him devise the plan for the *Athenian Mercury.* One day, while walking in a park with two male friends and trying to keep his mind off an injury he had suffered, he was struck "on a suddain" with a novel notion. Initially, he recounted, "it was no more than *a confus'd Idea of concealing the Querist and answering his Question.*" But later, at home, he *"brought it into form, and hammer'd out a Title for 't, which happened to be extremely lucky."* That title, employing the term *Athenian,* he explained, drew on Acts 17:21: "For all the Athenians and strangers which were there spent their time in nothing else, but either to tell, or to hear some new thing." Describing the project in his autobiography, he asked proudly, what "cou'd be more agreeable, than that which promises, at least, to open the *Avenues,* raise the Soul, as 'twere, into DAYLIGHT, and restore the Knowledge of *Truth* and *Happiness,* that had wandered so long unknown, and found out by few? This was the great Design of our *English Athens,* which was a Thought intirely (if you'll forgive me the Vanity) *of my own Creation.*"[7]

Dunton's clever and original idea was, in brief, to promise to answer in the *Athenian Mercury* any questions readers submitted on any subject. He called it "the Question Project." As a habitué of coffeehouses himself, the printer knew that they appealed to a clientele interested in talking about politics, current events, science, religion, and numerous other topics. Coffeehouse patrons read and discussed many ephemeral publications; Dunton recognized

Figure 3.1. "The Coffeehouse Mob," frontispiece to part 4 of *Vulgus Britannicus,* by Edward Ward (London, 1710). Although the patrons at this coffeehouse seem to be engaged in a more animated exchange than would have been common, the scene itself is typical. Patrons at tables read newspapers and broadsheets such as the *Athenian Mercury,* and in the rear a woman (the only one in the room) serves coffee to the guests. This item is reproduced by permission of the Huntington Library, San Marino, California.

that his periodical, asking for their inquiries on any topic that concerned them, would quickly attract widespread attention and interest. Thus he hired "Mercury Women" to sell his periodical in the coffeehouses, and when he later printed and bound individual volumes of the *Mercury*, he assumed that the collective copies would be available at such establishments for patrons to pore over, to contemplate past questions and answers, and perhaps to submit still more inquiries. Appropriately, the "address" of the *Mercury* was itself a coffeehouse: correspondents were directed to send their questions to James and Mary Smith's coffeehouse, located near Dunton's shop.[8]

Dunton knew that he could not handle the project without assistance and that he needed to recruit helpers. He turned first to a brother-in-law, Richard Sault, a mathematician, and soon to two additional men: another brother-in-law, the cleric Samuel Wesley, and a Dr. Norris, perhaps a physician. A few weeks after he began publication, Dunton started terming the four men a "Society," later to become the "Athenian Society." Dunton maintained their anonymity and, initially, his own as well; he was not revealed as the publisher until the title page of the first collected volume, produced four months after the appearance of the first number. Although other London printers must have known the composition of the group, not until he published *Life and Errors* did Dunton formally reveal the names of its members or its small size. He left readers with the impression that their queries were being answered by a large organization of men who met regularly to consider the responses carefully. Instead, his contract with Sault and Wesley (Norris participated only occasionally, and without pay) reveals that he paid them piecework rates for answers they drafted individually, although both men were to review all responses before publication.[9]

The *Athenian Mercury,* a two-sided broadsheet, was an immediate success, quickly changing from a weekly to a twice-weekly in response to high demand. The first issue, published on March 17, 1691, described its "Design" as "to satisfy all *ingenious and curious Enquirers* into *Speculations,* Divine, Moral, and Natural &c." It explained, too, that by making both questions and answers anonymous it hoped to "remove...that shame or fear of appearing ridiculous" in front of associates which might prevent people from asking certain questions publicly. Undoubtedly Dunton intended the *Mercury* to respond primarily to queries about religion, science, and other topics requiring some degree of knowledge. He almost certainly did not anticipate another consequence of the promised anonymity: that he would receive inquiries about the sort of intimate problems that men and women commonly discussed only with their closest friends and family members, if at all. But a survey of the *Mercury*'s content suggests that as many as one-third of the questions addressed to the periodical eventually fell roughly into that category.[10]

In the first issue, Dunton supplied some model questions and answers focusing mainly on religion. One asked, for example, where was Lazarus's soul while he was in the grave for four days? Another had social as well as legal implications, foreshadowing what would become a prominent theme in the *Athenian Mercury*. Dunton (or Sault, his sole collaborator for the first two numbers) asked himself: Could a man beat his wife? The response: Yes, legally, but doing so was nevertheless a bad idea. When the second number appeared a week later, one of the earliest readers had posed a follow-up question: could a woman beat her husband if he was a drunkard? No, came the answer, for husbands had the "Prerogative" of familial power. By the time the second issue was published, questions had already begun to pour in to the editors, for in addition to informing readers why the sea was salty and why a compass always pointed north, among other things, Dunton supplied a list of questions that would be answered in the next number: Are there witches? What causes the tides? Was polygamy lawful for the Jews? Such eclectic collections of inquiries characterized most two-page issues of the *Mercury*, even though occasionally Dunton grouped related questions together. Each number responded to between ten and twenty requests for information or advice.[11]

At the beginning of the second volume, in May 1691, Dunton and his collaborators attempted to bring some order to the chaotic circumstances they then evidently confronted. Revealing that they had a huge backlog of questions awaiting answers, they instructed their readers that for the time being they would give priority to inquiries needing a speedy response or to those in some respect "remarkable" or "extraordinary." After explaining why they could not take the time or space to list the questions received, they provided a set of negative directions: they would not reply to "Obscene Questions" or solve riddles. They would not answer more than a limited number of requests sent simultaneously by the same person. They would not print anything, "the Answer of which, may be a Scandal to the Government, or an Abuse to particular Persons." Urging their readers to consult the index of the first volume to ensure that they were not submitting questions that had already been answered, they observed that as long as their correspondents avoided "whatever may be destructive to the Principles of Vertue and Sound Knowledge," they would reply to any inquiries. Finally, the editors declared that no other people would be admitted to their society and that they intended to continue their anonymity. Clearly, correspondents had both asked them to reveal their identity and volunteered to join the Athenian Society.[12]

The preface to the third volume contained another lengthy message from the Athenians to their readers. They observed, "some find fault with us for meddling with things too *trifling* and *low,* others with things *too high.* Some that we have nothing but *old Stuff* which the World has been tired with a Thousand times over, and others again that our Notions are *daring and new,* and not safe to be Published." And so they asked: how can these contradictory objections to the *Mercury's* content be true simultaneously? How could the Athenian Society possibly manage to please everyone? The preface then addressed the contention that some of the questions they answered should not be "common *Chatt and Entertainment on a Coffee-house-board."* But, they replied, "why mayn't Discourses of this Nature be as proper for *Coffee-houses* as others?" At the very least, the editors argued, discussions of the questions posed to them might "serve to hinder People from talking of what's worse." And any fault surely lay with their correspondents, not themselves.[13]

Although such long and detailed passages certainly suggest that the collaborators faced a plethora of genuine submissions from their audience, readers of the *Athenian Mercury* then and now have wondered—as a 1695 correspondent put it—"whether ye have told most stories, false or true?" The Athenians' reply insisted on their sincerity and claimed that some of the published questions were superior to any they might have concocted themselves.[14]

Any attempt to interpret the "Question Project" must directly address three issues. First, who was responsible for the answers printed in the *Mercury?* The contract signed in April 1691 did not specify subject divisions, but Sault presumably handled the questions relating to mathematics and science, with occasional aid from Norris, and Wesley those dealing with religion and theology. Under the contract, Wesley and Sault were required to meet each Friday afternoon to review and approve the answers they had drafted and to receive questions for the following week. Dunton would certainly have distributed those questions, although his presence at the meeting was not mentioned in the agreement. Each man was to deliver to Dunton two separate sets of questions and answers, each set sufficient to fill one side of a printed sheet. Those materials would then constitute the contents of the next week's two issues.[15]

Many of the *Mercury's* correspondents asked questions of a sort not anticipated by the contract and outside the realm of expertise of Sault, Wesley, or Norris. Who replied to those queries is unclear, but because Dunton received and handed out the questions and had overall direction of the enterprise, he probably drafted many of the longer responses to personal inquiries. He certainly wrote the textual asides that addressed the *Mercury's* readers and contributors. That Dunton was largely responsible for both seems all the more likely because the contract provided that he "shall have power to intermix and place the said Questions as he pleases," and because of the printer's own interest in women and their roles, evident throughout the body of his work over the years. Regardless of who wrote what answers, though, the *Mercury* always employed the editorial "we."

The second issue is, did Dunton and his collaborators construct their own queries and then respond to them? Perhaps, but only rarely. Unless Dunton wholly invented thousands of questions and the numerous textual asides in which he directly addressed readers, the Athenians actually received large numbers of requests for information and advice. Furthermore, some surviving letters in Dunton's papers relate to *Mercury* submissions.[16]

The third issue is more complex. Assuming the *Mercury's* correspondents were real, did they accurately portray their circumstances? Probably, but one must acknowledge that some letter writers surely shaded the truth or altered certain facts. Once people realized that the *Mercury* would preserve their anonymity, they undoubtedly became more likely to reveal intimate details of their own or their friends' lives. Many claimed to consult the Athenian Society on behalf of "friends"; whether the writer or an associate was involved in the situation described was, though, largely irrelevant to the truthfulness of the overall circumstances. Regardless of whether the specific facts laid out in the letters were wholly accurate, the questions revealed concerns pervasive in late-seventeenth-century culture.[17]

Certainly the utter novelty of reading about and being able to discuss other people's often complicated and fascinating personal problems must have contributed greatly to the positive contemporary reception of the *Athenian Mercury*. Dunton attributed the *Mercury's* success to its role in educating the public about an eclectic set of topics. But, as already noted, nearly one-third of all questions revolved around personal relationships, and religion (the next most frequent subject) constituted just one-fifth of the whole, with other subjects such as science, literature, and history lagging far behind. The *Athenian Mercury's* openness to personal questions undoubtedly led readers to favor it over the several short-lived competitors it quickly spawned. One competitor, the *London Mercury*, lampooned the Athenians, as did a play, *The New Athenian Comedy*, but neither dented the popularity of Dunton's periodical. The idea that hit him "on a suddain" as he walked with friends that day in London had indeed struck a resonant chord with Dunton's contemporaries, and not just with other Londoners. Questioners came from provincial towns and rural areas in addition to the city, and there are even occasional references to readers in the American colonies.[18]

An Emblem of ye Athenian society. 1692.

A. behind ye scenes sit mighty we
nor are we known nor will we be
the world and we exchanging thus,
while we find chat for y'they work [for us]
B. dy'e see that lady in ye mask.
wee'l tell ye what she comes to ask
tho an unconscionable task
tis how her lover fast to bind [wind]
false as her selfe false as ye faithless
C. that other brings her favorite fles [ordue]
with golden fetters lock and key.
if thas a fling our thoughts does haue.
or only a tongue as other females
D. thinking our notions too ieiune

some take their aime at madam [moon]
some bring hard queryes which [we crack]
and throw the gazeing world a [Kernels back]
E. heres honest tarr who would his [crown afford]
were he paid off'ere he returns [aboard]
to know what he must ask in vain
when we shall beat ye french again [despaird]
F. euclid where art the'twas before [squard]
now maist thou haue thy circle [wind]
but art is long and thou must [stay]
nor Rome was built nor athens [in a day]
G. we know St but too well your [in ye case]
some powrfull faction right or [wrong embrace]
or starue and dye without a [place]

H. auoid you ront of noisy fools [rules]
once more you are not in our [few]
could we but please y learned [dispence w. you]
which send from far we couid [would you run]
I. whither, lost wretches whither [londou]
by guilt or by unhappy loue
what need you perish or despair [you where]
if you'd haue aid an angel shows
K. this quers quickly understood [good]
he only asks-aye think his coffee [doet]
yet woud croud in tho iust by th [in no more]
or woud heed take our letters
L. these dainty nuts i must not loose [dear pug]
nor burn my paws-b your leaue

if those that put em there enqu
twas you notj that robbil yf fir
how sweet is interlopers hire [he]
M. oll englands rarities are gathe
from unknown earth fire wate
thousands agree in such a glorio [stry]
or else a moments work woud lg
N. with beak and talons j infett
those cuckoes that invade my n
and if minerva yet supply
my antient gift in prophecy.
all scabd and old they in some
-hollow tree shall dye

London Printed For John Dunton at ye Rauen in ye Poultrey

The freshness of Dunton's enterprise needs to be underscored for readers in a modern era accustomed to columns by Ann Landers or her successors such as Amy Dickinson. The airing of personal problems in a public setting, even anonymously, was unprecedented in the seventeenth century other than for accused criminals, who often recited tangled tales of woe to explain their illicit behavior. Those who asked the Athenians' counsel about personal relationships were ordinary men and women who had erred in some way and wished to rectify their mistakes or extricate themselves from difficult circumstances in the least disruptive manner possible. In a rapidly changing age, people understandably sought guidance about life's tribulations (large and small) from experts—and the Athenians purported to offer their readers authoritative opinions on many topics.

John Dunton and Women

As they began the *Athenian Mercury,* Dunton and his collaborators seem to have assumed that their reading audience would be composed of men. After all, the patrons of the coffeehouses at which the publication was primarily aimed were largely, if not exclusively, male; and the Athenians' goal of furthering understanding of (as Dunton had put it in the first issue) "Divine, Moral, and Natural" subjects accorded with what they regarded as men's interests.

Yet women began reading the *Mercury* soon after it started publication. The "advertisement" at the bottom of the second page of the thirteenth number of the first volume read as follows:

> *We have receiv'd this week a very* Ingenuous *Letter from a* Lady *in the* Country, *who desires to know whether her* Sex *might not send us Questions as well as men, to which we answer, Yes, they may, our design being to answer* all manner of Questions *sent us by* either Sex, *that may be either useful to the publick or to particular Persons.*

FIGURE 3.2. "Emblem of the Athenian Society," 1692, engraving by Frederick Hendrik van Hove, frontispiece to *The Young Students Library,* published by John Dunton. The symbolic view of the Athenians shows hordes of questioners appealing to the row of learned gentlemen at the table. The first group of supplicants is bewigged and well dressed, the second (lower) group of lesser rank. In the middle a man being attacked by a woman shouts, "help help noble athenians," and the long caption below details some of the circumstances and queries indicated by the capital letters. The caption begins, "behind ye scenes sit mighty we / nor are we known nor will we be," emphasizing the initial anonymity of members of the Athenian Society. This item is reproduced by permission of the Huntington Library, San Marino, California.

Dunton asked that women wait to submit questions until he indicated that all queries already in hand had been answered, but the female readers must have been impatient. In issue 17—just two weeks later—Dunton published the first question explicitly identified as coming from a woman, and in that same number he commented, "The several Ingenious Questions lately sent us by a Young Gentlewoman, (they relating chiefly to the *Fair Sex*) shall be speedily answered all together in one Paper." He was as good as his word: in the next issue, just four days later, appeared twelve questions from the "young Gentlewoman," accompanied by yet another "advertisement":

> Whereas the Questions we receive from the *Fair Sex* are both *pressing* and *numerous,* we being willing to oblige 'em, as knowing they have a very *strong party* in the world, resolve to set apart the *first Tuesday in every month* on purpose to satisfie Questions of that Nature.

Thus began the *Athenian Mercury*'s practice of publishing designated "Ladies Issues," which continued through early January 1692.[19]

Dunton's decision (for it was surely his) to open the pages of the *Mercury* to inquiries from women led to complaints from some male readers, most notably a man Dunton guessed was either a *"disappointed Lover;* or else a grave Philosophical Don." In September 1691, that man asked: "Whether it does not weaken the Credit of the *Athenian Mercury,* that the Authors of it descend to such a pittiful Employment as to take Notice of Feminine Impertinencies"? Dunton responded (fittingly, in a "Ladies Issue") that if the writer read the letters the *Mercury* received, he would find "Ten, perhaps a Hundred *Masculine Impertinencies* to one Feminine." But he also defended the important content of women's correspondence. Weighty letters from women, he revealed, had required considerable thought and effort to answer. Some of those queries "not only have an Influence on the Happiness of particular Men, and the *Peace of Families,* but even the good and welfare of larger Society, and the whole Commonwealth, which consists of Families and single Persons."[20]

That Dunton would endorse the importance of women and their (assumed) concerns is not surprising. While he published the *Mercury,* his first wife, Elizabeth, whom he greatly esteemed, served as his competent financial manager. A good deal of evidence attests to Dunton's interest in and respect for intellectual women generally—the very women who submitted questions to his periodical.

For example, a year after Elizabeth's death, Dunton prepared for publication a manuscript purporting to consist of letters he had written during a five-month stay in New England in 1686. To escape the clutches of creditors attempting to collect a debt for which he had stood surety, the printer took a cargo of books to Boston and set up a temporary shop there. Whatever actual letters he might have written to friends and family in that period have long since been lost; the version that remains—not published until 1867—plagiarized long passages from a variety of English and American sources. Accordingly, as previous commentators have observed, his New England letters cannot be trusted as a firsthand account of late-seventeenth-century Boston.[21]

But if the so-called correspondence does not divulge much about Massachusetts and its residents, it does reveal a good deal about Dunton's attitudes. Male travelers of his day rarely wrote at length about women, yet Dunton devoted many pages to the exemplary women he encountered in Boston. (So exemplary, in fact, that his descriptions of "a Virgin, a Wife,... a Widow" are taken nearly word for word from Richard Allestree's portraits of ideal types in *The Ladies Calling* [1673]!) At the outset, he insisted, "I ever thought Women as fit for Friendship as Men," and he proceeded to prove the truth of that assertion in page after page filled with praises for the real women whom he described using Allestree's language. Further, when the bookseller recounted that a Boston customer asked him for recommendations of the best English authors, after listing such men as John Bunyan and John Dryden he added, "nor must we here forget to do justice to the Fair Sex." He then claimed to have named Katherine Philips, Aphra Behn, and "the Incomparable Philomela" (the poet Elizabeth Singer, later Rowe).[22]

Moreover, surviving letters from Englishwomen show that during the run of the *Mercury* Dunton corresponded privately with those who had submitted questions or poems to the journal. He both encouraged and flirted with them, intriguing them enough to draw them into extended epistolary exchanges. One such woman was Elizabeth Singer, who in 1695 indicated that she found his communications "charming," declaring that he had gained "all the pure and intellectual part of my affections." She regularly sent poems to the *Athenian Mercury*, which printed many separately before Dunton published a volume of her verse in 1696. Dunton dubbed her the "Pindarick Lady" and dedicated volume 15 of the *Mercury* to her. She returned the esteem, in 1695 penning "A Pindarick, to the Athenian Society," which concluded with the following lines:

> Oh, could my verse
> With *equal flights,* to after times rehearse,
> Your *fame:* It should as bright and Deathless be;
> As *that immortal flame you've raised in me.*

. . . .

A friendship so exalted and immense,
A *female breast* did ne're before commence.[23]

In 1704, Dunton published what he described as "an intire Series of *Pla-tonick Courtship* [letters] between several *Philosophical Gentlemen and Ladies.*" He remarked that "the Letters were really sent to the *Athenian-Society;* and we here promise that the Ladies Names shall be for ever conceal'd." The texts he printed show that Sault and Wesley too engaged in correspondence with female contributors. He obviously was concerned that the women in question would be outraged by the publication of their missives to the Athenians, for he added that anonymity kept their letters "as great a *Secret* as they were formerly when handed to us by private Messengers." Just as with the textual asides in the *Mercury* itself, such comments (and in this case, their evident urgency) suggest that the substance of Dunton's claims to the authenticity of the publication was truthful. The correspondence further demonstrates that well-educated women were attracted to the *Mercury* and its creators precisely because of the respect it showed them and because the publication was uniquely open to women's inquiries and writings.[24]

Dunton's exchanges with another 1695 correspondent, who called herself "Anonyma," suggest something of the allure the periodical held for such women. She submitted a poem, "An Hymn to Learning," which Dunton quickly published. Her explanatory subtitle, "Written upon occasion of La-dies Despising it [Learning] in Womankind &c Dedicated to the Athenian Society," revealed her purpose both for writing the verses and for sending them to the *Mercury*. In his editorial note Dunton observed that the author "is resolved to stand up for the interest of her Sex, and give the Age an idea of what might be expected from it, if their Education was agreeable to their Capacity and Merit"; and he asked that she inform the Athenians how to contact her directly. The poem began, "Hail Sacred Learning!" After praising learned men, it arrived at its point:

Each Age produceth many a learned she;
With thy Celestial Fire,
The fair the tender Sex thou dost inspire

. . . .

Out of reach of those,
That are learn'd Man or Woman's Foes,
Let me securely sit,
Accompany'd by Learning, Books, and Wit

. . . .

There with few Books and Learning's help will I
Study, first how to live; then how to die.[25]

When Anonyma wrote again to the Athenians as Dunton requested, she asked for "some Instructions for the encouragement of my studies." Although she thus invited a correspondence, she pronounced herself unhappy with Dunton's subsequent proposal to go beyond discussing such topics "incognito" and instead arrange a meeting in person. Possibly, she implied, not all the correspondence of women and the Athenians was truly "Platonick." Revealing in another letter that she knew John Dunton personally, Anonyma threatened to tell his wife about his attempt to "Act the Lovers part and court a Young Lady." She declared that she would "laugh heartily" the next time she saw him, because he did not know her identity while she was well aware of his, although he had hidden behind a pseudonym. Without Dunton's half of the correspondence it is impossible to know whether Anonyma correctly interpreted his intentions, but in any event she was sufficiently interested in her interaction with him to continue to exchange letters, and indeed even to write for one of his later publications.[26]

After several years of publishing the *Mercury* and receiving such correspondence, Dunton clearly came to understand that women composed a significant proportion of his readers and contributors. And so, hoping to build on the success of the *Mercury* in reaching that female reading public, in May 1694 he announced the impending publication of *The Ladies Dictionary,* "being a pleasant Entertainment for the *Fair Sex,* a Work never attempted before in *English.*" In July he promised that the book would "be serviceable to them in all their Concerns of *Love, Marriage, Dress, Behaviour, Business, Life, Houses, and Conversations.*" It was thus much more than a dictionary, defining terms but also including brief biographies of illustrious or notorious females and didactic essays—for instance, "Anger in Ladies, &c., discommendable and hurtful"; "Fame, Her Character, with a Caution to the Fair"; "Gracefulness"; and "Obedience of Virgins, &c to Parents in matters of Marriage." The author, purportedly one "N.H.," but surely in more than one entry Dunton himself, declared, "I should esteem the World but a Desert were it not for the Society of the *Fair* Sex." Men, he wrote, "are wrapt in a Circle of obligations to them for their Love and good Offices" throughout their lives. Flattering his female audience, he asserted that men and women were intellectually equal and observed that there has been "no Age or Nation but has produced some Females Renowned for their Wisdom or Vertue."[27]

The Ladies Dictionary failed to achieve the popularity Dunton had anticipated (a projected second volume never appeared), but the *Athenian Mercury* itself probably more than made up for the dictionary's lack of success. Its readership, male and female, remained sufficiently intrigued by the "Question Project" that publication continued until well into 1697, thus making the *Mercury* the longest-running English periodical of the seventeenth century. Its audience—primarily young, single urban dwellers of middling rank, interested in improving themselves—surely used the *Mercury* as a source for topics of interesting conversation and as a guide to acceptable and unacceptable behavior. Its continuing and widespread appeal is revealed not only by the success of the original periodical but also by the repeated reprintings of the collected volumes of questions and answers published in 1703 and thereafter by Andrew Bell, to whom a debt-encumbered Dunton sold the copyright. The interest extended across the Atlantic into North America. The three volumes, titled *The Athenian Oracle: Being an Entire Collection of All the Valuable Questions and Answers in the Old Athenian Mercuries,* were regularly advertised for sale by American booksellers from 1733 to 1794, and American newspapers occasionally published selected excerpts from the volumes. In an additional indication of the popularity of the material, the records of a lending library in a small Pennsylvania town indicate that the *Athenian Oracle* was checked out regularly between 1763 and 1774.[28]

John Dunton's publication, it seems clear, achieved that remarkable success at least in part because of its appeal to women—and to men concerned about personal relationships. Accordingly, it is important to examine in detail the questions and answers on gendered topics that appeared in the *Mercury*. Too often historians have looked only at prescriptive literature in an attempt to discern the gender norms of a particular time. But for late-seventeenth-century England, the inquiries published in the *Mercury* allow an investigation of pressing concerns articulated by young people from the middling ranks of society. The responses of Dunton and his colleagues constitute some of the earliest attempts to outline what were to become the standard components of the eighteenth-century notion of the feminine private sphere. That was certainly one reason (in addition to possible prurient interest in tales with potentially lurid overtones) why the collected volumes remained so popular—so relevant—that they were still being purchased and read in the new United States a century after the questions were originally posed and answered.

Women and "Ladies Issues" in the *Athenian Mercury*

The Athenians formally insisted on the essential intellectual equality of men and women, a position pleasing to their female readers. Rejecting the casual and pervasive misogyny of the past, they instructed questioners that many women were "as truly great, as brave, as learned, and as capable of any accomplishments as those of Men: and in Fact have managed Affairs as well, even when *plac'd upon Thrones.*" Although acknowledging that men had been given a superior position on earth, they remarked that such superiority would disappear after death. In eternity, souls would have no sex.[29]

Yet the *Athenian Mercury's* stance on gender similarity was more ambiguous than it might seem at first glance. Even its statement of ultimate equality admitted that in life men and women necessarily occupied unequal positions. Although the Athenians repeatedly stressed the mutual obligations of courting and married couples and rejected the sexual double standard, the *Mercury* also firmly based its treatment of topics pertaining to love and marriage on a newly conceptualized division between female and male roles inside and outside the household. That division Dunton himself would characterize a few years later by invoking the terms *public* and *private* in such a context for the first time.

Returning briefly to the traditional view of the English family reveals the innovation of Dunton's formulation. When Richard Cleaver, in *A Godlie Forme of Householde Government* (1598), considered his subject, he devoted scant attention to love or affection in any household relationship. To his mind, instead, husbands and wives, as family governors, had to fulfill obligations to each other and to their children and servants. "The husband and wife are Lords of the house," he declared, with an appropriate division of authority between them. He detailed the husband's responsibilities, then observed, "The wife is ruler of all other things, but yet under her husband." Contemporary understandings in late-sixteenth-century England thus defined *households* with men at the head.[30]

By contrast, for John Dunton a century later all questions relevant to love, courtship, marriage, and the household from women *or* men qualified for inclusion in the monthly "Ladies Issues." In effect, he excluded men from his definition of the family. The topic of the query rather than the identity of the inquirer determined the placement of the questions. Even if the requests for advice on such matters came from men (and many did), Dunton slotted most of them into his "Ladies Issues." Courtship, marriage, and the family, he implicitly indicated, were to his mind the sole province of women, even though they directly and necessarily involved men.[31]

Such topics were, moreover, of minor importance when compared with the "more *serious* and *weighty* *Meditations*" that filled other numbers of the *Athenian Mercury.* When in early 1693 Dunton attempted to establish the *Ladies Mercury,* a new publication aimed solely at female readers and writers, he made that attitude explicit and belied his stated insistence on gender equality. He explained that the Athenians would retain as their focus "that fair and larger *Field,...*indeed the whole *World,*" whereas the new periodical would confine "our narrow *Speculation,* to only that little Sublunary, *Woman."* It would deal exclusively with "*Martha's* humbler part, a little homely *Cookery,* the dishing up of a small Treat of *Love.*"[32]

Perhaps the *Ladies Mercury* constituted Dunton's response to some male patrons' continuing complaints about the Athenians' willingness to respond to "the Impertinence of *Foolish Tatlers* and *Gossips,* that have sometimes debased your Pens," but the periodical intended only for a female audience lasted just four issues. Possibly misled by his own categorization, Dunton himself had perhaps not realized how many men (by definition excluded as correspondents of the new publication) had contributed relevant questions on courtship, marriage, and personal relationships to the *Athenian Mercury.* He thus failed to understand that a successful publication could not be based on queries about such topics submitted by women alone. Or, alternatively, his stated rationale for the new publication, which dismissively characterized its focus as the "*Trifles* and *Vanities*" no longer of interest to the Athenians, alienated the very audience of women he needed to attract. In either case, the failure of the *Ladies Mercury* meant that the parent publication continued to respond to requests for advice on personal matters from both male and female correspondents.

Indeed, the initial set of such questions came from a man; Dunton published them in the issue of May 5, 1691, the same one in which he acknowledged receiving the first inquiry asking if the Athenians would respond to queries from women.[33] "*A Gentleman having lately proposed several Questions relating to Love and Marriage, to oblige the* fair Sex *and* him, *we think fit to Answer 'em here altogether,*" Dunton wrote. Thus from the very beginning of the *Mercury's* treatment of such topics, and before his designation of "Ladies Issues," the editor was already defining personal inquiries as "feminine" and assuming that women would be especially interested in the questions—and the answers.

The "gentleman's" questions raised themes that would recur repeatedly in the pages of the *Athenian Mercury* in succeeding years. The correspondent asked whether parents could insist that their children marry certain people, whether marriages could legitimately be based on money rather than affection, how men or women could subtly let potential partners know their feelings for each other, and whether married women were worse off than married men. All his inquiries were phrased generally, and so too were the answers. "*Parents are not to dispose of their Children like Cattel,* nor to make 'em *miserable,"* replied the Athenians. As for wives' position: *"Nature* has generally given the *fair Sex* Art enough" that women can hold their own with their husbands if they so wish.

Similarly, the first set of questions from *"a young* Gentlewoman" answered together later in May were mostly phrased impersonally: Is beauty "real or imaginary"? Why do children tend to resemble fathers rather than mothers? What is platonic love? Would an army of women conquer an army of men? Yet two had more specific implications and probably stemmed from the experience of the questioner or her acquaintances. First: Could parents force a woman who was of age and had been supporting herself to break an engagement she had entered into after "Honourable Courtship"? (The answer, couched in biblical terms and thus probably Wesley's, suggested an ambiguous no.) Second, introduced as coming from a poor woman who could not afford to consult an attorney: Must a married woman respond to a subpoena from a Chancery Court? (Answer: yes, or "great inconvenience" would ensue.)[34]

Although such numbers themselves verged on the promised "Ladies Issues," the first formally so designated was that of June 3, 1691. Dunton introduced it by explaining that he was setting aside the first Tuesday of each month *"to answer all the* Reasonable Questions *sent us by the fair Sex, as also any others relating to* Love and Marriage." He added that the responses to the sets of queries from the "gentleman" and "gentlewoman"—the terms were used not to connote gentry status but as respectful forms of address for correspondents—had been *"favourably receiv'd, as appears by many Letters lately sent us on that subject."* All eleven questions the issue contained were posed from either a masculine or an ungendered stance; nine addressed impersonal topics (Is marriage a divine or a political institution? Were there marriage ceremonies prior to Moses?), while two raised more intimate matters. A man admitted that he had publicly proclaimed his love for one woman but now loved another. The Athenians agreed with him that it was better to break off the relationship with the first and thus to make her unhappy briefly, rather than to marry her and render them both miserable until one or the other died. The second male questioner laid out a more serious problem: what should he do about his wife and her adulterous partner? Should he challenge the man to a duel? In response, the Athenians declared it "absurd" for a man to risk his life for a dishonored wife. They recommended that their correspondent instead "slight and scorn" both his wife and her lover, "to let 'em know we thought 'em not worth our Concern, and to trust their Punishment to t'other World." Since the law would not help him, only "Heaven" could.[35]

An "advertisement" at the end of that first "Ladies Issue" showed that the *Mercury* had quickly achieved a reputation as an authoritative source of information. Dunton reported receiving a question from a man about an illegitimate birth *"lately laid to his Charge (under very improbable Circumstances of being his)."* The editor expressed some hesitancy about replying publicly but promised to do so in the forthcoming supplement to the first volume because the correspondent insisted that his *"Reputation in a great measure depends upon our* determination." The *Mercury's* readers were surely teased by the prospect of this question and answer, and they would just as surely have been titillated when the exchange appeared.[36]

Is it possible, the man asked, "to lose a Maidenhead and conceive a Child at the same time?"—because the woman had claimed to be a virgin before they had sexual intercourse. The response graphically described an initial sexual experience for both parties, even though the man said nothing about *his* having been a virgin at the time. For a woman to become pregnant during her first sexual intercourse was possible but highly unlikely, replied the Athenians, for "a Maid the first time undergoes too much of the rack and Torture to be capable of acting her part Effectually, and a Young Mans Eagerness pushes him on to do that is natural for him to do before the Critical time." They went on to assert in definitive terms that the woman's claim was "amongst those things that are next to Impossibilities, especially in an Age which produces a Sex more delicate and tender than ordinarily." Clearly, whoever drafted this reply—most likely Richard Sault or Dr. Norris—accepted the then-common belief that a woman could conceive only if she reached orgasm during intercourse, which the author thought improbable in such circumstances. Therefore, if the woman formally testified under oath in court that the questioner had fathered her child, the Athenian concluded, most listeners would find her statement not credible.[37]

The Athenians' stated respect for women did not extend on this occasion to believing a mother's testimony about the paternity of her child. Yet the implications of their rejection of her claim that the questioner had fathered the baby were not entirely clear. Was the correspondent suggesting that she was not a virgin at the time they had sex? But then—under the theory he and the Athenians advanced—she was *more* likely to have become pregnant during that instance of intercourse since it would not have been her initial experience. Or was he claiming that she *was* a virgin when they first had intercourse but that a later sexual partner must have fathered the child? His query was clearly open to a more ambiguous interpretation than the firm response appeared to allow. And the negative tone of the answer stands out from other, later statements by the Athenians, which tended to be sympathetic to women who had borne children out of wedlock. Perhaps this early exchange provoked objections that led Dunton and his colleagues to avoid such hard-edged replies in subsequent numbers of the *Mercury*.

Unlike the first one, later "Ladies Issues" attracted inquiries identifiably from women. The queries continued to range from the theoretical and general (what is love? is fornication a venial sin?) to the specific (if a sailor who has been at sea for eighteen months returns to find his wife married to another man, whose wife is she? [Answer: his, if he still wants her.] Where is the best place for a woman to find a husband? [Answer: the colonies.]). Some posed amusing conundrums: if a man's mother and his mistress are "in equal danger" at the same time, whom should he save? The Athenians, entering into the spirit of the coffeehouse wags who had undoubtedly coined that one, responded: "we esteem it more generous, were it possible, to die himself than lose either."[38]

Others were far more serious. A woman with a brutal husband who had abandoned her for his mistress asked whether it would be a sin to accept "the offer of a single *Gentleman that will* maintain her very well." The Athenians were unyielding: "Is't any *Case of Conscience,* whether a Woman ought to turn Whore because her Husband is a Whoremaster?" She should maintain herself by "painful *Labour,* nay almost by begging it self," rather than accept such an arrangement.[39]

Even before Dunton abandoned the practice of designating "Ladies Issues" in early 1692, such questions also spilled over into other numbers of the *Mercury*. The themes of all the inquiries and the Athenians' responses provide considerable insight into the chief personal concerns of people of middling rank at the close of the seventeenth century. A plethora of courtship queries addressed the relative importance of love and money in contracting marriage, proper behavior by both parties during courtship, the appropriate role of parents in young people's decision making, and the tangles that could arise when courting couples made verbal commitments to each other, only to have one member change his or her mind thereafter. Husbands and wives asked not only about how to deal with sexual infidelity, brutal spouses, or general marital discord but also about household management and marriage law. And both parents and young people inquired about education—how to educate children or themselves.[40]

The Athenians provided consistent answers to most such questions:

- Parents can prevent dependent children from making marriages of which they do not approve, but cannot legitimately force children to marry anyone against their will. In the event of an impasse, the child should remain single until the parent dies. If young people have already achieved financial independence, they have somewhat more freedom to marry against their parents' wishes, but should still seek approval for their choices before entering marital unions.[41]

- Both love and adequate resources are preferable for a good marriage, but ultimately love (or at least the likelihood of affection) and good character are more important than money.[42]

- Courting couples should be careful about what promises they make to each other, because in doing so they incur moral obligations that they are duty-bound to keep unless released by the other party. At the same time, illicit promises are not binding.[43]

- Because of the difficulty of obtaining a divorce and the impossibility of legal remarriage in nearly all cases, women (or, less often, men) involved in abusive marriages need to find ways of coping with their circumstances. In the worst cases, legal separation can be sought.[44]

- All irregular and unlawful sexual relationships, before or after marriage, are forbidden, regardless of the circumstances.[45]

- Couples, married or not, should not try to prevent conception other than through abstinence, nor should they seek abortions.[46]

Underlying the Athenians' responses was a stress on the need for honest dealings and the recognition of mutual obligations in personal relationships. Yet despite such an emphasis on mutuality and their often-stated respect for women's intellect, Dunton and his colleagues did not ignore differences between men and women. They directly addressed such gender divergence primarily in their discussions of two topics: education and household roles.

In June 1694, an Athenian responded to a questioner who wanted to know what subjects a young man should study. That depends on his "Fortune, Constitution, Genius," and what he already knows, came the reply. In general, though, a young man should have a reading knowledge of Latin and French; he should also study mathematics, metaphysics, natural philosophy, geography, history, and "Morality." After he had a good comprehension of those topics, he could proceed on his own, keeping in mind that the goal was to "avoid Prejudice, and never receive anything before we are convinced of its truth."[47]

A follow-up question in a subsequent issue requested similar guidance for young women. "Women have, undoubtedly, the same Principles of Reason with Men, and therefore, whatever would tend to the Accomplishing of Men (some particular publick Business excepted) would be useful to Women," the response declared. Even so, the specifics that followed contradicted that initial assertion of near-equality. The Athenian first mentioned "Vertue and Piety" as "the most preferable Study"—a topic not listed for young men. He also recommended learning the art of conversation, especially with "Wise and Good" persons, because "to read Persons, makes a deeper and more lasting impression, than Books." Again, the importance of conversation (and the preference for it, over books) was not a part of the earlier prescription. He went on to list theoretical mathematics (which "open the Mind"), but added that "the practical parts... would be almost useless." It would be sufficient for women to study geometry, algebra, geography, and history for an hour a day for a year. A further two hours a day for about eighteen months should be devoted to "Philosophy, Logick, and a little Metaphysicks." He added that the young woman should learn "so much Dancing as is absolutely necessary for a good Carriage and decent Deportment to all Persons." Summing up, he wrote that "Afternoons for Converse and innocent Diversions, and Mornings for Studies, would do well."[48]

Thus the Athenian who responded to the query about education for young women seems to have believed that he was prescribing similar studies for the two sexes, but obviously he was not. Not only did he fail to mention instruction in foreign languages for a female student, he also insisted on the importance of conversation and dancing, while suggesting, for women, restrictions of topic or time on the subjects that men and women should both learn. For her: "a little" metaphysics and no "practical" mathematics, with at most half a day devoted to schooling for less than two years. For him: no expressed limitations on any subject, and encouragement for future independent work. Another answer about education supplied the likely reason for the difference. Every son would grow up to be a father: "has not the Master of every Family a Trust reported upon him both by God and his Countrey? And has he not indeed himself something still left of the *natural Patriarchal Power?* Is he not to teach as well as to govern his Family"? That comment made particular sense when added to the Athenian's initial interpolation of one difference—"some publick Business excepted"—in the uses of men's and women's educations. Men had roles in both nation and household that women did not.[49]

The same themes also emerged in a debate Dunton published in a 1697 book titled *The Challenge, ... or the Female War.* Featuring arguments between purported male and female contributors on a variety of gender-differentiated topics, *The Challenge,* declared Dunton, was "*a peice of Diversion for Ladies.*" It accordingly did not matter, he asserted, whether the debates were "real or *feigned.*" Even so, he insisted that the female authors (who included Anonyma) were actual women. He did not make the same claim for the essays attributed to men, and he himself might have written some or all of the most provocative. Regardless, the debate format helped to establish a firmer boundary between men and women than had previously been evident in his work.[50]

In one debate, a "Thomas Harcourt" allegedly submitted a diatribe "Against Learning in Women." The "Harcourt" essay, an over-the-top attack, informed women that "you are neither *qualify'd* for *Learning,* nor *equal* to it" and asserted that for them education was neither *"necessary"* nor *"useful"* but rather "mischievous and hurtful." He bluntly advised women: "Forget not Oeconomicks and the care of your own Houshold." (The seventeenth-century definition of *oeconomics* was "the science or art of household management; domestic economy.") In response, "Madam A.H." declared that education usefully improved women's minds and taught them self-control, even if it did not help "in making a *Pudding, threading a Needle, and teaching Domestick affairs."* Women, she furthermore averred, knew that men like himself should not attempt *"to instruct their Wives in Family Business,"* about which they knew little or nothing.[51]

Thus A.H. replied to Harcourt by challenging what he said about the household as well as by arguing about education, the nominal subject of the debate. A.H. firmly rejected the traditional notion that husbands could teach their wives about "Family Business," thus explicitly adopting the same position that Dunton did implicitly by his organizing category for the *Mercury's* "Ladies Issues." The "natural Patriarchal power" referred to in the previous answer by an Athenian had vanished, and in its place was the notion that women were better informed than men about certain aspects of "Family Business."

The Athenians' stance on the relationship of husbands and wives within the household was accordingly complicated, even contradictory. On the one hand, a *Mercury* essay (probably by Samuel Wesley) insisted that God had rendered wives subordinate to their husbands in matters both "Political" and "Oeconomical." On the other, in the *Ladies Dictionary* John Dunton counseled men not to meddle with "Houshold Government," except "by way of Advice and Assistance," rather than "Superiority." Do not become involved in "finding fault with the Feminine Jurisdiction," he recommended; and he plagiarized a key phrase penned by the Marquis of Halifax six years earlier: a husband's "province is without doors," and to him "the Oeconomy of the House would in some degrees be indecent." So when the Athenians were asked their opinion of a distinguished man who had caused controversy by his second marriage to a servant, one replied that *"Domestical concerns"* could not "fairly be brought into a mans Character" unless—as was possible in the case at issue—he had displayed "Imprudence" in his actions. Dunton thus by the mid-1690s was perceiving a pronounced separation between men's and women's familial roles.[52]

That split became even more obvious when Dunton considered a wider context: the world beyond the household. His key statement on women and the public realm in the *Mercury* came in November 1693, in response to a question submitted by a man who expressed skepticism about women's capacity for study and "solid reasoning." Dunton unsurprisingly endorsed the view that women and men had equal "Understanding," but he then broached the subject of fundamental differences between the sexes, offering in the process a crucial and novel rationale for women's education:

> Now if it be true, that Politicks and Oeconomicks, are founded upon the same Principles, and there needs as much Knowledge to preserve as to acquire; then since women are in a Family, what Men are in a State, and are destined to keep what Men get, why should they not have the Knowledge of the same Maxims, as Men have by Study and Theory; insomuch as the reservedness and Modesty of their Sex, allows them not to have the Experience thereof, by frequenting the World?[53]

Women are in a Family, what Men are in a State....Politicks and Oeconomicks [household management] *are founded upon the same Principles:* those remarkable statements separating the equivalents family and state, while linking one exclusively to women and the other solely to men, represented the origins of the modern gendered public/private distinction. Dunton had not yet adopted that language, but he would do so less than a decade later, just as a new monarch ascended the throne.

The Explication of the Public-Private Divide

Before John Dunton, only one other English author—the royalist Margaret Cavendish, Duchess of Newcastle—had even come close to making such a distinction. Uniquely for an Englishwoman of the time, she remarked in 1653 that "the *Sphear* of our *Sex*" excluded "*Politicks of State,*" but she did not then define what women's sphere *included.* A negative opinion of ordinary women's opposition to Charles I in the 1640s underlay the noblewoman's observation. "Our Sex in this age, is ambitious to be State-Ladies," she averred, "that they may be thought to be Wise Women; but let us do what we can, we shall prove our selves Fools." Even though women had not themselves borne arms during the Civil War, they had rallied men against the government, with "evil" consequences. The aristocrat thus concluded that "women in State-affairs...can disorder a State."[54]

Two years later Cavendish clarified her observations by differentiating between "most of our Sex...bred up to the Needle and Spindle" and the smaller number of high-ranking women like herself "bred in the publike Theatres of the World." Despite her seemingly broadly applicable exclusionary language in 1653, therefore, the Duchess of Newcastle indicated that she in fact adopted the traditional view affirming high-status women's role as state actors while denying such standing to lower-ranking females. She complained that "we" (by whom she meant herself and her high-status peers) were not "imployed either in civil nor marshall affaires" and lamented that "our" advice was "despised" by conceited men. She furthermore positively assessed the impact of powerful female rulers. "Let us take the advantage," she declared, "and make the best of our time, for feare their reigne should not last long, whether it be in the Amazonian Government, or in the Politick Common-wealth, or in flourishing Monarchy."[55]

Cavendish's usage of *private* in her essays was entirely conventional. Declaring that politics was outside ordinary women's sphere did not lead her to new terminology about females' familial role. She employed the common seventeenth-century dichotomy *private family–public commonwealth* to separate the household from the larger society; and she also used *private* to designate personal affairs, which she defined as men's and women's "Wealth, Ordering their Families, their Pleasures, or their Discontents." She never advanced a gendered meaning for *private,* nor did she privilege its connection to the household.[56]

By contrast, John Dunton broke sharply with such traditional language in his 1702 pamphlet, *Petticoat-Government, in a Letter to the Court Ladies.* The publication constituted Dunton's contemplation of the accession to the throne of Queen Anne, a Protestant daughter of James II and younger sister of Mary. In one sense the succession was unexceptional: England had had recent experience with three queens, Elizabeth and two Marys. But Anne was unusual in one respect: she was a queen whose husband was not the king. Mary I had briefly been married to Philip II, the king of Spain; Elizabeth famously never married; and Mary II, although a more direct heir of her father, James II, than her cousin and husband, William III, had acquiesced when William insisted on the primacy in their dual reign. But Anne's husband, Prince George of Denmark, was not and would not be king. England was thus confronted with a monarch who on the one hand was a wife, legally subject to her husband under the law, and who on the other was the supreme ruler of the land, in which her husband had no political authority. How could that contradiction be resolved? Dunton did it by explicitly separating her *public* role as queen from her *private* role as wife. In his remarkable publication, readers can follow his thought process from utter confusion to (somewhat greater) clarity as he worked out the implications of his argument.[57]

Unsurprisingly, Dunton began by praising women in general, denying any sexual difference in minds or souls, as the *Athenian Mercury* always formally did. Then he quickly turned to Queen Anne. "She was made purposely for our Crown and Scepter...Her Authority is just and deserved...'tis nothing more than God and Nature intended, *That Women should Govern as well as the Men.*" Anne exhibited both "Vertue and Greatness," essential qualities in a monarch of either sex.[58]

Dunton immediately addressed the key issue. After pointing out that a king's wife became queen, he observed that the reverse was not true: the queen's husband did not necessarily become king. The French, he observed, had by the Salic law forbidden women from taking the throne. If they had provided instead *"That no private Woman shou'd wear the Breeches, or pretend to Govern her Husband,* they had done well," he noted approvingly, "For, it must be own'd That Husband who lets his Wife RULE (except when she has a Right to do so) deserves to wear the *Petticoat,* having renounc'd the Prerogative of his Sex." Still, that did not apply in this case because "Government is not only lawful and tolerable in Women, but *justly, naturally, and properly Theirs."*[59]

Dunton next embarked on an eclectic, conceptually confusing commentary detailing women's many virtues and contending that men did not appreciate women's true value or importance. He reinterpreted the creation story from Genesis to favor Eve, cited the Virgin Mary and the Sabine women, and even asserted that *"no Men can be so fit for Government, as Women are,"* in large part because women would bring new and desirable qualities to the task: "their Heads are not troubl'd about the making of *Wars,* enlarging of *Empires,* or founding of *Tyrannies."* Instead of political factions, they would introduce *"Pleasure* and *Liberty"* to public life, along with *"Balls* and *Amorous* Appointments." Such an emphasis on gendered cultural differences called into question his basic premise of the equality of male and female rulers and rendered his central argument less than compelling. Tellingly, other authors who praised queens offered no similar contentions.[60]

Perhaps having recognized the inadequacy of his discussion thus far, in mid-pamphlet Dunton developed a new device to help him systematize his hitherto disorganized thoughts: he outlined three different meanings for his title phrase *Petticoat-Government.* First, "when Good Women Ascend the Throne, and Rule according to Law, as is the case of the present Queen"; second, "the discreet and housewifely *Ruling* of a House and Family; for *the Husband's*

Province lies without Doors and therefore tis the Place of the Mistress to *Govern the Kitchen*"; and third, "when Bad Women Usurp an Authority over their Husbands, as is the case of Shrews, and such as *Command,* and (perhaps) *Beat their Husbands.*" In the end, he devoted so many pages to the first two that he passed quickly over the third.[61]

First, then, he returned to his main theme: petticoat government "as it relates to Women in a *Publick Capacity.*" Conventionally, Dunton cited examples of female rulers from the Old Testament, ancient history, and English history, ending with Elizabeth I and Mary II. Noting that Prince George had sworn allegiance to Anne, he reverted, but in a novel way, to a familiar theme from the 1640s: other men too, he predicted, could expect to live happily under "the mild and gentle *Government* of *Queen Anne.*" He expressed his certainty that if the queen summoned "a *Parliament of Women,*" both women and men would readily agree to be ruled by such a body. That was certainly not the vision of a ladies' parliament depicted by Henry Neville or his imitators, and the fact that Dunton presented it as a positive prospect for men reveals the depth of his commitment to supporting Anne's right to rule.[62]

Dunton then had to compose a transitional paragraph to introduce his discussion of his second definition, and in doing so he initiated the equation of *private, female, sphere,* and *household:* "I am next to treat of *Petticoat-Government,* as it relates to *the Discreet and Housewifely Ruling of a House and Family;* and this part of my Essay chiefly concerns *Women* in a PRIVATE, or Lower Sphere." Dunton's language in that sentence linked *women, family,* and *private* in a novel way.[63]

He was not yet finished. Dunton went on to discuss what *"She-Governors"* should and should not do in a household context. Although stressing—as the *Mercury* did—that wives were legally subject to their husbands, in his second section Dunton used such phrases as *"a right Governing Wife"* and a wife's "right to Govern the Family." Reverting to the theme of his introductory paragraph, he explained, like the Marquis of Halifax in 1688, that a husband's *"Business is without-doors"* while a wife's was "properly within-doors." And so he reached his climax. Whereas he had modified previous references to the wife's supervisory role in the household with cautionary phrases about her need to show *"constant Obedience"* to her husband, this time he did not—and for the first time introduced the notion of separate spheres, even hinting at that very language by his expansive phraseology. Breaking decisively with long-standing tradition and going beyond Halifax's formulation, Dunton declared that men should not in any sense be viewed as household governors: "In the House," he averred, "her very Husband lives under *Petticoat-Government.*"

After hastening to add that such circumstances must not leave a woman "puft up with Pride and Boasting," he returned to his praise of a good wife. "A *She-Governor* thus accomplish'd, is like a Star with five Rays," he asserted, listing "*Devotion, Modesty, Chastity, Discretion* and *Charity.*" Such women, he concluded, "*are in their Houses, as the Sun in his proper Sphere.*"[64]

John Dunton thus in 1702 outlined what became the modern Western world's division of labor between men and women, developing both the *public/private* split in its modern form and laying out the first definition of *separate spheres,* which bore a remarkable resemblance to the domestic ideal prevalent in the nineteenth century.[65] Other seventeenth-century authors, Margaret Cavendish and the Marquis of Halifax prominent among them, had verged on a similar formulation but stopped short of a full explication. Although *Petticoat-Government* was internally contradictory and confusingly argued, the fact that Dunton was led to his conclusion by a meditation on the accession to the throne of a queen whose husband was not the king reveals the significance of thinking about the *public* to the initial equation of *private, female,* and *household.*

The section of the pamphlet in which Dunton arrived at that equation nominally failed to apply to Anne, for it considered his second definition of *petticoat government,* which was distinct from the consideration of the rule of "Good Women [like Anne] . . . according to Law." Yet, even so, his equal division between the husband's role "without doors" and the wife's familial authority certainly implied that if men had little power to govern the household, women who were not legitimate monarchs had little power outside it.

In 1715, after Anne's death, Dunton made that position explicit in a virulent attack on Abigail Masham, one of Anne's favorite courtiers. His pamphlet *King-Abigail* railed against illegitimate female rulers, and Dunton—although insisting he was impugning neither Anne's memory nor "*the Female Sex in general*"—asserted broadly that "it is ever a Sin and a Curse to the Kingdom, *when Women shall Rule over them.*" Women, he insisted, "have oftentimes proved the most dangerous to the State, because tho' the weaker Sex, their Passions and Enchantments are ever strongest." Thus he carried his ideas to their logical conclusion: not only were men's and women's roles complementary and distinguishable, but women in general were incapable of political involvement.[66]

John Dunton's early-eighteenth-century pamphlets focusing on Queen Anne and Abigail Masham thus put a symbolic period to a long history of women's political activism in seventeenth-century England, a history that stretched back to the first collective petitions of the Civil War years. The publications constituted one man's definitive and ultimately influential answer to women's claims of the right to engage in political activity—and ironically so, because Dunton's nominal purpose in the first was to legitimize a married woman's right to rule as sole monarch. But the conceptual relegation of *all* women, including aristocrats and excluding only hereditary monarchs, to a *sphere* termed *private* that was confined to familial affairs would for many decades to come stand as a significant barrier to women's engagement with the public realm.[67]

Mistress Sarah Kemble Knight and Her Journal, 1704

Mistress Sarah Knight, a thirty-eight-year-old Bostonian, set out in early October 1704 to travel to New Haven to settle the estate of her sister's husband, and then in December went on to Manhattan to perform similar tasks related to the estate of her oldest brother. She traveled by horseback on the post road, accompanied by the post rider or by local guides. The journey itself was unusual enough for a lone woman, but what made it truly remarkable was the journal that described her experiences, which she probably composed after her return to Boston from notes she made each night en route. The journal is not introspective; it was obviously written for an audience of other people, and surely it subsequently circulated among her friends and relatives, becoming the subject of much interest and conversation. Perhaps she read it aloud at Boston social gatherings to considerable acclaim. The journal was not published until 1825, after a copy of the manuscript came into the possession of its earliest editor, Theodore Dwight Jr.[1]

Sarah Knight's journal is the earliest known diary of any sort kept by an American woman. Only a few other female Americans wrote journal-like documents before 1760; all were younger than Sarah Knight, and their writings tended to be religious and self-reflective in nature.[2] Knight's journal, by contrast, is secular and picaresque, recounting her journey with an eye to telling amusing tales about her travels and the people she encountered. She was clearly an educated, well-read woman, for references in the journal demonstrated her familiarity with many English publications.[3] Yet, even so, her language differed strikingly from that of her English contemporary, John Dunton. Writing two years after the publication of *Petticoat-Government,* the female colonist seemed unaware of the gendered cultural developments it reflected. Nowhere did she employ *fair sex,* one of Dunton's favorite locutions, nor did she ever refer to *spheres* in any context. Her prose consistently stressed status rather than gender differences.[4]

Relatively little is known of her life. The daughter of Thomas Kemble, a wealthy merchant with extensive landholdings in Maine and New Hampshire, Sarah became the second wife of Richard Knight, described in Boston records as a "carver" (probably a woodworker), in 1688, around the time of her twenty-second birthday. Her husband seems to have been considerably older than she; at least, a man of the same name was in business with her father in New Hampshire as early as 1659. They had one child, Elizabeth, who was born the year after their marriage.[5]

Sarah Knight was given the high-status title *Mistress* (Mrs.) in the Boston court records, presumably because of the wealth she inherited from her father, who died in early 1689. She had excellent handwriting and engaged in copying legal documents and witnessing wills for others. Clearly a woman of great energy and enterprise, she also kept a shop, took in boarders, and perhaps taught writing. Journal entries reveal her familiarity with business practices; some sources demonstrate that she was already managing family finances before her husband's death, which occurred after October 1701. In 1707, the Boston census listed her as a widowed household head with a house, shop, and several boarders, identifying her widowed mother (Elizabeth Kemble) and widowed sister (Mary Trowbridge) as her tenants. After her daughter married John Livingston in 1713, Sarah relocated to New London, Connecticut, running an inn, tavern, and shop, in addition to purchasing and renting out various tracts of land. She died and was buried in New London in 1727, leaving her daughter a sizable estate.[6]

Her 1704 journal is lively and witty, filled with incisive observations of the people she met and the places she visited. Mistress Knight adopted a detached stance; as a person of rank, she commented humorously on the foibles of her social inferiors. She often complained about the bad manners of innkeepers and their family members, sometimes reconstructing conversations with them she thought comical. Once when she arrived late at a tavern, she recorded the exclamations of the innkeeper's startled daughter thus: "Law for mee—what in the world brings You here at this time a night?—I never see a Woman on the Rode so Dreadfull late, in all the days of my 'versall life. Who are You? Where are You going? I'me scar'd out of my witts." And after she recounted the story of a "Bumpkin" couple who were tongue-tied when trying to deal with a shopkeeper, she observed that although such country people had "as Large a portion of mother witt" as city folk, the "want of emprovements, Render themselves almost Ridiculos."[7]

One of the journal's most striking passages about social hierarchy pertained to household practices she witnessed in rural Connecticut. The farmers and their families "Generally lived very well and comfortably," she wrote, "But too Indulgent . . . to their slaves: sufering too great familiarity from them, permitting them to sit at Table and eat with them, (as they say to save time,) and into the dish goes the black hoof as freely as the white hand." Her singular use of "hoof," with its animalistic connotations, revealed much about her attitude toward enslaved people. She followed up that observation with a story about a farmer who had not fulfilled a promise to one of his slaves. The bondsman had taken the matter to local officials, which led arbitrators to order the farmer to pay the "black face" forty shillings and to admit his error, which he had "honestly" done. She appended no comment; to her, it appears, the tale was sufficiently outrageous to require none.[8]

Mistress Knight's language in both passages raises the question whether she owned slaves of African descent. None were listed in her household in the 1707 census, but Mary Trowbridge, her widowed tenant and sister, had an "Ind-boy" slave. Further, her grandfather owned three black slaves at the time of his death (when Sarah was nine), and when her older brother died intestate in 1684 on a voyage from Barbados to Boston, he left as one of his most valuable possessions "1 Negro boy." Since Thomas Kemble administered his son's estate, he probably incorporated that "Negro boy" into his household, which then included the eighteen-year-old Sarah. Regardless of whether she or her husband ever personally owned bondspeople, then, Mistress Knight had had contact in her youth with enslaved Africans owned by her relatives, and she had clearly formed definite opinions about the importance of maintaining a proper distance between masters and slaves.[9]

Sarah Knight's criticisms of her inferiors and her praise for the genteel were equally ungendered. With the exception of a remark about one "surly old shee Creature, not worthy the name of woman" she encountered, she commonly failed to differentiate between the male and female objects of her derision. Likewise, in similar phraseology she extolled both the "very kind and civill Gentlewoman" who had "very handsomely and kindly entertained" her, and the clergyman who "very handsomely and plentifully treated" her. The latter, she observed, had a reputation of being "the most affable, courteous, and best of men," which she could confirm from her own experience. She had arrived unannounced late in the evening at his house (as she had arrived late at that inn earlier in her journey), yet he warmly invited her to stay overnight on very short notice. The contrast with the uncouth innkeeper's daughter could not have been more sharply drawn. She, like Lady Frances Berkeley and other genteel colonists, greatly valued such hospitality.[10]

If awareness of rank thus pervaded the text of the journal, awareness of gender did not. Some of her entries focused more on the women she met than on their male counterparts, but she rarely referred to herself explicitly as a woman. Three passages comprise nearly the whole of her relevant observations. While crossing a river in a canoe, she had a comic vision of herself if the canoe had tipped her into the water as "a holy Sister Just come out of a Spiritual Bath in dripping Garments." When she was traveling through some "dolesome" woods alone one night, her guide having gone on ahead, she remarked on her lack of "a more Masculine courage"; similarly, a frightening stretch of "steep and Rocky Hills and precipices" on another day proved "Buggbears to a fearful female travailer." Yet she could also mention being scared without reference to gender, as occurred twice when she encountered flooding rivers just before reaching Boston on her return trip.[11]

The relative absence of gendered comments and the focus on rank revealed Sarah Knight to be a woman of the seventeenth rather than the eighteenth century, and an American of her day rather than a resident of London. Even though she appeared well acquainted with English publications, the gendered language and general approach to life evident in John Dunton's *Athenian Mercury* and its "Ladies Issues" found little place in her writing. Only once did she offer a remark of the sort that might have made its way into the *Mercury*. Commenting on how relatively easy it was to obtain a divorce in Connecticut, she averred that some tales she had heard about marital breakups "are not proper to be Related by a Female pen, tho some of that foolish sex have had too large a share in the story."[12]

Both phrases with gendered connotations—"Female pen" and "foolish sex"—stand out as unusual in her prose. And not just hers: only one of Sarah Knight's American contemporaries used Dunton's favorite term *fair sex* in print: Cotton Mather, in a 1704 funeral poem. After that single example, *fair sex* as such did not appear again in a publication of American origin until 1721. But later that decade it and other novel patterns of thought and terminology that first emerged in Britain began to be incorporated into colonists' published writings. The primary vehicles for transatlantic cultural transmission were colonial newspapers founded in the 1720s and thereafter, whose editors eagerly reprinted essays taken from English periodicals. By the mid- to late 1730s, residents of the colonies and the home country were composing observations on gender with essentially identical content.[13]

❦ CHAPTER 4

Women and Politics, Eighteenth Century–Style

In 1697, an anonymous pamphleteer published *A Letter to a Gentlewoman concerning Government,* directed to a possibly apocryphal elite female Protestant who still aligned herself with the deposed James II. Why, he asked, when "the best and wisest Statesmen" in England supported King William, did "Ladies, who generally know little or nothing of State Affairs," support the ousted Stuart monarch? Flattering the addressee by terming her "very sensible," he carefully laid out arguments for William and Mary's claim to the throne and reasons to reject a strict hereditary succession, which would have favored the son born to James in 1688. If his discussion did not wholly convince her, the author reminded her that nevertheless "Silence becomes your Sex . . . especially in a matter so much above your Capacity and Reach." Insisting that "the most commendable Quality of a Woman" was agreeing with her male relatives on political topics, he urged her and any female counterparts to keep their opinions to themselves, "never suffering your tongues to get the Mastery of you." After all, as women, their circumstances were preferable to those of men, who had to swear formal allegiance to the new monarchs and who could lose their estates and positions if they failed to do so. He advised such women to keep negative opinions about the current succession to themselves and to appreciate their privileged position.[1]

Just thirty years earlier in Virginia, no one thought that politics was "above the Capacity and Reach" of Lady Frances Berkeley nor that she knew "little or nothing of State Affairs." No one directed her to defer to her husband or suggested that she or her female contemporaries hold their tongues when political subjects were being discussed. Sarah Grendon had erred by speaking "foolish and indiscreet" words, but her situation was likened to, rather than differentiated from, that of her male contemporaries. Clearly, in the intervening years a marked change had occurred in attitudes toward elite Anglo-American women's role as state actors.

Although *Letter to a Gentlewoman* instructed the female gentry to defer to their better-informed husbands, brothers, and fathers in political affairs and denigrated their capacity to comprehend such subjects, the pamphlet's very existence acknowledged that elite women still had political opinions that mattered. Ever since ordinary English women had first petitioned Parliament in the 1640s, men had denied them the role of rightful political actors. Because status trumped gender in mid-seventeenth-century English political culture, high-ranking women did not at the time suffer from such an exclusion. Indeed, petitioners occasionally tried to claim high-status leaders in an attempt to add credibility to their appeals. The intended audience for the 1697 pamphlet revealed the persistent vestiges of that attitude. But over the course of the eighteenth century, recognition of high-ranking women's appropriate role as state actors largely disappeared from Anglo-American culture. It was replaced by satires and essays dismissing the possibility that women might legitimately work to advance a political agenda.

Letter to a Gentlewoman was apparently the last serious, freestanding English or American publication on the subject of government and politics aimed at a female readership until after 1800.[2] That the culture at large failed to acknowledge the legitimacy of high-ranking women as state actors did not mean that they—particularly English aristocrats—ceased all such endeavors. But it did mean that for the most part politically involved women pursued actions less directly linked to public affairs, especially in the 1740s and thereafter. Instead of formally petitioning Parliament or publishing statements describing their positions, English women covertly sought patronage for their relatives or hosted social gatherings with political overtones. Rather than publicly questioning the judgment of colonial courts, American women largely confined their opinions to diaries and correspondence. In such writings, female colonists signaled their understanding of a cultural precept that proscribed any feminine political activity.[3]

The immediate context for the onset of the change in attitudes toward women and public affairs was provided by the successive reigns of James II's two Protestant daughters, Mary II and Anne. The nominally joint monarch Mary, in an un-queen-like but feminine manner, deferred to her husband,

William, who had a lesser claim to the throne than she. Anne, though initially popular when John Dunton discussed her accession in 1702, attracted more and louder criticism in the years just before her death in 1714. A substantial share of that criticism revolved around her relationships with her successive female favorites, Sarah Churchill, Duchess of Marlborough, and Abigail Masham. In a highly politicized era with ten parliamentary elections in as many years, the duchess allied herself with the Whigs and Masham with the Tories. Their bitter rivalry affected the public's image of the queen, for she came to be seen as weak and easily manipulated by the women of her bedchamber. Both men and women were politicized by the widening division between the parties, and political rhetoric began to reflect gendered concerns. As Rachel Weil has observed, by the time of Anne's death, "negative perceptions of the queen were now connected to broader anxieties about the place of women in political life."[4]

The swiftness of the shift in attitudes can best be highlighted by contrasting two publications—one from 1692, the other from 1709, just seventeen years later. In the early 1690s, even as John Dunton was paying little attention in the *Athenian Mercury* to women and the public realm, his contemporary Nahum Tate, poet laureate and dramatist, insisted that many women "have exerted their useful Influence beyond the Sphere of their private Houses: They have many times been beneficial to States and Kingdoms, to their Country and mankind." This use of *sphere* in its novel meaning demarcating women's domestic role indicated that Tate had absorbed some of the same cultural currents that moved Dunton. At the same time, though, his tract—*A Present for the Ladies: Being an Historical Vindication of the Female Sex*—adopted the traditional view by asserting that women matched men in their political abilities. Tate listed familiar female heroines of the past—Deborah and Esther from the Old Testament, the Sabine women, Boadicea, and especially Queen Elizabeth—and asked his readers, "After such Illustrious Precedents of *Female Worth,* can it possibly be a Question, Whether Women are capable of *Government?*" To Tate, the answer was obvious: women could unquestionably rule as well as men.[5]

Yet when Bernard Mandeville in 1709 penned a series of dialogues between a maiden aunt and her niece which touched occasionally on public affairs, he revealed the altered climate by inserting an apology for portraying such politicized female characters. "I expect to be Censured for letting Women talk of Politicks," Mandeville commented. His fictional women not only discussed public matters but also conversed about the fact that they were doing so. In one dialogue, Antonia (the niece) observed that "every Cobler and Tinker talks Politicks," yet her aunt Lucinda would "never talk to me about State-Affairs."

Lucinda replied, "That is, because you are not fit for it, nor I neither." Subsequent dialogues made it clear that Lucinda believed she and Antonia were unfit to discuss "State-Affairs" because they had inadequate knowledge of political and military matters. So Lucinda asked her niece, "don't you see how little Politicks agrees with young Ladies, *Antonia?*" and the younger woman responded, "I must own, that much of 'em would soon tire me, and something that is more delightful, and requires less Attention, suits my Humour better." The notion that women preferred topics that did not require much attention and were "more delightful" than "State-Affairs" soon became deeply embedded in standard ways of thinking, in part because of the extraordinary cultural influence on both sides of the Atlantic of two early-eighteenth-century British periodicals.[6]

The *Tatler* and the *Spectator*

Richard Steele and Joseph Addison, founders of the *Tatler* and the *Spectator*, were active to varying degrees in Whig politics throughout much of their adult lives. Both born in 1672, they first met and became friends when studying at the same school; they then attended Oxford more or less simultaneously, though at different colleges. Their paths diverged for a time as Steele failed to complete a degree and joined King William's army while Addison persisted in his studies, earning degrees and preparing for a diplomatic career. The two ended up in London early in Anne's reign, and both made names for themselves as writers of plays and Whiggish political essays. Addison contributed some articles to Steele's *Tatler* in 1709–10; subsequently, they together founded the immensely popular and influential *Spectator*, which appeared six days a week from March 1, 1711, to December 6, 1712, with a brief, unsuccessful revival in 1714.[7]

Steele's outspoken political essays in other venues enveloped him in controversies, especially when the Tories were in power. Thus the two men prudently and publicly disavowed partisanship in the *Spectator*, even while covertly continuing to advance a Whig agenda. Yet their evident neutrality in the partisan wars of the era did not and could not fully explain their aversion (especially evident in Addison's essays) to women's involvement in political matters, broadly defined. The authors maintained nominal neutrality in the Whig-Tory disputes but showed no similar neutrality toward whatever interest in public affairs their female readers might manifest.[8]

Like the *Athenian Mercury*, both journals defined their reading audience as partially female. Also like the *Mercury*, they defined topics other than politics as those relevant to "ladies."[9] In the first issue of the *Tatler* Richard Steele made that exclusion explicit. He explained that even though he had chosen its title to honor women, his journal was "principally intended for the Use of Politick Persons, who are so publick-spirited as to neglect their own Affairs to look into Transactions of State." Then he added, "I resolve also to have something which may be of Entertainment to the Fair Sex."[10]

Steele thus assumed that women did not number among the "publick-spirited" people who interested themselves in "Transactions of State." To his mind, the "Fair Sex" needed to be "entertained," not informed. For the convenience of what he presumed would be two gender-differentiated sets of readers with diverse interests, he even announced that he would head his essays with the names of different coffeehouses to signal the subjects that followed: distinctive datelines would identify commentary on "Gallantry, Pleasure, and Entertainment"; "Poetry"; "Learning"; "Foreign and Domestick News"; and a miscellaneous category. Thus women would not have to read pieces on the classics and politics in order to be entertained by accounts of pleasure and gallantry; and men could readily skip remarks on cultural subjects while focusing on the news. Only the heading "from my own Apartment," designated for the miscellany, would potentially draw readers of both sexes.

Twice in the *Tatler* Steele commented on the phenomenon of women's interest in widely publicized trials. When many female spectators crowded into the sensational impeachment trial of Dr. Henry Sacheverell before the House of Lords in February–March 1710, Steele drafted observations with tongue firmly in cheek. The ladies "at present employ their Time with great Assiduity in the Care of the Nation," he wrote; "it is not to be expressed how many cold Chickens the Fair Ones have eaten since this day Sevennight for the Good of their Country." The spectacle of women frequenting prosecutions for rape prompted more serious reflections. Isaac Bickerstaff, Steele's alter ego, proposed that half the jurors in rape cases should be female, since all-male juries in effect represented the accused criminals. Yet he also argued that until the day when female jurors were impaneled, women who chose to attend such trials violated their requisite modesty, a key attribute of womanhood. Whereas Steele began with a potentially revolutionary speculation about women's potential as jurors in one category of crimes, then, he ended with an assertion of the importance of maintaining a modest feminine stance.[11]

Further, Steele disdainfully dismissed any notion that women could think rationally about politics. In October 1710, Bickerstaff recounted observing an undoubtedly fictional debate between two women employing "a Jargon of Terms" they did not understand but which they believed were relevant to the current disputes between Whigs and Tories. Isaac was nonplussed when they purportedly asked him to explain the difference between "Circumcision" and "Predestination." Before he could respond, Bickerstaff indicated, they resumed their quarrel, "lay[ing] open the whole State of Affairs, instead of the usual Topicks of Dress, Gallantry, and Scandal." These days, he reported, "the very silliest of the Women" were aligning themselves with the parties. Yet women could not win. Steele and other male cultural arbiters also excoriated them for spending too much time gossiping with each other about fashion and scandal. They were damned if they talked politics, and damned as well if they did not.[12]

Steele's writing partner, Joseph Addison, was even more outspoken on the subject of how ludicrous was the notion that women, including high-ranking ones, could reasonably be involved with politics and partisanship. In the *Spectator* he addressed the subject directly several times. In early May 1711, he introduced a lengthy discussion by alluding to a passage in *The Iliad*. Hector, he noted, had told his wife to "mind her Spinning" after she attempted to comment on an upcoming battle. Addison explained that thereby Homer insisted "that Men and Women ought to busie themselves in their proper Spheres, and on such Matters only as are suitable to their respective Sex." He warned women to avoid "Party Rage," which had recently come to occupy too much of their conversation. Excessive partisanship, a vice even for men, was "altogether repugnant to the Softness, Modesty, and those other endearing Qualities which are natural to the Fair Sex." Addison even contended at length that "there is nothing so bad for the Face as Party Zeal." Observing that he never knew a female partisan who retained her beauty for as long as a year, he advised his female readers to avoid all political disputes, "as they value their Complexions." Perhaps women accepted his message: a letter to the *Spectator* from "Helena" declared that "everybody" among her acquaintances "commended" the essay.[13]

Less than a month later, Addison tackled the subject again by mocking female attendees at the Haymarket Theatre who sat on different sides of the auditorium and wore face patches precisely placed to identify their partisan affiliations: "the Body of *Amazons* on my Right-Hand, were Whigs, and those on my Left, Tories." Referring to the Sabine women's success in persuading the Romans (their husbands) and the Sabines (their brothers and fathers) to establish peace, Addison recommended that British women follow that example instead of adopting men's partisanship. Reminding his readers that Roman women donated their jewelry to finance the nation's wartime defense, he developed an argument pointing up the relationship between women's exclusion from politics and their domestic role:

> As our *English* Women excell those of all Nations in Beauty, they should endeavour to outshine them in all other Accomplishments

proper to the Sex, and to distinguish themselves as tender Mothers and faithful Wives, rather than as furious Partizans. Female Virtues are of a Domestick turn. The Family is the proper Province for Private Women to Shine in. If they must be showing their Zeal for the Publick, let it not be against those who are perhaps of the same Family, or at least of the same Religion or Nation, but against those who are the open, professed, undoubted Enemies of their Faith, Liberty, and Country.[14]

In that comprehensive passage Addison made it clear that the "Accomplishments proper to the Sex" were "Domestick" and excluded "furious" partisanship. The only political course available to women, whose "proper Province" was the family, was to support the nation against its external enemies. Women were, by definition, *private;* that is, they had no appropriate public role, except perhaps sacrificing their personal possessions for the common good, as Roman women had done when their country faced particular peril.

Addison continued to fulminate against women's involvement in public affairs after the *Spectator* ceased publication. In the *Freeholder,* a series of political essays first published in 1716 and reprinted repeatedly until 1790, he again addressed the topic. Although Addison patted himself on the back for paying unique attention to women as "Members of the Body Politick," he complained that "Coquette Logician[s]" did not know how to reason about public affairs. It was difficult to dispel the errors and biases in women's political thinking, he averred, because "Arguments . . . are of little use" with them. Any author who tried to use "strong Reasonings" in "State Controversies" with the "Fair Sex" was foolish. Instead, women had to be made to laugh at their own ridiculous political ideas. As an example, he recounted the same tale of alleged legal bigamy that had served as the basis for the 1646 pamphlet *The Parliament of Women,* the risible results of which—he claimed—had led Roman women to forgo political involvement thereafter. Convincing partisan English women of their inability to be state actors, he implied, would have similar consequences.[15]

Addison's skepticism about all female politicians became fully evident in those *Freeholder* articles that reiterated a theme of his *Spectator* essays: vocal partisanship rendered women "unamiable" and unattractive to men, especially when a "pretty Bosom [was] heaving with such Party-Rage." Following the logic of his *Spectator* statement that partisanship and the household were antithetical, he linked household disorder to a woman's interest in politics: "we may always observe that a Gossip in Politicks, is a Slattern in her Family." An "angry Stateswoman" who paid attention only to public affairs would inevitably neglect her children and produce a chaotic household. Therefore,

Figure 4.1. "The Devonshire Amusement," 1784. A satirical cartoon produced when Georgiana Spencer, Duchess of Devonshire, campaigned for Charles James Fox in the parliamentary election of 1784. The right-hand image shows the consequences predicted by Joseph Addison decades earlier: the duke is diapering a baby, exclaiming, "Ah William every one must be cursed that like thee, takes

a Politic Mad Wife." The image is completed by the document dangling from his pocket, labeled "Letters to Married Women," and the picture of the cuckold hanging on the wall. Courtesy of the Lewis Walpole Library, Yale University.

women should adopt "perpetual Neutrality" in politics. He insisted that women's recent involvement with partisanship had led to both "the Ruin of good Huswifery" and the "visible Decay of the National Beauty." So, Addison concluded, a "States-woman is as ridiculous a Creature as a Cot-Quean [effeminate man]. Each of the Sexes should keep within its particular Bounds, and content themselves to excel within their respective Districts." He proposed that a female parliament devise rules for all women to observe, among them that "the Discoursing of Politicks shall be looked upon as dull as Talking on the Weather," and that "no Woman of any Party presume to influence the Legislature."[16]

Not all of Addison's contemporaries agreed with him; Bernard Mandeville, for one, filled the pages of the *Female Tatler* in 1709–10 with accounts of female worthies who had been "famous for Wisdom, Politics and Prudence in Government" in ancient times.[17] Yet on both sides of the Anglo-American Atlantic, Addison's view of women's political incapacity would prevail over Mandeville's opposite position. The ideas Joseph Addison forcefully expressed in his essays in the first two decades of the eighteenth century came to dominate Anglo-American thinking on the subject of women and politics. They can be summed up as follows: all women, high-ranking or not, should eschew involvement in politics. Engagement in political talk would render them unfeminine and ugly. Such women crossed gender boundaries in ways both ridiculous and dangerous—ridiculous, in that they could not reason properly about political subjects and so adopted absurd positions; dangerous, in that political passions led them to neglect their domestic responsibilities, causing chaos in their families. To maintain social order, all women had to focus on households, remaining neutral in politics while glorying in their freedom from responsibilities to the public. Men would handle such matters. Women needed only to be "amiable" and to cultivate those "Accomplishments proper to the Sex," to be "tender Mothers and faithful Wives, rather than . . . furious Partizans."[18]

When the young Benjamin Franklin, an aspiring writer in Boston in the early 1720s, chose a model for the essays he wrote at night after work in his brother's printing establishment, he picked the *Spectator.* He "read it over and over," he recalled, "and was much delighted with it," especially the writing style. After taking brief notes on an essay and mixing them up, he attempted to re-create the contents without reference to the original. "This was to teach me Method in the Arrangement of Thoughts," he explained. To improve his vocabulary and use of language, he practiced turning the essays into verse and several weeks later into prose again. By the end of the process,

Franklin began to think he "might possibly in time come to be a tolerable English Writer, of which I was extremely ambitious."[19]

The brilliant teenager studied the *Spectator* more intensively than most residents of North America, but others too found its prose attractive and entertaining. Information about its appeal in America at the time of initial publication is lacking, both because little correspondence survives from that period and because the only newspaper then being published in the colonies devoted itself almost exclusively to commercial topics. Yet by the middle decades of the century, increasingly prosperous Americans were using the *Spectator* as an unparalleled guide to proper behavior and genteel modes of living. Probably the most widely advertised publication in the colonies, it was owned, borrowed, and read by Americans from South Carolina to New England even after independence was won. Its sentiments would echo for years through the pages of those American newspapers whose contributors, like Franklin, sought to imitate its form, style, and content. The *Spectator* and the notions it expressed found eager colonial audiences everywhere in North America by the 1730s.[20]

Evidence of Addison and Steele's influence abounds in colonial sources. Almost as many southerners owned copies of the *Spectator* as owned the Bible, and editions of it outnumbered editions of Shakespeare in South Carolina book collections by three to one. More than one-third of all colonial libraries for which catalogs survive had copies of Addison's *Works,* which included the *Freeholder,* and 15 percent had independent editions of those political essays. The books did not simply sit on the shelves; they were read and remarked on by American readers. One woman, for instance, recommended the *Spectator* to her son (then a student at Princeton) as containing "an inexhaustible store of elegant instruction"; another willed a copy to her great-niece; and a young North Carolina lawyer penned a long entry in his journal defending Addison and Steele against the negative judgments of Henry Fielding. Addison, he insisted, was a far better writer than Fielding. Addison's "Genius, His Learning, the incomparable Grandeur and Sublimity of his Sentiments on the highest subjects," he remarked, "added to an unerring attention to the interests of Virtue, both in his Writings and his Conduct, certainly declare him to all unprejudiced Minds to have been one of the most respectable, amiable, and endearing Characters that ever lived!"[21]

Such British publications as the *Tatler,* the *Spectator,* and the *Freeholder* were ubiquitous in the colonies because they filled a void for American readers, who had little locally written published material available to them.

The few colonial printers—not until midcentury was there even one in every province—devoted themselves primarily to producing official documents and printed forms and possibly a sermon or two. Newspapers were difficult for their editors to sustain for long; most survived only a few years before disappearing or merging with others. Accordingly, imported (or reprinted) English books and periodicals composed much of the reading material available to literate colonists throughout the century. Middling and elite Anglo-Americans sought to enhance their ties to the mother country by following its cultural trends closely; the *Spectator* and its later imitators set the tone for the "Anglicization" of the colonies, a process through which provincials did their best to replicate British life on American shores. That it sometimes took a decade or two for the trends to make their way to North America is hardly surprising, given the difficulties of travel and slow patterns of communication. But as time passed, colonial and metropolitan cultures tended to converge, in part because of the influence of British publications on the American audience.[22]

Wit and Misogyny in the *New-England Courant* and *New-York Weekly Journal*

The earliest American newspapers—the *Boston News-Letter, American Weekly Mercury* (Philadelphia), and *Boston Gazette,* all begun before 1720—filled their pages with dispatches from Europe and commercial information. Aimed at a readership composed of the political and economic leaders of the northern and middle colonies, all three ignored the local news and commentary that elite men would have obtained from daily conversations with their peers in taverns, coffeehouses, and countinghouses, and on the docks or in the streets. Appearing weekly with news compiled by their editors from a variety of sources, such papers focused on the comings and goings of ships and reports of conditions in Britain or on the Continent that might affect the workings of commerce. They stressed practical matters to the exclusion of other topics.[23]

James Franklin's *New-England Courant,* founded in August 1721, had different aims. Initiated to voice skepticism about the efficacy of smallpox inoculations in the midst of a controversy then raging in Boston at the same time as a major epidemic, the *Courant* also opened its pages to essayists and correspondents who imitated contemporary English authors. Franklin and a small group of other writers—eventually including Benjamin, his younger brother and apprentice—supplied articles and purported letters to the editor on a variety of subjects. The most important contributors had been born or educated in Great Britain, and many had ties to the Church of England. They prided themselves on their sophisticated taste, attempting to amuse and entertain their fellow Bostonians with witty commentaries. Like his competitors, James Franklin published advertisements, current shipping information, and European news, but his emphasis was elsewhere. Perhaps the key indicator was the fact that the top left-hand column on the front page of the *Courant* was typically devoted to an essay by a local or an English author.[24]

The *Courant,* along with publishing satires on such topics as courtship, marriage, and female gossipers, became the first American newspaper to address the issue of women's public role, echoing themes in the *Tatler,* the *Spectator,* and the *Freeholder.*[25] The earliest piece came from the pen of James Franklin, who adopted the pseudonym "Ichabod Henroost," surely mimicking Richard Steele's use of "Nathaniel Henroost" in a 1711 essay. Early in 1722, Ichabod complained about his wife, who had become "an Informer against the Anti-Inoculators" and was spending each day talking to the "vile Fellows of the Town." He feared her obsession with inoculation would ruin their home life. In her absence "the Management of Affairs in the House is left wholly to the Servants, who within this Three Weeks have broke Fourteen earthen Mugs and a Looking-Glass, melted Five Plates, and burnt Two good Brooms." Ichabod thus rendered concrete the warning that Joseph Addison had sounded in the *Freeholder* six years earlier: a woman's involvement in a major public controversy produced chaos in her household.[26]

Another parody mirrored Steele's account of female spectators at the Sacheverell trial. The Boston parallel was the prosecution of a group of pirates in the Court of Admiralty in mid-May 1724. "A Company of Ladies of the first Quality" attended the entire trial, reported a correspondent, "to the great Anoyance of his Majesty's good Subjects the Male Auditors, who were unmercifully squeez'd together upon that unusual Cry in a Court of Justice, *Make way for the Ladies.*" After a humorous account of the women's huge hoop petticoats, the author expressed concern about the results if "the Trulls and Gossips of the vulger Herd" imitated high-status women. "Should this [practice] of Women's attending Courts of Justice become general," he predicted, "a noisy Court" would be commonplace at any trial that drew public interest. He then supplied a lengthy interlocking dialogue in which he imagined what would occur on such occasions:

(This is a) *speak softly* (mighty pretty Lace of yours; what did it cost a Yard?).... *That's a pretty Man,* (Law, he'll hear ye) *he in Black there! I don't care if he* (Is your Sister) *does not I* (brought to Bed yet?) *No Madam,*

(Is that the Sheriff?) *but she looks every Day,* (Yes,) *Where's the* (how old is her) *Constable?* (youngest Child?)....*I wish every Body'd hold their Tongue,* (Aye perswade them to it,) *I'm sure I wou'd* (Do be quiet,), *if the rest wou'd.*[27]

With all the talk, the correspondent wrote, "my head begins to turn." His clever narrative left his readers with a verbal picture illustrating the inappropriateness of women's presence at such events. Women, he indicated, would not (could not?) concentrate on such serious matters as a trial that could lead to the execution of criminals. Rather, female spectators would devote their time to gossiping about men, clothes, and their families, disrupting the court with their idle chatter. Better, then, that women should simply stay away when men were administering justice—as Steele had, in effect, advised.

That other early colonial newspapers (four more were founded in mainland North America before the end of the decade) did not also stress the same theme and that it disappeared from the pages of the *Courant* as well for the remainder of its relatively brief existence suggest that the relationship of women and the public realm was not of pressing interest to male cultural arbiters in the colonies during the 1720s. But that was to change during the following decade when New Yorkers became enmeshed in a major political confrontation.

In August 1732, New York acquired a new governor, William Cosby, whose wife, Grace Montagu, was an English aristocrat—first cousin of the Duke of Newcastle, sister of the Earl of Halifax. Accustomed in England to the continued political involvements of female contemporaries with similar high standing even at that late date, she behaved in Manhattan as she undoubtedly would have in London. In some ways her actions mimicked those of Lady Frances Berkeley over fifty years earlier. One contemporary even went so far as to claim that she had "the Intire management of that weak madman her husband." In reaction, male New Yorkers not only penned parodies resembling those in the *New-England Courant* in the preceding decade, but also produced a definitive statement asserting women's incapacity for public affairs, the first such essay authored in North America.[28]

Governor Cosby quickly aroused controversy by becoming involved in a lawsuit over salary arrears with a local man of Dutch descent who had served as interim governor before Cosby's arrival. Lewis Morris, the chief justice of the Supreme Court, refused to back Cosby, who suspended and replaced him with James DeLancey, previously an associate justice. Morris then assumed the role of opposition leader, as New York's politicians lined up for or against Cosby. By late 1733, the province was deeply divided into partisan camps and the opposition had started to publish a newspaper, the *New-York Weekly Journal,* printed by John Peter Zenger; both parties vigorously worked to recruit adherents.

That Grace Cosby, like Lady Frances Berkeley, wielded hospitality as a political weapon becomes clear in the letters Abigaill Levy Franks, the wife of a wealthy Jewish merchant in Manhattan, wrote to her son in London during Governor Cosby's tenure. Having read Addison, Abigaill followed his advice and informed her son that although she privately favored the opposition, she publicly remained neutral in the "Perfect war" that had engulfed the town. The governor and his wife were "Very much disliked," she reported, but the governor was attempting to win allies "by being Affable & Courteous." The Cosbys hosted frequent dinner parties at their residence in Fort George with guest lists largely composed of merchants of Dutch heritage. Grace Cosby, for her part, held weekly visiting days for such men's wives. Abigaill disclosed that she had often been invited to the fort for afternoons or evenings but that she had never accepted, "for I desire noe more honour then the rest of my fellow Cit[izen]s." She described Grace's "Agreeable Courtly Method," which the governor's wife had employed to flatter a member of the assembly so successfully that it put him into an "Extacy" of pleasure. Abigaill recounted that one woman who called daily on the Cosbys had become an object of spiteful mockery; she rode in the governor's coach so often, some people joked, "She has Allmost forgot to walk a foot."[29]

In the midst of her account, Abigaill commented, "As You will observe, the Jounalls are Very merry upon These feasts." She was referring to a parody of the governor's hospitality campaign that appeared in Zenger's *Weekly Journal.* On January 21, 1733/4, the "Widows of this City" complained that although they were "House keepers, Pay our Taxes, carry on Trade," the governor had neglected them. "The Husbands that live in our Neighbourhood are daily invited to Dine at Court," they observed, insisting that they could be just as "Entertaining" as the men. Why, then, were they being excluded? was their implicit question. "Tho' we don't understand the Law, we do the Gospels," the "widows" concluded, citing Proverbs 23:1–7, verses "lately put up near the Markett Place." That passage made the author's point crystal clear: "When thou sittest to eat with a ruler, consider diligently what is before thee.... Be not desirous of his dainties: for they are deceitful meat.... Eat and drink, saith he to thee; but his heart is not with thee."[30]

Anyone reading the article who failed either to recall or to look up the contents of Proverbs 23:1–7 in the Bible would have missed the most pointed part of the satire. Had those verses actually been posted "near the Markett Place"? It is impossible to know for certain in the absence of other contemporary sources. But the "petition" cleverly cited relevant scriptures to attack the governor, who must have been incensed at the implication of such phrases as "deceitful meat," yet would surely have felt himself unable to challenge publicly a passing reference to an Old Testament passage. Further, the use of "widows" as spokespeople for the governor's critics was inspired. Had the author chosen instead to represent the purported petitioners as an anonymous group of men, their exclusion from gubernatorial entertainments could have been (mis)interpreted by readers as whiny complaints coming from some merchants who were not in the Cosbys' inner circle. That widows were the nominal authors exposed the covert political aims of the governor's seemingly generous hospitality. All that differentiated the female traders and housekeepers (who were not invited to the fort) from the neighboring men (who were welcomed there as guests) was one factor: the men were voters and state actors; the women were not. Any careful reader of the *New-York Weekly Journal* could easily reach the conclusion that the governor was engaged in a "deceitful" campaign to woo New York's political leaders.

As the "Party rage" and the "Vast deall of Polliticall Dissentions" (in Abigaill Franks's words) persisted and the anti-Cosby critiques in Zenger's paper became more pointed and less amusing, the governor charged Zenger with seditious libel. Several issues of the *New-York Weekly Journal* were publicly burned; the affair culminated in Zenger's famous libel trial and acquittal in August 1735. The ongoing discord led to a "most dreadful breach" between Grace Cosby and some of her female acolytes, one male observer reported, but he gave no specifics as to the cause.[31]

Grace continued her politicking, and when her husband fell seriously ill in late 1735, she, like Lady Frances Berkeley during the illness of *her* husband in 1677, began to take actions on his behalf. Grace Cosby's meddling outraged others, including the governor himself. "It is whisper'd," remarked Daniel Horsmanden, a New York attorney, "that he upbraided Madams Conduct in Such Lively Colours, that She fell in a Swoon."[32] Grace had opened and read a packet of letters that arrived from London addressed to her husband at a time when he was too sick to act. Among them was a missive from several members of the Board of Trade indicating that they intended to remove his opponents from the colony's council, thus suggesting that he had won a clear victory in New York's partisan conflict. The removal was not yet final, but Grace reported it as having been completed.

Just as Frances Berkeley had spread negative information about Nathaniel Bacon, so Grace Cosby gossiped about the ousting of her husband's adversaries from their official positions. Furthermore, she did so long before the governor himself had read the letter in question. Horsmanden, who noted that the letter "was Shown about to a great many," including himself, termed Mrs. Cosby and those who believed her "Novices in polliticks" who had to be "undeceive'd" about its contents. But surely Grace, who was no political novice despite Horsmanden's characterization, knew exactly what she was doing. She and Frances Berkeley—who was similarly called to account for her gossip mongering—both used talk as a mechanism for supporting their husbands. The difference was that Governor Cosby himself "upbraided" his wife more or less publicly whereas Governor Berkeley probably covertly colluded in his wife's actions, at least until they became a public embarrassment after Bacon demanded a formal explanation and apology.

In this context of partisan confrontation and Grace Cosby's political activism, Zenger's *New-York Weekly Journal* published the first American essay that did not just satirize women's involvement with politics but asserted explicitly that women should not be state actors.[33] The untitled, unsigned article appeared in August 1734, in the midst of the issues of the *Weekly Journal* that led to Zenger's prosecution. After an ungendered epigraph, "Study thy self, learn in what Rank and State / The wise Creator has ordain'd thy Fate," the author directly addressed the newspaper's female readers. He hoped he would not offend them by asserting that "Poli[ti]cks is what does not become them; the Governing Kingdoms and Ruling Provinces are Things too difficult and knotty for the fair Sex, it will render them grave and serious, and take off those agreeable Smiles that should always accompany them." The author's initial stress on "Governing Kingdoms" and "Ruling Provinces" was not coincidental; Grace Cosby had brought to New York an aristocratic woman's traditionally activist style, which was unusual in mid-eighteenth-century North America and clearly had aroused considerable antagonism in the colony.

The essayist then recounted two anecdotes, neither of which pertained to female rule or governance and the first of which strongly resembled the story Steele told in the *Tatler* of encountering two women having an animated argument about public affairs. After expressing deep concern about every day hearing "Numbers of fair Ladies contending about some abstruce Point in Politicks, and running into the greatest Heats about they know not what," he described a meeting with two women who were arguing about politics over tea. They were so incensed that he barely escaped "without being scalded," he reported. The second tale pertained to women "shewing their Resentments in the publick Streets"; his target was a woman who instructed her children not to show any signs of respect when they walked past the house of a member of the party she opposed. Once she arrived home, she purportedly "could not help exulting at . . . how pretty the Children had behaved" in following her directions. While admitting that men should "shew a just Disregard for all those Tools of Power that endeavour to contribute to their Slavery," and that women should always be contemptuous of "any Man that appear'd a Tool," the author nevertheless insisted that women should not follow her example.

Hastening to add that female readers should continue to peruse the *Weekly Journal,* the author advised them to teach their children "the Principles of Liberty"—but also "good Manners," as the mother in his second story had not. "I think a Woman never appears more agreeable then when she is discharging the Duties incumbent upon a Mistriss of a Family, when through her Management her Friends partake of a Genteel Frugality," he asserted. Such behavior "will redound much more to their Honour than by Discommoding their pretty Faces with Passion and Resentment."

The themes of the essay thus bore a striking resemblance to the earlier arguments of Joseph Addison. Like Addison, the New Yorker declared that "the fair Sex" could not understand the "abstruce" points of politics, which were "too difficult and knotty" for them; that they should avoid partisan "Heats"; that their "pretty Faces" would be ruined if they became too "grave and serious," talking with "Passion and Resentment" and thus losing their "agreeable Smiles"; and that they would be much better off if they focused on "discharging the Duties incumbent upon a Mistriss of a Family."

Such points were then driven home by other publications in the *Weekly Journal.* A month later a reader signing himself "A.B." submitted to Zenger a poem by the Englishman George Lyttelton, "Advice to a Lady." Among other words of wisdom, the poet told "Belinda," whom he was addressing:

> Seek to be good, but aim not to be great;
> A Woman's noblest Station is Retreat;
> Her fairest Virtues fly from publick Sight,
> Domestick Worth! That shuns too strong a Light.
> To rougher Man Ambition's Task resign,
> 'Tis ours in Senates and in Courts to shine
>
> . . . .
>
> One only Care your gentle Breasts should move,
> The important Business of your Life is Love.[34]

A few months later, a correspondent claiming to be a woman apologized for writing for publication, then complained of men "setting up for Politicians." In women's presence, she remarked, "instead of saying those pretty Things that I think we deserve, they are talking of Deeds, Property, Lawyers,

Courts, and Judges...that we poor Girls can't comprehend." Such men, she declared, were "mere *Woman-Haters,*...cold and indifferent." Men—as the August essayist had argued—should of course defend New Yorkers' privileges, but they should do it "in the proper Places and not fill our Ears with...the Lord knows what." Men who talked to women about current political affairs, she averred, would be far more congenial if they discoursed instead about "the Beauties of a married State, and all the Pleasures and Happiness that attend it." She ended her untitled article with a long poem celebrating women's and men's mutual positive influence on each other, to the benefit of all concerned.[35]

The message to Zenger's female readers was unmistakable. It was, indeed, the same message conveyed nearly two decades earlier by Joseph Addison: women should stay out of partisan disputes and even political discussions, which were appropriately the sole province of men. Instead, they should focus on their domestic responsibilities and glory in their roles as sweethearts, wives, mothers, and mistresses of families. In the 1730s, American women and men clearly grasped that message. In May 1736, shortly after Governor Cosby's death, Cadwallader Colden, a New York councillor, praised his wife, Alice, for her nonpartisan socializing: "I am pleas'd that you know nothing of parties but visit & converse without any regard to them." Soon thereafter he likewise advised his daughter, Elizabeth DeLancey, to avoid "being a party Woman A Lady never looks more re[di]culous to men of Sense than when she sets up for a Politicean & never more betrays her Judgement than on such Occasions."[36]

The Anglo-American Debate over Women's Political Role

In early-1720s Boston and mid-1730s New York, such misogynist publications questioning women's capacity for politics went unanswered. By contrast, the late 1730s and early 1740s brought a flurry of publications in England and America debating the issue. In each case, the dialogue began with an essay attacking some aspect of women's claim to a public role, and now those essays occasionally—though not always—elicited responses, all of which came from authors claiming to be female. Much more is said about the contours of this device, *rhetorical femininity,* in the next chapter; here it is sufficient to observe that nearly every defense of women's political acumen appearing in the middle of the century employed it. That contrasts sharply with similar publications of three to five decades earlier. Men such as Nahum Tate and Bernard Mandeville readily revealed themselves as men in the text even if they published their works anonymously. That by the late 1730s support for women's claim to a public role came primarily from nominal women speaks volumes about the growing gender divide in Anglo-American society.[37]

In September 1737, an anonymous contributor to *Common Sense, or the Englishman's Journal,* a periodical series reprinted in part in the *Gentleman's Magazine* and later appearing as a separate two-volume set, published essays on the theme of affectation in men and women. The latter focused in large part on delineating the "natural" role of women in such a way as to exclude them from the public realm. Both essays were eventually republished in the American press, so colonial editors clearly believed that the sentiments expressed would interest their readers.[38]

In the first essay, the author roundly attacked those men he termed "self-created" coxcombs, or men who pretended to have talents they in fact lacked, offering prose portraits of men to whom he gave such names as Fatuus and Ponderosus. Fatuus, he declared, had the "Post of Honour" among the others; one key fault was that "he talks Politicks to his Women." That foreshadowed the major theme of the second essay, which criticized women who failed to recognize that "each Sex has its distinguishing Characteristick" and that women should not abandon "their natural Characters" to act like men. His descriptions of women included Agrippina, who read just enough to talk "absurdly" on any subject; and Canidia, who "talks Politicks and Metaphysicks, mangles the Terms of each, and, if there be Sense in either, most infallibly puzzles it."

The author declared that he intended to "advise and reform" his female readers rather than offend them. But, he insisted, "their Sphere of Action is more bounded and circumscrib'd" than "Men's Province," which was "universal, and comprehends every Thing, from the Culture of the Earth, to the Government of it." His aim, he declared, was to convince women to "act their own natural Parts, and not other Peoples." And he clearly outlined women's "natural" role: "Women are not form'd for great Cares, themselves, but to sooth and soften ours"; they provided men with a "desirable Retreat from Study and Business. They are confined within the narrow Limits of Domestick Offices and when they stray beyond them, they move excentrically, and consequently without grace."[39]

Just how "excentrically" such graceless women moved, in the opinion of the author, became obvious when he began to discuss women in myth and history who "have made very considerable Figures in the most heroick and manly Parts of Life." In most such cases, he averred, the tales of their exploits were "so mix't up with Fables, one is at Liberty to question either the Facts or the Sex." Strikingly, he then went on to question not the facts but the sex. Citing a purported treatise on hermaphrodites, he insisted that its author had proved definitively that "all the reputed Female Heroes of Antiquity were of this Epicene Gender," although in deference to his female readers' modesty he would refrain from detailing the evidence for that assertion. He also gave two more recent examples: Queen Christina of Sweden, for whom "the Masculine was so predominant" that she even adopted man's dress; and, most significantly, Queen Elizabeth, "of whose Sex we have abundant Reason to doubt, History furnishing us with many Instances of the Manhood of that Princess, without leaving us one single Symptom or Indication of the Woman." Women who insisted on "going beyond the Bounds allotted to their Sex," he declared, should publicly admit that they were hermaphrodites, and until they did so he would not permit them to "confound Politicks."[40]

Such extraordinary language was deliberately intended to shock his reading audience. Women who dared to venture into the public realm were literally unsexed; by stepping outside the "natural" and "narrow" boundaries of the domestic sphere into the broadly expansive province of men, they violated not just cultural and social but biological norms. The contrast to the woman who knew her proper place could not have been sharper. She displayed "native Female Softness" and had "a natural Chearfulness of Mind, Tenderness and Benignity of Heart." His ideal woman, Flavia, bore little resemblance to the earlier negative pictures. She was superior to others but concealed that superiority carefully, adapting readily to any company or circumstances. "Tho' she thinks and speaks as a Man would do, still it is as a Woman should do; she effeminates (if I may use the Expression) whatever she says, & gives all the Graces of her own Sex to the Strength of ours." Women, in sum, "should content themselves with the private Care and Oeconomy of their Families, and the diligent Discharge of Domestick Duties."

Given the heavy-handed argument in the *Common Sense* essay, it is unsurprising that no one in America (and seemingly no one in England either) dared to challenge it publicly. Any woman who penned and published a response would have left herself open to the charge of hermaphroditism, for the mere act of contradicting the author in print would have moved a woman beyond the limits of "domestick offices" and into sexually uncharted territory, or so the author would assert. A man coming to women's defense might well have found himself branded a "Cott-Queen," also a target of the anonymous author, who warned men against intruding on "Female Detail."

Yet a 1739 essay in the same series, which was reprinted in New York the following year, elicited replies from English and American authors adopting a pose of rhetorical femininity. *Common Sense* 135 reflected on the wisdom of Roman law, "by which Women were kept under the Power of Guardians all the Days of their Lives." Women were so fickle, ignorant, and flighty that they could destroy marriages and families if given too much freedom; they were unable to govern themselves. "The right Use of full Liberty is only known to Men," the author insisted. Women were most appropriately confined to the household: a woman's "true Eclat is a private Life, and the Oeconomy of a Family her solid Glory—Women risque too much to go out of that little Circle of Action to which Decency has confined them." Moreover, if men ever admit that women are our equals, he warned, "they will immediately want to become our Mistresses," which would lead to disaster.[41]

Common Sense 135 addressed women's public role only implicitly, by its emphasis instead on women's appropriately restricted "private Life." The "constant female reader" of Zenger's *New-York Weekly Journal* who replied to the essay adopted the same approach. She challenged the author's negative characterization of women, argued that men too often made poor decisions, and asserted that "there are bad Husbands who destroy the Happiness of the Matrimonial state, as well as bad Wives." She therefore accepted the terms of the debate as the *Common Sense* author stated them.[42]

An English author who responded to the same essay took a very different tack, going beyond asserting that women were capable of governing themselves to contend that they were also capable of ruling others. In thus broadening her focus, she revealed the linkage between the two seemingly diverse roles: confining a woman to "a private Life" necessarily involved preventing her from exercising her talents in the public realm. And *that* she wanted to challenge.

Sophia, "a person of quality," cited *Common Sense* 135 several times in her 1739 pamphlet, *Woman Not Inferior to Man,* which is widely regarded as the most important English predecessor of Mary Wollstonecraft's *Vindication of the Rights of Woman* (1792). Sophia's identity remains a mystery. She presented a frontal challenge to the author of *Common Sense* 135 and other misogynists of the mid-eighteenth century, and did so with sweeping claims of women's competence in many fields of endeavor. Whoever Sophia was, she had a copy of François Poulain de la Barre's 1677 tract, *The Woman as Good as the Man,* in front of her as she wrote, but she was not wholly dependent on its contents.[43]

Sophia divided her work into seven chapters, three of which explicitly addressed the question of women's political abilities: "Whether the Men are better qualified to govern than Women, or not"; "Whether the Women are fit for public Offices, or not"; and, unusually, "Whether Women are naturally qualified for military offices, or not." In these chapters Sophia argued that women were "as much qualified... by nature" to hold public office as "the ablest of *Men*." She exposed what she termed the "very great absurdity" of men's circular reasoning on the subject of women's education: "Why is *learning* useless to us? Because we have no share in public offices. And why have we no share in public offices? Because we have no *learning*." Since England has had "glorious" queens, she contended, could women not also fill "the subordinate offices of ministers of state, vice-queens, governesses, secretaries, privy-counsellors, and treasurers?"[44]

Men, Sophia argued, excluded women from public positions only because of "custom and prejudice," and because women did not engage in the same "violence, shameless injustice, and lawless oppression" as they did. Freed from "the disadvantages imposed upon them by the unjust usurpation and tyranny of the *Men*," women would be fully capable of serving the public in civil or military affairs. The most radical part of Sophia's argument, a section that drew on Poulain de la Barre, pertained to women's capacity for military leadership. Why, she asked, should it be more surprising "to see [a woman] preside in a council of war, than in a council of state"? Surely, she declared, "the military art has no mystery in it beyond others, which *Women* cannot attain to." All men were not sufficiently strong to endure the hardships of a campaign, nor were all women too weak to participate in military operations. Moreover, most women were naturally as courageous as most men. She concluded that only men's "brutal strength" gave them a superior position in the world, and that did not entitle them to "engross all *power* and *prerogative* to themselves."[45]

"A Gentleman" replied to Sophia in *Man Superior to Woman,* published later that same year. In misogynist prose, he cited "all the greatest Sages of Antiquity," who had seen women as "less noble, less perfect, and consequently inferior to *Men*." Analogizing between household and polity, he observed that "those poor pretty Creatures must make a very sorry Figure in Government and publick Offices, who appear so universally unqualified for the Administration of private Oeconomy." As for holding military rank, that was wholly "unnatural and out of Character" for women. In reasoning echoing that in the 1737 *Common Sense* essay, he implied that any woman who sought military office would unsex herself. "It is no Praise then, but rather a Disgrace, to any of that soft Sex to be qualified for military Offices."[46]

Sophia did not let the attack go unanswered, replying in yet another publication, *Woman's Superior Excellence over Man,* which restated and partially modified her earlier position. When she began her writing project, she explained, she had expected to find "the sphere which *Women* are capable of acting in very narrow," but she had soon realized her mistake and had drafted *Woman Not Inferior to Man* to show what she had learned. Sophia declared firmly, "I am resolved to shew my adversary, and all his sex, that there is at least one *Woman* capable of preferring truth to flattery, sense to sound, and who dares assert her right in the face of usurpation, tho' harden'd by custom into tyranny." She disdainfully rejected the "impotent endeavours" of her opponent, crowing that his "weak defence" had made "a bad cause worse." Characterizing his argument as "an idle collection of foul-mouth'd scurrilities from the Ancients," Sophia boldly turned her opponent's household-polity analogy back on himself. If he insisted that all women were unfit for rule because certain women could not manage their households properly, she could just as well contend that because of some men's "indiscretion in private life . . . all his sex are disqualified from public government." She did, though, modify her comments on women and military leadership. She did not intend to imply that women should actually participate in the military, she declared, but rather only to reveal "the excessive silliness" of men's arguments that all women were "naturally cowards."[47]

It is telling that the one position from which Sophia retreated in her second pamphlet was the most unusual assertion in the first, and that which was most dependent on her seventeenth-century predecessor, Poulain de la Barre. Was she accurately describing her original intention? The answer is not clear. But what is clear is that for all her insistence on women's capacity for assuming civic responsibility and their intellectual equality, Sophia also accepted eighteenth-century notions of sexual difference. Her ultimate goal, she declared in her conclusion to *Woman's Superior Excellence,* was to show other women "that if the *Men* have by fraud and violence gain'd a superiority of power over us; we still retain our original superiority of sense and virtue over them." Honest men, she averred, had to admit that they could not equal women's "perfections of soul" or their "charm of personal beauty and graces."[48]

The 1751 one-volume republication of the three Sophia pamphlets, titled *Beauty's Triumph,* was advertised for sale three times in Boston a decade later.[49] Those advertisements constitute the only evidence that colonists had access to the terms of the Sophia debate. But American newspapers carried other opinion pieces reprinted from English sources that addressed the subject of whether women had an appropriate role in the public realm and, if so, what the contours of that role might be. America produced no local Sophia to champion women's ability to participate in public affairs. Instead, the authors whose works were later published in the colonies were unanimous in their opinion: either women should stay out of politics altogether or they should participate only in an appropriately feminine manner.

The writers who advocated women's total exclusion from the public realm took several different approaches, many of them mocking. One wit offered a description of a "political Ballance" that would accurately weigh the abilities of various public figures; he placed 999 women on the scale at once, yet "they were all found *wanting;* except one and her I found dead in the Scale." A misogynistic poet translated into verse Joseph Addison's calumny about women's uncomprehending use of political terminology: "her arguments directly tend / Against the side she would defend / ... And, to defend the whiggish cause, / Her topics from the tories draws." Another author turned the absence of a law preventing women from taking the English throne into a satirical petition from "Dame Catherine High-Blood" and others contending that they "may be no more shut out from private than publick Power" and outlining the circumstances under which women should be entitled to "wear the Breeches" in a variety of families.[50]

Others took the matter more seriously. One tack was to discuss various female rulers but not to mention their skill at governance, focusing instead on other aspects of their lives, such as their learning or—as when Caroline, George II's politically astute queen, died in 1737—to celebrate only their "prudent Family Government."[51] Another was to denigrate the political roles of the wives or mistresses of powerful men. An English essay reprinted in the *New-York Weekly Journal* in early 1751, for example, contended that "the greatest Ministers never had Wives," because wives could not keep secrets and employed manipulative wiles behind the scenes. "There is no Enemy so dangerous as a Woman," the author warned; a determined female could entice men into "Snares" that belied their "pretended Strength and Resolution." As an example, he cited Mark Antony's passion for Cleopatra, which had led to "the depth of Misfortunes." Insisting that a government wholly excluding feminine influence would be best, he failed to mention that Cleopatra was a powerful ruler in her own right.[52]

Those who foresaw that women could be a positive force in the public realm sharply restricted the scope of such activism. An English essay republished in Boston in 1739 advised contemporary women to look to heroines of the past to learn how to be "useful Subjects" and lauded those ancient "Female Patriots" who had sacrificed their personal interests for their country's good. Yet the author's main point was that times had changed. Queens had once led conquering forces, but "our modern polite Ladies" had no need of "Military Virtues." Long ago, governments had called on "Female Power."

Now, though, women would fulfill their patriotic obligations not as "Warriors and Heroines" but instead as "Wives, Mothers, Sisters, and Daughters" who knew how to sew and cook and who purchased "the Manufactures of [their] Country" instead of imported goods.[53]

A similar call for women to devote themselves to domesticity and frugality for patriotic reasons dominated a pamphlet first published anonymously in London in 1746 and thereafter reprinted several times before the end of the decade in Britain and America. James Burgh's *Britain's Remembrancer* appeared in America in the year of its initial publication under the title *A Serious and Earnest Address to the Gentry, Clergy, and the Other Inhabitants of the British Nation. Also a Faithful and Pathetick Expostulation to the Women....* Burgh, writing in the immediate aftermath of the Jacobite rebellion of 1745 and in the middle of the War of the Austrian Succession, argued that British society needed thorough reformation. As the American title suggested, he admonished clergymen and magistrates, then addressed "my fair Countrywomen." He accused women of devoting too much attention to the "Pleasures of Theatrical and Musical Entertainments, to the Neglect not only of all that is spiritual and sacred, but also of those domestic Cares which are your proper Province." Pursuing even seemingly innocent diversions would remove women from their "only natural Sphere... originally intended by the Ordination of Heaven"—in short, their familial and household responsibilities. To be anything other than "dutiful Daughters, loving Wives, tender Mothers, prudent Mistresses of Families, faithful Friends, and pious Christians" would be "quite out of Nature," Burgh insisted. So how could women best help themselves and the nation? Quite simply, they had the power to reform men.

> Upon the whole, if you will resolve to retrench your Extravagancies, to employ your Time at home in the Works of domestick Oeconomy, Charity, Virtue, and Piety, and filling up the Place you hold with regard to your Friends, your Relations, and your God: you will contribute what is properly in your Power toward the Reformation, and consequently the saving of your unhappy Country.[54]

Thus, for James Burgh, women's most appropriate public role in the end came down to this: fulfilling their domestic responsibilities and reforming men through their own virtuous conduct. The boundaries of women's sphere, natural and ordained by God, confined them so tightly to the family that only through personal relationships with husbands, children, and others could they contribute to public well-being. By the late 1740s, through such works as these, all women were being theoretically excluded from the realm of public affairs.

That Burgh's argument must have carried particular resonance in North America is suggested by the fact that his work was reprinted nearly as often in the colonies as in Great Britain. Even though a good part of the content (for example, complaints about women's frequenting the Covent Garden theater or the Ranelagh pleasure garden) bore little relevance to life in Boston, New York, Williamsburg, or Philadelphia, printers in those towns produced new editions of his pamphlet, presumably because local readers wanted to purchase them or because the printers thought a local audience would find them appealing.[55]

No American Sophia challenged the new gender-role strictures in print. After the departure of Grace Cosby, only one woman in the colonies, the prominent Pennsylvania Quaker Susanna Wright, is recorded as engaging in open politicking. During a heated contest for Lancaster's seat in the colonial assembly in 1742, she reportedly helped to write a political pamphlet and then distributed not only it but also "Lies & Tickets [marked ballots]" from a tavern on election day. She thus earned a critic's complaint about her "unbecoming" and "unfemale" political activities.[56]

Susanna Wright's actions stood out dramatically because other colonial women in the middle decades of the century confined their reflections about political matters to their diaries and correspondence, or to personal conversations with close friends and family members. Even if they therefore failed to avoid discussing politics entirely (as Joseph Addison would have preferred), they expressed their interest in muted tones and did not translate that interest into action. Moreover, their language revealed that they were well aware that political topics were "out of their sphere."[57]

Colonial Women on War and Politics

For several reasons, surviving letters penned by colonial women during the decades before the American Revolution are relatively scarce. Fewer women than men could write, especially early in the century; paper was scarce and expensive; and the difficulty of dispatching correspondence meant that people wrote letters primarily when they were separated from loved ones for months at a time at a considerable distance. Such lengthy separations were relatively rare in the years before the Revolutionary War. Diary keeping by women was even more rare, for the act of writing to oneself (as a diary is, in effect) demanded a high level of literacy and the availability of time for reflection.

Accordingly, written evidence of colonial women's reactions to political and military affairs is exceptionally sparse and scattered before the 1740s. But then the onset of near-continuous warfare between 1739 and 1763, and the subsequent beginnings of the resistance movement that culminated in the struggle for independence, impinged directly on women as well as men.[58]

Some women, the New Yorkers Abigaill Franks and Alice Colden among them, avidly read colonial and English newspapers and reported what they learned to distant correspondents or, conversely, thanked those correspondents for sending newspapers. When they had additional news gleaned from other sources that would supplement the "prints," they passed that on too.[59]

Those who lived in places where papers were harder to acquire eagerly sought information from friends and tried to separate rumor from fact. One such consumer of news was Esther Edwards Burr, a resident of Princeton, New Jersey, who during the Seven Years' War was deeply concerned about the fate of her parents, then living on the frontier in Stockbridge, Massachusetts. Esther filled the long journal-letter she wrote seriatim to her close friend in Boston, Sarah Prince, with information about the war she learned from her husband and others. After an Albany resident told her bluntly in September 1754 that the Indians wanted "to kill all the people in Stockbridge," she exclaimed, "I am almost out of my witts! What will become of my Dear father and his afflicted family!" The defeat of General Edward Braddock in July 1755 caused her confusion, for she had "many different accounts" on successive days. She first heard that Braddock had been killed and the army routed, then that he had not died though he had been defeated, and finally the "sertain News" that the initial report had been correct after all.[60]

Female correspondents and diarists most often simply recorded the military or (less frequently) political news, but sometimes they also offered their opinions. Abigaill Franks in 1742 advocated forcing Sir Robert Walpole to "Answer for his past Conduct" and "Suffer, for his Mismanagement." For her part, the Philadelphia Quaker and pacifist Hannah Callender lamented in her diary the "Wickedness...perpetrated by our Army" during the Seven Years' War. One especially outspoken commentator was Eliza Lucas Pinckney of South Carolina, who was educated in Great Britain and also spent part of the 1750s there, as a widow overseeing the education of her young sons. When she returned to America late in that decade, she continued to correspond with her friends in England, and she frequently assessed the political and military abilities of her colony's leaders as they fought the neighboring Cherokees. Most notably, she approved of the governor's actions (though others criticized him), asserting that he demonstrated "courage" and "great spirit" and "gained much honour" from a campaign against the Indians. As victory in North America neared in summer 1760, she presciently warned her English friends that in seeking "new conquests in America" the British should not "neglect the protection of their old Colonys."[61]

Yet even while they were writing about public affairs, colonial women were acutely aware that they were violating cultural norms in doing so. Both Hannah Callender and Esther Burr signaled that awareness in the 1750s. After detailing a conversation she and her mother had in 1758 with three other women on "the universal Topic of the Town now"—a French frigate that was lying just off the coast and capturing American merchant vessels sailing from New York and Philadelphia—Hannah explained to herself, "Women either by connections of Husband or Father &cc cant help interesting themselves in Politics." Then she added, whether she believed it or not: "I woud always avoid it, and think that the duties of our Station would be much more agreeable Conversation." Esther Burr was more forthright. In December 1755, she indicated her unwillingness to assume that men always knew best:

> I am perplexed about our publick affairs. The Men say (tho' not Mr Burr he is not one of that sort) that Women have no business to concern themselves about em but trust to those that know better and be content to be destroyed because that they did all for the best—Indeed if I was convinced that our great men did act as they realy thought was for the Glory of God and the good of the Country it would go a great ways to meke me easy.[62]

Although women before the 1760s thus did not ignore public events in their personal writings, three striking aspects of their remarks need to be highlighted: first, most of them recorded events without giving their own viewpoints. In so doing, they were, in effect, imitating the newspapers they read. Second, if they did offer opinions, like Esther Burr they tended to focus on the implications of the news for their own families and friends rather than presenting more disinterested commentary. And third, although they followed the progress of the Anglo-American armies in the field, they usually did not remark on the colonial or British policymakers whose decisions had shaped those army movements. Only rarely did women reveal interest in, or knowledge of, the political maneuvers that lay behind the events they reported.[63]

Soon after the end of the Seven Years' War, British policy toward the colonies changed in ways that began to politicize the entire American populace, including women, regardless of whether they reacted positively or negatively to the resistance movement. In the early years of revolutionary agitation, women responded as might be anticipated in light of prevailing mid-eighteenth-century notions of women's restricted sphere. They either eschewed the discussion of politics, explicitly stating that they did so because women were not supposed to deal with such matters; or they offered political opinions but then made the same disclaimer. Take, for example, the following excerpts from correspondence of the period:

> This is my Private opinion, but how I came to give it is a Mistry, for Politicks is a puddle I never choose to dabble in. (1769) [concluding a conservative analysis of events in Boston]
>
> Let me see what is the present Reigning Topick amongt us— Politicks—Avaunt, Ill have nothing to do with such things, as they are not only out of my Sphere, but above my ability. (1772) [a woman who failed to discuss politics]
>
> The management of our publick affairs is in very good hands, and all that is requir'd of you is your Prayers and exhortations for a general reformation. It is not my province to enter into politicks, but sure I am that it is not your Duty to do or say any thing that shall tend to distroy your usefulness. (1774) [from a female revolutionary sympathizer to her loyalist-leaning male cousin][64]

John and Abigail Adams, so deeply involved in politics in the 1760s and 1770s, and also so influenced by the conventional wisdom that accepted a sharp division between the public realm of men and the familial province of women, epitomized such trends. Among other similar statements, Abigail's double apology in one letter stands out. When she drafted a political letter to a member of the Continental Congress in 1779 while John was abroad, she wrote that she thought it important to convey certain political news from Massachusetts, remarking, "I intreet your pardon for touching upon a subject more properly belonging to your sex." At the end she appended an additional justification: "the absence of a very near and dear Friend I must plead as a further Excuse for addressing any other gentleman upon a subject which may be considerd as foreign to my sex." That even Abigail Adams felt the need to explain herself not just once but twice when she dared to broach political subjects in correspondence with a man not her husband underscores the impact of the eighteenth-century belief that women should be excluded from the public realm.[65]

Likewise, when in 1776 John Adams seemingly endorsed women's engagement with politics, he in fact adopted a position that echoed Addison's in some respects: "The Ladies I think are the greatest Politicians that I have the Honour to be acquainted with, not only because they act upon the Sublimest of all the Principles of Policy, viz., that Honesty is the best Policy, but because they consider Questions more coolly than those who are heated with Party Zeal and inflamed with the bitter Contentions of active public Life."[66] Women were good "politicians," then, in Adams's opinion, precisely because—just as Addison had advocated—they were not "heated with Party Zeal" and had no involvement with "the bitter Contentions of active public Life." Addison would not have approved of Adams's alteration of his ideas, because the American ultimately praised female politicians. But that Adams viewed women's gender identity as distancing them from partisanship revealed his debt to Addison's arguments.

Even for this most political of families—and for a man accustomed to his wife's interest in and knowledge of current events—women's proper place was therefore to be positioned somewhat apart from the public realm. Instead, women should focus their attention on household and family—newly dubbed "private" in the eighteenth century, though not previously designated by that term. The long-standing multiple oppositions expressed by the dichotomy public/private were acquiring a new and enduring meaning by midcentury, one that is explored in the next chapter.

Lady Chatham and Her Correspondents, 1740s–1760s

Few if any eighteenth-century women in Britain or America could claim better political connections than Hester Grenville Pitt. Born in 1720 and married in 1754, she was the sister of one prime minister (George Grenville), wife of another (William Pitt the elder, Lord Chatham), and mother of a third (William Pitt the younger). She grew up surrounded by politics; her oldest brother, Richard, later Earl Temple, entered Parliament when she was just fourteen. Her brothers Richard and George and her husband-to-be, William Pitt, who was first elected to Parliament in 1735, were avid critics of Sir Robert Walpole during the 1730s and early 1740s, and after Walpole's ouster in 1742 they moved into (and out of) various leadership positions in successive governments through the 1760s and into the 1770s. If anyone might have been expected to be a British version of Abigail Adams, it would accordingly be Hester Pitt, her somewhat older contemporary.[1]

But she was not, and the reason for that most likely lies in the fact that she *was* older. Her worldview formed in her young adulthood in the 1740s and 1750s, before the revolutionary agitation that turned Abigail Adams into a political commentator in her own right. Hester Pitt saw her role differently, more in accordance with the prescriptions laid down by Joseph Addison and his successors. She was certainly knowledgeable about politics, but her primary role in public affairs was to act as her husband's adjunct and secretary during his repeated bouts of illness and depression. She offered few of her own political opinions in the letters she wrote to her husband, her brothers, or her female friends. Her male relatives kept Hester informed of current events when she was in the country and they in London, yet she rarely responded with comments about public affairs.

From the 1740s (before her marriage) through the 1760s, Hester wrote to her brother, George, exclusively about such topics as mutual friends and the health of family members. When once, in June 1760, she passed on some news from the Quebec campaign, then nearing its climax, she added, "Mr. Pitt has desired I wou'd send you this account." In light of the breach that opened between her husband and her brother when Pitt resigned from the government in 1761 while Grenville continued to serve George III, her apolitical missives to her brother after that point could be interpreted primarily as an attempt to maintain family ties in spite of political divisions. That her earlier letters had similar content, though, suggests that her avoidance of political topics did not stem solely from such motives. There is little indication that George wrote to her about political topics; perhaps she primarily let him take the lead on the contents of their exchanges.[2]

Her other brothers, Richard and James, by contrast, shared political commentary with her. They, unlike George, initially remained her husband's allies. In a letter to Hester in early 1764, Richard sarcastically termed George "this great minister" and accused him of "haranguing half an hour with great indecency, fallacy, &c. &c" in the Commons; he was "not only unsupported, but deserted by the whole House," Earl Temple told her with evident satisfaction. Hester's husband, too, wrote to her about politics, keeping her up-to-date on war news while the Seven Years' War continued, and informing her triumphantly of the repeal of the Stamp Act in early 1766. "Joy to you, my dear love," she replied in a similar vein. "The joy of thousands is yours, under Heaven, who has crowned your endeavours with such happy success." Venturing a rare political opinion of her own while tying it to a personal observation, she added, "All my feelings tell me that I hate oppression, and that I love zealously the honour of my dear husband."[3]

By then, Earl Temple had reconciled with his younger brother, George, and he did not follow Pitt's lead in calling for repeal of the act the colonists had protested. The breach between Richard and Hester was evident from their correspondence in January 1766. "I refer myself only to your recollection of what has passed betwixt you & me in many unreserved conversations," he told her, explaining that he would not comment on events after "the Day of my Dissent from Mr. Pitt." Although he regretted the "family Disunion," Richard declared, "I know the Purity of my own Intentions, sufficient to vindicate me to myself."[4]

In mid-1766, after Earl Temple refused to join the ministry when Pitt (now Lord Chatham) again became leader of the government, the breach widened. Hester wrote first, expressing her satisfaction that Richard had behaved "with the greatest kindness and friendship imaginable" to her husband even while rejecting his invitation for a political alliance. But her brother was not appeased, responding that he found it "indispensably necessary" to inform her of his "indignation" at having been asked to join a ministry surrounded by "cyphers, all named by Mr. Pitt, of a different complexion for me, with some of whom I had so essentially differed on many accounts." He canceled their planned "reciprocal country visits" while still assuring her of his "warmest affection," and if letters passed between them over the next twenty months, they have not survived. The political division that led to "family Disunion" was not healed until the fall of 1768, nor did their regular correspondence resume until the winter of 1768–69.[5]

Notably, nothing in the surviving letters suggests that Hester felt herself to be directly involved in the political rupture between her husband and her brother. Although she always allied herself politically with her husband, she—in accordance with Addison's counsel to women in such instances—attempted to heal the schism rather than take part in the family quarrel.

When William Pitt fell ill, which happened with increasing frequency in the 1760s and 1770s, Hester acted as his secretary and surrogate correspondent. She wrote political letters on her husband's behalf and received others in return, some addressed directly to her rather than to him. Presumably at her husband's dictation, in spring 1770 she drafted a petition that was presented to George III on behalf of John Wilkes, the radical who had been refused a seat in Parliament despite his election from the City of London. Although she was thus an active participant in political dialogues, the surviving correspondence only occasionally provides clues to what she herself thought about public events. In one undated letter to William, probably from the early 1770s, she wrote, "I can express nothing about the scene which our patch'd ministry treat the public with. Sure it is too gross!" Another undated letter to him, probably from 1775, offered the following inaccurate prediction about Lord North, then the prime minister: "I think the Doubts he has betray'd as to the Line of Conduct he pursues, together with the wretched Figure he has made, will induce his being removed, or removing himself." And always she gloried in any praise for her husband and his "Artfull Arguments" in Parliament. She was pleased by the "Publick Joy" about his presence in the House of Lords, she wrote in another undated missive to him; "all are *Chatham,* and no Hope *without* him," one man had reported.[6]

So if Hester Pitt did not for the most part comment about politics, what did occupy her thoughts and fill her correspondence? Just as eighteenth-century essayists advised, she appears to have focused her major efforts on her household and social life. In letters to her husband, the health of their children and household affairs in general took center stage—as did the same subjects in letters he wrote to her.[7]

Surviving letters that Lady Chatham exchanged with a close personal friend and near contemporary, Elizabeth Robinson Montagu, confirm that her interests were largely apolitical. Elizabeth, a wealthy author and well-known hostess, was the wife of a member of Parliament during the period they associated with one another, but neither woman discussed political matters in their correspondence. Instead, their letters revolved around their social interactions and mutual interests. Elizabeth—whose only child, a son, had died as a toddler—showed great affection for Hester's children. She took them to the theater and on other excursions in London; in 1774, Hester told her, "it is impossible to say, my Dear Madam, whom you have made the proudest, or the happiest, ourselves, or our Adventurous Youths. All of us are especially sensible of the honor it was to such *Youngsters* to be *so* invited, and mix'd in such a society." For her part, Elizabeth expressed concerns about Lord Chatham's health, either hosted or visited the Chathams regularly, and passed on books she thought would interest Hester. She once sent a copy of a new play by Voltaire, but remarked that the leaves were "uncut, & by her unread." It was unfortunate, she remarked, "to think a man of great & universal genius should have addicted himself to such a manner of writing that one cannot venture to read any of his works till one has been assured by some person of daring curiosity that they are not shocking to religion & morals." Elizabeth clearly had not been that "person of daring curiosity," but perhaps she thought that Lord or Lady Chatham might be.[8]

A letter Lady Chatham addressed to Earl Temple in October 1777 best summed up her attitude toward her own political role and illustrated her essential affinity for the position advanced by Addison early in the century. By the time she wrote, her husband and her brother had once again developed political disagreements over American policy. "Let me Lament that my Lord and you meaning the same great object of public happiness, shou'd think the road to it so different," she wrote, as they awaited news from America of Burgoyne's campaign in northern New York. William hoped that afterward reconciliation would still be possible whereas Richard wanted to see America "reduced... into a beaten Enemy." She added that "as you will allow a Lady ought, [I] wish Peace and good will among all Men," including the two of them, expressing the hope that the news, when it arrived, would find them in agreement over the results. Having adopted the stance of a disinterested observer, appropriate for a woman who formally eschewed partisan politics, she then appended the standard disclaimer: "When I set down to write I never propos'd the saying a Syllable on the Subject that I have gone on upon.... You will forgive me I am sure for letting my Pen follow my Thoughts."[9]

More commonly, Lady Chatham's thoughts led her to household and family. And the same was true of other eighteenth-century women in the colonies before the American Revolution. As the notion of women's private sphere gained credence over the course of the first half of the century, it came to dominate women's lives in wide-ranging ways.

⚘ CHAPTER 5

Consolidating the Feminine Private

The sixteen-year-old Benjamin Franklin entered the world of publishing in an April 1722 issue of the *New-England Courant* in the guise of Silence Dogood, the widow of a rural clergyman.[1] Informing her readers that before her marriage she had been the ward of her older husband, Silence explained that the clergyman "endeavour'd that I might be instructed in all that Knowledge and Learning which is necessary for our Sex, and deny'd me no Accomplishment that could possibly be attained in a Country Place." Widowed after seven years of marriage during which she bore three children, Silence described herself as "an Enemy to Vice, and a Friend to Vertue," revealing that she had "a natural Inclination to observe and reprove the Faults of others."[2]

When Franklin decided to become an older, single woman canvassing others' failings, he adopted a pose of rhetorical femininity. Subsequent colonial writers were to make a similar choice. Whether or not those authors were in fact female, the topics and contents of their essays reveal much about the developing notion of the feminine private, which was consolidated in the first half of the eighteenth century on both sides of the Anglo-American Atlantic. Authors who presented themselves to the public using female pseudonyms typically wrote about a restricted range of subjects and adopted a limited set of approaches to their topics. They thereby underscored the validity of the observation of the anonymous Englishman who penned the 1737 *Common Sense* essay on women's role: it was "bounded and circumscrib'd," whereas men's realm was "universal, and comprehends every Thing."[3]

But perhaps because Franklin wrote before the outline of the appropriate feminine private sphere was complete or perhaps simply because he was a male teenager of outstanding ability, Silence Dogood addressed topics that, in the long run, would prove to be unusual for a nominally female author. Indeed, Silence herself acknowledged receiving criticism of an essay in which she charged that Harvard students graduated "as great Blockheads as ever, only more proud and self-conceited." A correspondent objected not to the content of the critique, but rather to Silence's boldness in addressing the topic at all. "Ephraim Censorious" contended, she reported, that she should "censure the Vices and Follies of my own Sex, before I venture to meddle with yours." Specifically, Ephraim advised Silence to "let Female Idleness, Ignorance and Folly (which are Vices more peculiar to your Sex than to our's) be the Subject of your Satyrs, but more especially Female Pride, which I think is intollerable." Whether a reader or Franklin himself produced the purported communication is irrelevant, because it emphasized one of the key conventions of rhetorical femininity: female writers should focus their attention primarily on women.[4]

In response, Silence challenged Ephraim's assertions and argued that men were more idle, ignorant, and proud than women. Yet her next essay dealt with female pride, and two others focused on widows and on an old maid seeking a husband—in other words, on topics more obviously aligned with Silence's feminine identity. Although publicly questioning Ephraim's strictures, in short, Franklin complied with his request to take a more conventional approach in some of the Dogood essays.[5]

In so doing he followed a practice set by Richard Steele in the *Tatler,* one not adopted earlier by John Dunton. The Athenian Society never presented its membership other than as all-male, but Steele created "Jenny Distaff," Isaac Bickerstaff's much younger half-sister, to be a rhetorically feminine commentator on her sex.[6] Jenny's inclusion in *Tatler* essays in 1709 presaged the further elaboration of the convention later in the century, but with respect to what became the standard language of the feminine private, Steele and his writing partner, Joseph Addison, were less prescient. They failed to employ *private* as a gendered word despite their oft-stated insistence that women had no place in the exclusively masculine public realm. The two influential authors wrote women out of the *public,* in brief, but did not create a gendered definition of *private.* That task was left to their successors in England and America.

Once Anglo-American men had defined a feminized private realm, women developed its meaning. Others have examined the contours of domestic ideology in England;[7] in this chapter the primary focus is the North American colonies. Not only in rhetorically feminine writings (some of which can be definitively attributed to women), but also in their actions, colonial women elaborated on the feminine sphere even as it was being consolidated. Whereas men equated the *feminine private* with the *domestic* and the *household,* women's own definition expanded to include relationships with their female friends. Large families composed of men, women, children, and male and female servants crammed into small eighteenth-century houses made the notion of a specifically feminine *private domestic sphere* more metaphorical than real. But within those same houses colonial women could and did create feminine spaces, most notably in and around that quintessential place for domestic socializing, the tea table. Both men and women recognized that the tea table was a feminine location, one that women dominated and controlled even when men were present. Accordingly, although households in general were only theoretically feminine, women's creation of tea-table society constituted their own contribution to the construction of the feminine private.

The Emerging Language of the Feminine Private

John Dunton's adoption of the language of the feminine private, initially formulated in 1702 in the context of his commentary on Queen Anne, was ignored by his immediate successors as cultural commentators, Richard Steele and Joseph Addison. Neither man employed the word *private* in the gendered way invented by Dunton. Insistent that women had no place in the public realm, they nevertheless failed to complete the binary by assigning *private* to the female sex. Instead, it took approximately four decades after Dunton published *Petticoat-Government* for the now-familiar dichotomy equating *public* and *men, private* and *women,* to develop fully on both sides of the Anglo-American Atlantic.

In the seventeenth and early eighteenth centuries, English and American authors alike commonly contrasted *public* and *private,* but in ungendered ways. In such traditional usages, the word *private* carried the implication of the individual apart from the whole, of a subject that was or should be concealed rather than generally open to view, of a person or an act not authorized by government, or—most notably in this context—of someone who did not hold political office or of an institution that had no formal relationship with the government. The ungendered usages would persist, but the last two would over time give birth to the gendered *feminine private*. Once the *public* was successfully defined as solely masculine, even a high-status woman could not be classified as an appropriate state actor with political responsibilities. After the adoption of Lockean thought caused the family and the state to be seen as disparate rather than analogous, *private* was utilized to modify *family* with greater frequency. And since women were identified culturally with the family and domesticity, the consequence was the development of the *feminine private*.[8]

Demonstrating the absence of a concept is always difficult, but a promising possibility is to seek places where an idea or a term most likely would have been employed had it been available to an author or speaker. One such location is a 1712 *Spectator* essay by Richard Steele, which used *public* but not *private* when discussing women:

> We have indeed carryed womens Characters too much into publick Life, and you shall see them now A-days affect a sort of Fame: But I cannot help venturing to disoblige them for their service, by telling them, that the utmost of a Woman's Character is contained in Domestick Life; she is Blameable or Praise-worthy according as her carriage affects the House of her Father or her Husband.

Here Steele employed the classic meaning of *public* as *widely known,* as was evident from his reference to "a sort of Fame," and he logically could have used *private* to denote the hidden, household-based opposite of that statement, but he did not. Even someone as committed as he to notions of sexual difference did not have the gendered language of *public* and *private* to draw on in 1712 as he discussed women's lives. A contemporary example on the other side of the Atlantic came from a funeral sermon the Reverend Increase Mather delivered in 1711 for a judge and his wife, who died a few days apart. Mather described the husband's role "in his Publick Capacity," using the meaning for *public* that applied the term to an officeholder with responsibilities to the people. Although he also described the childless wife's activities (for example, showing "Mercy and Charity" to the poor), he did not employ the word *private* with reference to her.[9]

The same absence was evident in a quotation cited earlier, although at first glance it might not appear so. When Joseph Addison wrote in 1711, "the Family is the proper Province for Private Women to Shine in," he was not equating *private* and *domestic;* in the context of a passage denigrating female partisanship, *private* referred to someone who had at most a limited and disinterested public role. In effect, he was observing that women should devote themselves wholeheartedly to their families because they had no formal civic responsibilities. Employing the word in a like manner in 1729, a Philadelphia essayist referred to "many People of both Sexes in their private Capacities." Such remarks show that the standard terminology of *public* and *private* had not by then acquired gendered meanings.[10]

That dichotomy did have other implications, with the latter half of the *public/private* opposition developing a negative inflection, as "Publick good" was contrasted—in one clergyman's words—to *"private selfish views."* The usage was pervasive in the colonies during the first half of the eighteenth century. A New England cleric exhorted his congregation not to advance their own "little private narrow Interests only." A New Yorker warned against political leaders who might "prostitute their *Power* to their own private *Avarice* or *Ambition."* Such rhetoric that universally contrasted *public* and *private* in a political or monetary context consistently favored *public* over *private* and saw the latter as *selfish, little, narrow, avaricious,* and so forth—implications that would carry over into the public/private divide once it became fully gendered. Men could have the interests of the whole society at heart whereas women's concerns came to be seen as *little* or *narrow,* contrary to such community interests. Thus the English authors of the 1737 and 1739 *Common Sense* essays could write readily of "the narrow Limits of Domestick Offices" or "that little Circle of Action" to which women were rightly confined.[11]

The absence of a gendered public/private language did not mean that early-eighteenth-century Anglo-Americans lacked concepts of sexual difference. Quite the contrary: such ideas permeated the *Tatler* and *Spectator.* Addison and Steele presupposed the existence of separate but nominally equal male and female "Natures." Steele, who believed that "there is a Sort of Sex in Souls," insisted that "the Soul of a Man and that of a Woman are made very unlike, according to the Employments for which they are designed." For women, that was "manag[ing] well a great Family"; for men, "execut[ing] a great Employment." Although Steele also indicated that it would be "Partiality" to rank masculine virtue above feminine and asserted that men's minds were "not superior" to women's, he persistently denigrated women while seeming to defer to them. For example, the true nature of his praise for women's "easy Flow of Words" became obvious when his exemplar of feminine talk, "Lady Courtly," earned his acclaim for speaking of fashion "with so excellent an Air and Gesture, that you would have sworn she had learn'd her Action from our *Demosthenes."* The exaggerated tribute made clear his ultimate disdain, since Steele frequently criticized as frivolous and insignificant women's purported focus on fashion and dress in their conversation.[12]

Addison and Steele in the *Spectator* continued the pattern of gender-differentiated commentary established in the *Tatler*. In a July 1711 *Spectator* essay, for instance, Addison discoursed at length on the sexes' "different Inclinations and Endowments." Women were naturally "much more gay and joyous than Men," perhaps because "their Fibres [were] more delicate, and their animal Spirits more light and volatile." Women accordingly needed to seek out men who would "moderate and counter-ballance" that natural volatility. Addison concluded that the best marriages were those in which the husband bore "the main Burden" and the wife employed "all the little Arts of soothing and Blandishment" given her by nature to "chear and animate her Companion." In his vision of the ideal couple, "the Wife grows Wise by the Discourses of the Husband, and the Husband good-humoured by the Conversations of the Wife." Such a balanced marriage, he declared, was "like a Ship that is duly trimmed," needing "neither Sail nor Ballast."[13]

Thus despite the absence of a rhetoric invoking the gendered opposition public/private, Addison and Steele conveyed to their Anglo-American reading audience an understanding of deep and abiding differences between men's and women's natures. Colonists could access such cultural commentary in the 1720s and thereafter not only in *Tatler* and *Spectator*, but also in their weekly newspapers. The *New-England Courant*'s successors in American journalism tended to copy James Franklin's paper rather than its more mundane predecessors. They prominently published didactic essays, many of them deliberate imitations of Addison and Steele, along with such bread-and-butter items as local shipping news, advertisements, and the latest "advices from London." Desperate for attractive literary content, editors throughout the colonies opened their pages to contributions of a variety of sorts, printing works by local authors, essays originally published elsewhere in the American press, and articles from British newspapers and magazines, sometimes properly attributed, sometimes not, and sometimes reportedly forwarded by their readers. The editors all drew on the same pool of publications and information, which led to a remarkable similarity of theme and content in colonial papers generally. The time lag in colonists' usage of current locutions evident in Mistress Knight's 1704 journal dissipated as American editors quickly republished British material and the language of those essays was copied by local writers. Except in unusual circumstances—such as those that enveloped John Peter Zenger in New York in 1734–35—editors did not take sides in local controversies, for they could not afford to alienate any paying customers. In fact, they seem to have published all submissions they regarded as being in good taste. In 1740 and thereafter, largely because of the onset of war with Spain, printers began to emphasize political and military news and opinion, and so the papers included fewer cultural analyses.[14]

Before 1740, though, the newspapers' literary aspirations and the absence of other outlets for such commentary, along with the editors' eclectic choices of material, make their pages an unparalleled source for the ideas circulating among literate colonists and accessible to elite and non-elite Americans alike. Although most colonial newspapers printed no more than six hundred to seven hundred copies of each issue, they had a wide readership. The newspapers were read and discussed in coffeehouses and taverns and passed from hand to hand and household to household, exposing many Americans to a wider world of ideas than had been available to them before the early 1720s. For people whose previous reading would have been largely confined to the Bible, devotional literature, almanacs, and perhaps a conduct book, the essays in the newspapers must have provided revelatory openings to new ways of thinking, in addition to informing them about developments in Europe and elsewhere in America. Aside from the newspapers, colonists would have encountered cultural and moral commentary only in some scattered pamphlets—many originally published in England—and a few locally produced publications such as funeral sermons.[15]

Unlike the *Athenian Mercury,* the *Tatler,* and the *Spectator,* the editors of colonial American newspapers aimed their works at a largely male audience, even though—on the rare occasions they addressed their "fair readers" directly—they acknowledged that women also sometimes perused the papers. Articles about women rarely appeared on the printed page, and topics assumed to be of interest primarily to women (such as child rearing and household management) were largely absent. Instead, editors produced their newspapers for wealthy or middling men, the voters and property owners dominating the colonies' polities and economies. The worldview of such men, reflected in the papers, presupposed the natural superiority of genteel white Protestant men, the necessity of maintaining order in state and household, the importance of protecting private property, and the need to be industrious, frugal, honest, and pious.[16]

Why, it might be asked, were eighteenth-century Britain and America so different in publishers' assessments of their audiences? Surely a key explanation was the editors' accurate assumption that adult colonial women in the 1720s and 1730s were less likely than men either to be literate or to purchase newspapers for their own use. Further, despite the ubiquity of didactic and satirical essays in colonial newspapers, their chief attraction for purchasers must have been the supply of recent political and commercial news from Britain and the European continent. The papers gained their currency from useful information that could not be obtained from local knowledge. That no American magazine (a format limited to cultural commentary) survived more than a year or two before the 1780s supports the conclusion that merchants and professional men with utilitarian goals largely composed the actual as well as the presumed reading audiences for American periodicals.[17]

Colonial newspapers joined the *Tatler* and *Spectator* in the beliefs that men and women differed fundamentally, and that men were superior. Indeed, those beliefs were so unquestioned by the 1720s that they were rarely stated explicitly. Instead, assumptions of sexual difference and male superiority permeated essays on disparate topics. One author in the *New-England Weekly Journal* in 1729 laid out the common way of thinking in an article on women that nominally proclaimed them superior to men because of their natural beauty but that otherwise judged women wanting. He praised "the superiour Greatness of Mens Souls" and men's "greater Strength of Imagination and Memory," as well as their superior ability to concentrate. Such qualities allowed men to "assert our Dominion at all Times," except when they were in the throes of love. Although he averred that he had placed men as "Supream in the Throne of Reason and Fancy...principally to obviate the Charge of Partiality [to women]," the thrust of his argument ran counter to that claim.[18]

The same was true of the well-known pamphlet *Reflections on Courtship and Marriage,* published in America by Benjamin Franklin in 1746. Although the author insisted at the outset that women's perceived deficiencies resulted from their inadequate upbringing rather than their inherent nature, the rest of the text assumed innate feminine inferiority. Women lacked "the requisite Fund of *substantial Worth* to raise the Thought, and touch the Heart; to be an agreeable Companion, and a steady Friend," he declared, alluding to their "little narrow-spirited Way of Thinking," their "low and pitiful Artifices," and their "lurking Sort of Cunning." Admitting that he assumed male superiority in "Knowledge and Understanding," he insisted that men therefore had "a directing Power in the more difficult and important Affairs of Life." In an ideal *"harmonious"* marriage, the writer argued, the husband knew how to control his wife without appearing to do so, and women had to recognize that men "are best capable of directing and judging in the important Concerns."[19]

Many newspapers conveyed messages of gender differentiation, even if they avoided obvious references to sexual superiority and inferiority. A male/female binary, in short, undergirded published colonial discourse about women and men in the early decades of the eighteenth century.[20] As time passed, that male/female binary was increasingly linked to the roles of men and women outside and inside the home, and to the new meanings of the long-standing conceptual binary public/private. A careful examination of the evolution of Anglo-Americans' usage of language in the middle decades of the eighteenth century reveals the trend.

On both sides of the Atlantic in the early 1730s, novel phraseology began to emerge in essays on political and familial topics alike—"Private Life," "private Family"—and those terms became linked to *domestic* and *household*. "Meanwell's" discussion of patriotism, published in the *New-York Gazette* in 1734, observed that "in publick" men talked of patriotism in the same way as "in private Life...a Master of a Family harangue[s] in Praise of Oecon-omy"; in both cases, he remarked, *"Saying and doing are two Things."* By 1737, the anonymous author who penned the *Common Sense* essays on affectation could write that women "should content themselves with the private Care and Oeconomy of their Families, and the diligent Discharge of Domes-tick Duties." For him, *private* modified *care and oeconomy,* which both he and "Meanwell" used in its traditional sense as "the art or science of household management, esp. with regard to expenditure." By the late 1730s, *private* thus was linked to *family* and *domestic* in a way it had not been for Addison and Steele in the early 1710s.[21]

When in 1739 a British author (perhaps the same one who wrote the 1737 comments just quoted) declared that "women risque too much to go out of that little Circle of Action to which Decency has confined them," he con-trasted men's freedom with women's necessary restriction to the household. A woman's "true Eclat is a private Life," he insisted, "and the Oeconomy of a Family her solid Glory." Such language soon became commonplace, as did the explicit opposition between men's roles in *public* and women's in *private.* Thus that same year the author of *Man Superior to Woman* voiced the *public* = government-and-men, *private* = household-and-women equation when he wrote, "Those poor pretty Creatures must make a very sorry Figure in Gov-ernment and publick Offices, who appear so universally unqualified for the Administration of private Oeconomy."[22]

In the following decade, the phraseology began to appear regularly in the colonies. One poet, describing himself as a "Constant Reader and Hum-ble Servant," wrote in 1745 of a woman who "adorns each State of private Life!/A Daughter, Mother, and what's more—a *Wife,*" then went on to de-scribe how that wife, "far from the busy thoughtless World retir'd," and "unconcern'd, can view the Pomp of *State*/And how Men strive, and bustle to be *great." Private life* for women was thus delineated by the successive roles of daughter, wife, and mother; and that *private life* was explicitly conceptual-ized as "retired" from the world, "unconcerned" with politics, and separated from the busier, bustling world of male strivers, a world in which women were observers rather than participants.[23]

Three years later, a reader submitted an article to the *South Carolina Gazette* titled "Offences against Common Sense in the Ladies, particularly Wives," which, like Joseph Addison, warned women against "deviat[ing] into Politicks, or begin[ning] to redden with Party Rage" and proscribed additional topics of conversation. He then described his ideal wife in terms that readers a century later would have found congenial: "Her Life is a just Mixture of domestick Care and innocent Diversion. In the former, she is indefatigably busied in embellishing private Life, and bringing him, whose Felicity is her chief Aim, to look upon her company, and his own Home, a sure *Assylum* from the Noise, Fatigues, and Crosses of the World."[24]

By the late 1740s, therefore, the transition to a novel way of thinking about the relationship of male/female and public/private had been completed on both sides of the Atlantic. Images eventually associated with the nineteenth-century cult of domesticity—the household as a quiet haven from a busy world, the wife as the tireless manager caring for her husband's needs and wants—had entered the Anglo-American lexicon. As the term *private life* came to be newly equated with family and household, the role women traditionally played in that household came to be deemed *private,* a word never previously connected to women in a gendered fashion. The negative implications of *private interests* (as opposed to *public good*) coalesced with notions of the narrow limits of *women's sphere,* as distinguished from men's broader public responsibilities. A newly constructed variant of the long-standing binary opposition public/private, which also had many other guises, was thus mapped onto the male/female binary. The resulting gendered dichotomy had immense staying power and lasting consequences for men and women alike.

The Pose of Rhetorical Femininity

When colonial editors assumed their audience was wholly male, they marginalized females as both readers and contributors. How most colonial women responded to newspaper essays that adopted a uniformly male perspective is unknown. But one female Philadelphian, "C.W.," recorded her reaction to presumptions of universal masculinity in a 1736 commentary in the *American Weekly Mercury* that began: "Tho' I am of the *Female Sex,* yet I am a Constant Reader of *News-Papers.*" C.W. clearly understood that the *Mercury's* editor would see her as unusual in the amount of attention she paid to the press. And surely he found the contents of her essay to be equally unusual.[25]

C.W. explained that she was submitting her essay in response to an article that had appeared not in the *Mercury* but in its competitor, Benjamin Franklin's *Pennsylvania Gazette*. The author of the *Gazette's* recent piece on the character of a good man and the benefits of a social conscience, C.W. complained, had erred in his choice of words. She objected to his repeated references to men's need to aid their "FELLOW-MEN," which omitted "the Assistance of WOMEN." She recommended instead employing the term "MANKIND, which comprehends both Sexes." She concluded that the use of "fellow men" was "a great Indignity done to the FEMALE SEX, obliquely reflecting upon them as Creatures not fit to have a Place or Name amongst MANKIND,—which seems to be a very great Contempt to the Divine Wisdom, who thought fit to Place them on the same Level."

C.W., then, perceived the masculine-inflected language of the article in the *Gazette* as insulting in its omission of women. Her interpretation of the anonymous author's terminology was undoubtedly correct; he had, for example, said of his ideal man that "a generous Ambition glows in his Breast of being a publick and extensive Blessing to the World," the sort of statement never contemporaneously applied to a woman. Even if she reached an incorrect conclusion, however, her essay highlighted the common exclusion of women from the rhetoric of colonial newspapers. And it showed that at least one eighteenth-century American woman regarded that exclusion as "a great Indignity."

Presumably C.W. accepted the notion that politics and the public realm were "out of women's sphere," so—if she chose to read such pieces—articles addressing public policy questions that assumed an exclusively male readership would not have offended her to the same extent as the *Gazette* essay on desirable personal characteristics and the importance of social interactions. But what about a series of articles in a Boston paper in 1728 that discussed the management of household expenses without ever mentioning the role of the wife and mother in such "oeconomy"? Or the many essays that dealt with themes of courtship and marriage solely from a male point of view, by offering suggestions for choosing a wife but neglecting criteria for selecting a husband? Or ubiquitous biting satires about women? The consistently misogynistic views expressed in the newspapers surely had an impact on women other than C.W.[26]

Whereas Dunton's *Athenian Mercury* celebrated its female readers and welcomed contributions from women by its publicly stated attention to women's concerns, colonial newspapers conveyed the opposite message through their overwhelmingly male-oriented content. Yet, even so, some rhetorically feminine authors ventured to contribute essays to the press.

Analysis of such articles—and of the published reactions to them—helps to reveal the boundaries of the newly consolidated feminine private sphere, whether or not the works were actually written by women. Recognizing what a nominal woman could, and could *not,* say publicly in print adds depth to the understanding of the gender definitions established in the middle decades of the eighteenth century. That the barriers between male and female were rigid and unyielding became dramatically evident in an exchange of letters in the *South Carolina Gazette* in early 1732. Even before the adoption of the gendered language of public and private, the dialogue revealed the existence of a rigidly constructed male/female binary.[27]

"Martia," describing herself as a young woman of sixteen who had been raised by "a good Father," responded to the editor's request for correspondence from readers by offering observations on some of her male contemporaries, including her own brother.[28] She commented on "a set of young Gentlemen...whose Concerns in Life particularly require a steady and judicious Conduct" in business transactions and personal behavior. Certainly, she asserted, such conduct was "the very corner Stone of their Building" for anyone who wanted to succeed in the mercantile field. Yet the young men, she charged, displayed too much "Levity" in conversation, which potentially could detract from the "Credit" needed to cultivate their reputations. She hastened to add that she was "a merry Girl" and did not object to "mirth and well-tim'd Humour," but she nevertheless insisted that some of the exchanges the young men viewed as witty could instead have the effect of damaging their good names. She had tried giving them "private Hints" to alter their language, but without success, and so she chose to admonish them publicly in hopes of reforming their behavior.

Martia admitted that her warning perhaps "comes awkwardly from a Female Pen," but she expressed the hope that her identity as a young woman would deflect "too severe Reparties" from those she criticized, for she believed that "none can be so impolite, as to Attack Youth and Beauty in Petticoats, with such improper Weapons." Martia thus tried to use her feminine identity as a shield, but the ploy did not work. Assuming that Martia actually was the young woman she claimed to be—which seems likely, although it is impossible to discover her identity—the "Reparties" she received in response gave her a quick and telling lesson in the rules of rhetorical femininity.

In the *Gazette's* next issue, "Rattle" replied not to Martia but rather to "Miss Martia's Papa," a unique insult. His daughter was quite a "forward Lass," Rattle exclaimed, and she needed to concern herself primarily with her *own* reputation, rather than the young merchants' social standing. A good name was the "*Corner-stone* in the *Fabrick* of the *Fair,*" and once lost, it was gone forever. Likening Martia's reputation also to a building and making an unambiguous, innuendo-laced comment, Rattle declared that "once broke down...it must be an uncommon *Structure* that, after a *successful Attack,* stands whole and tight, beyond *Nine* [months] at most." Instead of venturing to critique the young men, Martia would do better to learn *"the making of a Pudding"* like any "good Housewife." Rattle predicted that her father would find it hard to locate someone to marry the unmanageable young woman.[29]

In her reply Martia showed that she was shocked by the vehemence of Rattle's reaction, despite the concern already evident in her defensive comments about the impoliteness of any attack on "Youth and Beauty in Petticoats." Martia revealed that she had burned two other letters forwarded to her by the *Gazette*'s editor, intending to prevent their publication. Claiming that Rattle had misconstrued her meaning, she declared that she would never repay her father's careful upbringing with "the Guilt of *personal Scandal,*" thus demonstrating that she had no difficulty interpreting Rattle's innuendo. She insisted that Rattle was "not worth my Notice," yet she apologized for the fault she deemed "imaginary." Asking forgiveness from anyone she had offended, she expressed the wish that "the *Example,* in this particular, may be of more Force, than the well meant *Precepts* of *Martia.*" The apology, then, was Martia's legacy, rather than the initial letter daring to criticize her male contemporaries in print. And she would try in the future to avoid giving the least hint of similar behavior.[30]

The replies to Silence Dogood from Ephraim Censorious and to Martia from Rattle highlighted the restrictive conventions of rhetorical femininity, as did the essayists' responses to their critics. Authors who adopted female personas to submit articles to colonial newspapers could address only a limited range of topics, and when they strayed outside such boundaries they encountered stiff opposition. Rattle's attack on Martia far outdid Ephraim Censorious in its highly charged condemnation of Martia's criticism of the youthful Charleston merchants. By analogizing her contribution to the *Gazette* to engaging in illicit sex and by contending that her writing made her a less desirable marriage partner, Rattle dramatically turned the tables on Martia. *She,* not the young men, became the issue; and she, shamed, quickly retreated into silence. Other rhetorically feminine authors never ventured such gambits in the colonial press. Instead, they confined their remarks to subjects thought relevant to women, including courtship, marriage, and household affairs. They, like C.W., also penned responses to published statements they perceived as misogynistic.[31]

Although nearly all editors adopted apolitical stances to avoid antagonizing potential male readers, they appeared unconcerned about alienating

their possible female audience. Remarkably few articles presented a rhetorically feminine viewpoint, even though some authors constructed artificial
male-female dialogues intended to amuse readers. The relative paucity of
submissions from nominal women almost certainly derived from two related
factors: the restricted subject matter allowed to such essayists (why under
most circumstances would a man choose to write as a woman, when selecting a male pseudonym would give him a much wider field to analyze?); and
women's hesitancy to enter publicly a realm implicitly defined as exclusively
male. Only when a woman had a strong motive—for example, responding
to an insulting essay—would she make such a move.[32]

Contributions to colonial newspapers from rhetorical women fell into
two broad categories: essays that introduced a subject relevant to women,
and those that replied to negative characterizations of "the fair sex." Of the
first group, some—almost all of English origin—were overtly satirical, including supposed petitions from groups of single women criticizing "old
bachelors" who resisted marriage, or from "Ladies of Quality" who objected
to Sunday observances that prevented them from attending card games, plays,
and other diversions.[33] Some rhetorical women focused on critiquing their
own (nominal) sex, just as Ephraim Censorious had advised Silence Dogood
to do.[34] Other essays, a few evidently drafted locally, offered complaints of
various sorts about personal relationships with men. Authors employing female pseudonyms expressed grievances about wastrel or unfaithful husbands,
"bashful" or unappealing suitors, or treacherous seducers.[35] Even though such
pieces criticized men, unlike Martia they did so in a customary context. They
did not attack men for their behavior in the company of other men, as she
had, but rather accused them of abusing women. Such charges could legitimately originate with women.

Two poems of English origin in which women protested their lot proved
popular with colonial printers and their readers. "The Lady's Complaint,"
which came from a play first performed in London in 1700, declared,
in part:

Men to new Joys and Conquests fly,
    And yet no Hazard run,
Poor we are left, if we deny,
    And if we yield, undone.
Then equal Laws let Custom find,
    And neither Sex oppress,
More Freedom give to Womankind,
    Or give to Mankind less.

Another, which originally appeared in the *Gentleman's Magazine* in 1733, began:

> How wretched is a *Woman's* Fate,
>> No happy Change her Fortune knows,
> Subject to Man in every State.
>> How can she then be free from Woes?[36]

Both poems elicited verse responses that challenged their premises: to the first, a South Carolina man insisted that all the author needed was "some dear, simple, homely Swain" to ease her mind; to the second, "A Gentleman" countered,

> How happy is a *Woman's* Fate,
> Free from Care, and free from woe,
> Secure of Man in ev'ry State,
> Her Guardian-God below!"

The seemingly radical critiques of women's lives in the newspapers, in short, were quickly offset by replies that would have pleased a culturally conservative audience of male readers. The ultimate message was comforting, not disquieting, and nothing in the press would have shaken colonial men's complacency about the correctness of their relationships with women. Like similar prose pieces, such poetic exchanges were amusing rather than challenging.[37]

Yet a nominally feminine viewpoint could also create an opening for pointed remarks on matters of public concern. Just as the rhetorical femininity of New York "widows" made possible the clever attack on William and Grace Cosby's 1734 hospitality campaign, so too that stance proved fruitful for a critic of the Great Awakening revivals during the following decade. Because the Reverend George Whitefield attracted so many female followers, letters from a rhetorical woman provided an ingenious means of censuring him.

One "Deborah Sherman" twice addressed Thomas Fleet, editor of the *Boston Evening Post* and an opponent of the revival, asking Fleet to "be fair, and print [articles] on both Sides" regarding the controversial preacher. Deborah's letters, though, were astute parodies that underscored how women's enthusiasm for Whitefield wreaked havoc in their households. In the first, she insisted that women were Whitefield's "best Friends, if they fall off all is gone." When St. Paul told women to "keep at home, and mind their

Families," she averred, surely he "did not mean this when dear Mr. *Whitefield* preach'd." Even if Paul had meant to proscribe such devotion, she exclaimed, women would go anywhere to hear Whitefield, even possibly following him back to his Georgia base. Her second letter, welcoming Whitefield's return to Boston after some months away, overflowed with yet more praise. "O, how tedious have been the hours of your Absence!" she gushed; "how dull all the Preaching I have heard!" How she envied the women to whom he had been speaking in the interim! "Methoughts I saw you, as we us'd to do here, leaving Husbands, Children, Family Concerns, and all the vain Cares of life, and crowding after the dear, the heavenly Man, listning to the charming Musick of his Tongue, and drinking in the melodious Sounds." The letters' subtext was unmistakable: Whitefield endangered the maintenance of household order. Left unchecked, he would entice wives away from their duties and threaten ordinary men's control of their families.[38]

Religious leadership, the topic of the Deborah Sherman correspondence, was commonly regarded as "beyond woman's sphere."[39] Yet the picture those letters drew of neglected households abandoned by mistresses who had been lured away by a silver-tongued orator placed the subject firmly within the usual constructs of rhetorical femininity. The adroit lampoons made the author's point subtly, but with humor and more force than a direct approach.

One subject discussed by rhetorical women raised no questions of suitability—and that was women themselves. The ability of women to reply to published observations on their sex was never publicly called into question. Most of the essays that appeared under women's names in the colonial press dealt with three popular topics that regularly aroused comment in newspaper columns: fashion, tea drinking, and courtship or marriage.

For instance, an article titled "A General Review of *Female Fashions* Address'd to the *Ladies*," which was published in two different papers in the early 1730s, elicited a response from "Betty Pert," who, instead of defending such items of clothing as hoop petticoats, declared that if men wanted to criticize women they should "show us the Example first, and reform *your* dress." She made fun of men's wigs; and whereas the essayist had accused women of wearing "masculine" clothing, she charged men with "effeminacy" in their own dress. In short, Betty made it clear that two could play at the game of accusing the other sex of cross-dressing. At the same time, she implicitly confirmed the existence of rigid contemporary gender boundaries.[40]

Confronted with criticisms of women's penchant for drinking tea, authors assuming the guise of rhetorical femininity replied by defending the healthfulness of tea and by contending that men's habit of drinking alcohol was far more damaging to individuals and society. Many an exchange on the topic appeared more contrived than real, presented (as one editor put it) "in hopes it [might] prove diverting" to readers. Take, for example, the letter from "Amy Prudent" in the *American Weekly Mercury* in 1729. Amy, claiming to speak for the twenty wives of members of a punch-drinking men's club, complained of their habits; the men responded by attacking "the noxious streams of that Paralytick Herb, [which] create Disorders in the Brain and Nerves." Two years later in New York, "Suckey Goodtaste" rejected any deprecation of "such pleasant and delightful Amusements" and insisted that "if you would complain against Drink, let it be against such Liquor whose spiritous Fumes intoxicate the Brain." Undoubtedly these humorous charges and countercharges indeed amused colonial newspapers' readership.[41]

In contrast to the dialogues on tea (or punch) drinking, published interactions on courtship and marriage appear more genuine and highly charged. In early 1731, the Philadelphian Elizabeth Magawlay, writing as "Generosa" in the *American Weekly Mercury,* challenged the "groundless" charge that most women preferred *"Fools and Coxcombs"* to men of character and intelligence. Magawlay insisted that only "Coquets and Romps" liked coxcombs, asserting that "Women of Sense" instead favored men of their own caliber. They toyed with "Fops and Fools" only from "meer Necessity," because most men failed to recognize the value of conversing with intelligent women. She thus turned the critic's comments back on himself: any fault lay with men, who lacked the "Courage" to deal with women who were not "their imaginary Goddesses."[42]

Another woman—"Andromache"—responded with a similarly heated letter in 1737 when the *Virginia Gazette* reprinted a variant of Benjamin Franklin's "Rules and Maxims for Promoting Matrimonial Happiness," which had originally appeared in Franklin's own *Pennsylvania Gazette* in 1730. Franklin's "maxims" included admonitions to women not to manipulate their suitors or husbands; to remember that their husbands were men, not angels; and to avoid arguing with their spouses. "Study his Temper, regulate your own,... sooth his Cares, and by no Means disclose his Imperfections.... Read often the Matrimonial Service, and overlook not the Important Word OBEY," Franklin advised, recommending that women always wear their wedding rings and look at them frequently to remind themselves of their duties.[43]

Andromache's commentary revealed that she regarded the "maxims" as "animadversions on the FAIR SEX." She thought it "hard" that women "should be attacked with a Weapon we are unacquainted with (I mean the Pen)," and she insisted that every woman understood her duties without looking at her wedding ring. Sarcastically exclaiming that the author's "Genius" was so superior to Addison and Steele's that their essays would now be deemed "trifling," Andromache offered an adroit riposte: the author had in effect admitted that women "have the greater Share of Sense" because he believed that they could readily manipulate their husbands. She suggested that the author should admonish other men, "for I don't doubt but the Cox-comb, the Indolent, and the Sloven, may be met with among his, as well as the Cockquett, the Gossip, and the Slattern, may be found among our Sex." *Her* maxim, she declared, was that "a good Husband makes a good Wife," and that "where the Head is furnish'd with Prudence, the other Part of the Body can't fail of being happy." Accordingly she, like Generosa a few years earlier, defended women not only by rejecting critical comments but also by turning the arguments around to offer a negative appraisal of men. If good husbands produced good wives, then a poor wife should not be blamed for her evident failings: her husband bore the ultimate responsibility for those.[44]

Contributions to the press like Andromache's, though serious and seem-ingly deeply felt, nonetheless fell into the pattern of the amusing and fre-quently artificial exchanges on such topics as fashion and tea drinking. Critiques of coxcombs and coquettes were common and often exaggerated for effect; regular newspaper readers would have seen many of them over the years. Why only a few of those elicited a response is unknown and unknow-able, except in the case of the dialogues contrived by James Franklin and other printers such as his brother Benjamin. Similarly, why some offensive essays—such as one from 1730 that advised men to choose a wife who was "tame" and "helpless" and "thinks herself overpaid by any little Return of Kindness from her Master"—did *not* provoke published reactions is equally mysterious. However stylized and erratic, though, the exchanges on women in the colonial press helped to produce the cultural construction of the eighteenth-century feminine private and to outline the perceived parameters of women's lives.[45]

Those dialogues made it clear that women should confine their attention to the narrow range of topics and concerns defined as feminine in nature: personal relationships with friends and family, household affairs, and the con-sumption of certain gendered items like women's clothing and tea. If other subjects could be made relevant to that limited list (as George Whitefield's appeal to women became a cautionary tale about neglected family respon-sibilities), then public commentary from women would pass unnoticed. But venturing onto men's turf without such a justification was forbidden, as Mar-tia learned when she dared to publicly chastise a group of young Charleston merchants for their levity. Any topic seen as beyond woman's sphere, not just politics, was off limits in public discourse.

Creating a Space for the Feminine Private

The first houses in seventeenth-century America were small and simple, with just one or two rooms on the ground floor and a "chamber" or two above, under the roof.[46] Colonists, logically enough, tended to construct homes that resembled those in the disparate regions from which they had emigrated, and by the end of the century local American variants had begun to emerge. Specific forms varied from place to place along the Atlantic coast, but all resembled each other in limited size and the basic arrangement of rooms. Even though by the mid-eighteenth century some colonists acquired considerable wealth, the finest American homes never matched their British counterparts in dimensions or opulence.

In such small colonial houses, women's and men's lives intermingled of necessity. Sometimes the master and mistress slept on a bed (with or without curtains) in the same room used for cooking and eating, which was known as the hall. Young children and servants might sleep on trundle beds nearby or in the chambers overhead. The second room, usually termed the parlor, was also a possible site for the best bed, along with whatever better furniture or other items for display the family might possess. In homes with two ground-floor rooms, the parlor served as the location for more formal socializing and for some family privacy while servants, slaves, or laborers worked in the hall. Such houses continued to be built and inhabited throughout the seventeenth and eighteenth centuries, but in the late seventeenth century and thereafter some colonists expanded their homes, adding rooms on both the first and second floors.[47]

In that process in New England, kitchens were moved to lean-tos at the back of the house. Alternatively, the hall might become more or less exclusively a kitchen, thus separating cooking activities and smells from a space devoted to other work and socializing, and partially dividing men's and women's work spaces. That development occurred even more dramatically in the Chesapeake, where kitchens migrated to new, small buildings located some distance from the main house. The move helped to prevent the dangers of fire as well as rendering the house cooler in the heat of southern summers, but it also notably relocated a major work space inhabited primarily by female subordinates, at the same time as enslaved people of African descent were replacing English indentured servants on Chesapeake farms.

By the early eighteenth century up and down the American Atlantic seaboard, larger houses with four or more ground-floor rooms (each often with a chamber above) began to be constructed in towns and some rural areas as well. Many such homes had central or side hallways, so that residents could access

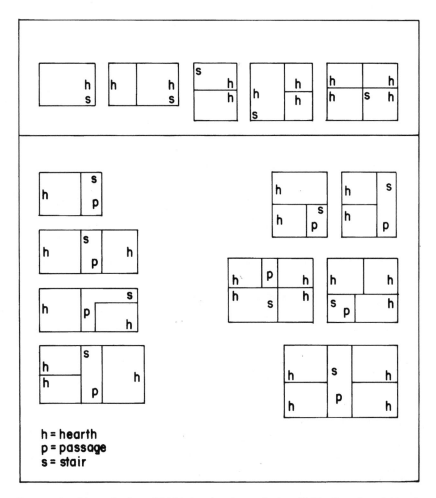

FIGURE 5.1. Schematic plans of British-American houses in the mid-Atlantic region, eighteenth century. The introduction of stair hallways allowed for a wide variety of arrangements and rooms with specialized uses. Kitchens and other service areas might have been placed in wings, separate buildings, cellars, or the rooms located away from spaces used for formal entertaining. The layout of rooms on the second level ("chambers") most often mimicked that of the floor below. From Bernard L. Herman, *Architecture and Rural Life in Central Delaware, 1700–1900* (Knoxville: University of Tennessee Press, 1987), 27. Courtesy of Bernard L. Herman.

rooms in the rear of the building without going through those in the front. Yet not all these rooms were used year-round. The central hallway served in the Chesapeake as an open passageway for cooling breezes during the summers. Such hallways were increasingly inhabited as hot-weather living spaces by southern gentry families. Concomitantly, in cold weather New Englanders congregated in just a few rooms so they would not have to maintain fires throughout the house.

As the number of rooms expanded, their functions became more differentiated. Wealthy or learned men, for example, acquired offices or studies. The bedroom of the master and mistress became only that instead of a room with multiple purposes; it was used primarily for sleeping or possibly for entertaining intimate friends. Socializing in larger groups occurred in rooms designed specifically with that end in mind.[48] Yet except for the kitchen, which would have been largely off-limits to men other than male servants or slaves engaging in heavy labor of some sort, few or none of these homes contained spaces exclusively for women's use. Accordingly, although Anglo-American culture by the 1740s defined the household as *feminine* and *private,* in actuality it was neither. The mistress of a household shared her bedroom with her husband; and daughters would have shared bedrooms with each other, perhaps with their brothers while the children were young. Then, too, living spaces changed in function because of seasonal crowding in northern winters or southern summers. Only in widowhood or if she did not marry would a woman have a space she could regard as hers alone.[49]

One pious wife in Newport, Rhode Island, Sarah Haggar Osborn, found a solution to this problem. In 1767, she reported to a friend that after her husband rose in the morning, she proceeded "to Make my bed my closet, curtains drawd Except Just to Let in Light. I do not Lie there but turn upon my knees my stomach soported with bolster and Pillows, and I am thus securd from the inclemency of all Seasons and from all interruptions from family affairs. There I read and write almost Every thing of a religious Nature."[50]

The word *closet* referred to small, private spaces used by colonial women or men for quiet reflection and writing, and other eighteenth-century women possibly used curtained beds in the same way. If women had an available room, or if—like Sarah Osborn—they were able to improvise such spaces, they would have had places to retreat from their busy households. But even if they could not find solitude, colonial women could create a private space for themselves and their friends around that feminized object, the tea table.[51]

Tea was first introduced to England on a large scale after Charles II's 1662 marriage to Catherine of Braganza, the Portuguese princess who brought Bombay as part of her dowry. The beverage became fashionable, but tea was not linked culturally to women for several decades. As early as the 1690s, though, Englishwomen began meeting to drink tea around six o'clock in the evening, at the same time their menfolk were conducting business in coffeehouses. In the early eighteenth century, the trope of tea-drinking women at home was employed in literature and art to balance the image of coffee- or ale-drinking men at coffeehouses or taverns. References to women's tea-table conversations filled the *Spectator.* By the early 1720s, satires on tea-drinking themes appeared in American newspapers. Still, it was not until the 1730s that the rise of direct trade between England and India increased the supply of tea significantly. The previously high price of tea dropped, making the beverage affordable for all, rather than just the wealthy. By 1747, one elite New Englander was complaining that even *"Maids* and *Washer-Women* follow this *polite* Custom, and every common Jilt treats with Tea."[52]

Drinking tea involved far more than simply making and imbibing a hot, stimulating beverage. Doing so properly required not only a kettle to heat the water, a pot to brew the tea, and the tea itself (with a canister for storage), but also the appropriate utensils. A full tea service included containers for sugar and milk or cream, sugar tongs, perhaps a tea strainer, a slop bowl (into which the dregs of a cup could be poured before a fresh cup was served), and of course the cups and saucers themselves. Fashionable teacups had no handles and were referred to as "dishes"—thus, one drank a dish of tea. Teapots and sugar bowls could be silver or ceramic; blue and white porcelain seems to have been especially popular. The tea equipage could sit on a tea board placed on another, larger table or, preferably, on the iconic round or rectangular tea table. Clearly, not every woman who served tea to her friends, especially those who lived in ordinary small houses, had all that equipment.[53]

Still, probate inventories and similar records demonstrate that the emphasis on tea drinking in the American press by the 1730s was not misplaced. The 1720s were the crucial decade marking the appearance in colonial inventories of new tableware at all economic levels—knives, forks, and glassware in addition to tea equipment, which implies increased use of the home for socializing over food and drink. In rural Massachusetts and Connecticut alike, tea boards and tea tables first appeared in lists of decedents' property in the 1730s, followed later by teapots and storage devices such as chests and canisters.[54]

Various contemporary sources attest to American women's love of drinking tea. In 1748, a foreign traveler commented that tea "is drunk here in the morning and afternoon, especially by women, and is so common at present that there is hardly a farmer's wife or a poor woman who does not drink tea in the morning." Women's diaries recounted numerous meetings with female friends for tea, and surely many men who traveled to England brought tea back as a gift for their wives. Women expected tea to be served using the appropriate utensils and ingredients. One New Englander, eating breakfast at a house where she was lodging for a few nights, later described to her sister the inadequate service: "a large Square pine table some Bohea tea on it, Sugar Near the Colour of Mollasses, the Water Boil'd in a porridge pot & laded out, pewter spoons the Colour of led." Clearly, she regarded everything about that experience as wrong, except perhaps the Bohea tea itself: a large, rough, square table and brown (rather than white) sugar, along with the absence of a kettle, teapot, and silver spoons, added up to an experience that was decidedly déclassé. That she wrote that description nearly six weeks after the breakfast in question suggests how inappropriate—and noteworthy—she had found it to be.[55]

So in the 1780s, when loyalist refugee women presented claims to a British commission established to compensate them for property confiscated by the rebels, they recounted the loss of such obviously beloved objects as "1 compleat set blue and white Tea and Table China"; "a Silver Tea Pot, Sugar Bason"; "Mahogany Dining Tables, Tea Tables"; and "1 Japan Tea Board." The wife of a baker from Charleston, South Carolina, lost a set of tea china and several tables on which she might have used it; a carpenter's wife from Manhattan lost two brass kettles, eighteen cups and saucers, and a silver milk pot; even a poor farming household listed losses of two "puter Basons" and "1 tea pot." Among the most extensive claims for tea-related items came from the widow of a wealthy landowner who had lived near Saratoga, New York; she told the commission she had lost a large mahogany tea table with mahogany chairs, a full set of china, four tea trays, and "One large Tea Urn Silver top and Mahogany stand." She would have entertained a great many acquaintances had she used all those possessions at once.[56]

When the Philadelphian Hannah Callender married Sammy Sansom in 1762 and they moved into their new home, Hannah recorded in her diary that she placed the mahogany tea table in the front parlor. In so doing she mimicked the choice of most of her contemporaries, judging by probate inventories that listed items room by room and by other descriptions of the placement of tea tables. Even when the term *parlor* was not employed by estate appraisers, being replaced by "lower room" and the like, the descriptions of the furniture and other objects in the rooms with tea tables made it clear that those rooms were, for the most part, designed for entertaining. The inventories also indicate that tea equipage commonly sat out on the tables. Thus, for example, the 1750s appraisal of the estate of Samuel White of Brookline, Massachusetts, showed, in the "East lower room," a tea table, kettle, teapot, and cups and saucers, along with a mirror, two other tables, and twelve chairs. Some inventories placed tea tables in rooms (on lower or upper floors) that also contained beds. Presumably, women entertained only their closest female friends in such contexts.[57]

Tea tables themselves were often quite small, and a proper tea service would take up much of the surface area. The hostess would sit in a chair somewhat offset from the table and serve her guests individually from the tea equipage prominently displayed there for all to admire. With the hostess thus occupying that dominant position, the visitors would sit or stand in various locations around the room. The person pouring the tea (slowly and carefully, so as not to shatter the fragile porcelain cups with hot liquid) was not always the oldest woman of the house; it might be her daughter, or, in the case of a postwedding ritual described in 1753 by Grace Growden Galloway, it might be a female friend. Galloway, who decried the "ceremonious farse" she was obligated to observe in Philadelphia, informed her sister that after her wedding she had to stay home for a month to receive female guests every afternoon. She had to wear a white satin gown and behave with great formality at all times. Meanwhile, the maid of honor from her wedding came each day "to make Tea & entertain the company & after Tea to put Up large peices of Cake in white paper which is handed to every Lady after Tea." After the month was over, Grace would "by the Laws of Politness" return the visits, and her ordeal—for she saw it as such—would at last be finished.[58]

Regardless of where they placed their tea tables or how they served the tea, women would surely have agreed with "Fidelia" (Hannah Griffits), a Philadelphia poet, who at some time in the mid-eighteenth century penned the following lines on tea "extempore":

Blest Leaf whose aromatic Gales dispence,
To Men, Politeness, & to Ladies Sense
Gay Wit, Good-Nature, circulate with thee,
Doctors & Misers, only rail at Tea.

Griffits's poem decried tea's critics and praised not only the "Blest Leaf" with "aromatic Gales" itself, but also the "Gay Wit" and "Good-Nature" the drink promoted—the "Sense" it brought to women, the "Politeness" it brought to men fortunate enough to be included in the sociability of the tea table. Yet first and foremost, the tea table was women's private space, and as such it was celebrated (by women) and satirized (by men).[59]

Male wits attacked the tea table with gusto. Even though Richard Steele, one of their models, had written in an early number of the *Spectator* that it would be his "greatest Glory" if his essays became the topic of *"Tea-Table Talk"* among "reasonable Women," Anglo-American moralists mercilessly satirized women's tea-table conversations, finding in them no redeeming qualities. One British poet visualized "Our Madam o'er her Ev'ning-Tea; / Surrounded with her noisy Clans / Of Prudes, Coquets, and Harridans," with the resulting talk consisting of "Inuendo's, Hints and Slander's, / Their Meanings lew'd, and double Entanders."[60]

FIGURE 5.2. "The Tea-Table," a British satirical engraving, undated but c. mid-eighteenth century, John Bowles, London. A group of well-dressed ladies sit at a tea table, gossiping, as two men eavesdrop at the window. The long caption below decries the setting and the talk: "Chief Seat of Slander! Ever there we see, / Thick Scandal circulate with right Bohea." The book open on the table is labeled "Chit-Chat," and a demon hides at the feet of the lady on the right. At the left rear, Envy chases Truth and Justice out of the room. Courtesy of the Lewis Walpole Library, Yale University.

Others wrote of "the insipid *Tittle Tattle* of a *Tea Table,*" of "Ladies…at a Tea Table emploied in their usual Business of Scandal and Detraction," or how—once fashions and household matters had been disposed of—at a tea table "it is very well if you escape hearing a long roll of your Neighbour's Faults, which either are not true, or if so would better be buried in Silence." One essay of English origin, reprinted twice in the colonies, insisted that women who agreed on little else at the tea table concurred in "the vile Practice of *Slander.*" For his part, a Rhode Islander declared that if gossip were banned, "a Company of Females at a Tea Table, would look like so many fair China Statues, as dumb, dull and unactive as their Cups and Saucers."[61]

Benjamin Franklin took particular aim at tea tables and their aura of extravagance and slander in three clever satires in the *Pennsylvania Gazette* in the early 1730s. His alter ego Anthony Afterwit, "an honest Tradesman," reported that his wife's "strong Inclination to be a *Gentlewoman*" had led her to insist on buying a fashionable mirror and several tables and chairs, including a tea table "with all its Appurtenances of *China* and *Silver,*" so that she could entertain her visiting female friends. When he realized that her purchases were sending him into debt, he took the opportunity of her prolonged absence to exchange all those objects for more useful items. Anthony replaced the tea table with a spinning wheel, following Franklin's lead in real life: Benjamin gave his sister Jane such a wheel as a wedding present instead of a tea table, because "the character of a good housewife was far preferable to that of being only a pretty gentlewoman."[62]

Later Franklin wrote as "Alice Addertongue," describing her role as a purveyor of gossip. A "young Girl" of thirty-five who lived with her mother in Philadelphia, Alice declared that she tried to censure someone each day as her contribution to the public, for "none ought to have a greater Share of Reputation than they really deserve." Her devotion to slander led to a split with her mother: "we parted Tea-Table, and I concluded to entertain my Acquaintance in the Kitchin." She spread scandal but her mother did not, so her mother's guests became bored, subsequently joining her in the kitchen. Eventually her mother moved as well, and their tea table was once again united by scandalous talk. In the third essay, which appeared in May 1733, Franklin admitted that tea had some merit, for "Patience Teacraft" described how she had reformed her hard-drinking, gambling-addicted husband by brewing him repeated cups of "good strong Tea."[63]

On one occasion a rhetorically feminine author attacked tea-table talk in the guise of defending it, just as "Deborah Sherman" had criticized George Whitefield while seeming to praise him. "Penelope Aspen," a correspondent of the *South Carolina Gazette,* wrote to complain when the editor insisted that women should seldom speak in company. She exclaimed in response, "What! debar us from those sweet Topicks of Conversation, *Dress,* and *Fashions,* and the dear delightful Satisfaction of railing at our Neighbours? Fie upon ye, even *Addison* himself were he here, dared not to have said so much." After nodding to those who charged that men gossiped as much as women, and suggesting that the editor should criticize men too, Penelope offered unusual reasoning to support her request: women did not appreciate the "Encroachments" of "those mimick Tattlers in Breeches." She called on men to acknowledge women's supremacy as gossipers and to "secure to Us the sole Property of exercising this our antient Prerogative of the *Tea-Table*." The satire thus went a step further than most, while remaining consistent in its portrayal of gossip and tea tables as exclusively feminine.[64]

Of course, that image was in many ways inaccurate. Women's and men's diary entries show that the two sexes often drank tea together and discussed a variety of topics in that context.[65] Yet the parodies expressed a larger truth: tea tables, whether peopled by women alone or by men and women together, *were* governed by women. The hostess or her female surrogate presided over the event and directed the flow of conversation. Susan Stabile has termed this the "gynecocracy of the tea table" and has emphasized that women's talk "broke the masculine monopoly on cultural representation." Women understood tea-table rituals whereas men could feel out of place and confused in such a female-dominated setting. That, at least, was the message of a purported 1729 statement by young tradesmen in Philadelphia (or New York, where it was republished two years later, with appropriate emendations). The "young men" revealed that they sought wives of their own rank but were unacquainted with "the Politeness of Assemblies" and consequently felt "excessively awkward and rediculous" in the company of women who seemed to be of higher status than they. They explained that they could not distinguish between green and Bohea tea and that they did not truly like the beverage, "besides which there are great Variety of Utensils belonging to the Tea-Equipage which your Petitioners despair of ever learning the Name and Use of." Without assistance, they complained, they despaired of ever being able to see past the "China-ware" on the tea table and to identify appropriate partners for themselves.[66]

Dr. Alexander Hamilton, a Scots physician who had settled in Annapolis, Maryland, remarked in the 1750s that "among the fair Sex, ceremony is a mighty favorite." And among the ceremonies he cited, drinking tea stood out for its importance. "A lady displays a great deal of benevolence in deigning to visit another lady, as she pays her a decent respect, and puts her upon an equality with herself, by discoursing over a dish of tea with her, on an Infinity of triffles," Hamilton observed. Even if "there be not real friendship,... yet the keeping up the form and Ceremony of going to see one another, turn about, shows a benevolence and respect." His insightful cultural commentary revealed the probable dynamics of the afternoon tea parties hosted in 1734 by Grace Cosby in New York: the intimacy implied by invitations from the governor's wife would have been hard to resist for any woman less determined to maintain political neutrality than Abigaill Franks.[67]

Yet most such occasions attended by women were not so ceremonious or contrived. One of the best sources for uncovering women's own attitudes toward tea-table socializing is the diary of Hannah Callender, later Sansom, especially during the period before her marriage, because she often wrote not only about whom she saw but also about what they discussed and how she felt about their relationship. One such person was Caty Howel, "the Friend of my Youth, with whome I have passed many happy Hours." After one evening at Caty's, "none but she and I," Hannah wrote, "'the conversation of a friend brightens the eyes' a pretty metaphor." Another night at Caty's, the two of them and a third woman drank tea and had "a good deal of conversation concerning some matches." Among other topics, they discussed "popes opinion Every Woman is a Rake at heart." Hannah signaled her awareness of the common cultural constructions of such sessions when she commented one winter afternoon that she, Caty, and two other women had "talked of the Gentry of the Town, yet twas not 'in Scandel over the Tea,' no base Innuendues hinted at, but the true desighn of Conversation, was endeavoured at, mutual Pleasure. we talked of Authers." Yet on other occasions it is clear that local scandals were indeed the topics of tea-table talk: after she and her mother had tea with a neighbor, she wrote, "some talk on keeping [of mistresses], a wretched instance of it in there next Neigh: a man of credit till caught by that bait of Saten, the fear of being shackled for life." And following afternoon tea with two women and an evening with a third, she once penned without further explanation: "those men are encroachers. 'tis hardly possible for Girls to be too careful of there Company. There are so many of the Sex that lead a life of repentance, for the neglect of this Caution." The obvious implication was that at a tea table the women had exchanged information about men with dubious reputations.[68]

A cynic might contrast such accounts of actual tea-table scandalous talk, in which women usefully informed each other about untrustworthy men, to men's accounts of such conversations (in which the subjects always seemed to be trivia or other women), and conclude that male moralists' primary aim was to prevent women from communicating key pieces of information to each other outside the presence of men.

The often-reprinted "Letter to a Very Young Lady on her Marriage," by Jonathan Swift, advised a new wife in no uncertain terms to avoid the company of other women, even those of higher rank. Indeed, he warned, such high-status women might well lead her to "Foppery, Affectation, Vanity, Folly or Vice." At most, she would need six female friends, whom she could see twice a year. "Your Company at home should consist of Men rather than Women," he averred, observing, "I never yet knew a tollerable Woman to be fond of her own Sex." It went almost without saying that her husband should choose her male companions; she certainly should not follow her female friends' lead. Swift acknowledged that a "mixt and well Chosen" group of men and women could engage in "an intercourse of Civillity and good Will," which could make for congenial and informative conversation. But, by contrast, "a knot of Ladies got together by themselves, is a very School of Impertinence and Detraction," and participation in such gatherings should always be avoided.[69]

Swift declared that women *should* not have female friends; other eighteenth-century men insisted that women *could* not experience friendship among themselves comparable to that which men commonly enjoyed with each other. One Mr. Ewing, a tutor at the College of New Jersey in the 1750s, had the misfortune to say as much to Esther Edwards Burr, wife of the college's president, when he offered the opinion that women *"were hardly capable of anything so cool and rational as friendship."* In recounting the incident in a letter to her close friend, Sarah Prince, Esther revealed that she had "talked him quite silent." She wrote: "My Tongue, you know, hangs pretty loose, thoughts Crouded in—so I sputtered away for dear life" and "retorted several severe things upon him before he had time to speak again." Yet he did not give ground in the hour-long dispute, Esther reported. In the end, he simply "got up and . . . went off."[70]

Unknown to Mr. Ewing, on the previous day Annis Boudinot, Esther's youthful local admirer, had handed her a poem lauding their relationship as "above the treasures of the Main." "Burrissa Oh my soul aspires / And clames a kin with yours," Annis exclaimed; "When first I knew thy Heavenly Mind / I felt the sacred Flame / [Of] Friendship rising in my Brest." Commenting on the verse, Esther modestly informed Sarah that Annis's regard for her was "overgrown" and "absurd," but she was obviously pleased with the praise. Less than twenty-four hours later, she was not prepared to let a tutor inform her that she could not enjoy close relationships with other women.[71]

Manuscript collections of eighteenth-century American families include not only correspondence among male and female family members, but also many letters that passed between female friends like Esther and Sarah, ranging in age from teenagers to adults. Women's correspondence from the 1760s contains such deeply felt declarations of mutual affection as the following: "What would I not give just now, for an hours sweet conversation [with you]"; "[when I read your most recent letter] tears of heart felt joy and satisfaction dim'd my eyes and [I felt] expressions of Love and admiration at the condvencion, constancy and tenderness of my dear Nancy's Friendship"; "I look upon my thoughts as Safe in the Breast of my Friend as my own and upon that Consideration Shall Give you my opinion with out Reserve"; and "I know the Pleasure you give your Friends is not to be express'd by words, but why should it burst forth in Tears and yet I declare you never do or say a kind thing but it has that effect."[72]

Befriending other women was a high priority for the South Carolinian Eliza Lucas Pinckney, who, when she listed a set of "resolutions" to guide her future behavior, included—along with being a good wife, mother, and sister—"I am resolved to be a sincere and faithful friend." After one of her female friends fell victim to insanity, she recalled with a sharp sense of loss her friend's once "cheerful temper, good sence, natural and pleasing vivacity" and lamented no longer being able to experience their "many happy times" together. Likewise, when Esther Burr died of smallpox in the prime of life, Sarah Prince was nearly inconsolable. "My whole dependance for Comfort in this World [is] gone," Sarah wrote in her personal book of meditations. Esther "was dear to me as the Apple of my Eye—she knew and felt all my Griefs.... she was made for a Refin'd Friend. How faithfull? how sincere? how Open hearted? how Tender how carefull how disinterested—And *she was mine!* O the tenderness which tied our hearts!"[73]

In forging and maintaining such friendships with each other in violation of the strictures propounded by male cultural arbiters, eighteenth-century American women created an important component of the developing feminine private sphere, a virtual space for themselves that was even more important than were the evanescent actual spaces they could occasionally craft in their houses or around tea tables. Whereas men insisted that women always subordinate themselves to fathers and husbands and follow men's directions throughout their lives, women recognized that intimate relationships with other women offered them necessary support in a male-dominated world. They deliberately cultivated such relationships, regardless of whether their female friends lived nearby (as did the Philadelphians Caty Howel and Hannah Callender) or far away (like Esther Burr in Princeton and Sarah Prince in Boston).

Men characterized eighteenth-century women's domestic roles as *little* and *narrow,* and indeed they could well have been such—had women fully accepted men's definitions. But they did not. Even in the unwelcoming, overtly hostile pages of colonial newspapers, rhetorical women (many of whom were surely actual women) defended their sex's intellectual abilities and cultural interests. While men sought to confine the *private* to the household, Anglo-American women expanded that concept to include their female friends, rejecting the limits men tried to impose on them. They developed a key cultural institution—the tea table—which they controlled and to which men were awkward intruders. After the mid-1760s, when tea gained explosive symbolic significance in the aftermath of the Townsend Duties (1767) and Tea Act (1773), that beverage and the female networks it created ironically thrust colonial women into the very sort of public role from which men had long attempted to exclude them, for women organized effective boycotts of the beverage identified with them. Soon after the *public = male, private = female* divide had been fully developed, in brief, events worked to break down those gendered barriers, and colonial women for a time assumed the role of state actors.

Conclusion

Defining "Women"

Before approximately 1700, ordinary female Anglo-Americans were likely to be thought of—and to think of themselves—not as a single group denominated *women,* but rather in a series of different roles, primarily defined by a sequence of family relationships: maid, wife, mother, widow, and the like. Female aristocrats of any age or marital status, for their part, were commonly lumped together as "gentlewomen," an indication that for them rank generally took precedence over other determinants of social standing. Thus the early 1640s petitioners to Parliament termed themselves "gentle-women and trades-men's wives," "trades-mens wives and widdowes," or stated, in the longest such self-description: "some of us have husbands, others none, some are poore trades mens wives, and widdowes, and others handicraft trades mens wives and widdows, most of us have many children and servants." Even when the titles of the documents identified the supplicants as *women,* the petitioners went on to describe themselves in considerable detail by their familial and marital statuses.[1]

Such terminology also abounds in seventeenth-century conduct books. Take, for example, Hannah Woolley's 1673 guide, *The Gentlewoman's Companion,* which despite its title was aimed at women of somewhat lesser rank than the aristocracy. It outlined in a lengthy subtitle the various roles women were expected to fulfill: "Children to Parents. Scholars to Governours. Single to Servants. Virgins to Suitors. Married to Husbands. Huswifes to the

House. Mistresses to Servants. Mothers to Children. Widows to the World." Woolley then summed up: "the whole being an exact Rule for the Female Sex in General." She clearly regarded it as impossible to prepare "an exact Rule" for her readers without specifying distinct aspects of their lives, for the "whole" required attention to the individual parts. Likewise, Richard Allestree's popular *The Ladies Calling,* also published in 1673, had two sections: the first described general desirable qualities, the second was divided by roles: virgins, wives, widows. A three-volume compilation, *The Ladies Library,* which appeared early in the eighteenth century, followed a similar pattern: the second volume detailed the successive duties of daughter, wife, mother, widow.[2]

What was true in England was true in the colonies as well. Cotton Mather's *Ornaments for the Daughters of Zion* (1692), the first American-authored conduct book for women, adopted the same formulaic organizational scheme as its English predecessors. After a general introductory section, Mather laid out prescriptions for the behavior of "vertuous" maids, wives, mothers, and widows. Eliza Lucas Pinckney, born in Antigua in 1722, continued in that traditional vein when in the "resolutions" she drafted during the 1740s to guide her future conduct she outlined "the several Stations wherein Providence has placed me." In order, those were wife, child (of her mother), mother, sister, mistress of servants (by which she meant slaves), and friend. It did not appear to occur to her to write of the need to be a good *woman.*[3]

Eliza Lucas's birth date, 1722, placed her on the cusp of change in eighteenth-century gender definitions: after Richard Steele and Joseph Addison had laid out guidelines for female Anglo-Americans, but before those definitions had been fully consolidated or incorporated into Anglo-Americans' worldview. Her list resembled works by her seventeenth-century predecessors more than those by her eighteenth-century successors. For Eliza in young adulthood, as for Hannah Woolley, no single rule would suffice for "the Female Sex in General." Eliza Pinckney found it impossible to think of one set of maxims that would cover every aspect of her life. Each of her responsibilities had to be defined and listed separately.

Yet even during Eliza Pinckney's lifetime—and indeed later in her own prose—the terminology shifted. Novel conceptualizations of gender difference constituted integral parts of broader cultural developments that straddled the last decades of the seventeenth century and the first decades of the eighteenth. As political thought moved from a familial to a contractual model, as commercial capitalism took hold in the English economy, and as new ways of understanding the human body were adopted, the categorization of males and females was also transformed. Although the changes are subtle, it is possible to trace them in Americans' published and unpublished writings during the period from 1700 to 1760.[4]

One way to establish a baseline for systematic comparison of seventeenth- and eighteenth-century linguistic practice is to begin by consulting the works of the New England poet Anne Bradstreet. Her large corpus of published verses provides unparalleled access to the mind of an educated woman who lived through much of the seventeenth century and who wrote poetry that often (though not always) focused on household, husband, children, grand-children, and the like. What words did Bradstreet employ to describe herself and other females? A concordance to her complete works answers that question. She most commonly used *mother(s)* (63 times), less frequently *daughter(s)* (34) and *wife* or *wives* (32). *Woman* or *women* appeared in her entire range of poems just 8 times, and *female* only 3, in contrast to *man* or *men,* which appeared a total of 173 times. Even acknowledging that in her era the latter term was often used generically to refer to all humans, the difference in terminology is striking. That *father(s)* (65 references) and *husband(s)* (24) are roughly comparable to *mothers* and *wives* underscores just how rarely Bradstreet joined all females together in a single word, in contrast to her practice with males.[5]

More than three decades ago, Laurel Thatcher Ulrich demonstrated that New England clergymen's funeral sermons for women in the seventeenth century celebrated their subjects' ungendered virtues and similarities to men, and she then showed that as time passed—especially by the 1730s—ministers became more likely to place greater emphasis on the deceased's distinctive feminine qualities. One of the earliest such sermons, delivered by the Reverend Benjamin Colman in 1711, listed qualities he termed "peculiarly obliging, decent and ornamental" to all women, as a consequence of both *"Nature"* and *"Custom"*: "an Eminence in Modesty, reserve, purity, temperance, humility, truth, meekness, patience, courtesie, affability, charity, goodness, mercy, compassion: Discretion, prudence, Piety and Devotion." Yet even though Colman attributed such characteristics universally to women, only a few items on his list—among them modesty, reserve, purity, and meekness—would have been out of place as descriptors for pious men as well.[6]

When Colman's own daughter, Jane Turell, died in 1735, aged twenty-seven, he used traditional role-related terminology to describe her as one who as "a child, a Wife, a Mother, a Sister, a Mistress, and a Friend...found Grace to carry her self in a laudable and exemplary manner," but he added an observation in line with his 1711 list of feminine virtues: she always acted "under the Veil of great Modesty and Reserve."[7] Jane's husband, the Reverend Ebenezer Turell, exhibited a more up-to-date sensibility when he expressed the hope that New England daughters would read Jane's writings,

published in conjunction with her father's sermon, "that they may understand what true *Beauty* is, and what the brightest Ornaments of their Sex are,
and seek them with their whole Desire."

Such phrases were unusual in the context of formulaic sermons, as were
the contents of some of Jane's own writings printed in the pamphlet. In one
poem, she expressed her admiration for Elizabeth Singer Rowe (John Dunton's Philomela), of whom she wrote,

> Surpriz'd I view, wrote by a *Female* Pen,
> Such a grave Warning to the Sons of Men
>
> .   .   .   .
>
> A *Woman's* Pen strikes the curs'd *Serpent's* Head,
> And lays the Monster gasping, if not dead.

On another occasion, Jane Turell admitted that she aspired to imitate other
female poets like Mrs. Rowe: "O let me burn with *Sappho's* noble Fire,. . . /
And let me rival great *Orinda's* Fame, /Or like sweet *Philomela's* be my Name."
Her husband observed, "she was sometimes fir'd with a laudable Ambition
of raising the honour of her *Sex,* who are therefore under Obligations to
her." With such phrases both Jane and Ebenezer—who came of age in the
1720s—revealed that they had been influenced by the new linguistic practices that ascribed similarities to all *women,* by using that word, *female,* or
the sex, instead of one or more of the previous lengthy series of terms. They
expressed a newly gendered essentialism in their characterization of Jane
Colman Turell's identity.[8]

The same transitions in language are evident in condolence letters on the
deaths of the two wives of Henry Lloyd exchanged among members of the
extended Lloyd family of Long Island, in 1728 and 1749. The earliest missives
describe the death of Henry Lloyd's first wife as "a heavy burthen" and an "Ir-
reparable" loss to the family, but use no gendered rhetoric. By contrast, when
Lloyd's second wife died twenty-one years later, his relatives employed very
different phrases. One quoted a few lines of poetry beginning, "Thou best
of all thy Sex!"; another termed her "obliging & Tender"; and her son from
her first marriage described her in a memorial publication thus: "Her *Aspect*
was lovely, serene and pleasant. . . . The Politeness of her Address, the Vivacity
of her Conversation, joined to the Benevolence of her Disposition, captivated
all Companies." Her mode of expression, he proclaimed, "raised her above the
greatest Part of the Sex." He also made a point of observing that "She never
affected a *public Appearance* beyond the Decency of her Station; nor interfered
with Affairs, foreign to her Sex."[9]

Surviving letters from the 1750s of another New York extended family, the Coldens, suggest that other women besides Mary Lloyd sought to avoid encroaching on "affairs, foreign to their sex." The correspondence that passed among Cadwallader and Alice Colden and their adult children and spouses had markedly gendered content. When women wrote to other women, with rare exceptions they conveyed only family news. When women wrote to men, they primarily discussed the same topic but sometimes added comments on politics or military affairs. Men addressing other men focused on political or military information, whereas when they communicated with women they emphasized family matters, with an occasional reference to politics or war.[10]

Such content appeared, too, in letters that Cadwallader Colden exchanged with other men about his daughter Jane's scientific talents. He consistently explained his encouragement of her study of botany in gendered terms. "I thought that Botany is an Amusement which may be made agreable for the Ladies who are often at a loss to fill up their time," Colden told one correspondent. "Their natural curiosity & the pleasure they take in the beauty & variety of dress seems to fit them for it." He proposed the same solution for others in similar terms: "Perhaps from her example young ladies in a like situation may find an agreable way to fill up some part of time which otherwise may be heavy on their hand May amuse & please themselves & at the same time be usefull to others." Such language was never employed to characterize the studies of Jane Colden's male contemporaries.[11]

Even Eliza Lucas Pinckney, who thought about herself in different family-related roles in the 1740s, employed more modern rhetoric when she discussed other women two decades later. For example, writing to one woman about a mutual friend in 1762, she commented, "She is certainly a worthy and most amiable woman. Her real and unaffected piety and goodness of heart is a noble foundation for all her other virtues, of which I think she has as many as can come to one womans share, besides being clever in every thing; for that she is one of the most ingenius ladies I ever knew." Although she later added, "happy is the man that has made her his wife, Blessed is the Child that calls her mother," what primarily stands out in Eliza Pinckney's language of praise is the use of *woman* twice and *lady* once in a short passage. Her admiration for her acquaintance was real, but it was now inflected with gendered considerations once absent from her phraseology.[12]

Yet the impact of changing conceptions of *women* and *womanhood*—and the general application of such terms—is best seen in the writings of Pinckney's younger contemporaries. Hannah Callender Sansom, born in 1737 (and thus fifteen years Eliza Pinckney's junior), provides an excellent example.

Callender began her diary in 1758, when she was twenty-one, and she filled her entries with language found but rarely in Pinckney's letters. Take the following selected phrases from 1758, all of which express the new gendered sensibility through the use of "the sex" to refer to women: "coud wish with all my heart the sex gave less proofs of there passion"; "the behaviour of some of the Ladies, made me think of a Satire, cast on the Sex"; "I know not what's the matter with the Sex, they cant reconcile themselves to a single state"; and "no wonder the men laugh at the Sex." Unsurprisingly, therefore, when Hannah wrote of her marriage four years later, she put it this way, employing *woman* where *wife* would previously have been standard: "on this day we began the Important affair of Housekeeping, In which the Woman's care is to make the house agreable to her husband." And less than a year later, when the marriage had already proved to be far from ideal, she penned in a like vein, "Poor woman let thy Happiness take its rise in Resignation. for thou will never wittness it otherways."[13]

The language of Hannah Callender Sansom's journal differs significantly from the poetic rhetoric of Anne Bradstreet or even from the letters penned by Eliza Lucas Pinckney, Hannah's older contemporary. Hannah represented the future: women whose lives were defined by the new ideology of *womanhood* and the *feminine private* as well as by the demands of their lives as wives and mothers, women who did the best they could to create personal space for themselves amid the demands of their households, and women who just a few years hence would have to confront and cope with the disruptions of the American Revolution. By their very nature, those disruptions would challenge the newly consolidated, gendered *public/private* divide. Just as the Civil War of the 1640s brought English women together for a public purpose, the war in America led women to attempt to form the first national all-female organization, the Ladies Association of 1780, which raised a considerable sum of money to support the Continental Army. Even so, the *public/private* divide would not collapse. Ultimately, that divide would gain new strength through a broadened redefinition.[14]

In the immediate aftermath of independence, though, such an outcome appeared unlikely. As partisan conflict engulfed the new republic, women as well as men took sides in battles over foreign policy. How should citizens react to the French Revolution or the Jay Treaty? Such questions deeply divided Americans of both sexes in the 1790s, and Federalist and Republican men competed openly for the political allegiance of the nation's women. But after 1800, mimicking Joseph Addison's promotion of feminine nonpartisanship as an antidote for the negative impact of party discord in the reign of Queen Anne, America's male politicians began to argue that a disinterested patriotism was the most appropriate stance for women. Like Addison, they contended that women should become peacemakers and mediators among their menfolk, and that engaging in partisan politics would "unsex" them, distracting them from their domestic duties. Even though American men failed to adopt Addison's overt misogyny, they also in effect banished women from the political realm.[15]

Yet definitions of the *private* came to encompass a covertly political role: that of the republican wife and mother who by her work in the domestic realm allowed her husband to fulfill his responsibilities to the public outside the household, and who carefully raised her children—especially her sons—to be good citizens of the new nation. In such an ideological context, some women found scope for social activism as an extension of their domestic responsibilities; for example, they formed female charitable or religious organizations to aid widows and orphans or support missionary endeavors. But by the late 1820s such outlets were no longer adequate for women who wanted to have a more direct impact on political matters of concern to the nation as a whole. And so, like their predecessors in Civil War–era England, they became state actors through renewed involvement in partisan activities and through novel petitions to Congress: first on the subjects of Indian removal and the abolition of slavery, and eventually on women's rights.[16]

Those American women were worthy heirs of the petitioners two centuries earlier on the other side of the Atlantic. In seventeenth-century Anglo-America, women divided by rank and marital status could not long sustain all-female groups, especially when they came under attack from hostile newsbook editors and clever pornographic parodists like Henry Neville. Indeed, that ordinary women joined together as *women* in the 1640s was remarkable in the first place, probably a result of their prior association in dissenting congregations in London and environs.

But female members of the gentry and aristocracy, the sole group of women who at the time would have been viewed as legitimate state actors, did not participate in such activities. The royalist Margaret Cavendish, Duchess of Newcastle, explicitly decried the Civil War petitioners. Lady Frances Berkeley, too young to have been involved during the 1640s, showed through her actions in Virginia what seventeenth-century female aristocrats could accomplish in the public realm. In the 1670s, she did not have to confront the chorus of complaints generated just over a century later by the activism of a prominent English noblewoman, Georgiana Spencer, Duchess of Devonshire. When the duchess campaigned vigorously for Charles James Fox in the parliamentary election of 1784, the negative reactions to her politicking demonstrated that eighteenth-century gendered understandings of women's appropriate roles were by then being applied to gentlewomen as well as to ordinary females. Aristocratic women of the Duchess of Devonshire's era were expected to express any political interests solely in the context of household and family.[17]

The newly gendered sensibility that culminated in the *feminine private* of the mid to late eighteenth century formulated by John Dunton, Joseph Addison, and Richard Steele initially expelled all women from the public realm. Ironically, that same sensibility later gave American female political activists the gendered solidarity that their predecessors had lacked. It also supplied them with the ability to persist in their efforts for long periods despite confronting vocal criticism from many men and some women. Seeing themselves, and being seen, as *women*—rather than as gentlewomen, wives, mothers, or widows—brought women together in new ways and allowed them to identify as a gendered group with unified interests. In the absence of that conception of sexual separation and solidarity, nineteenth-century American women would not have been able to combine effectively as state actors to seek the rights of citizenship for themselves. The *feminine private* thus sowed the seeds of its own eventual destruction.

✒ Notes

Preface

1. Originally published by Little, Brown in 1980; reprinted, with a new introduction, by Cornell University Press in 1996.

2. Ibid., esp. chaps. 1, 4, and 6.

3. Elizabeth Cook, *Literary Influences in Colonial Newspapers, 1704–1750* (New York: Columbia University Press, 1912), discusses the influence on newspapers of English authors generally and *The Spectator* in particular.

4. See Ellen Hartigan-O'Connor, *The Ties That Buy: Women and Commerce in Revolutionary America* (Philadelphia: University of Pennsylvania Press, 2009); Ann Smart Martin, *Buying into the World of Goods: Early Consumers in Back Country Virginia* (Baltimore: Johns Hopkins University Press, 2008); T. H. Breen, *The Marketplace of Revolution: How Consumer Politics Shaped American Independence* (New York: Oxford University Press, 2004); Richard L. Bushman, *The Refinement of America: Persons, Houses, Cities* (New York: Alfred A. Knopf, 1992); Sarah Knott, *Sensibility and the American Revolution* (Chapel Hill: University of North Carolina Press, 2009).

5. *Founding Mothers and Fathers: Gendered Power and the Forming of American Society* (New York: Alfred A. Knopf, 1996; Vintage Books, 1997); hereafter cited as *FM&F.* On the absence of a gendered dimension to public/private distinctions, see 20–24; on the public roles of high-ranking women, see esp. chaps. 3 and 8, and sec. 3, prologue. On seventeenth-century behavioral prescriptions, see C. Dallett Hemphill, *Bowing to Necessities: A History of Manners in America, 1620–1860* (New York: Oxford University Press, 1999), 13–62; and Laurel Thatcher Ulrich, "Vertuous Women Found: New England Ministerial Literature, 1668–1735," *American Quarterly* 28 (1976): 20–40. Such practices were reflected in the similar sentences for criminal conduct imposed on men and women in the colonial north, though the southern colonies exhibited a different pattern; see *FM&F,* chap. 7.

6. *In the Devil's Snare: The Salem Witchcraft Crisis of 1692* (New York: Alfred A. Knopf, 2002). I originally thought the analysis would be more focused on gender than turned out in the end to be the case, although the book employs a gendered analysis when appropriate. But, as friends have observed, the Wabanakis "abducted" it.

7. Since its appearance in English, Jürgen Habermas, *The Structural Transformation of the Public Sphere,* trans. Thomas Burger (Cambridge, Mass.: MIT Press, 1989), has had a major impact on the work of both literary and historical scholars studying the early modern world; it was first published in German in 1962. Feminist critics have accurately observed that although Habermas portrayed the early modern public sphere as wholly masculine, by his own criteria many women in Anglo-America actively participated in it. That point was made effectively by Mary P. Ryan with respect to the nineteenth century and conceded by Habermas; see Ryan, "Gender and

Public Access: Women's Politics in Nineteenth-Century America," in *Habermas and the Public Sphere,* ed. Craig Calhoun (Cambridge, Mass.: MIT Press, 1992), 259–88; and Habermas's comment that her work was "very convincing," 466. Among many useful commentaries are the essays in Calhoun, *Habermas and the Public Sphere;* Anthony J. LaVopa, "Conceiving a Public: Ideas and Society in Eighteenth-Century Europe," *Journal of Modern History* 64 (1992): 79–116; Johanna Meehan, ed., *Feminists Read Habermas* (New York: Routledge, 1995); and Joan B. Landes, "The Public and the Private Sphere: A Feminist Reconsideration," in *Feminism, the Public and the Private,* ed. Landes (Oxford: Oxford University Press, 1998), 135–63. *FM&F,* esp. chap. 5, "Amongst the Neighbors," 240–77, discusses colonial men and women as participants in what I term the *informal public,* or community opinion about people and topics of general concern, including but not limited to politics.

8. This is a more restrictive definition than that used by some other historians, notably Cynthia Kierner, *Beyond the Household: Women's Place in the Early South, 1700–1835* (Ithaca: Cornell University Press, 1998), 2. I have adopted it because of its clarity; it directly addresses what I see as the core of the public/private divide. Not considered here are other public realms of concern to some scholars, such as the writing practices that increasingly placed women in the public eye during the eighteenth century. See, for example, Elizabeth Heckendorn Cook, *Epistolary Bodies: Gender and Genre in the Eighteenth-Century Republic of Letters* (Stanford, Calif.: Stanford University Press, 1996). Other Early American historians have voiced similar complaints about vague uses of Habermasian terminology; see the comments in John L. Brooke et al., "Forum: Alternative Histories of the Public Sphere," *WMQ,* 3rd ser., 62 (January 2005): 92–112. In *FM&F* I employ the phrase *formal public* to mean *government.* I take "state actors" from Margaret R. Hunt, "Men, Women, and the Eighteenth-Century English State," unpublished paper, 1995. Thanks to my friend Margaret for allowing me to read and cite her work in progress.

9. *Separated by their Sex* confines itself to Britain and its mainland North American colonies. Scholars who have looked at related (though not the same) questions in France and elsewhere in Europe have reported somewhat different findings. See, for example, Dena Goodman, *The Republic of Letters: A Cultural History of the French Enlightenment* (Ithaca: Cornell University Press, 1994); and Karen Offen, *European Feminisms, 1700–1950: A Political History* (Stanford, Calif.: Stanford University Press, 2000), part 1.

10. The prime examples are G. J. Barker-Benfield, *The Culture of Sensibility: Sex and Society in Eighteenth-Century Britain* (Chicago: University of Chicago Press, 1992); and Michael McKeon, *The Secret History of Domesticity: Public, Private, and the Division of Knowledge* (Baltimore: Johns Hopkins University Press, 2005), which—despite its subtitle—focuses almost exclusively on domesticity. See also (on France) Phillipe Ariès and Georges Duby, eds., *A History of Private Life,* vol. 3: *Passions of the Renaissance,* ed. Roger Chartier, trans. Arthur Goldhammer (Cambridge, Mass.: Harvard University Press, 1989); and (on America) Knott, *Sensibility and the American Revolution.*

11. *OED,* q.v. "public," "private."

12. Useful observations on historians' uses of the language of *public* and *private spheres* are Linda K. Kerber, "Separate Spheres, Female Worlds, Woman's Place: The Rhetoric of Women's History," *Journal of American History* 75 (1988–89): 9–39;

Amanda Vickery, "Golden Age to Separate Spheres? A Review of the Categories and Chronology of English Women's History," *Historical Journal* 36 (1993): 383–414; Leonore Davidoff, "Regarding Some 'Old Husbands' Tales': Public and Private in Feminist History," in Landes, *Feminism, the Public and the Private,* 164–94; and "Women's History in the New Millennium: Rethinking Public and Private," a forum in *Journal of Women's History* 15, no. 1 (spring 2003): 10–69. See also the insightful theoretical articles by Susan Moller Okin, "Gender, the Public and the Private," in *Political Theory Today,* ed. David Held (Stanford, Calif.: Stanford University Press, 1991), 67–90; and Susan Gal, "A Semiotics of the Public/Private Distinction," in *Going Public: Feminism and the Shifting Boundaries of the Private Sphere,* ed. Joan W. Scott and Debra Keates (Urbana: University of Illinois Press, 2004), 261–77.

13. For examples of historians utilizing such categories simultaneously for contemporary analysis and past description, see Dena Goodman, "Public Sphere and Private Life: Toward a Synthesis of Current Historiographical Approaches to the Old Regime," *History and Theory* 31 (1992): 1–20; Lawrence E. Klein, "Gender, Conversation, and the Public Sphere in Early Eighteenth-Century England," in *Textuality and Sexuality: Reading Theories and Practices,* ed. Judith Still and Michael Worton (Manchester: Manchester University Press, 1993), 100–115; and Robert B. Shoemaker, *Gender in English Society, 1650–1850: The Emergence of Separate Spheres?* (London: Longman, 1998). Near the end of a volume intended to challenge the perception that by 1850 English society was organized along separate-sphere lines, Shoemaker nevertheless admits that he defined the content of his chapters according to "an implicit distinction between private and public spheres of activity" (305), thus demonstrating the pervasiveness of the metaphor even when it is being questioned.

14. For three scholars who have asked questions related to mine, see John Brewer, "This, That and the Other: Public, Social and Private in the Seventeenth and Eighteenth Centuries," in *Shifting the Boundaries: Transformation of the Languages of Public and Private in the Eighteenth Century,* ed. Dario Castiglione and Lesley Sharpe (Exeter, U.K.: University of Exeter Press, 1995), 1–21; Lawrence E. Klein, "Gender and the Public/Private Distinction in the Eighteenth Century: Some Questions about Evidence and Analytic Procedure," *Eighteenth-Century Studies* 29 (1995): 97–109; and Erica Longfellow, "Public, Private, and the Household in Early Seventeenth-Century England," *Journal of British Studies* 45 (April 2006): 313–34.

15. As the late Jeanne Boydston observed in her article "Gender as a Question of Historical Analysis," *Gender and History* 20 (2008): 578, "the primaryness of gender in a given situation should be one of our questions, rather than one of our assumptions." I reached this same conclusion in the late 1980s, during my research on the seventeenth-century colonies; at that time, a crucial conversation with Joan Wallach Scott helped to crystallize my thinking. Cf. Leonore Davidoff and Catherine Hall, *Family Fortunes: Men and Women of the English Middle Class, 1780–1850* (Chicago: University of Chicago Press, 1984), 29, on the timeless predominance of gender categories.

16. Cf., for instance, Clare A. Lyons, *Sex among the Rabble: An Intimate History of Gender and Power in the Age of Revolution, Philadelphia, 1730–1830* (Chapel Hill: University of North Carolina Press, 2006); Cara Anzilotti, *In the Affairs of the World: Women, Patriarchy, and Power in Colonial South Carolina* (Westport, Conn.: Praeger, 2002); Karin Wulf, *Not All Wives: Women of Colonial Philadelphia* (Ithaca: Cornell

University Press, 2000); Kierner, *Beyond the Household;* Kathleen M. Brown, *Good Wives, Nasty Wenches, and Anxious Patriarchs: Gender, Race, and Power in Colonial Virginia* (Chapel Hill: University of North Carolina Press, 1996); and Cornelia Hughes Dayton, *Women before the Bar: Gender, Law, and Society in Connecticut, 1639–1789* (Chapel Hill: University of North Carolina Press, 1995).

Introduction

1. For Filmer, see Margaret J. M. Ezell, *The Patriarch's Wife: Literary Evidence and the History of the Family* (Chapel Hill: University of North Carolina Press, 1987), appendix 1: Sir Robert Filmer, "In Praise of the Vertuous Wife," 183. The essay in the 19 August 1734 *New-York Weekly Journal* is untitled and appears on p. 1. On *fair sex,* see below, n. 9.

2. See Gordon J. Schochet, *Patriarchalism in Political Thought: The Authoritarian Family and Political Speculation and Attitudes Especially in Seventeenth-Century England* (New York: Basic Books, 1975); and James Daly, *Sir Robert Filmer and English Political Thought* (Toronto: University of Toronto Press, 1979).

3. For the hierarchical nature of seventeenth-century England, see Keith Wrightson, *English Society, 1580–1680* (London: Hutchinson, 1982). Neither Wrightson nor the scholars who have studied Filmer discuss women at any length; this paragraph summarizes my argument in *Founding Mothers and Fathers: Gendered Power and the Forming of American Society* (New York: Alfred A. Knopf, 1996), introduction and passim (hereafter cited as *FM&F*).

4. On Margaret Brent, see *FM&F,* part 3, prologue, "His Lordship's Attorney." For early modern Englishwomen who engaged in politics in various ways, see Barbara J. Harris, *English Aristocratic Women, 1450–1550: Marriage and Family, Property and Careers* (New York: Oxford University Press, 2002); Amanda Vickery, ed., *Women, Privilege, and Power: British Politics, 1750 to the Present* (Stanford, Calif.: Stanford University Press, 2001), 6–8; Diane Purkiss, *Literature, Gender and Politics during the English Civil War* (Cambridge: Cambridge University Press, 2005), 244n10; Sara Mendelson and Patricia Crawford, *Women in Early Modern England, 1550–1720* (Oxford: Clarendon Press, 1998), 56, 347; and Antonia Fraser, *The Weaker Vessel* (New York: Alfred A. Knopf, 1984), 230–34. Thus Anthony Fletcher was incorrect to assert in *Gender, Sex, and Subordination in England, 1500–1800* (New Haven, Conn.: Yale University Press, 1995) that "women in this society had no public roles as persons in themselves" (263).

5. One of the best studies of the mechanics of transatlantic cultural transmission is Ian K. Steele, *The English Atlantic, 1675–1740: An Exploration of Communication and Community* (New York: Oxford University Press, 1986). On literacy rates and the pursuit of genteel English values by colonists, see 265–71. A useful survey of books that were aimed at women and found in American libraries is Kevin J. Hayes, *A Colonial Woman's Bookshelf* (Knoxville: University of Tennessee Press, 1996).

6. [Richard Cleaver], *A Godlie Forme of Householde Government…* (London: Felix Kingston, 1598), 19, 176 (see also 61–87); George Savile, Marquis of Halifax, *Advice to a Daughter* [orig. pub. 1688 as *The Lady's New Year's Gift*], in *Miscellanies* (London: W. Rogers, 1704), 35, 38. Halifax's language was copied by other prescriptive writers; see, e.g., *The Ladies Library,* 3rd ed., 3 vols. (London: Jacob Tonson, 1722 [orig.

pub. 1714]), 2:265–66. Michael McKeon gives numerous examples of other authors who described the "housewife as [sole] governor" in *The Secret History of Domesticity: Public, Private, and the Division of Knowledge* (Baltimore: Johns Hopkins University Press, 2005), 181–94.

7. Karen Harvey points out the lack of continuity in the subjects of studies of early modern Englishmen in her review essay, "The History of Masculinity, circa 1650–1800," *Journal of British Studies* 44 (April 2005): 296–311. See also Alexandra Shepard, "From Anxious Patriarchs to Refined Gentlemen? Manhood in Britain, circa 1500–1700," ibid., 281–95; and Shepard, *Meanings of Manhood in Early Modern England* (Oxford: Oxford University Press, 2003). John Tosh, "The Old Adam and the New Man: Emerging Themes in the History of English Masculinities, 1750–1850," in *English Masculinities, 1660–1800,* ed. Tim Hitchcock and Michèle Cohen (London: Longman, 1999), 217–38, argues that men continued to be actively involved in domestic affairs. Fletcher, in *Gender, Sex and Subordination,* 322–23, points out the significance of *masculinity* as a neologism of 1748. For American men, see Lisa Wilson, *Ye Heart of a Man: The Domestic Life of Men in Colonial New England* (New Haven, Conn.: Yale University Press, 1999); Kathleen Brown, *Good Wives, Nasty Wenches, and Anxious Patriarchs: Gender, Race, and Power in Colonial Virginia* (Chapel Hill: University of North Carolina Press, 1996), esp. chaps. 8, 10; Anne S. Lombard, *Making Manhood: Growing Up Male in Colonial New England* (Cambridge, Mass.: Harvard University Press, 2003); and Thomas A. Foster, *Sex and the Eighteenth-Century Man: Massachusetts and the History of Sexuality in America* (Boston: Beacon Press, 2006).

8. The discussion that follows has been greatly facilitated by the ability to conduct keyword searches in the online databases EEBO, ECCO, AHN, and EAI. The databases are not yet comprehensive, so the results reported herein should be regarded as suggestive rather than definitive. (Searches were conducted at various times during 2008.)

9. The English imprint that initially employed *fair sex* was a play, John Fletcher, *The Wild-Goose Chase a Comedie*...(London: Humphrey Moseley, 1652), 52. A keyword full-text search on *fair sex* in EEBO showed twenty-five examples in the 1680s.

10. *OED,* q.v. "province"; Halifax, *Miscellanies,* 35; Nicolas Malebranche, *Father Malebranche's Treatise Concerning the Search after Truth...,* trans. T. Taylor (Oxford: L. Lichfield, 1694), 67. Another contemporary translation omitted *province* or a similar word: "'Tis for Women to determine Fashions...," it read. See Richard Sault, trans., *Malebranch's Search after Truth*...(London: John Dunton, 1694), 161.

11. J. Olivier, pseud., *A Continuation of the Life and Adventures of Signor Rozelli*...(London: Will Taylor, 1724), 122. The earliest similar published use of *province* ("the Business, or Province of a *Woman*") found in EAI is a reprint of a London edition of a translation from the French: François Fénélon, *The Archbishop of Cambray's Dissertation*...(Philadelphia: Andrew Bradford, 1738), preface, xlv–xlvi.

12. *OED,* q.v. "sphere"; George Savile, Marquis of Halifax, *Some Cautions Offered*...(London: [no pub.,] 1695), 28; Ebenezer Pemberton, *The Divine Original and Dignity of Government Asserted*...(Boston: B. Green, 1710), 13; John Wise, *The Churches Quarrel Espoused*...(New York: William Bradford, 1713), 109. Later in the century, governors adopted the same language when confronting restive assemblies; see, e.g., *The Speech of his Excellency Lewis Morris, Esq...the 10th of December 1743* (Philadelphia: Benjamin Franklin, 1743), 4; *A Journal of the House of*

Representatives of the Province of New-Hampshire (Boston: J. Bushell, B. Allen, & J. Green, 1745), 21.

13. "On the Death of the Queen. By my Lord Cutts," in Matthew Prior, *State-Poems...*, 2nd ed. (London: [no pub.,] 1695), 200. See also similar uses of *sphere* in such works as Gilbert Burnet, *An Essay on the Memory of the Late Queen* (London: Richard Chiswell, 1695); and Robert Gould, *A Poem Most Humbly Offered to the Memory of Her Late Sacred Majesty, Queen Mary* (London: Jacob Tonson & Francis Saunders, 1695).

14. Edward Ward, *Nuptial Dialogues and Debates...*, 2 vols. (London: H. Moore for T. Morris, 1710), 1:23; *Conversations Moral and Entertaining...*(London: John Hawkins, 1740), 72; Sophia, *Woman's Superior Excellence over Man...*(London: John Hawkins, 1740), unpaginated preface. See also an essay in the *London Magazine,* September 1742, 443: "she has made herself absolute Mistress of that Part of it [literature] which can properly come within a Woman's Sphere."

15. *A Serious and Earnest Address to the Gentry, Clergy, and Other Inhabitants of the British Nation...*(Boston: Rogers & Fowle, 1746), 12; *Reflections on Courtship and Marriage: in Two Letters to a Friend...*(Philadelphia: Benjamin Franklin, 1746), 51.

16. Blandina [Grace Growden, later Galloway], "On a very Bad Preacher But a good Woman ML," 1747, Joseph Galloway Papers, Library of Congress Manuscript Division; *South Carolina Gazette,* 14 May 1753, identified as originally published in London. Also printed in Benjamin Franklin, *Poor Richard...for...1760* (Philadelphia: Benjamin Franklin, 1759), unpaginated; quotations from pages for April–May (poem begins in March, ends in December).

17. In *FM&F* I advanced the contention that seventeenth-century Chesapeake society, because of its peculiar demographic makeup, constituted a nascent Lockean culture, in that political authorities showed little interest in regulating family life. See *FM&F,* 58–62, 97–101, 140–47, and part 3 passim. For analyses of Locke's ideas, see Rachel Weil, *Political Passions: Gender, the Family, and Political Argument in England, 1680–1714* (Manchester: Manchester University Press, 1999), esp. chaps. 1, 2; and Carole Pateman, *The Sexual Contract* (Stanford, Calif.: Stanford University Press, 1988). See also Susan Kingsley Kent, *Gender and Power in Britain, 1640–1900* (London: Routledge, 1999), 43–44; and McKeon, *Secret History of Domesticity,* chaps. 1–3.

18. Scholars who connect changing gender definitions to commercial developments (not all in the same way) include E. J. Clery, *The Feminization Debate in Eighteenth-Century England: Literature, Commerce, and Luxury* (New York: Palgrave Macmillan, 2004); Kent, *Gender and Power,* 54–74; and G. J. Barker-Benfield, *The Culture of Sensibility: Sex and Society in Eighteenth-Century Britain* (Chicago: University of Chicago Press, 1995). Ruth H. Bloch links concern with women's moral authority in eighteenth-century America not to commerce but rather to the combined influences of evangelical religion, the Scottish Enlightenment, and sentimental fiction. See Bloch, *Gender and Morality in Anglo-American Culture, 1650–1800* (Berkeley: University of California Press, 2003), esp. 4–13 and 154–66.

19. See Thomas Laqueur, *Making Sex: Body and Gender from the Greeks to Freud* (Cambridge, Mass.: Harvard University Press, 1990), 194–207; Londa Schiebinger, *The Mind Has No Sex? Women in the Origins of Modern Science* (Cambridge, Mass.: Harvard University Press, 1989), 214–44; Michael McKeon, "Historicizing Patriarchy:

The Emergence of Gender Difference in England, 1660–1760," *Eighteenth-Century Studies* 28 (1995): 295–322; Karen Offen, *European Feminisms, 1700–1850: A Political History* (Berkeley: University of California Press, 2000), 27–33; and Nancy Leys Stepan, "Race, Gender, Science and Citizenship," *Gender and History* 10 (1998): 26–52. Stepan observes that the production of racial categories was part of the same process that created gender categories, a contention supported by Margot Minardi, "The Boston Inoculation Controversy of 1721–1722: An Incident in the History of Race," *WMQ*, 3rd ser., 61 (2004): 48–76. But cf. Karen Harvey's critique of Laqueur, "The Substance of Sexual Difference: Change and Persistence in Eighteenth-Century Representations of the Body," *Gender and History* 14 (2002): 202–23.

20. For instance, although McKeon (above, n. 19) emphasizes changing definitions of sexuality, he also connects his analysis to political developments; and Clery (above, n. 18), who emphasizes commerce, ties her argument to Laqueur's findings.

1. Lady Frances Berkeley and Virginia Politics, 1675–1678

1. T. M. [Thomas Mathew], "The Beginning, Progress, and Conclusion of Bacon's Rebellion, 1675–1676," in *Narratives of the Insurrections, 1675–1690,* ed. Charles M. Andrews (New York: Charles Scribner's Sons, 1915), 29–30, is the source of quotations in this paragraph. For other eyewitness accounts, see William Sherwood and Philip Ludwell to [Sir Joseph Williamson], 28 June 1676, *Virginia Magazine of History and Biography* (hereafter *VMHB*) 1 (1893–94): 171–74, 182–86. Bacon's own account of the encounter was disingenuous; see Bacon to [?], 18 [*sic;* 28] June 1676, *WMQ*, 1st ser., 9 (1900): 8–9.

2. John Berry and Francis Moryson, "A True Narrative of the Rise, Progresse, and Cessation of the Late Rebellion in Virginia...," in Andrews, *Narratives,* 115; text of Bacon's submission, in *The Papers of Sir William Berkeley, 1605–1677,* ed. Warren M. Billings (Richmond: Library of Virginia, 2007), 532–33. According to Mathew, the wily governor restored Bacon to the council to keep an eye on him, and Bacon belatedly realized as much; see "Beginning, Progress, and Conclusion," 27.

3. On the significance of body control and body language in the colonies, see Melvin Yazawa, *From Colonies to Commonwealth: Familial Ideology and the Beginnings of the American Republic* (Baltimore: Johns Hopkins University Press, 1985), chap. 3; and C. Dallett Hemphill, *Bowing to Necessities: A History of Manners in America, 1620–1860* (New York: Oxford University Press, 1999), part 1, esp. 25–26, 43, 57.

4. The relationship of Lady Berkeley and Nathaniel Bacon is mentioned but not emphasized in standard discussions of the rebellion: Thomas Jefferson Wertenbaker, *Torchbearer of the Revolution: The Story of Bacon's Rebellion and Its Leader* (Princeton, N. J.: Princeton University Press, 1941); Wilcomb E. Washburn, *The Governor and the Rebel: A History of Bacon's Rebellion in Virginia* (Chapel Hill: University of North Carolina Press, 1957); Edmund S. Morgan, *American Slavery, American Freedom: The Ordeal of Colonial Virginia* (New York: W. W. Norton, 1975), chap. 13; and Stephen Saunders Webb, *1676: The End of American Independence* (New York: Alfred A. Knopf, 1984), part 1. Even Terri L. Snyder, who devotes much of chapter 1 of *Brabbling Women: Disorderly Speech and the Law in Early Virginia* (Ithaca: Cornell University Press, 2003), to Lady Berkeley, fails to stress her kinship to Bacon, nor does Kathleen M. Brown, in

Good Wives, Nasty Wenches, and Anxious Patriarchs: Gender, Race, and Power in Colonial Virginia (Chapel Hill: University of North Carolina Press, 1996), chap. 5.

5. For example, Susan Westbury, "Women in Bacon's Rebellion," in *Southern Women: Histories and Identities,* ed. Virginia Bernhard et al. (Columbia: University of Missouri Press, 1992), 30–46, does not single Lady Berkeley out for special attention. The most detailed discussion is in Snyder, *Brabbling Women,* chap. 1. Wertenbaker, *Torchbearer,* mentions her on four pages; and Washburn, *Governor and the Rebel,* on just three. Webb, in *1676,* declares that "women led both the Berkeleyan and Baconian camps," but he devotes only two pages (5–6) to that subject, subsequently mentioning Lady Berkeley on only two more pages.

6. Basic biographical information in this and subsequent paragraphs comes from Jane Carson, "Berkeley, Lady Frances," *NAM* 1:135–36; Terri L. Snyder, "Berkeley, Lady Frances," *ANB* 2:648–49; and Fairfax Harrison, "Proprietors of the Northern Neck," *VMHB* 33 (1925): 145, 238, 348–52. See also Lady Frances's surviving papers reprinted in Billings, *Papers of Berkeley,* appendix 2, which was published after I completed the research for this chapter. Billings modernized some spelling, capitalization, and punctuation in a different way than I have done. I read the original documents but have nevertheless added citations to his page numbers for reference purposes. His transcription of some hard-to-read phrases occasionally diverges from mine.

7. H. R. McIlwaine, ed., *Minutes of the Council and General Court of Colonial Virginia, 1622–1632, 1670–1676…*(Richmond, Va.: Colonial Press, 1924), 211, 514; Billings, *Papers of Berkeley,* 626. On prenuptial agreements in general, see Mary Beth Norton, *Founding Mothers and Fathers: Gendered Power and the Forming of American Society* (New York: Alfred A. Knopf, 2002), 155–56 (hereafter *FM&F*). Lady Deborah Moody, a Massachusetts religious dissenter in the 1630s and 1640s, also used the title.

8. The comment on Lady Berkeley came in 1684 from a later governor of Virginia: Warren M. Billings, ed., *The Papers of Francis Howard, Baron Howard of Effingham, 1643–1695* (Richmond: Library of Virginia, 1989), 115. On her relationship to nieces and nephews by blood and marriage, see n. 12, below. For some contemporary English analogues to Lady Frances, see the letters of noblewomen in the Hastings Papers, HEHL, esp. boxes 34–35.

9. Biographical information from Warren M. Billings, *Sir William Berkeley and the Forging of Colonial Virginia* (Baton Rouge: Louisiana State University Press, 2004). For the remark on the marriage: "Complaint from Heaven with a Huy and crye and a petition out of Virginia and Maryland," 1676, in *Archives of Maryland,* 64 vols., ed. William Hand Browne (Baltimore: Maryland Historical Society, 1883–1972), 5:134. The word I read as "todeinge" (after consultations with experts) has been transcribed variously; the printed version has it as "fools-age." The original document is in Colonial Office, Class 1, vol. 36, no. 119, TNA (hereafter cited as CO 1/36). Mathew's narrative discreetly implied a similar interpretation of the marriage: "Beginning, Progress, and Conclusion," 20.

10. Biographical information in this and the next paragraph from Wilcomb E. Washburn, "Bacon, Nathaniel," *ANB* 1:851–52; Washburn, *Governor and the Rebel,* 18; Wertenbaker, *Torchbearer,* 39–50; and Billings, *Sir William Berkeley,* 232–34.

11. Quotations from Bacon to Sir William Berkeley, 18 September 1675, Coventry Papers, Longleat House, vol. 77, f. 6; and Berkeley to Bacon, 21 September 1675,

ibid., f. 8 (hereafter cited as Coventry Papers), reprinted in Billings, *Papers of Berkeley,* 491–93. I have silently expanded contractions and minimally modernized spelling in these and subsequent quotations. I have been unable to identify the exact nature of the kin connection between Frances Berkeley and Nathaniel Bacon, but it seems to have been through their mothers' families. Both paternal families (Bacon and Culpeper) have been extensively researched and show no obvious familial tie; also, there is no evidence that Lady Berkeley ever acknowledged kinship to Nathaniel Bacon Sr., who was related to the younger Nathaniel through the paternal line. Further, William Byrd I was termed "cousin" to both Nathaniel the younger and Lady Berkeley; his wife was related to Frances through her mother's family (see n. 12, below). That suggests that Nathaniel's familial connection to Frances had a similar maternal origin. Frances was distantly related to William Penn's wife, Gulielma Springett, whom she also called "cousin"; see Billings, *Papers of Berkeley,* 637–38.

12. First quotation: Berry and Moryson, "True Narrative," 110. Lady Berkeley's two extant letters to Filmer the younger are in Filmer Papers, U120 C14, Kentish County Council Archives, Maidstone, and reprinted in Billings, *Papers of Berkeley,* 627–28; her letters to Danby (son of her sister Anne) in the 1680s and 1690s are in the Cunliffe-Lister Muniments, Bundle 69, sec. 11, Bradford Art Museum, Bradford, U.K. (reprinted in Billings, *Papers of Berkeley,* 627–28, 634–36, 640–42). Mary Horsmanden Filmer, later Mrs. William Byrd I, was the granddaughter of Frances Berkeley's maternal aunt Ursula St. Leger.

13. My account of Bacon's Rebellion summarizes the consensus of the works cited in n. 4, above, along with the first historical assessment, Robert Beverley, *The History and Present State of Virginia* [1705], ed. Louis B. Wright (Chapel Hill: University of North Carolina Press, 1947), 74–78. Beverley was the son of one of Berkeley's strong supporters; his wife, Ursula, was Lady Frances Berkeley's first cousin twice removed, the daughter of Mary Horsmanden Filmer and William Byrd I. His narrative has a strong pro-Berkeley bias yet is nevertheless valuable for its near-contemporary perspective. See "Grievances of Virginia," *VMHB* 21 (1913): 124, for a list that includes the taxes to support the agents in London, as well as "A Repertory of the General County Grievances of Virginia . . . ," 15 October 1677, CO, Class 5, vol. 1371 (hereafter cited as CO 5/1371), ff. 295, 303, 306, 319, 321, 324, 328. This volume largely but not entirely duplicates a secretary's summary book, Bibliotheca Pepysiana 2582, Magdalene College, Cambridge, published (after I completed my research for this chapter) as Michael Oberg, ed., *Samuel Wiseman's Book of Record: The Official Account of Bacon's Rebellion in Virginia, 1676–1677* (Lanham, Md.: Lexington Books, 2005). Many of the original documents transcribed in both Pepys 2582 and CO 5/1371 are in volumes of CO 1, which is organized chronologically; that classification includes some documents found in neither of the transcribed volumes. As with Billings's *Papers of Berkeley,* I have added notes to Oberg's volume for reference purposes.

14. Bacon to Berkeley, 18 September 1675, Coventry Papers, 77:6 (Billings, *Papers of Berkeley,* 491). On Indian trade, see "Grievances of Virginia," *VMHB* 21 (1913): 125; "Repertory of General County Grievances," CO5/1371, f. 321; "Mr. Bacon's acct of their troubles in Virginia . . . ," *WMQ,* 1st ser., 9 (1900): 6; "Nathaniel Bacon Esq'r his Manifesto . . . ," *VMHB* 1 (1894–95): 57–58.

15. Berry and Moryson, "True Narrative," 105–9.

16. "Repertory of the General County Grievances," CO 5/1371, f. 322; "A Review, Breviary, and conclusion from the foregoing Narrative . . . ," ibid., ff. 411–12. The March laws are printed in William Waller Hening, ed., *The Statutes at Large . . . ,* 13 vols. (New York: R., W., & G. Bartow, 1819–1823), 2:326–40. The story of the New Kent volunteers and Lady Berkeley is recounted in Webb, *1676,* 138, but without a reference. Webb has discarded his notes and drafts for the book and is unable to supply me with information about the source (personal communication, 10 January 2005). I have not located the original document. Lady Berkeley, though, treated protesters from Nansemond County more kindly in May 1676 when they came to Green Spring; she wrote to her absent husband on their behalf, giving them "Satisfaction." See "Nancymond First Grievances," CO 1/39, no. 96.

17. Berry and Moryson, "True Narrative," 110–11; Berkeley to [Thomas Ludwell], 1 July 1776, Coventry Papers, 77:144 (Billings, *Papers of Berkeley,* 536–37); "Review, Breviary," CO 5/1371, f. 412. See also, on the choice of Bacon as leader, Beverley, *History and Present State of Virginia,* 78.

18. Nathaniel Bacon to Sir William Berkeley, 25 May 1676 (copy), Coventry Papers, 77:89 (Billings, *Papers of Berkeley,* 523–24). For a detailed discussion of the exchange between Bacon and Berkeley of which this letter was a part, see Billings, *Sir William Berkeley,* 236–39. On slander and gossip as a woman's weapon, see the discussion in *FM&F,* sec. 2; and Snyder, *Brabbling Women.*

19. All quotations from Frances Berkeley in this paragraph and the next three come from a copy of her undated statement, written after 25 May 1676, Coventry Papers, 77:91, reprinted with the omission of a phrase (accusing Bacon of "expressing a kind of Aspersions upon his [William Berkeley's] Courage & conduct in the Governmt of this Country") in Billings, *Papers of Berkeley,* 628–29.

20. Virginia Council to [Lords of Trade?], 31 May 1676, Coventry Papers, 77:96.

21. See *FM&F,* 258–59, on defamation law, including the Virginia statute; and Clara Ann Bowler, "Carted Whores and White Shrouded Apologies: Slander in the County Courts of Seventeenth-Century Virginia," *VMHB* 85 (1977): 411–26.

22. A contemporary account of the events between July 1676 and the end of the rebellion, including Bacon's burning of Jamestown in September, is Berry and Moryson, "True Narrative," 119–40. See also the works cited in n. 4, above. Under the Julian calendar, 25 March began the new year; during the seventeenth century and early eighteenth century, dates between 1 January (New Year's Day in the newer and more accurate Gregorian calendar) and 25 March were written using both years.

23. Quotations: Lady Frances Berkeley to the king, [30 November 1676], Coventry Papers, 77:308, enclosed in her letter of that date, f. 307 (Billings, *Papers of Berkeley,* 631–32). For two of the planning documents, see Coventry Papers, 77:281–82; and Francis Moryson to William Jones, October 1676, in Oberg, *Wiseman's Book,* 125–28. A letter Frances received in England was sent to Secretary of State Henry Coventry (Coventry Papers, 77:117); see Billings, *Papers of Berkeley,* 629–31.

24. See Sir John Berry to Sir William Berkeley, 29 January 1676/7, announcing their arrival; and Berry and Moryson to same, 2 February 1676/7, containing a list of directives to Berkeley, in Billings, *Papers of Berkeley,* 565, 573–75. McIlwaine, *Minutes of the Council and General Court,* 454–55, details the trials and executions of twelve men between 11 January and 24 January, along with the banishment of another man

and the confiscation of his property. Billings, *Sir William Berkeley,* chap. 14, provides an excellent discussion of the relationship between Berkeley and the commissioners and how it deteriorated over time.

25. Quotations in this paragraph and the next from Berry and Moryson to secretaries of state, 2 February 1676/7, in Oberg, *Wiseman's Book,* 59–61. They reported that twenty men had been executed. For Berkeley's account of the rebellion, written to Sir Henry Coventry on the same day, see Billings, *Papers of Berkeley,* 568–73.

26. His proclamation, issued 10 February 1676/7, added a general exemption for any (unnamed) men who had circulated oaths of allegiance to Bacon among other Virginians; see Billings, *Papers of Berkeley,* 580–82. On Sarah Grendon (or Grindon), see below, nn. 56–60. For convictions and compositions in March, see McIlwaine, *Minutes of the Council and General Court,* 456–58.

27. The quotation: Jeffreys to Sir Henry Coventry, 2 May 1677, Coventry Papers, 78:44. For specific complaints from individuals and county groups, see Oberg, *Wiseman's Book,* 207–88 passim. One infuriated Virginian, formerly a Berkeley supporter, sympathized with many "poore planters" who had been forced to enlist with Bacon and were now suffering the consequences. In his opinion, they deserved a pardon instead of punishment (William Sherwood to [Sir Joseph Williamson], 13 April 1677, CO 1/40, no. 43).

28. The governor's health was mentioned several times in exchanges with the commissioners; see Oberg, *Wiseman's Book,* 64 (quotation), 78, 79, 125. For the quotations about postwar conditions and repairs at Green Spring, see Lady Frances Berkeley to Abstrupus Danby, 27 September 1678, Cunliffe-Lister Muniments, Bundle 69, sec. 11, and an earlier letter to the same, 26 January 1677/8, both reprinted in Billings, *Papers of Berkeley,* 634–36 (he and I disagree about the date and the addressee of the quoted letter). In this correspondence she revealed that she had lost a court case and was being forced to reimburse several owners of confiscated property. On Jenkins, see Oberg, *Wiseman's Book,* 258 (for full documentation: CO 1/40, nos. 17–19).

29. Moryson to Frances Berkeley and vice versa, both 25 March 1677, in Oberg, *Wiseman's Book,* 117. See, too, Moryson to "worthy Sir," n.d. [1680], and Robert Jones, petition to Charles II, both in CO 1/45, no. 3. Jones had been condemned on 8 March (McIlwaine, *Minutes of the Council and General Court,* 457).

30. Berkeley to commissioners, 7 March 1676/7; commissioners to Sir Henry Coventry, 27 March 1677, in Oberg, *Wiseman's Book,* 94–95, 99. The increasingly acerbic correspondence is most easily consulted in ibid., 56–133 passim. All correspondence to or from Berkeley himself is reprinted in Billings, *Papers of Berkeley.*

31. Moryson to Berkeley, 21 April 1677, CO 5/1571, f. 211 (Oberg, *Wiseman's Book,* 122, differs slightly, omitting "ill").

32. This paragraph and the next are based on commissioners to Thomas Watkins, 4 May 1677, CO 5/1371, ff. 224–26 (original in CO 1/40, no. 66); it is not in Oberg, *Wiseman's Book.*

33. Commissioners to Berkeley, in Oberg, *Wiseman's Book,* 123. One Maryland man escaped execution for multiple felonies only by being ordered to serve as the colony's executioner; for a reference to this case, see *FM&F,* 456n67.

34. Quotations in this and the next two paragraphs are from William Berkeley to commissioners, 23 April 1677, CO 5/1371, ff. 214–15, and Frances Berkeley to same, 23 April 1677, ibid., f. 217; reprinted in Billings, *Papers of Berkeley,* 608–9, 633. Oberg,

Wiseman's Book, 123–24, differs slightly, substituting "fall" for "face." Susan Westbury, "Theatre and Power in Bacon's Rebellion: Virginia, 1676–77," *Seventeenth Century* 19 (2004): 69–86, also analyzes this incident, but she mistakenly conflates the "Negro" coachman with the hangman postillion, whereas it is clear from Frances Berkeley's letter of 23 April that they were two different people because Lady Frances disclaimed knowledge of the hangman yet admitted having spoken directly to the coachman. My thanks to Paula Backscheider for calling this article to my attention.

35. Moryson to Berkeley and Berkeley to Moryson, 25 April 1677, in Oberg, *Wiseman's Book,* 124–25.

36. Commissioners to Thomas Watkins, 4 May 1677, CO 5/1371, ff. 221–23.

37. Berkeley to Jeffreys, 7 [i.e., 28] April 1677, Coventry Papers, 78:34 (Billings, *Papers of Berkeley,* 610–11); Jeffreys to Sir Joseph Williamson, 11 June 1677, CO 1/40, no. 104. See also same to Sir Henry Coventry, 11 June 1677, Coventry Papers, 78:64–65.

38. Berkeley to Jeffreys, 7 [i.e., 28] April 1677, Coventry Papers, 78:34 (Billings, *Papers of Berkeley,* 610–11).

39. This paragraph and the next two are based on Frances Berkeley to Sir William Berkeley, 9 August 1677, Alderman Library, University of Virginia, Autograph Collection, box 1. (Billings, Westbury, and Snyder did not locate this letter.) I thank the staff of the library for supplying me with a photocopy of this important letter, and Ben Ray for facilitating the process. Frances's brother, Alexander Culpeper, used information from the letter in fall 1677, when he presented a formal response to the commissioners' criticisms of Sir William Berkeley (CO 1/41, no. 119). Jeffreys's wife repeated to Moryson one of Lady Berkeley's remarks about him; for his sarcastic response, and for a report of how Lord John Berkeley accused him of ingratitude, see Moryson to Thomas Ludwell, 28 November 1677, in John Burk, *History of Virginia...,* 4 vols. (Petersburg, Va.: Dickson & Pescud, 1804–16), 2:266–67. Warren Billings has observed to me (personal communication) that Lady Frances perhaps felt especially betrayed by Moryson, who had been her husband's long-time associate.

40. Wilcomb E. Washburn investigated this case in detail; even though his account reads like a legal brief supporting Sir William Berkeley, it is useful for its careful investigation of Sarah Drummond's claims and its identification of the property to which she referred. See Washburn, "The Humble Petition of Sarah Drummond," *WMQ,* 3rd ser., 13 (1956): 354–75. General details about the case in this and the following three paragraphs are based on Washburn, in addition to the documents cited in the notes. The original of her petition (quotations) is in CO 1/41, no. 74.

41. Privy Council minutes, 19 October 1677, Privy Council 2/66, ff. 133–35, TNA (hereafter PC 2); Moryson to Thomas Ludwell, 28 November 1677, in Burk, *History of Virginia,* 2:266. Emboldened by her success, Mistress Drummond quickly submitted another petition, this one directed to the Privy Council and asking that certain goods taken from her by Sir John Berry be returned. Berry responded that he had used some wine and brandy for the king's service, but that he would return the rest of her possessions (or the money made from selling them), and the Council concurred. See CO 1/41, nos. 76, 91; and PC 2/66, f. 156.

42. Francis Moryson to "Honored Sir," 24 December 1677, CO 1/41, no. 137. And see Moryson to Thomas Ludwell, 28 November 1677, in Burk, *History of Virginia,* 2:266; and [William Blathwayt?] to [Moryson], draft, 2 January 1677/8, CO

1/42, no. 1, replying that the Lords of Trade and Plantations understood that Berry and Moryson were not referring to the innocence of Drummond and that the decision had been based on "compassion" for the widow and nothing more.

43. General Court, minutes, 8 June 1678, CO 5/1371, ff. 531–32; [Herbert Jeffreys], "A Narrative of Some Affaires in Virginia…," c. June 1678, Coventry Papers, 78:168; Sarah Drummond to Francis Moryson, 8 July 1678, CO 5/1371, ff. 533–42. As Sarah Drummond knew, one of the councillors present, Nathaniel Bacon Sr., had been among those who tried and condemned her husband on 20 January 1676/7. Cf. the 8 June 1678 minutes and those of 20 January 1676/7, in McIlwaine, *Minutes of the Council and General Court,* 454.

44. The discussion in this and the next paragraph is based on Sarah Drummond to Francis Moryson, 8 July 1678, CO 5/1371, ff. 533–42; and on Drummond's two petitions to the governor and council of Virginia, both c. June 1678, CO 5/1371, 523–26, 527–30. Mistress Drummond's case became a topic of conversation at Green Spring on 9 June 1678; see Paul Williams, deposition, 6 July 1678, Coventry Papers, 78:272. An inventory of the Drummonds' possessions prepared by representatives of the commissioners is in CO 5/1371, ff. 457–60. Drummond reported to Moryson that the court dismissed her case in June, but it was reheard subsequently. McIlwaine, *Minutes of the Council and General Court,* 521, indicates that the records included a letter of hers dated 30 August [1678]. Hening, *Statutes at Large,* 2:558, which discloses that Mistress Drummond won the case, does not give a date for the hearing or the decision. Possibly, though, the September 1678 letter to her nephew in which Lady Frances complained that she was being required to reimburse people from whom her husband had seized goods refers to the judgment in this case. See n. 28, above.

45. This is my reconstruction based on the brief comments in Hening, *Statutes at Large,* 2:558. Unfortunately for future historians, Hening decided that a lack of space prevented him from reprinting the entire case record, which, he declared, "goes fully into the character of Sir Wm. Berkeley, of Drummond and his wife, during the rebellion, and discloses many curious facts in relation to those times."

46. For the quotations in this paragraph, see Herbert R. Paschal, ed., "George Bancroft's 'Lost Notes' on the General Court Records of Seventeenth-Century Virginia," *VMHB* 91 (1983): 355–59; and Hening, *Statutes at Large,* 2:558. Judging by the folio numbers Bancroft noted, the case occupied at least twenty-three pages. If Frances disputed Sarah's accounting of the seized property, neither Hening nor Bancroft noted it.

47. For years, Lady Frances actively pursued a claim to the three months' salary she argued was due her husband for the time he had stubbornly remained in Virginia after having been ordered to return to England. Not until 1682 did Susanna Jeffreys win the battle of dueling petitions. The dispute may be traced in Coventry Papers, 77:431, 78:91, 169, 217, 268–69; CO 1/43, nos. 143, 152, 155; CO 1/44, no. 4; CO 1/45, no. 8; CO 1/46, no. 85; and PC 2/68, ff. 248, 318; PC 2/69, f. 590. See also Billings, *Papers of Berkeley,* 634.

48. Herbert Jeffreys to [Sir Henry Coventry], 11 February 1677/8, Coventry Papers, 78:206; same to unknown, 31 March 1678, ibid., f. 215; same to [Francis Moryson?], 1 April 1678, ibid., f. 214. See also "An abstract of a Letter from Col Herbert Jeffreys… to Col. Francis Moryson dated the 30th of December 1677," CO 1/41, no. 138; William Sherwood to [Sir Joseph Williamson], 1 July 1678, CO 1/42, no. 103.

49. [Herbert Jeffreys], "Narrative of Some Affaires," c. June 1678, Coventry Papers, 78:168–69. Warren M. Billings, *Virginia's Viceroy: Their Majesties' Governor General; Francis Howard, Baron Howard of Effingham* (Fairfax, Va.: George Mason University Press, 1991), esp. 27–28 and 71, discusses the opposition to Jeffreys and his successors in Virginia, and briefly considers Lady Frances's crucial role.

50. [—Parke] to Sir Joseph Williamson, 3 January 1677/8, CO 1/42, no. 17. See also Jeffreys to [Sir Henry Coventry], 11 February 1677/8, Coventry Papers, 78:206.

51. Various documents pertaining to this incident are in Coventry Papers, 78:134, 135 (the slander), 172 (Ludwell's account), 173 (the dueling statements). Jeffreys's letters to England in the first months of 1678 all contained progress reports on the affair; see his missives dated from February to June, ibid., ff. 168–69 ("Effronts…"), 207, 214–17. For "scandalous," see McIlwaine, *Minutes of the Council and General Court,* 521.

52. Jeffreys to [Sir Henry Coventry], 4 July 1678, Coventry Papers, 78:268; William Sherwood to [Sir Joseph Williamson], 8 August 1678, CO 1/41, no. 117. Jeffreys's last surviving letter, 7 August 1678, Coventry Papers, 78:283, reiterates the same theme as all those that preceded it: the troubles being caused him "dayly" by "the Greenspring Factious Caball."

53. Thomas, Lord Culpeper, to Judith Culpeper, 14 May 1680, Wykeham-Martin Papers, Kentish County Council Archives, Maidstone, U.K. For Chicheley's comment about his "high esteeme" for Lady Berkeley, see his letter to Lord Culpeper, 13 July 1679, Coventry Papers, 78:397. For biographical information, see Paul David Nelson, "Culpeper, Thomas," *ANB* 5:845–46.

54. For some correspondence mentioning her in these years, see Billings, *Papers of Francis Howard,* 81–82, 115, 235; William Fitzhugh to Nicholas Hayward, 3 November 1690, *VMHB* 3 (1895–96): 253 (quotation); Marion Tinling, ed., *The Correspondence of the Three William Byrds of Westover, Virginia, 1684–177,* 2 vols. (Charlottesville, Va., 1977), 1:12–121 passim; and her letters to her nephew Sir Abstrupus Danby, Cunliffe-Lister Muniments, Bundle 69, sec. 11. Her last known letter, to Danby, is dated 31 May 1695 (Billings, *Papers of Berkeley,* 640–42). Biographical information: Lindley S. Butler, "Ludwell, Philip," *ANB* 14:107–8.

55. The most comprehensive treatment is Westbury, "Women in Bacon's Rebellion" (see n. 5, above). For the "white aprons," see Berry and Moryson, "True Narrative," 135; and "The History of Bacon's and Ingram's Rebellion, 1676," in Andrews, *Narratives,* 68–69. A major source of information about the activities of women of all social ranks in Charles City County is Col. Edward Hill's defense of his actions, drafted in May 1677 to respond to grievances submitted to Berry and Moryson by his neighbors. For example, he indicated that the wife of Mr. Anthony Haviland was "an excellent divulger of News," who "was sent post up & downe the Country as Bacon's Emissary to Carry his declarations & papers." The lengthy document was published in *VMHB* 3 (1895–96): 239–52, 341–49; 4 (1896–97): 1–15.

56. "Sir Wm Berkeleys Proclamation," 10 February 1676/7, CO 5/1371, f. 284, reprinted in Billings, *Papers of Berkeley,* 536–38. For some biographical details about Sarah, who had two previous husbands and was to have a fourth after Thomas's death, see Westbury, "Women in Bacon's Rebellion," 39–41. But Westbury omitted the

close family ties between Sarah and William Byrd I through her first husband's family. See Tinling, ed., *Correspondence of the Three William Byrds,* 2:826.

57. Case of Thomas Grendon, "Personal Grievances of divers inhabitants . . . ," 15 October 1677, CO 5/1371, f. 339, reprinted with small changes in Oberg, *Wiseman's Book,* 260–61.

58. Berry and Moryson to Sir Joseph Williamson, 27 March 1677, in Oberg, *Wiseman's Book,* 104; Sarah Grendon, petition to the commissioners, n.d. [but before 10 May 1677], Coventry Papers, 78:6.

59. Case of Sarah Grendon, "Personal Grievances," 15 October 1677, CO 5/1371, f. 340; reprinted with small changes in Oberg, *Wiseman's Book,* 261.

60. Case of Sarah Grendon, "Personal Grievances," 15 October 1677, CO 5/1371, f. 340; reprinted with small changes in Oberg, *Wiseman's Book,* 262. On the restoration of their property, see Privy Council minutes, 12 December 1677, PC 2/66, f. 189.

Mistress Alice Tilly and Her Supporters, 1649–1650

1. My discussion is drawn generally from Mary Beth Norton, "'The Ablest Midwife That Wee Knowe in the Land': Mistress Alice Tilly and the Women of Boston and Dorchester, 1649–1650," *WMQ,* 3rd ser., 60 (1998): 105–34. There were six petitions in all; the first, extremely brief and consisting of only two questions, was signed by five women and three men, including two spousal pairs. No man signed any of the five petitions at issue in this discussion. The six petitions included 294 signatures from the 217 women; 47 women signed two petitions, and 14 signed three. David Zaret, *Origins of Democratic Culture: Printing, Petitions, and the Public Sphere in Early-Modern England* (Princeton, N.J.: Princeton University Press, 2000), chap. 4, discusses traditional individualized English petitioning practices.

2. The three petitions discussed in this and the next paragraph are reprinted in Norton, "Ablest Midwife," 122–26. Because most of the court records in this period have been lost, the precise content of the charges against Mistress Tilly is unknown. For her arrest, see ibid., 111.

3. The two 1650 petitions are reprinted in ibid., 126–29; for scattered information about Alice Tilly's subsequent life in Boston, see ibid., 114–15.

4. The Dorchester petitions are in ibid., 123–24, 126–27. On Greenaway and her daughters, see ibid., 117.

5. For these Boston petitions, see ibid., 122–23, 127–29. The lack of expertise in phrasing suggests that women themselves drafted all the petitions, even if (as seems likely) male scribes copied three of them.

6. See ibid., 116 and n37, on the signers of the second Boston petition of 1649. The petition closed, "And Soe Humbly expecting a gratious Answere which if you grant wee shall for ever bee bound to bee thankfull to God and remaine yors in the Lord" (125). Ursula and David Yale's son, Elihu, the later benefactor and namesake of Yale College, was born in early April 1649, so Alice Tilly probably supervised his birth during one of her absences from jail before her trial.

7. For the quotations in this paragraph, see (in the following order) Norton, "Ablest Midwife," 128, 126, 124, 127–28.

8. Norton, "Ablest Midwife," 128.

2. English Women in the Public Realm, 1642–1653

1. "The humble petition of many poore distressed women in & about London" to House of Lords, 1 February 1641/2, HO/PO/JO/10/1/115, Parliamentary Archives, Houses of Parliament, London; *To the Right Honorable the high Court of Parliament: The Humble Petition of many hundreds of distressed Women, Trades-mens Wives, and Widdowes* (London: John Hammond, 1642); hereafter cited as *Humble Petition of Many Hundreds*. Unless otherwise noted, all contemporary political publications cited in this chapter, such as this one, are from Thomason Tracts, BL.

2. Judith Bennett (personal communication, November 2008) has called my attention to several petitions to the authorities by groups of fourteenth- and fifteenth-century female Londoners, but they dealt with matters of personal finance (such as debts owed them by the monarch's household) rather than politics. Some sources report female-only crowd actions, but no secular political petitions signed only by women; see Ralph Houlbrooke, "Women's Social Life and Common Action in England from the Fifteenth Century to the Eve of the Civil War," *Continuity and Change* 1 (1986): 171–89.

3. On traditional petitioning patterns, see David Zaret, *Origins of Democratic Culture: Printing, Petitions, and the Public Sphere in Early-Modern England* (Princeton, N.J.: Princeton University Press, 2000), 68–99. For aristocratic women's tradition of political activity, see, e.g., Barbara J. Harris, *English Aristocratic Women, 1450–1550: Marriage and Family, Property and Careers* (New York: Oxford University Press, 2002); and Sara Mendelson and Patricia Crawford, *Women in Early Modern England, 1550–1720* (Oxford: Clarendon Press, 1998), 56, 347. Elaine Hobby, *Virtue of Necessity: English Women's Writing, 1649–88* (London: Virago, 1988), 14–18, briefly discusses individual and collective petitions.

4. This paragraph summarizes the major arguments of Zaret in *Origins of Democratic Culture*. He contends, 217–65, that the Civil War petitions were crucial to the constitution of public opinion and democratic culture, but he does not consider the gendered implications of his argument. On levels of literacy and the history of newsbooks, see ibid., 151, 185–96; and Joad Raymond, *The Invention of the Newspaper: English Newsbooks, 1641–1649* (Oxford: Clarendon Press, 1996), esp. 241–53. A thoughtful discussion of such themes is Raymond, "The Newspaper, Public Opinion, and the Public Sphere in the Seventeenth Century," in *News, Newspapers, and Society in Early Modern Britain,* ed. Raymond (London: Frank Cass, 1999), 109–40. See also Peter Lake and Steve Pincus, "Rethinking the Public Sphere in Early Modern England," *Journal of British Studies* 45 (April 2006): 270–92.

5. Diane Purkiss, *The English Civil War: Papists, Gentlewomen, Soldiers, and Witchfinders in the Birth of Modern Britain* (New York: Basic Books, 2006), is a lively and unusually wide-ranging general narrative of the era and is the source for information given in this chapter on the progress of the Civil War. For the immediate pre-war period, see David Cressy, *England on Edge: Crisis and Revolution, 1640–1642* (New York: Oxford University Press, 2006). Also relevant is Michelle Anne White, *Queen Henrietta Maria and the English Civil Wars* (Burlington: Ashgate, 2006).

6. *Humble Petition of Many Hundreds;* surely any such previous petitions had been presented to the Long Parliament just a few months before. The first newsbook was published in late November 1641, so the absence of surviving commentary on earlier

appeals is not surprising; see Raymond, *Invention of the Newspaper,* 108–11. Useful studies are Patricia Higgins, "The Reactions of Women, with Special Reference to Women Petitioners," in *Politics, Religion, and the English Civil War,* ed. Brian Manning (London: Edward Arnold, 1973), 179–222; and Ann Marie McEntee, "'The [Un] Civill-Sisterhood of Oranges and Lemons': Female Petitioners and Demonstrators, 1642–1653," in *Pamphlet Wars: Prose in the English Revolution,* ed. James Holstun (London: Frank Cass, 1992), 92–111. For the broader context of women's political conversations at the time, see Dagmar Friest, "The King's Crown Is the Whore of Babylon: Politics, Gender, and Communication in Mid-Seventeenth-Century England," *Gender and History* 7 (1995): 457–81; Lois G. Schwoerer, "Women's Public Political Voice in England, 1640–1740," in *Women Writers and the Early Modern British Political Tradition,* ed. Hilda L. Smith (New York: Cambridge University Press, 1998), 56–74; and Bernard Capp, *When Gossips Meet: Women, Family, and Neighbourhood in Early Modern England* (Oxford: Oxford University Press, 2003), 267–319.

7. *Journal of the House of Commons,* 10 vols. (London: His Majesty's Stationery Office, 1802) 2 (1640–1643):404–5, 407 (hereafter cited as *Commons Journal*); Henry Oxenden to Henry Oxenden, n.d. [early February 1641/2], Oxenden Family Correspondence, Add. MSS 28000, f. 48, BL, including the estimate of five hundred representing five thousand. *The True Diurnal Occurrances, or, The Heads of the Proceedings of Both Houses in Parliament,* 31 January–7 February 1641/2, estimated the crowd at four hundred. That newsbook, but no other source, stated that the women presented a petition with the same content to the House of Lords on 31 January.

8. *True Diurnal Occurrances,* 31 January–7 February 1641/2. A less sympathetic account termed the women "a rude multitude" and their behavior with Lennox "impudent." See Robert Fox to Sir John Pennington, 3 February 1641/2, *Calendar of State Papers, Domestic…1641–43* (London: Her Majesty's Stationery Office, 1887), 274. The duke, a loyal cousin of Charles I, left the House of Lords on February 2, never to return. See David L. Smith, "Stuart, James, fourth duke of Lennox and first duke of Richmond," *ODNB* 53:159–61.

9. Among many modern editions, see Aristophanes, *The Congresswomen (Ecclesiazusae),* trans. Douglass Parker (Ann Arbor: University of Michigan Press, 1967). There appears to have been no English translation in the seventeenth century, but the duke could have read it in another language or simply been aware of its theme.

10. *The Petition of the Weamen of Middlesex…* (London: William Bowden, 1641). The only extended scholarly discussion of this satire is Georgia Wilder, "The Weamen of Middlesex: Faux Female Voices in the English Revolution," in *Shell Games: Studies in Scams, Frauds, and Deceits (1300–1650),* ed. Mark Crane et al. (Toronto: Centre for Reformation and Renaissance Studies, 2004), 163–83, but much of Wilder's analysis revolves around the erroneous assumption that *Weamen* preceded all the actual women's petitions.

11. *A True Copy of the Petition of the Gentle-women, & Trades-mens wives In, and about the City of London, Delivered to the Honourable, the Knights, Citizen and Burgesses of the House of Commons, assembled in Parliament, Feb. 4, 1641[/2]* (London: J. Wright, 1642), unpaginated preface, 6 (hereafter cited as *True Copy*). See Patricia-Ann Lee, "Mistress Stagg's Petitioners: February 1642," *Historian* 60 (Winter 1998): 241–56. Lee identifies Stagg as the wife of Giles, a brewer and City of London freeman, and observes that the women's concerns resembled those expressed by men at the same time.

12. *True Copy*, esp. 1–3. The words *humble* or *humbly* occurred six times in the text of this petition, but only once each in those of 1 February, in addition to the uses in the titles.

13. Ibid., 5–6.

14. For discussions of the religious foundations of women's petitions, see Sharon L. Arnoult, "The Sovereignties of Body and Soul: Women's Political and Religious Actions in the English Civil War," in *Women and Sovereignty*, ed. Louise Olga Fradenburg (Edinburgh: Edinburgh University Press, 1992), 228–49; and Patricia Crawford, "Public Duty, Conscience, and Women in Early Modern England," in *Public Duty and Private Conscience in Seventeenth-Century England: Essays Presented to G. E. Aylmer*, ed. John Morrill, Paul Slack, and Daniel Woolf (Oxford: Clarendon Press, 1993), 57–76.

15. *True Copy*, 4 ("new" petitioners); *True Diurnal Occurrances*, 31 January–7 February 1641/2; *Commons Journal* 2 (1640–1643):413.

16. Pym's statement is printed at the end of *True Copy; Journal of the House of Lords*, 10 vols. (London: His Majesty's Stationery Office, 1802) 4 (1629–1642):562 (hereafter cited as *Lords Journal*). On the crowds that regularly gathered at the Houses of Parliament, see Jason Peacey, "Print Culture and Political Lobbying during the English Civil War," *Parliamentary History* 26, pt. 1 (2007): 30–48.

17. *The Resolution of the Women of London to the Parliament…*([London: no pub., 1642]); [dated 26 August], title page, A2. George Thomason, who bought these publications now located in the BL, wrote dates of purchase on most of the political tracts he acquired; such dates are indicated in subsequent notes, as in this one. On the real and mock women's petitions of the 1640s, see Marcus Nevitt, *Women and the Pamphlet Culture of Revolutionary England, 1640–1660* (Aldershot, U.K.: Ashgate, 2006), 164–69.

18. *The Mid-wives Just Petition…*(London: [no pub.,] 1642/3) [dated 26 January], title page, A3v, A2r, A2v; *The Virgins Complaint for the losse of their Sweet-Hearts…*(London: Henry Wilson, 1642/3) [dated 31 January], 5; *The Humble Petition of Many Thousands of Wives and Matrons of the City of London…*(London: John Cookson, 1642/3) [dated 2 February]; *The Widowes Lamentation for the Absence of their deare Children, and Suitors…*(London: John Robinson, 1642/3) [dated 8 February].

19. *Humble Petition of Many Thousands*, title page, 3; *Mid-wives Just Petition*, A2r.

20. Edward [Hyde], Earl of Clarendon, *The History of the Rebellion and Civil Wars in England…*, 6 vols., ed. W. Dunn Macray (Oxford: Clarendon Press, 1888; reissued 1992), 3:135–39, esp. 136; Sir Simonds D'Ewes, Diary, 7 August 1643, Harleian Manuscripts 165, ff. 146a, 147a, 148a, BL. The House of Lords adjourned early that day, complaining that it regarded "the coming down of People in this Manner as a great Breach of Privilege of Parliament." See *Lords Journal* 6 (1643): 172. Ian J. Gentles contends that Londoners were at the time deeply divided over the war: Gentles, "Parliamentary Politics and the Politics of the Street: The London Peace Campaigns of 1642–3," *Parliamentary History* 26, pt. 2 (2007): 139–59.

21. Clarendon, *History*, 3:139; D'Ewes, Diary, 8 August 1643, f. 149b. Several newsbooks described the white silk ribbons; see below, n. 25.

22. Clarendon, *History*, 3:139; *Mercurius Civicus*, 3–11 August 1643; *Certain Informations from severall parts of the Kingdome*, 7–14 August 1643; *Kingdomes Weekly Intelligencer*, 8–15 August 1643. Clarendon called the demonstrators *silly*, a word some

historians have read as a critique, applying its modern meaning, but the *OED* defines it in this context as "defenseless."

23. *Mercurius Civicus,* 3–11 August 1643. See the comment that "little exception" could be made to the contents of the petition, in *Kingdomes Weekly Intelligencer,* 8–15 August 1643.

24. Quotations: Sir John Coke the Younger to Sir John Coke, 9 August 1643, Historical Manuscripts Commission, *Twelfth Report, Appendix, Part II: The Manuscripts of the Earl Cowper, K.G.* (London: Her Majesty's Stationery Office, 1888), 336; *Mercurius Civicus,* 3–11 August 1643. See *Commons Journal* 3 (1643–44): 199. The most detailed account of the riot is in *Kingdomes Weekly Intelligencer,* 8–15 August 1643.

25. *Mercurius Civicus,* 3–11 August 1643; *Kingdomes Weekly Intelligencer,* 8–15 August 1643. See also *Certain Informations,* 7–14 August 1643.

26. D'Ewes, Diary, 9 August 1643, f. 150a. See also Thomas Knyvett to Katherine Knyvett, 10 August 1643, Add. MSS 42153, f. 118, BL; Walter Yonge, Parliamentary Journal, 9 August 1643, Add. MSS 18778, ff. 13v–14, BL; and Lawrence Whiteacre, Diary, 9, 11 August 1643, Add. MSS 31116, ff. 69r–v, BL. See an acidic royalist assessment of these events and the cowardice of pro-war men in *Mercurius Aulicus,* 6–12 August 1643.

27. *Parliament Scout,* 3–10 August 1643. *Mercurius Civicus* claimed that one of the women taken to Bridewell had "an old rusty blade by her side," but that was the only weapon a contemporary linked to any demonstrator other than rocks or objects that could be thrown (*Mercurius Civicus,* 3–11 August 1643).

28. Lady Brouncker, who seems to have remained in London while her husband was at Oxford, is mentioned in a biography of her son: G. S. McIntyre, "Brouncker, William, second Viscount Brouncker of Lyons," *ODNB* 7:998–99; on the Earl of Holland, see R. Malcolm Smuts, "Rich, Henry, first earl of Holland," *ODNB* 46:664–67.

29. *A Continuation of certain Speciall and Remarkable Passages informed to the Parliament,* 10–18 August 1643; *Commons Journal* 3 (1643–44): 203.

30. On the House of Lords' inquiry into the 7 August demonstrators, see *Lords Journal* 6 (1643): 172–73. If a newsbook account of the encounter between the demonstrators and the Earl of Holland on 9 August is correct, they do not appear to have had prior contact with each other (see *Certain Informations,* 7–14 August 1643). Patricia Higgins remarks that the women were "probably committed to neither side and genuinely anxious to end the war," although they might have been "exploited" by royalists (Higgins, "Reactions of Women," 199). See also the assessment in Gentles, "Parliamentary Politics," 156.

31. Gerolamo Agostini to Doge and Senate, 28 August 1643, in *Calendar of State Papers...in the Collections of Venice..., 1643–1647* (London: His Majesty's Stationery Office, 1926), 11 (see also 8); *Commons Journal* 3 (1643–44): 202.

32. The three mock petitions to Parliament from women appeared in August and September 1647: *The Maids Petition. To the Honourable Members of Both Houses...* ([London: no pub.,] 1647) [not purchased by Thomason]; *A Remonstrance of the Shee-Citizens of London...* ([London: no pub.,] 1647) [dated 28 August 1647]; *The City-Dames Petition...* ([London: no pub.,] 1647) [dated 28 September 1647]. Later pamphlets and broadsides parodying women's authorship and employing "petition" in the title did not direct their complaints to Parliament or indeed to any official body until 1681

and the publication of *The Petition of the Ladies at Court, Intended to be Presented to the House of Lords: against the Pride and Luxury of the City Dames* ([London]: R. J., 1681). All such later "petitions" are replete with sexual content but lack political allusions.

33. This and the following paragraph are based on the unpaginated *The Parliament of Women: With the merrie Lawes by them newly Enacted*...(London: W. Wilson, 1646) [dated 14 August 1646]; and the reprint, *A Parliament of Ladies: with their Lawes Newly Enacted* ([London: no pub., 1647]) [dated 16 April 1647]. Later reprints with minor variations followed. Some sources claim that a pamphlet titled *Parliament of Women* was published in 1640, but if so, no copies seem to have survived, and thus it is not clear whether (if it existed) it was identical to the 1646 text. On Aristophanes' play, see n. 9., above; and Parker, *Congresswomen*. Cf. the discussions of pamphlets employing the "parliament" trope in Mary Fissell, *Vernacular Bodies: The Politics of Reproduction in Early Modern England* (Oxford: Oxford University Press, 2004), 191–94; and Hilda L. Smith, *All Men and Both Sexes: Gender, Politics, and the False Universal in England, 1640–1812* (University Park: Pennsylvania State University Press, 2002), chap. 3, esp. 125–27.

34. Thomason did not acquire the first printing of *The Parliament of Ladies* ([London: no pub.,] 1647), but its preface is dated 26 March 1647. He did purchase the other 1647 publications mentioned in this paragraph and the next, which are discussed below in more detail. Thomason dated Neville's corrected second edition as 18 May 1647 and the sequel, *The Ladies, A Second Time Assembled, in Parliament* ([London: no pub.,] 1647), as 13 September 1647 (hereafter cited as *Second Time*).

35. For the republications of *Parliament of Women*, see above, n. 33. Thomason dated the pirated version, *The Ladies Parliament*, as 18 July 1647. The mock petition, not acquired by Thomason, was *To the Right Honourable, the Ladies Ordinary and Extraordinary, assembled in Parliament, now sitting in Spring Garden* ([London: no pub.,] 1647). The response, dated by Thomason as 29 July 1647, is [Marchamont Nedham], *Match me these two...With an Answer to a Pamphlet, entituled, The Parliament of Ladies* ([London: no pub.,] 1647); see p. 13 for the quoted passage. Neville's pamphlet was reprinted in 1705, 1708, and 1768; and publications using related themes appeared in 1656 and 1684. Interest in the idea was not limited to England. Late in the seventeenth century, an Irish author writing in Gaelic created a female "parliament" that concerned itself with moral and cultural topics; see Brian Ó Cuív, ed., *Parliament na mBan* (Dublin: Institute for Advanced Studies, 1977); see esp. xxxi–xxxiv. I owe this reference to Mary O'Dowd.

36. See Nicholas von Maltzahn, "Neville, Henry," *ODNB* 40:499–501. Some authors and the English Short Title Catalogue attribute all or most of the *Parliament of Ladies*–themed pamphlets to Neville, but style and content suggest that he wrote only the first and its most obvious sequel, *Second Time*.

37. The quotation is from *Second Time*, 7. The only discordant note in either pamphlet appears at the end of the second (corrected) edition of *Parliament of Ladies*, in a passage printed in a different typeface and perhaps not written by Neville but instead added by the printer. In it, a monstrous female figure wearing a dildo invades a parliament composed of women and shaken by a "rumor of Doomsday"; see 13–15. At least one later reader's intense interest in Neville's pamphlets is revealed by his marginal annotations in the copies of both the second edition of *Parliament of Ladies* and *Second Time*, bound together and catalogued at the Bodleian Library, Oxford, as

Mal. 710 (1); internal references show that he made the notes after the Restoration. Purkiss notes that Anthony Wood, an Oxford resident, created a personal book catalog that included an entry for 'Wom Parl. Of'' as one of 139 items under "women"; see *English Civil War,* 277–78.

38. *Parliament of Ladies,* title page, 4. For biographical information on these women and their husbands, see R. Malcolm Smuts, "Rich, Henry, first earl of Holland," *ODNB* 46:664–67; G. D. Owen, "Cecil, William, second earl of Salisbury," *ODNB* 10:796–97.

39. *Parliament of Ladies,* 6–7. Neville liked the trope of the proposition about "weake persons" so much that he employed it again in *Second Time;* with only slight variations in wording, it was the subject of the "humble petition" of "Citizens Wives." See *Second Time,* 7. For biographical information, see Nabil Matar, "Blount, Sir Henry," *ODNB* 6:302–3; D. A. Orr, "Foster, Sir Robert," *ODNB* 20:523–24; and Michael J. Braddick, "Cranfield, Lionel, first earl of Middlesex," *ODNB* 14:1–6.

40. *Second Time,* 6–7; *Parliament of Ladies,* 14. On Harley's iconoclastic activities, see Purkiss, *English Civil War,* 201–3. For biographical information, see Andrew J. Hopper, "Grey, Henry, first earl of Stamford," *ODNB* 23:849–51; and J. T. Peacey, "Norton, Sir Gregory, first baronet," *ODNB* 41:170–71; Lord "Montague" was probably Lord Montagu of Boughton, whose wife died in 1642; Anne Cecil Grey, wife of Henry, the Earl of Stamford, was at least ten years older than he. (My thanks to Barbara Donagan for the information about Montagu and Grey.)

41. *An Exact Diurnall of the Parliament of Ladyes* ([London: no pub., n.d.]) [dated 6 May 1647]; *(Hey Hoe, for a Husband,) Or, The Parliament of Maides: Their Desires, Decrees, and Determinations* ([London: no pub.,] 1647) [dated 24 September 1647]; *Newes from the New Exchange; or the Common-Wealth of Ladies, Drawn to the Life, in their severall Characters and Concernments* (London: [no pub.,] 1650), 1 [not purchased by Thomason]. A BL copy of *Newes* (16567) has six manuscript pages of verse bound at the back; each quatrain focuses on a noblewoman's sexual misdeeds. Although a handwritten note asserts that the verses were "much too gross for publication," similar verses appeared in print at the end of the pirated *Ladies Parliament* in July 1647 (see n. 35, above). Like the annotations described in n. 37, above, the verses indicated readers' intense interest in the scurrilous tales. Although *Exact Diurnall* and *Newes* have been attributed to Neville, both are so inferior in wit and style to *Parliament of Ladies* and *Second Time* that I think those attributions erroneous. The libels in *Newes* elicited a published response proclaiming its author to be "a sworne profest enemy both to Vertue, Piety, and true Nobility." See *New News from the Old Exchange: or the Common-wealth of Vertous Laides…* ([London: no pub., 1650?]), 4.

42. Roger Thompson, *Unfit for Modest Ears: A Study of Pornographic, Obscene, and Bawdy Works Written or Published in England in the Second Half of the Seventeenth Century* (London: Macmillan, 1979), 104, dismisses these publications as nothing more than "good undergraduate bawdry." Cf. Susan Wiseman, "'Adam, the Father of all Flesh,' Porno-Political Rhetoric and Political Theory in and after the English Civil War," in Holstun, *Pamphlet Wars,* 134–57; and Diane Purkiss, *Literature, Gender, and Politics during the English Civil War* (Cambridge: Cambridge University Press, 2005), 64–70. Both offer evocative readings of the ladies' parliament literature but miss its full political and social implications.

43. For a useful discussion of the relationship of political and sexual inversions in *The Man in the Moon,* a royalist newsbook, see David Underdown, *A Freeborn People: Politics and the Nation in Seventeenth-Century England* (Oxford: Clarendon Press, 1996), 90–111.

44. For these developments, see Purkiss, *English Civil War,* 463–510; and Michael Mendle, ed., *The Putney Debates of 1647: The Army, the Levellers, and the English State* (New York: Cambridge University Press, 2001).

45. This paragraph summarizes *To the Right Honorable the Commons of England in Parliament Assembled. The humble Petition of divers wel affected Persons*…([London: no pub., 1648]), 1, 2, 6, 7, and passim [dated 15 September 1648].

46. Among such publications were *A plea for common-right and freedom…Or, the serious addresses…of…presenters of the late large-petition*…(London: Ja. and Jo. Moxon, 1648); *A copie off two letters…to his excellency Thomas Lord Fairfax; concerning the late large petition*…([London: no pub., 1648]).

47. It is thought that Walwyn had no hand in drafting the pamphlet for which the men were jailed. For excellent background on these Levellers, see Andrew Sharp, "Lilburne, John," *ODNB* 33:773–82; Ann Hughes, "Lilburne, Elizabeth," *ODNB* 33:772–73; B. J. Gibbons, "Overton, Richard," *ODNB* 42:166–71; Barbara Taft, "Walwyn, William," *ODNB* 57:225–31; and P.R.S. Baker, "Prince, Thomas," *ODNB* 45:395. The quotation is from *Juglers Discovered, In two Letters writ by Lieut. Col. John Lilburne*…([n.p.: no pub., n.d.]) [dated 27 October 1647].

48. *The Impartiall Intelligencer…,* 18–25 April 1649; *Perfect Occurrences of Every Daie Journal in Parliament…,* 20–27 April 1649; *Mercurius Pragmaticus…,* 17–24 April 1649. The account in *Perfect Occurrences* is one of only two reports of how signatures were obtained for *any* of the women's petitions in the 1640s; logically, "congregationall meetings" were involved, since such gatherings allowed efficient recruitment. The other account, in *Continued Heads of Perfect Passages in Parliament…,* 20–27 April 1649, claimed that "certain women [were] appointed in every Ward and Division" to collect the signed documents. See also, on the female Levellers and signature gathering, Stevie Davis, *Unbridled Spirits: Women of the English Revolution, 1640–1660* (London: Women's Press, 1998), 61–90, esp. 70; and Dorothy P. Ludlow, "Shaking Patriarchy's Foundation: Sectarian Women in England, 1641–1700," in *Triumph over Silence: Women in Protestant History,* ed. Richard L. Greaves (Westport, Conn.: Greenwood Press, 1985), 105–6.

49. For estimated numbers, see *The Kingdomes Faithfull and Impartiall Scout…,* 20–27 April 1649; *Impartiall Intelligencer,* 18–25 April 1649; *Mercurius Militaris, or The People's Scout…,* 17–24 April 1649. The petition summarized in this and the following two paragraphs is *To the Supream Authority of this Nation, the Commons assembled in Parliament: The humble Petition of divers wel-affected Women…(Affecters and Approvers of the late large Petition of the Eleventh of September, 1648)…*(London: [no pub.,] 1649).

50. Cf. Ann Hughes, "Gender and Politics in Leveller Literature," in *Political Culture and Cultural Politics in Early Modern England: Essays Presented to David Underdown,* ed. Susan Amussen and Mark Kishlansky (Manchester: Manchester University Press, 1995), 162–88, which stresses the familial themes and contends that the Leveller women's petitions were not as novel as the authors insisted. Yet the other 1640s petitions offered much more limited pronouncements on governmental matters than did this Leveller document.

51. *Perfect Occurrences,* 20–27 April 1649; *Mercurius Pragmaticus (For Charles II) …,* 24 April–1 May 1649. For other accounts of the women's "civil" departure, see, e.g., *The Moderate …,* 24 April–1 May 1649; and *Kingdomes Weekly Intelligencer,* 24 April–1 May 1649. One royalist paper commented that "they held their *tongues,* which was a wonder in their sex" (*Mercurius Pragmaticus …,* 24 April–1 May 1649).

52. *Mercurius Militaris,* 17–24 April 1649. A royalist newsbook also (but in very different language) reported a confrontation between Cromwell and the women; see *Mercurius Pragmaticus (For Charles II),* 24 April–1 May 1649.

53. *Perfect Occurrences,* 20–27 April 1649; *Mercurius Pragmaticus,* 23–30 April 1649; *Man in the Moon,* 16–24 April 1649. *The Moderate …,* 17–24 April 1649, allied with the Levellers, termed the petitioners "civil" and their language "humble, yet high."

54. *Continued Heads of Perfect Passages,* 20–27 April 1649. For other scornful newsbook accounts of the Leveller women, their petition, and the Commons' response, see *Mercurius Pragmaticus,* 24 April–1 May 1649; *Mercurius Elencticus …,* 24 April–1 May 1649; and *Man in the Moon,* 23–30 April 1649.

55. One royalist newsbook did use *public* and *private* in its commentary on the episode: the sergeant-at-arms "bad them goe home to their *housewiferie,*" it observed, "the *House* having no mind to deal with them in *publick* matters, whatever they mean [to do] in *private.*" In that sentence, only *public* conveyed the meaning at issue here; *private* referred not to women's household role but to MPs' personal relationships with their wives. See *Mercurius Pragmaticus (For Charles II),* 24 April–1 May 1649.

56. *A Perfect Diurnall of some Passages in Parliament …,* 30 April–7 May 1649.

57. This and the next two paragraphs summarize *To the Supreme Authority of England. The Commons Assembled in Parliament. The Humble Petition of divers well-affected Women …Affecters and Approvers of the Petition of Sept. 11 1648* ([London: no pub., 1649]) [dated 5 May 1649]. On Katherine Chidley, who was an active Leveller and an author of religious tracts, see Ian J. Gentles, "London Levellers in the English Revolution: The Chidleys and Their Circle," *Journal of Ecclesiastical History* 29 (1978): 281–309; Nevitt, *Women and the Pamphlet Culture,* 21–48; and Ian J. Gentles, "Chidley, Katherine," *ODNB* 11:410–12.

58. *A Modest Narrative of Intelligence …,* 5–12 May 1649; *Mercurius Militaris* [n.d., dated by Thomason 8 May 1649; tract E.554(13)]; *Mercurius Pragmaticus (For King Charls [sic] II),* 1–8 May 1649. McEntee misinterprets the final phrase as supporting the petitioners; see McEntee, "[Un]Civill Sisterhood," 103.

59. *Mercurius Britanicus …,* 1–8 May 1649; *England's Moderate Messenger …,* 2–9 May 1649; *Perfect Occurrences,* 4–11 May 1649. See also *Kingdomes Weekly Intelligencer,* 1–8 May 1649.

60. *Mercurius Militaris,* 22–29 May 1649.

61. On the history of newsbooks and the impact of the law, see Raymond, *Invention of the Newspaper,* chap. 1, esp. 72. Between 1649 and 1653, two other groups that included but do not seem to have been exclusively composed of women submitted petitions to Parliament or Cromwell. See *To the Supreme Authority of this Common-wealth, the Parliament of England: The humble Petition of the Creditors of such Delinquents whose Estates are propounded to be sold …* ([n.p.: no pub.,] 1650); and the allied *The Humble Petition of Severall of the Wives and Children of such Delinquents …* ([n.p., no pub.,] 1650) [both dated 1 August 1650]; and *The Womens Petition, To the Right Honorable, his Excellency, the most Noble and Victorious Lord General*

Cromwell ... ([n.p.: no pub., 1651]) [dated 30 October 1651]. The subtitle of the latter made it clear that men had also signed the petition: described as submitted by "many thousands of poor enslaved, oppressed and distressed Men and Women," it protested imprisonment for debt in general terms. In describing this petition, the contemporary author Bulstrode Whitelocke, *Memorials of the English Affairs ... A New Edition* (London: J. Tonson, 1732), 512–13, did not indicate that it came solely from women, although it has recently been so interpreted.

62. For these biographical details, see the *ODNB* article on Lilburne cited in n. 47, above.

63. *To the Parliament of the Commonwealth of England. The humble Petition of divers afflicted* WOMEN, *in behalf of M. John Lilburn Prisoner in Newgate* ([London: no pub., 1653]). Contemporary sources disagree about the precise dates of the two petitions; they also imply that there might have been a third address. Thomason dated the first 25 June 1653, but that date is clearly erroneous, since the petition refers to the ongoing trial. It is thought that he actually acquired it on 25 July. The first petition appears have been presented on 20 July, but see nn. 64, 65, below. See *Faithful Post,* 19–26 July 1653; and *The True and Perfect Dutch-Diurnall ...,* 19–26 July 1653.

64. *Unto every individual Member of Parliament: The humble Representation of divers afflicted Women Petitioners to the Parliament, on the behalf of Mr John Lilburn* ([London: no pub., 1653]) [dated 29 July 1653]. Contemporary sources refer to a petition presented on 27 July (which could be this one or the one acquired by Thomason on 25 July) but also to another, for which signatures were being gathered on 30 July (which could also be this one, or still a third, one that was not printed). See n. 65, below.

65. "Advertisements from London," 29 July 1653, Ms. Clarendon 46, f. 131b, Bodleian Library, Oxford. See also *A Perfect Account of the daily Intelligence ...,* 27 July–3 August 1653; *Faithful Post,* 26 July–2 August 1653.

66. *These Several Papers Was Sent to the Parliament The twentieth day of the fifth Moneth, 1659* ... (London: printed for Mary Westwood, 1659), a series of separate signed petitions against tithes from different Quaker women's meetings. The individual statements were primarily ungendered in their content. On these petitions, see Nevitt, *Women and the Pamphlet Culture,* 145–78.

Mistress Elinor James and Her Broadsides, 1681–1714

1. Paula McDowell is the only scholar who has examined James in any detail. See her excellent discussion in *The Women of Grub Street: Press, Politics, and Gender in the London Literary Marketplace, 1678–1730* (Oxford: Clarendon Press, 1998), part 2. McDowell has edited a comprehensive facsimile edition of James broadsides: Paula McDowell, ed., *Elinor James,* in *The Early Modern Englishwoman: A Facsimile Library of Essential Works,* part 3, vol. 11, series 2: *Printed Writings, 1641–1700,* ed. Betty S. Travitsky and Anne Lake Prescott (Aldershot, U.K.: Ashgate, 2004), hereafter cited as *EJ;* quotation, 83. The printer John Dunton termed James a "She-State-Politician" in *The Life and Errors of John Dunton, Citizen of London* ... (London: S. Malthus, 1705), 334. Recently (2010), a previously unknown James broadside has surfaced; undoubtedly more will be found in the future.

2. Biographical details: *EJ,* xvii–xxvi. For those titles and phrases, see 205, 137, 199.

3. The quotations come from broadsides she published in 1695, 1702, 1710, and 1712; see *EJ,* 91, 127, 135, 169, 199. She indicated that the encounters began in 1665 or 1666; see, e.g., 23, 129, 137, 160. McDowell notes that Charles II had a reputation for graciously receiving petitions from commoners; he seems to have been both amused and intrigued by James's statements.

4. *EJ,* 5, replying to a broadside reprinted on 263–64.

5. Quotations: ibid., 83, 121. For additional related recollections, see, e.g., 137, 160, 169, 176. Broadsides from the mid- to late 1680s with similar information are on 23–27.

6. *EJ,* 35–46 passim, esp. 38, 46. *A New Test…*is reprinted on 267–76. McDowell points out that Elinor James chose to hold her *Vindication* when her portrait was painted some years later, so she clearly took pride in this publication.

7. Thus, for example, a response to her *Vindication* attacked her arguments, not her female identity; see *EJ,* 277–78.

8. See *EJ,* 63–79 passim, for the many broadsides in which she worked out her thoughts on the transition in the monarchy. For her arrest and conviction, see Paula McDowell, "James, Elinor," *ODNB* 29:693–94. She supported the Hanoverian succession in 1714; see *EJ,* 205, 219, 231. For examples of broadsides addressed to Parliament and City officials, see ibid., 81–105 passim.

9. In 1710, James recalled one incident in the 1660s in which critics mentioned her sex (*EJ,* 169), but that is her only reference to such a comment early in her career.

10. *EJ,* 160, 173, 197, 233. See also, e.g., 209, 223.

11. Ibid., 133, 160, 223, 237–43.

12. On the gendered implications of Locke's theories, see Carole Pateman, *The Sexual Contract* (Stanford, Calif.: Stanford University Press, 1988).

3. John Dunton and the Invention of the Feminine Private

1. As a printer, John Dunton was notoriously casual about many things, including the pagination of his publications (as is evident in subsequent notes). The same was true of the title of this, his most successful work: after the first issue he was forced to change the name of individual numbers to *Athenian Mercury* because of objections from the official *London Gazette,* yet when he later printed conglomerate volumes he reverted to the original title. Like others, I employ *Athenian Mercury* (abbreviated *AM*). In *John Dunton and the English Book Trade: A Study of His Career with a Checklist of His Publications* (New York: Garland, 1976), 76, Stephen Parks observes that Dunton was "a brilliant popularizer, and he had a thorough understanding of the tastes and interests of his audience." (See also ibid., 189.) Two books have examined Dunton and the *Athenian Mercury:* Gilbert D. McEwen, *The Oracle of the Coffee House: John Dunton's Athenian Mercury* (San Marino, Calif.: Huntington Library, 1972); and Helen Berry, *Gender, Society and Print Culture in Late-Stuart England: The Cultural World of the Athenian Mercury* (Aldershot, U.K.: Ashgate, 2003). Excellent shorter treatments are Kathryn Shevelow, *Women and Print Culture: The Construction of Femininity in the Early Periodical* (London: Routledge, 1989), chaps. 2, 3; and E. J. Clery, *The Feminization Debate in Eighteenth-Century England: Literature, Commerce and Luxury* (New York: Palgrave Macmillan, 2004), chap. 2.

2. On coffeehouses and their patrons, including men and (possibly) women, see Steve Pincus, "'Coffee Politicians Does Create': Coffeehouses and Restoration Political Culture," *Journal of Modern History* 67 (1995): 807–34, esp. 814–16. Berry, unlike Pincus, believes that respectable women did not frequent coffeehouses; see *Gender, Society and Print Culture,* 56–58. An excellent commentary is Brian Cowan, "What Was Masculine about the Public Sphere? Gender and the Coffeehouse Milieu in Post-Restoration England," *History Workshop Journal* 51 (Spring 2001): 127–57. For colonial readers and Dunton's American connections, see nn. 18, 21, 28, below.

3. "The Duchess of Yorks Ghost," Ellesmere Manuscripts 8770, f. 78, HEHL. For a recent discussion of the unsettled political situation in England at the time, see Steve Pincus, *1688: The First Modern Revolution* (New Haven, Conn.: Yale University Press, 2009).

4. On the movement for the reformation of manners, see the balanced discussion in Margaret R. Hunt, *The Middling Sort: Commerce, Gender, and the Family in England, 1680–1780* (Berkeley: University of California Press, 1996), chap. 4. On male anxieties in this period, see Karen Harvey, "The History of Masculinity, circa 1650–1800," *Journal of British Studies* 44 (2005): 296–311, esp. 298–300. The challenges to traditional views listed in the text are Poulain de la Barre, *The Woman as Good as the Man...*, translated from the French by A.L. (London: T. M. for N. Brooks, 1677); Nahum Tate, *A Present for the Ladies...* (London: Francis Saunders, 1692); Mary Astell, *A Serious Proposal to the Ladies...* (London: R. Wilkin, 1695); [Judith Drake], *An Essay in Defence of the Female Sex...* (London: A. Roper and E. Wilkinson, 1696).

5. A good entry point into the vast literature on eighteenth-century gender is offered by G. J. Barker-Benfield, *The Culture of Sensibility: Sex and Society in Eighteenth-Century Britain* (Chicago: University of Chicago Press, 1992). On the importance of Dunton and his successors in creating "a developing discourse surrounding women that was reformulating sexual relations and the family based upon new criteria," see Shevelow, *Women and Print Culture,* 1–5 (quotation, 2).

6. There is no full-length published biography of John Dunton, but see the useful short summary by Helen Berry, "Dunton, John," *ODNB* 17:366–67. See also Theodore Merryman Hatfield, "The True Secret History of Mr. John Dunton" (Ph.D. dissertation, Harvard University, 1926) (copy at HEHL). Dunton eventually claimed to have published approximately six hundred works, and that figure might not have been too far off the mark; see Parks, *Dunton and the English Book Trade,* 43–44.

7. John Dunton, *The Life and Errors of John Dunton Late Citizen of London...* (London: S. Malthus, 1705), 249, 248.

8. See Parks, *Dunton and the English Book Trade,* 76–77; Berry, *Gender, Society and Print Culture,* 11–28 passim, esp. 13–16, 21. See also Dunton's contention that coffeehouses would please their customers by buying complete volumes in addition to purchasing the individual numbers as they appeared, in *AM* 2:3, 4 (3, 6 June 1691). He dedicated volume 11 to "the Worshipfull Society of Mercury-Women," on whom sales of the *AM* depended. See preface to volume 11 (11 July–21 October 1693).

9. Dunton's contract with Sault and Wesley is reprinted in full in Parks, *Dunton and the English Book Trade,* 81–82. Parks describes the initial history of the periodical and the process through which Dunton recruited early contributors (including, briefly, Daniel Defoe); see ibid., 78–80, 83–86. See also McEwen, *Oracle of the Coffee*

House, 23–26. Sault and Wesley (father of the founders of Methodism, John and Charles) were married to Dunton's younger half-sisters. E. J. Clery contends that "Dr. Norris" was Edward, a physician, not John, an academic previously identified as Dunton's collaborator. See *Feminization Debate,* 184n4, 186n20.

10. *AM* 1:1 (17 March 1690[/91]). On the importance of anonymity, see Shevelow, *Women and Print Culture,* 71–74. Berry, in *Gender, Society and Print Culture,* 244, table 1, summarizes the contents of the randomly selected volume 6 (January–May 1692): 31 percent of the printed queries related to courtship or marriage.

11. *AM* 1:1 (17 March 1690[/91]); ibid., 1:2 (24 March 1690[/91]). McEwen, *Oracle of the Coffee House,* surveys the eclectic overall contents of the *Mercury.*

12. *AM,* preface to volume 2 (30 May–18 August 1691). One woman sent a brief verse to ask about a female Athenian: "Have *you* not in this fam'd Society/A *womans Pen* to bear your Company?" The answer: "If *one* like *yours,* a great *Fel-i-ci-ty!*" See *AM* 17:22 (18 June 1695).

13. Ibid., preface to volume 3 (18 August–17 October 1691). Dunton did not specify which topics some readers thought inappropriate for coffeehouse conversations. See also the messages to readers in the prefaces to volumes 6 (30 January–10 May 1692), 8 (9 July–20 December 1692), 9 (20 December 1692–8 April 1693), 10 (8 April–11 July 1693).

14. *AM* 17:29 (9 July 1695).

15. This and the next paragraph are based on the contract as reprinted in Parks, *Dunton and the English Book Trade,* 81–82.

16. One question probably drafted by Dunton himself, in part because it differed significantly from most queries in the *Mercury* and in part because it revealed information from New England, where he had continuing contacts with Increase and Cotton Mather (see below, n. 21), was published in *AM* 12:29 (30 January 1694). The inquiry sought information about a peace treaty negotiated with the Wabanaki Indians at Pemaquid, Maine, in August 1693; the reply explicitly cited Dunton ("our Bookseller") as the source of the news. Another probably concocted question in 1692 asked the Athenians for their opinion of a book Dunton had just written, *The Post Boy Robb'd of His Mail;* the response termed it "both Pleasant and Witty" (*AM* 8:11 [4 October 1692]). For the surviving correspondence, see nn. 23, 25, 26, below.

17. Helen Berry reached the same conclusion (see *Gender, Society and Print Culture,* 36–49), as did Kathryn Shevelow (see *Women and Print Culture,* 38–42). A similar interpretive problem confronted my former graduate student Jackie Hatton in her dissertation on *True Story* magazine, and I acknowledge here my indebtedness to her reasoning about that analogous twentieth-century publication. See Jacqueline A. Hatton, "True Stories: Working-Class Mythology, American Confessional Culture, and *True Story* Magazine, 1919–1929" (Ph.D. dissertation, Cornell University, 1997). Hatfield, writing about John Dunton in 1926, recognized his similarity to Bernarr McFadden, publisher of *True Story;* see Hatfield, "True Secret History," 411.

18. For the statistics on content of a random volume, see Berry, *Gender, Society and Print Culture,* 244, table 1. On audience, imitators, and the play, which was published but never performed, see ibid., 20–23, 41; and Parks, *Dunton and the English Book Trade,* 94–98. In *Life and Errors,* 261, Dunton recalled that one noble admirer expressed an intention to send bound volumes *"into the Indies,* to his Friends." See

also *AM* 3:18 (26 September 1691) and 4:8 (24 October 1691), for a question from Maryland. Although I found no contemporary reference in American sources to the *Mercury,* the compiled three-volume set, titled *The Athenian Oracle* (London: Andrew Bell, 1703–4; reprinted several times thereafter), was advertised by colonial booksellers throughout the eighteenth century and is also recorded as having been read in at least one colonial lending library (see below, n. 28). (Hereafter abbreviated *AO.*) Because I was unable to consult all the original issues of *AM,* some questions and answers are cited to the reprints in *AO,* which are undated.

19. *AM* 1:13 (5 May 1691); 1:17 (19 April [*sic;* i.e., May] 1691); 1:18 (23 May 1691). The first question a woman asked was whether fleas sting or suck their victims. The Athenians accurately replied that the latter was correct.

20. *AM* 3:13 (8 September 1691). This response did not stop the criticism; the *AM* received more "Rebukes" from men objecting to "this *poor Love-paper,*" to which Dunton replied in 5:3 (8 December 1691).

21. See Hatfield, "True Secret History," 16–32, which convincingly dates the manuscript (now in Rawlinson Papers, D 71, Bodleian Library, Oxford) in 1698; Chester Noyes Greenough, "John Dunton's Letters from New England," *Publications of the Colonial Society of Massachusetts* 14 (1912): 213–57; and William Whitmore, introduction, John Dunton, *Letters from New-England* (Boston: Prince Society, 1867). During his sojourn in Boston, Dunton developed a cordial relationship with Increase and Cotton Mather, leading to his 1693 reprinting of their works on Salem witchcraft.

22. Quotations are from Dunton, *Letters from New-England,* 97, 160. For the lengthy (plagiarized) descriptions, see ibid., 98–116, 281. He could not have named Elizabeth Singer in 1686 because he did not know her until the 1690s, nor had she yet written anything noteworthy, but he could have named Philips and Behn. The citations in n. 21, above, especially the article by Greenough, identify the sources from which Dunton copied. Men's journals reprinted in Newton D. Mereness, ed., *Travels in the American Colonies* (New York: Macmillan, 1916), rarely mention women.

23. Elizabeth Singer to John Dunton, 1 August 1695, transcribed in part and summarized in part in Hatfield, "True Secret History," quotations on 82–83 (Hatfield unfortunately gives no source for this letter, but it is presumably located in the Rawlinson Papers, D 72); "A Pindarick, to the Athenian Society," *AM* 17:29 (9 July 1695). Dunton introduced the poem with the comment that all of Singer's writings have "a peculiar Delicacy of *Stile* and Majesty of *Verse,* as does sufficiently distinguish 'em from all others." For the dedication of volume 15, see *AM* 16:10 (19 January 1695). Other poems of hers appeared in such issues as 14:3 (29 May 1694), 18:22 (28 September 1695), and 19:18 (28 December 1695). Clery stresses the importance of Singer's contribution to the *AM* project: see *Feminization Debate,* 34–41.

24. [John Dunton], *The Athenian Spy* (London: R. Halfrey, 1704), part 1 introduction, last page of book (unpaginated).

25. "An Hymn to Learning…By a Young Lady," *AM* 18:28 (19 October 1695), reprinted in *AO* 3:212–14. Hatfield, "True Secret History," 66, quotes Anonyma's letter to Dunton after the poem appeared in print, 27 October 1695 (Rawlinson Letters 108, p. 362).

26. Anonyma to Dunton, 11 November 1695, Rawlinson MSS D 72, no. 39 (a subsequent letter from her is no. 40), as transcribed in Hatfield, "True Secret History,"

67–70. See also Berry, *Gender, Society and Print Culture,* 39–40, on the Anonyma exchange. "Anonyma" is listed as one of the authors in Dunton's publication, *The Challenge Sent by a Young Lady to Sir Thomas—&c, Or, the Female War* ... (London: E. Whitlock, 1697), unpaginated table of contents.

27. Quotations: *AM* 14:1 (29 May 1694), 14:17 (17 July 1694); N.H., *The Ladies Dictionary: Being a General Entertainment for the Fair Sex* ... (London: John Dunton, 1694), 450–52, essay titled "Sentiments of the Author, Concerning Women." The pagination for this volume is erratic; the quoted passages appear on the first set of pages with those numbers. Pages 161–240, 301–52, and 401–84 are all duplicated. The listed essays appear on 15–18, 233–34 [1st set], 170–76 [1st set], 341–46 [2nd set]. Hatfield, "True Secret History," 80, identifies "N.H." as "one of Dunton's most active employees." He probably compiled the definitions and biographical entries whereas Dunton drafted the longer didactic essays. See n. 60, below, on a later publication by Dunton that echoes the phraseology of an essay in *Ladies Dictionary.* Despite the claims of originality, part of the preface of the *Ladies Dictionary* and surely some of its content copied Hannah Woolley's *The Gentlewoman's Companion: or, A Guide to the Female Sex* (London: A. Maxwell, 1673). Cf. the two prefaces.

28. Berry, *Gender, Society and Print Culture,* chap. 4, esp. 103–4, reaches these conclusions about the composition of *AM*'s reading public. See Chester Hallenbeck, ed., "A Colonial Reading List from the Union Library of Hatboro, Pennsylvania," *Pennsylvania Magazine of History and Biography* 56 (1932): 289–340 passim, for eleven notations of borrowers of the *Oracle*. A keyword search on *Athenian Oracle* in AHN (accessed 19 December 2007) produced twenty-five hits for booksellers' advertisements in New England and the mid-Atlantic between 1733 and 1794. After that, interest appears to have dropped off precipitously. Bell reprinted the work three times before 1720, and another edition from a different printer followed in 1728. For an excerpt (about trade), see *Boston Gazette,* 19 February 1751, and *New York Evening Post,* 25 March 1751. In 1705, according to an entry in the English Short Title Catalogue, Samuel Sewall arranged for an excerpt on slavery to be published as a broadsheet in Boston by Bartholomew Green.

29. *AM* 5:3 (8 December 1691). On earlier misogyny in England, see Katharine M. Rogers, *The Troublesome Helpmate: A History of Misogyny in Literature* (Seattle: University of Washington Press, 1966), chap. 4; Linda Woodbridge, *Women and the English Renaissance: Literature and the Nature of Womankind, 1540–1620* (Urbana: University of Illinois Press, 1984); Katherine Usher Henderson and Barbara F. McManus, eds., *Half Humankind: Contexts and Texts of the Controversy about Women in England, 1540–1640* (Urbana: University of Illinois Press, 1985); and Pamela J. Benson, ed., *Texts from the Querelle, 1521–1640,* 2 vols., in *The Early Modern Englishwoman: A Facsimile Library of Essential Works,* ser. 3, ed. Betty S. Travitsky and Anne Lake Prescott (Burlington: Ashgate, 2008).

30. [Richard Cleaver], *A Godlie Forme of Householde Government: for the Ordering of Private Families* ... (London: Felix Kingston for Thomas Man, 1598), 19, 176. See also the discussion in Mary Beth Norton, *Founding Mothers and Fathers: Gendered Power and the Forming of American Society* (New York: Alfred A. Knopf, 1996), part 1 (hereafter *FM&F*).

31. Berry tallied the origins of the questions in ten "Ladies Issues" published in 1691–92: 45 percent came from men, 23 percent came from women, and in 33 percent

the sex of the inquirer was unspecified. See Berry, *Gender, Society and Print Culture,* 246, table 3. She includes in the table questions from the 5 and 23 May 1691 issues, before the formal designation appeared in the periodical. She (ibid., 59–62) disagrees with this interpretation of the "Ladies Issues," but Shevelow (*Women and Print Culture,* 66–69) concurs with my reading of their significance. Dunton even thought that questions involving male and female "Creatures" should be in "Ladies Issues"; see *AM* 4:17 (24 November 1691).

32. Quotations in this and the next paragraph come from the *Ladies Mercury* 1:1 (28 February 1693).

33. Quotations in this paragraph and the next from *AM* 1:13 (5 May 1691).

34. *AM* 1:18 (23 May 1691).

35. *AM* 2:3 (3 June 1691).

36. Ibid. For a questioner claiming that a woman would not agree to be courted by a man until the *AM* approved, see *AM* 2:6 (13 June 1691).

37. *AM* 1:30 (supplement; June 1691). On the need for a woman to achieve orgasm to conceive, see Thomas Laqueur, *Making Sex: Body and Gender from the Greeks to Freud* (Cambridge, Mass.: Harvard University Press, 1990), 42–52. See also *FM&F,* 76.

38. Quotations: *AM* 2:13 (7 July 1691). All cited questions come from this or the next "Ladies Issue," *AM* 3:4 (8 August 1691).

39. *AM* 5:13 (12 January 1691[/2]). See *AO* 3:350–51 for a similar case in which a woman abandoned by her husband asked for counsel about an offer from a man who loved her "passionately" and promised to maintain her children. The Athenians agreed that hers was a "sad Story" but responded similarly.

40. For a detailed discussion of the transition in the law and practice of marriage on both sides of the Anglo-American Atlantic in this era, see Holly Brewer, *By Birth or Consent: Children, Law, and the Anglo-American Revolution in Authority* (Chapel Hill: University of North Carolina Press, 2005), chap. 8, which traces the manifestations of concerns about parental consent and the need for formal marriage ceremonies, among other topics, in a very different context from the discussion here.

41. *AM* 8:11 (4 October 1692), 8:25 (22 November 1692) [two different questions], 14:2 (26 May 1694), 14:17 (17 July 1694), 17:24 (23 June 1695), 18:26 (12 October 1695); *AO* 2:227.

42. *AM* 4:8 (24 October 1691), 4:13 (10 November 1691); *AO* 2:482; 3:309–10, 543.

43. Moral obligations: *AM* 8:16 (22 October 1692), 17:10 (4 May 1695), *AO* 2:96–98, 156; promises that are not binding: *AM* 4:7 (20 October 1691), 5:9 (29 December 1691); *AO* 1:428, 2:467–68.

44. *AM* 4:2 (3 October 1691) [two questions], 3:21, 25 (both from supplement, post–26 September 1691), 8:19 (1 November 1692), 12:9 (21 November 1693); *AO* 1:62, 2:125–26.

45. *AM* 8:3 (19 July 1692), 8:5 (26 July 1692), 12:25 (16 January 1693[/4]), 17:25 (26 June 1695), 18:30 (26 October 1695); *AO* 1:420, 2:5–7, 3:325.

46. *AM* 8:4 (23 July 1692), 8:19 (1 November 1692), 8:20 (5 November 1692), 16:13 (29 January 1695[/6]); *AO* 2:240.

47. *AM* 14:7 (12 June 1694).

48. *AO* 2:288. See also ibid., 241; and *AM* 16:22 (2 March 1695[/6]). Once, when an Athenian recommended long books of poetry to Elizabeth Singer, he added, "if you have Patience." A subsequent questioner inquired about that phrase; the Athenian replied that because he was responding to a woman he thought "her Constancy might fail her in reading a work of that length, tho' indeed no more than is Necessary to a Poem of that Nature." See *AM* 12:1 (24 October 1693), 12:18 (23 December 1693).

49. *AM* 8:17 (25 October 1692).

50. Dunton, *Challenge,* unpaginated preface (for a full citation to this book, see n. 26, above). One of the few scholars to discuss this publication at any length is Clery; see *Feminization Debate,* 38–39.

51. Dunton, *Challenge,* 102, 106, 108 [2nd set of pages with those numbers]; *OED,* q.v. "economics, oeconomics."

52. Quotations: *AO* 1:98; *Ladies Dictionary,* 203 [2nd set], 250 [1st set] (see n. 27, above, on the erratic pagination of this volume); *AM* 16:2 (22 December 1694) (the man was the jurist Sir Matthew Hale). For Halifax, see introduction, n. 6.

53. *AM* 12:4 (4 November 1693), reprinted in *AO* 1:382–83. The questioner had read a "little tract" favoring women's education, probably either Poulain de la Barre's *Woman as Good as the Man* (1677) or Nahum Tate's *Present for the Ladies,* which had recently been published (see n. 4, above, for full citations to these works).

54. Margaret Cavendish, *Poems, and Fancies...* (London: T.R. for J. Martin and J. Allestrye, 1653), A5r (front matter); Margaret Cavendish, *CCXI Sociable Letters, written by the Thrice Noble, Illustrious, and Excellent Princess, The Lady Marchioness of Newcastle* (London: William Wilson, 1664), 12–13 (see also 27–28, 141, 145, 175, 367). Her use of *sphere* to denote women's place was extremely unusual and appears to be the earliest published instance of that terminology; see the discussion in introduction, nn. 12–14. See James Fitzmaurice, "Cavendish [née Lucas] Margaret, duchess of Newcastle upon Tyne," *ODNB* 10:633–36.

55. Quotations: Margaret Newcastle, *The Worlds Olio* (London: J. Martin and J. Allestrye, 1655), unpaginated front matter; Cavendish, *Poems, and Fancies,* Av [following 160]. Victoria Kahn, *Wayward Contracts* (Princeton, N.J.: Princeton University Press, 2004), chap. 7, usefully observes that Cavendish reveals both the illogic of the exclusion of women from the political contract and the presumptive relationship of political and sexual contracts. John Rogers links Cavendish's ideas of women's appropriate range of action to her philosophical trajectory; see *The Matter of Revolution* (Ithaca: Cornell University Press, 1996), chap. 6. (Thanks to Rachel Weil for these references.)

56. Quotation: Cavendish, *CCXI Sociable Letters,* 293. A similar statement is Cavendish, *Poems, and Fancies,* "To the Reader," unpaginated. For private family/public commonwealth, see, e.g., Newcastle, *Worlds Olio,* 75, 82. For her other (standard) usages of *private,* see Cavendish, *CCXI Sociable Letters,* 302, 332, 371.

57. A useful discussion is Charles Breem, "'I Am Her Majesty's Subject': Prince George of Denmark and the Transformation of the English Male Consort," *Canadian Journal of History* 39 (2004): 457–87. Dunton thus adopted for a female office holder the same language that had long been used to differentiate male officials' familial and public roles; see *FM&F,* 22. On Mary II, see Susan Kingsley Kent, *Gender and Power in Britain, 1640–1990* (London: Routledge, 1999), 37–41.

58. [John Dunton], *Petticoat-Government. In a Letter to the Court Ladies* (London: E. Mallet, 1702), unpaginated front matter, 1–2. I have located only one other commentary on the contents of this pamphlet: Kathryn Gleadle and Sarah Richardson, eds., *Women in British Politics, 1760–1860: The Power of the Petticoat* (New York: St. Martin's Press, 2000), 2–5.

59. Dunton, *Petticoat-Government,* 5–6. In an advertisement for a projected (but never published) second volume of *Challenge,* Dunton indicated that he had recruited combatants (Caliste, Mr. Valdo) for a debate "Against the Salique Law." See unpaginated list at end of *Challenge,* no. 110.

60. Dunton, *Petticoat-Government,* 7–50 passim; quotations, 20–21. There are no pp. 32–41 because of a pagination error (there is no missing text). Dunton's discussion here echoed his argument in *Ladies Dictionary* in the essay "Government Female asserted the best"; see 162–64 [2nd set of pages]. For other English authors' views of queens, see chapter 4 and n. 62, below.

61. Dunton, *Petticoat-Government,* 50–51.

62. Ibid., 52–75 passim (quotation, 75). For a conventional (and nearly contemporaneous) defense of women's potential as rulers that also refers to Mary II and Elizabeth I, see Tate, *Present for the Ladies,* 87–104 passim. Hannah Smith points out that other authors besides Dunton also referred to Anne's feminine qualities when they assessed her as a ruler; see Smith, "'Last of All the Heavenly Birth': Queen Anne and Sacral Queenship," *Parliamentary History* 28 (2009): 146.

63. Dunton, *Petticoat-Government,* 75.

64. Ibid., 87–102 passim (quotations, 87, 97–99, 100, 102). Cavendish, like Halifax (see introduction, n. 6), came close to this phraseology: in the unpaginated "Preface to the Reader" that preceded *Worlds Olio,* she wrote: "Man is made to Govern Common-Wealths, and Women their privat Families." Dunton's pamphlet inspired a reply, by some attributed to Dunton himself: *The Prerogative of the Breeches, in a Letter to the Sons of Men, Being an Answer to Petticoat-Government* (London: A. Baldwin, 1702). The author, whoever he might have been, made it clear that he was not challenging Queen Anne, only the "monstrous Heap and Medley of Inconsistencies" (unpaginated preface) that made up Dunton's argument. His major criticism highlighted the contradictory statements about whether wives or husbands should rule in households; he also asserted that most women had not "the least shadow of pretence to Government" (29).

65. The classic initial study of which, Barbara Welter's "The Cult of True Womanhood," is reprinted in her essay collection, *Dimity Convictions* (Athens: Ohio University Press, 1976); the characteristics of the "true woman" remarkably resemble Dunton's description.

66. John Dunton, *King-Abigail: or, The Secret Reign of the She-Favourite, Detected and Applied* ...(London: John Dunton, 1715), A2, 11, 15, and passim.

67. Another barrier that affected those few female aristocrats who had claimed the vote earlier in the seventeenth century was erected when George Petyt declared in 1690 that no woman, regardless of the size of her freehold, could vote for a member of Parliament: see G[eorge] P[etyt], *Lex Parliamentaria: or, a Treatise on the Law and Custom of the Parliaments of England* (London: Timothy Goodwin, 1690), 114. Likewise, Holly Brewer notes that all women and children were excluded from voting in Virginia by a 1699 law; see Brewer, *By Birth or Consent,* 360.

Mistress Sarah Kemble Knight and Her Journal, 1704

1. On the convoluted history of the journal, which for some years was thought to be fictitious, see Alan Margolies, "The Editing and Publication of 'The Journal of Madam Knight,'" *Papers of the Bibliographic Society of America* 58 (1964): 25–32. The journal was handed down in the family of the executor of Sarah Knight's daughter; see notes in folder 3, box 2, William R. Deane Collection, New England Historic Genealogical Society, Boston. For my conclusions about the business she was conducting, see below, n. 6. Of the available editions, I have used one of the most recent: Sargent Bush, ed., "The Journal of Madam Knight," in *Journeys in New Worlds: Early American Women's Travel Narratives,* William L. Andrews, gen. ed. (Madison: University of Wisconsin Press, 1990). (Hereafter cited as Bush, "Knight Journal"; see his excellent introduction, 69–83.) See also David S. Shields, *Civil Tongues and Polite Letters in British America* (Chapel Hill: University of North Carolina Press, 1997), 117–19. Although both the original manuscript and the copy from which Dwight produced his edition have been lost, editors concur that the surviving text appears to be accurate and more or less complete.

2. On early American women's diaries, real and fake, see Mary Beth Norton, "Hetty Shepard, Dorothy Dudley, and Other Fictional Colonial Women I Have Come to Know Altogether Too Well," *Journal of Women's History* 10, no. 2 (Fall 1998): 141–54. For some authentic colonial women's journals, see Barbara E. Lacey, ed., *The World of Hannah Heaton: The Diary of an Eighteenth-Century New England Farm Woman* (DeKalb: Northern Illinois University Press, 2003); Benjamin Colman, *Reliquae Turellae, et Laychrymae Paternae...* (Boston: S. Kneeland and T. Green, 1735), including excerpts from the journal of Colman's daughter Jane Turell, from the late 1720s; and Samuel Hopkins, *Memoirs of the Life of Mrs. Sarah Osborn...* (Worcester, Mass.: Leonard Worcester, 1799), which includes passages from a journal started in 1744. Esther Edwards Burr's so-called journal of the mid-1750s was actually an extended letter to her friend Sarah Prince; see Carol Karlsen and Laurie Crumpacker, eds., *The Journal of Esther Edwards Burr, 1754–1757* (New Haven, Conn.: Yale University Press, 1984).

3. For instance, one incident reminded her of "the Hero's in Parismus and the Knight of the Oracle." Bush identifies these as references to romances by the Elizabethan author Emanuel Forde (Bush, "Knight Journal," 90 and n. 5). Other scholars have noted her evident familiarity with contemporary poetic forms, picaresque works, and John Bunyan's *Pilgrim's Progress.* See Ann Stanford, "Images of Women in Early American Literature," in *What Manner of Woman: Essays on English and American Life and Literature,* ed. Marlene Springer (New York: New York University Press, 1977), 198–200; Peter Thorpe, "Sarah Kemble Knight and the Picaresque Tradition," *CLA Journal* 10 (1966–67): 114–21; and Kathryn Zabelle Derounian-Stodola, "The New England Frontier and the Picaresque in Sarah Kemble Knight's Journal," in *Early American History and Culture,* ed. Derounian-Stodola (Cranbury, N.J.: Associated University Presses, 1992), 122–31. Her only possible model was [Edward Ward], *A Trip to New-England, with a Character of the Country and People, Both English and Indians* (London: [no pub.,] 1699), but it is less lively and specific than Knight's journal.

4. In just the brief passages quoted in chapter 3, Dunton referred to *fair sex* nine times.

5. For biographical information in this and the following paragraph, see Bush, "Knight Journal," 70–74; Barbara E. Lacey, "Knight, Sarah Kemble," *ANB* 12:818–19; and Malcolm Freiberg, "Knight, Sarah Kemble," *NAM* 2:340–42. Bush and Lacey call her husband a "shipmaster," but Boston records copied in the Deane Collection, box 2, fol. 1, term him a "carver," as does Freiberg. On Thomas Kemble, Richard Knight, and their businesses, see Sybil Noyes et al., *Genealogical Dictionary of Maine and New Hampshire* (Baltimore: Genealogical Publishing Co., 1996), 400, 404.

6. On her familiarity with business, see Bush, "Knight Journal," 105–6, 110; and copies in the Deane Collection, box 2, fols. 1 and 3, which show that she at times served as attorney for both her mother and her husband. These documents demonstrate that Sarah thought her husband was alive as late as 22 July 1706, but his last recorded court appearance was 16 October 1701. He was presumably absent on a long trip when he died. The 1707 Boston census is available online at http://search.ancestrylibrary.com/search/db.aspx?dbid=6363 or in print in *A Report of the Record Commissioners of the City of Boston Containing Miscellaneous Papers* (Boston: Rockwell and Churchill, City Printers, 1886). Deane Collection transcripts, box 2, fol. 3, reveal that Sarah's trip to New Haven in 1704 was to settle the estate of Caleb Trowbridge, a wealthy, childless merchant whose wife's name is unknown but was certainly Mary, based on Mary's residence with Sarah in 1707. Sarah observed in her diary that business also required her to travel to New York (Bush, "Knight Journal," 107); copies in the Deane Collection (box 2, fol. 1) suggest that she went there to settle the estate of her brother.

7. Bush, "Knight Journal," 91, 106. Although Sarah found a woman and her daughter "divirting company" when she traveled with them, she nevertheless joked about them in her journal (ibid., 100).

8. Ibid., 104–5.

9. Information about slaveholding in the family is from Deane Collection, box 2, fol. 1. The pattern continued: when her daughter died in 1736, her estate included a black woman and an Indian man; see ibid., fol. 3. In addition, Sarah's father had dealt in Scottish prisoners captured by Cromwell in 1650 and sent to Barbados to be sold as indentured servants in 1651; see ibid. Other Boston households in 1707 had listings for Negroes or Indians, almost all of whom were enslaved (one free Indian woman was designated as such); see n. 6, above, on the census.

10. Bush, "Knight Journal," 110, 112, 102.

11. Ibid., 92, 94, 111, 116. When she described the clothing of New Yorkers, she remarked only on the differences between Dutch and English women, never mentioning men's dress; see 109–10.

12. Ibid., 105. Divorces were difficult to obtain in all the colonies, but Connecticut laws were, as she observed, more "Indulgent" than most other jurisdictions. Cf. Shields, *Civil Tongues,* 118–19.

13. Mather's poem was *Eureka. The Vertuous Woman Found…* (Boston: Bartholomew Green, 1704), 2. A 1713 New York almanac used the phrase "fair female sex"; see Daniel Leeds, *The American Almanack for…1713* (New York: William Bradford, 1713); see page for September. The newspaper with the American-composed article is the *New-England Courant,* 18–25 September 1721. Even so, *fair sex* seems to have lagged behind other American adaptations of English locutions: a keyword full-text search on *fair sex* in EAI produced no appreciable number of uses until the 1760s

(18). A similar search in AHN likewise showed a dramatic jump in the usage of the term in the 1760s, from 21 (1720s) to 205 (1760s). Not every colonial newspaper is available on series 1 of AHN, and the AHN search engine occasionally produces incorrect hits, both missing some and creating false positives. I did not check each of the 1760s results. The point is the relative incidence of use of the phrase, not the specific numbers.

4. Women and Politics, Eighteenth Century–Style

1. *A Letter to a Gentlewoman concerning Government* (London: E. Whitlocke, 1697), 2, 3, 27, and passim. By contrast, in Virginia in 1661, Quaker women were included in Governor William Berkeley's order to take an oath of allegiance or be jailed, an indication of changed attitudes by the 1690s; see Kathleen M. Brown, *Good Wives, Nasty Wenches, and Anxious Patriarchs: Gender, Race, and Power in Colonial Virginia* (Chapel Hill: University of North Carolina Press, 1996), 144.

2. That *Letter to a Gentlewoman* is seemingly the last such publication is suggested by the lack of relevant results to keyword title searches on women, government, and politics (and variants) on ECCO and EAI.

3. For various sorts of indirect political activity by wealthy women, see Elaine Chalus, *Elite Women in English Political Life, c. 1754–1790* (Oxford: Clarendon Press, 2005); John G. Kolp and Terri L. Snyder, "Women and the Political Culture of Eighteenth-Century Virginia: Gender, Property Law, and Voting Rights," in *The Many Legalities of Early America,* ed. Christopher L. Tomlins and Bruce H. Mann (Chapel Hill: University of North Carolina Press, 2001), 272–92; Sarah Fatherly, *Gentlewomen and Learned Ladies: Women and Elite Formation in Eighteenth-Century Philadelphia* (Bethlehem, Pa.: Lehigh University Press, 2008), 133–57; and Karin Wulf, *Not All Wives: Women of Colonial Philadelphia* (Ithaca: Cornell University Press, 2000), 181–210. A brief, astute commentary is Kathleen Wilson, *This Island Race: Englishness, Empire, and Gender in the Eighteenth Century* (London: Routledge, 2003), 40–43. See also Robert Shoemaker, *Gender in English Society: The Emergence of Separate Spheres?* (London: Longman, 1998), 227–32; and Edmund S. Morgan, *Inventing the People: The Rise of Popular Sovereignty in England and America* (New York: W. W. Norton, 1988), 190–95.

4. See Rachel Weil, *Political Passions: Gender, the Family and Political Argument in England, 1680–1714* (Manchester: Manchester University Press, 1999), chaps. 7 and 8 passim (quotation, 162); and, in general, Edward Gregg, *Queen Anne* (London: Routledge and Kegan Paul, 1980); Geoffrey Holmes, *British Politics in the Age of Anne,* rev. ed. (London: Hambledon Press, 1987); and Frances Harris, *A Passion for Government: The Life of Sarah, Duchess of Marlborough* (Oxford: Clarendon Press, 1991).

5. Nahum Tate, *A Present for the Ladies: Being an Historical Vindication of the Female Sex* (London: Francis Saunders, 1692), 87–100 passim (quotation, 96). Tate's employment of *sphere* in the household context is the earliest I have located using the full-text search function of EEBO. Although Tate did not refer to her, another exemplar of female political competence frequently cited by seventeenth-century authors was Queen Christina of Sweden; see, e.g., Joad Raymond, ed., *Making the News: An Anthology of the Newsbooks of Revolutionary England, 1641–1660* (Moreton-in-Marsh, U.K.: Windrush Press, 1993), 141–48.

6. Bernard Mandeville, *The Virgin Unmask'd: or, Female Dialogues Betwixt an Elderly Maiden Lady, and her Niece*...(London: J. Morphew, 1709), unpaginated preface, 132–33, 173–74 (see also 132–40 passim). Mandeville in his own persona later defended women's political abilities; see Bernard Mandeville, *By a Society of Ladies: Essays in The Female Tatler,* ed. M. M. Goldsmith (Bristol: Thoemmes Press, 1999), 31–32 and passim. See, on Mandeville's writings on women, E. J. Clery, *The Feminization Debate in Eighteenth-Century England: Literature, Commerce, and Luxury* (New York: Palgrave Macmillan, 2004), 60–73. Mandeville's 1709 apologia is one of two such statements that year located by ECCO full-text search functions (accessed December 2008–January 2009). The other was a brief remark in a play: Mary Pix, *The Adventures in Madrid: A Comedy*...(London: [no pub.,] 1709), 12. No earlier statements of the sort were located by either ECCO or EEBO full-text searches (accessed January 2009); *Letter to a Gentlewoman* is not yet included in EEBO.

7. See Calhoun Winton, "Steele, Sir Richard," *ODNB* 52:358–64; and Pat Rogers, "Addison, Joseph," *ODNB* 1:321–24.

8. A statement about observing "an exact Neutrality between the Whigs and Tories" appeared in the first *Spectator* essay, 1 March 1711; see Donald F. Bond, ed., *The Spectator,* 5 vols. (Oxford: Clarendon Press, 1965), 1:5. An insightful analysis of Addison and Steele's deliberately muted Whiggery is Brian Cowan, "Mr. Spectator and the Coffeehouse Public Sphere," *Eighteenth-Century Studies* 37 (2004): 345–66.

9. One key indication of such definitions was their lack of attention to exemplary female public figures. No issue of either periodical extolled Queen Elizabeth; even Queen Anne was seldom the subject of *Tatler* or *Spectator* essays. Most references to Elizabeth or Anne in the two periodicals were casual and brief; see, e.g., Donald F. Bond, ed., *The Tatler,* 3 vols. (Oxford: Clarendon Press, 1987), 2:336, 3:304; and Bond, *Spectator,* 1:424, 2:214, 216, 380; 5:44. The one long passage praising Anne (Bond, *Spectator,* 3:444), summarized the sermon at her accession to the throne. By contrast, Mandeville discoursed at length about Elizabeth when he defended women's political and military abilities in 1710 (*By a Society of Ladies,* 173–74). The absence of any comment about Queen Elizabeth in journals aimed partly at a female audience was telling. See John Watkins, *Representing Elizabeth in Stuart England: Literature, History, Sovereignty* (Cambridge: Cambridge University Press, 2002). (I owe this reference to Paulina Kewes.)

10. These quotations and those in the next paragraph are from Bond, *Tatler,* 1:15.

11. Ibid., 2:310–11 (no. 142), 32–33 (no. 84). On the complex issues involved in Sacheverell's impeachment and on the crowds that attended the trial, see W. A. Speck, "Sacheverell, Henry," *ODNB* 48:520–23.

12. Bond, *Tatler,* 3:202 (no. 232). See also two other essays by Steele that dealt with women's political talk: Bond, *Spectator,* 2:194–96, 3:73.

13. Bond, *Spectator,* 1:241–43 (no. 57); 2:247n2.

14. Ibid., 1:347, 349 (no. 81).

15. Joseph Addison, *The Freeholder,* ed. James Leheny (Oxford: Clarendon Press, 1979), 182–83. In some early *Freeholder* essays, Addison praised Whig "Female-Patriots," though humorously, but soon replaced that theme with the contention that women should remain out of politics. See ibid., 52–54, 71–74, 87–90, 103–6. The English Short Title Catalogue lists twenty-four editions of *The Freeholder* published in London, Glasgow, and Dublin between 1716 and 1790. These were occasionally

advertised for sale in the colonies, but less often than *Tatler* or *Spectator* (see n. 20, below).

16. Addison, *Freeholder,* 135–38, 146–47, 204–7 (quotations 137, 146–47, 205–7).

17. Mandeville, *By a Society of Ladies,* 116 (quotation). For accounts of female worthies, see 164–92, 198–202, and the editor's introduction, 54–62. The *Female Tatler,* as the title suggests, imitated Steele's *Tatler* and aimed solely at a female audience. Scholars disagree on the originator of that periodical, but it was later taken over by Mandeville and other (still anonymous) writers. See the discussion in editor's introduction to Mandeville, *By a Society of Ladies,* 33–48; Clery, *Feminization Debate,* 60–66; and Tedra Osell, "Tatling Women in the Public Sphere: Rhetorical Femininity and the English Essay Periodical," *Eighteenth-Century Studies* 38 (2005): 283–99.

18. For a discussion of similar positions advanced later in the century by Jean Jacques Rousseau, see Dena Goodman, "Difference: An Enlightenment Concept," in *What's Left of Enlightenment? A Post-modern Question,* ed. Keith Baker and Peter Hanns Reill (Stanford, Calif.: Stanford University Press, 2001), 129–47, esp. 140–41.

19. Leonard W. Labaree et al., eds., *The Autobiography of Benjamin Franklin* (New Haven, Conn.: Yale University Press, 1964), 62. That Franklin absorbed the contents as well as the style of Addison's essays was suggested by his June 1758 comment to his wife: "You are very prudent not to engage in Party Disputes. Women should never meddle with them except in Endeavours to reconcile their Husbands, Brothers, and Friends who happen to be on contrary Sides"; see Labaree et al., eds., *The Papers of Benjamin Franklin,* 39 vols. (New Haven, Conn.: Yale University Press, 1959–), 8:92.

20. A keyword search on advertisements in AHN, conducted 27 January 2009, located more than six hundred advertisements for the *Spectator,* along with another three hundred-plus for the *Tatler.* On the importance of *Tatler* and *Spectator* in eighteenth-century Virginia, see Richard D. Brown, *Knowledge Is Power: The Diffusion of Information in Early America, 1700–1865* (New York: Oxford University Press, 1989), 46, 62. John Hook, a storekeeper in backcountry Virginia, in 1772 imported two eight-volume sets of *Spectator* and one four-volume set of *Tatler;* see Ann Smart Martin, *Buying into the World of Goods: Early Consumers in Backcountry Virginia* (Baltimore: Johns Hopkins University Press, 2008), table 3.10, pp. 86–88. Probate inventories in the New York Public Library also reveal ownership of *Spectator* volumes; see Schuyler Papers, box 38, and Livingston Family Papers, estate of Henry Livingston.

21. Specific examples: Sarah Gibbes to John Gibbes, 10 September 1783, Gibbes Papers, South Carolina Historical Society, Charleston; Susanna Atkinson, will, 28 April 1794, Freeman Papers, New Hampshire Historical Society, Concord; James Iredell, Journal, 26 January 1773, in *The Papers of James Iredell,* 3 vols., ed. Don Higginbotham (Raleigh, N.C.: Division of Archives and History, 1976), 1:212–13. For the general patterns, see Richard Beale Davis, *A Southern Colonial Bookshelf: Reading in the Eighteenth Century* (Athens: University of Georgia Press, 1979), 113–15, 128; and David Lundberg and Henry F. May, "The Enlightened Reader in America," *American Quarterly* 28 (1976): 273–74. A study of books listed in 438 probate inventories in South Carolina before 1776 found 77 copies of *Spectator,* 30 copies of *Tatler,* and 15 copies of Addison's *Works.* See Walter B. Edgar, "Some Popular Books in Colonial South Carolina," *South Carolina Historical Magazine* 72 (1971): 178.

22. See Ian K. Steele, *The English Atlantic, 1675–1740: An Exploration of Communication and Community* (New York: Oxford University Press, 1986). On transatlantic

print culture, see Hugh Amory and David D. Hall, eds., *The Colonial Book in the Atlantic World,* vol. 1 of *A History of the Book in America* (Chapel Hill: University of North Carolina Press, 2007), esp. 349 (on the influence of Addison and Steele). See also Paul Giles, *Transatlantic Insurrections: British Culture and the Formation of American Literature, 1730–1860* (Philadelphia: University of Pennsylvania Press, 2001); Leonard Tennenhouse, *The Importance of Feeling English: American Literature and the British Diaspora, 1750–1850* (Princeton, N.J.: Princeton University Press, 2007). Jack P. Greene discusses Anglicization generally in "Search for Identity: An Interpretation of the Meaning of Selected Patterns of Social Response in Eighteenth-Century America," *Journal of Social History* 3 (1969): 189–220, esp. 205–18.

23. On these early papers, see Charles E. Clark, *The Public Prints: The Newspaper in Anglo-American Culture, 1665–1740* (New York: Oxford University Press, 1994), 77–83, 114–19. The *News-Letter* was founded in 1704, the other two in 1719.

24. Clark, *Public Prints,* 123–40 passim. See also Carla Mulford, "Pox and 'Hell-Fire': Boston's Smallpox Controversy, the New Science, and Early Modern Liberalism," in *Periodical Literature in Eighteenth-Century America,* ed. Mark L. Kamrath and Sharon M. Harris (Knoxville: University of Tennessee Press, 2005), 7–27.

25. For satires on marriage and the like in the *Courant* (hereafter *NEC*), see, for example, issues: 5, 22 March 1721/2; 2 April 1722. That its authors were attuned to contemporary English terminology is shown by their frequent and still-novel use of "fair sex" in their essays; see "Ben Treackle," 9 April 1722; and "Cornelius Easy," 28 October 1723, among others.

26. Ibid., 15 January 1721/2. For Steele as "Henroost," see Bond, *Spectator,* 2:194. The authors of some of the early *NEC* essays were identified by Benjamin Franklin in a document now in the BL; see Worthington Chauncey Ford, "Franklin's New England Courant," *Proceedings of the Massachusetts Historical Society* 57 (1923–24): 336–53, esp. 352.

27. *NEC,* 18 May 1724, from "Kitchen Stuff."

28. The best general accounts of the controversial Cosby administration, which inform my discussion in the next five paragraphs, are Stanley Nider Katz, *Newcastle's New York: Anglo-American Politics, 1732–1753* (Cambridge, Mass.: Harvard University Press, 1968), chap. 4; and Patricia U. Bonomi, *A Factious People: Politics and Society in Colonial New York* (New York: Columbia University Press, 1971), chap. 4. Neither devotes much attention to Grace Cosby, but the quotation (from Lewis Morris) is in *Newcastle's New York,* 78.

29. Edith B. Gelles, ed., *The Letters of Abigaill Levy Franks, 1733–1748* (New Haven, Conn.: Yale University Press, 2004), 17, 24–26; see the introduction, xv–xlii, for a biography of Abigaill Franks (xxxi on her reading). When the wife and daughter of Cadwallader Colden, a council member, first met Mrs. Cosby, she received them "very handsomly and kindly" in her husband's absence; see *Letters and Papers of Cadwallader Colden,* vol. 2, in *Collections of the New-York Historical Society* 51 (1918): 90 (hereafter *NYHS Colls*).

30. Gelles, *Letters of Franks,* 24–25; *New-York Weekly Journal,* 21 January 1733/4 (hereafter *NYWJ*); quotations from verses 1, 3, and 7 of Proverbs 23 in the King James Bible. Serena Zabin, "Women's Trading Networks and Dangerous Economies in Eighteenth-Century New York City," *Early American Studies* 4 (2006): 313, recognizes that the "widows' petition" was a parody linked to the controversy; other historians

of women have quoted it as genuine. A week later, New York's "maids" continued the parody in a more traditional manner by adding a pouting complaint: "the young Gentlemen are so taken up with Politics, that we hardly get one pretty Thing said to us in a Month" (*NYWJ*, 28 January 1733/4).

31. Gelles, *Letters of Franks*, 41, 45 (see also 36); *Letters and Papers of Colden* 2, in *NYHS Colls* 51 (1918): 143. On the Zenger trial, see James Alexander, *A Brief Narrative of the Case and Trial of John Peter Zenger*, ed. Stanley Nider Katz (Cambridge, Mass.: Harvard University Press, 1963); Stephen Botein, ed., *"Mr. Zenger's Malice and Falsehood": Six Issues of the New-York Weekly Journal, 1733–34* (Worcester, Mass.: American Antiquarian Society, 1985). The trial did not involve the issue of 21 January 1733/4. See also Alison Gilbert Olson, "The Zenger Case Revisited: Satire, Sedition, and Political Debate in Eighteenth-Century America," *Early American Literature* 35 (2000): 223–45; Michael Warner, *The Letters of the Republic: Publication and the Public Sphere in Eighteenth-Century America* (Cambridge, Mass.: Harvard University Press, 1990), 49–63.

32. Quotations in this paragraph and the next from *Letters and Papers of Colden* 2, in *NYHS Colls* 51 (1918): 144. William Cosby died in spring 1736. For additional political statements and actions by Grace Cosby, see ibid., 153; and William Smith, Jr., *The History of the Province of New-York,* 2 vols., ed. Michael Kammen (Cambridge, Mass.: Harvard University Press, 1972), 2:10, 24. She also was reportedly involved in elaborate machinations that successfully married off the Cosbys' daughter to the son of the duke of Grafton; see ibid., 2:23, and Gelles, ed., *Letters of Franks,* 22.

33. This paragraph and the next two are based on the essay appearing on page 1 of the 19 August 1734 issue of *NYWJ*. It is telling that the rival, semiofficial *New York Gazette* published nothing similar, thus underscoring the relationship of this essay to the opposition to Governor Cosby and his wife.

34. *NYWJ,* 30 September 1734. "A.B." claimed that the poem had never before been published and he did not give the author's name, but this is a well-known poem written by Lyttelton in his youth. Zabin also connects the publication of the poem to the satirical statements by the "widows" and "maids," but she does not mention the August 1734 essay on women and politics. See "Women's Trading Networks," 313.

35. Francis Ready, untitled, *NYWJ,* 12 May 1735. See also the letter from Andrew Merrill to Zenger, ibid., 15 March 1735/6. "Merrill" claimed to be a visitor to New York who was surprised by the fierce partisanship of local men, so he sought out women, only to find them "warmer than the Men." Yet he praised them for treating "their Antagonists, with pretty good Manners," and he did encounter some "no party Women." This letter was reprinted in the *Boston Evening Post,* 4 April 1736. None of the other essays discussed previously seem to have been published in other colonial newspapers.

36. *Letters and Papers of Colden* 8, in *NYHS Colls* 67 (1934): 240; Colden to Elizabeth DeLancey, c. 1739, DeLancey Papers, Museum of the City of New York. The message was received outside Manhattan too; on 26 March 1734, when Deborah Norris of Philadelphia reported some political news to her brother Isaac, then in London, she added: "when I first begun I Resolved not to meddle with politick but find I have been Involuntary Led in to say what I have," thus excusing her temerity in broaching a subject she knew would interest him but which she understood was

inappropriate for her to discuss. See Norris Family Papers, 1:23, Historical Society of Pennsylvania, Philadelphia.

37. See Osell, "Tatling Women," passim, for a useful discussion of rhetorical femininity. An ECCO keyword search produced only one result of a man who offered even a low-key defense of women's political capacity between 1730 and 1750, and then not as part of an exchange with another author; see *The Constitution and Government of the Germanic Body*… (London, 1745), 75–79.

38. The essays, no. 31 (on men) and no. 32 (on women), quoted in the next five paragraphs, were originally published on 3 and 10 September 1737 and appeared, slightly abridged, in *Gentleman's Magazine* 7 (1737): 549–55. They were reprinted in *Common Sense: or, the Englishman's Journal*…, 2 vols. (London: J. Purser & G. Hawkins, 1738–39), with no. 32 in 1:224–30. Lord Chesterfield, George Lyttelton, Henry Fielding, and even Oliver Goldsmith (who was too young) have all at various times been identified as the author of these two essays. They appeared in *New England Weekly Journal* (hereafter *NEWJ*), 7 and 14 February 1737/8, respectively, under the titles, "On Affectation, particularly in Men," and "Of Affectation, in Women." The second was printed again, with the title "Animadversions on the Affectation of ill-suited Characters among the Female Sex," in *American Magazine and Historical Chronicle* (hereafter *AMHC*) 2 (July 1745): 302–4. The editors of these two publications were Boston rivals; see Clark, *Public Prints,* 144–46, 157–61. Not every paragraph of the original was included in the American publications, which also did not entirely duplicate each other. The essays can conveniently be consulted in their entirety in Ioan Williams, ed., *The Criticism of Henry Fielding* (London: Routledge and Kegan Paul, 1970), appendix 3, 325–29.

39. The quoted phrases in this paragraph referring to women's sphere and man's province were not published in the *Gentleman's Magazine* or either American reprinting; the other quotations were included in both colonial versions of the essay.

40. *NEWJ* but not *AMHC* printed the paragraph in which Elizabeth and Christina were identified as undoubted hermaphrodites. Both published a reference to a mythical treatise titled *De Hermaphroditis*, by "Conrad Wolfgang Laboriosus Nugatorius."

41. *Common Sense* 135, 1 September 1739, as reprinted in *NYWJ,* 8 September and 22 September 1740. The author claimed that he was summarizing an ancient viewpoint, but his language made it clear that he concurred with the argument. For information on the original publication, see François Poulain de La Barre, *The Woman as Good as the Man; or, the Equality of Both Sexes,* trans. A.L., ed. Gerald M. MacLean (Detroit: Wayne State University Press, 1988), 26–27. A useful discussion of Poulain de la Barre is Karen Offen, *European Feminisms, 1700–1850: A Political History* (Berkeley: University of California Press, 2000), 34–35, 44–45.

42. "One of your constant Female Readers" to Mr. Zenger, *NYWJ,* 27 July 1741.

43. The full title: Sophia, A Person of Quality, *Woman Not Inferior to Man: or, a Short and Modest Vindication of the Natural Right of the Fair-Sex to a Perfect Equality of Power, Dignity and Esteem, with the Men* (London: John Hawkins, 1739). It is possible that Sophia had access to the original French version, *De l'Egalité des Deux Sexes* (Paris, 1673), rather than A.L.'s English translation, published in 1677. Gerald MacLean, in his edition of Poulain de la Barre's tract, cited in n. 41, above, claims, 28, that parts of *Woman as Good as the Man* "appear wholesale" in Sophia's pamphlet. Felicity Nussbaum, *The Brink of All We Hate: English Satires on Women, 1660–1750*

(Lexington: University Press of Kentucky, 1984), 8, goes further and contends that the Sophia pamphlets (there were two; see below for the second) were in fact translations of the French work. Yet a comparison of the texts shows that such claims are overstated. A later pamphlet by "A Lady," *Female Rights Vindicated: or the Equality of the Sexes Morally and Physically Proved* (London: printed for G. Burnet, 1758), resembles Poulain de la Barre's work more closely, though it is an updated revision coupled with a new introduction. (It does not mirror the Sophia pamphlets as fully.) See also Barbara Brandon Schnorrenberg, "Sophia: British Feminism in the Mid Eighteenth Century," paper delivered at the American Society for Eighteenth Century Studies, 1980, available at http://www.pinn.net/~sunshine/biblio/sophia2.html, which addresses the question of Sophia's identity and rejects such authorial possibilities as Eliza Haywood and Lady Mary Wortley Montagu. My thanks to Margaret Hunt for this reference.

44. Sophia, *Woman Not Inferior,* 45, 27, 48. Sophia admitted, 45, that "a positive law of God" prevented women from assuming religious leadership, but she cleverly argued that God might have favored men in this regard because their general irreligion meant they needed his extra attention. The last quotation in the paragraph mirrored one in Poulain de la Barre, *Woman as Good,* 123, but her statement calling the circular reasoning into question had no parallel in the earlier work, nor did her comment about women and religious leadership, which adopted the eighteenth-century stance that women had a "natural propensity" for "*virtue* and *religion*," a notion alien in the previous century.

45. Quotations: Sophia, *Woman Not Inferior,* 35–37, 49, 55. Even though her treatment of this topic is more heavily dependent than most of her prose on Poulain de la Barre, many of the paragraphs differ; cf. *Woman as Good,* 123–24, 133–34, and *Woman Not Inferior,* 49–56 passim.

46. [A Gentleman], *Man Superior to Woman: or, the Natural Right of the Men to Sovereign Authority over the Women...* (1739), as reprinted in *Beauty's Triumph; or the Superiority of the Fair Sex Invincibly Proved* (London: J. Robinson, 1751), 27–28, 38, 55, and passim. In the course of explaining why women could not keep secrets (and therefore could not be rulers), he cited, 31, the Roman tale that formed the basis of 1646's *Parliament of Women* and other subsequent opinion pieces about women's incapacity for government. Some have argued that Sophia herself wrote *Man Superior to Woman,* to set up an easily refuted straw-man "opponent."

47. [Sophia], *Woman's Superior Excellence over Man...* (1740), as reprinted in *Beauty's Triumph,* 1, 4, 5, 97, 58, 91 (separately paginated from *Man Superior...*).

48. Ibid., 111.

49. In both the *Boston Gazette* (twice in November 1761) and *Boston Post-Boy* (once in December 1761); search results from *AHN.*

50. "An Account of a Political Ballance," *New-York Evening Post,* 21 January 1744/5 (from *London Magazine* [April 1744], 195–96; also printed in *Pennsylvania Journal,* 29 December 1744); Jonathan Swift, "The Furniture of a Woman's Mind," *AMHC* 2 (June 1745): 226; "from the Champion, Publish'd by Hercules Vinegar, June 24, 1740," *American Weekly Mercury,* 18 December 1740. All these had an English origin, but see also the roughly contemporary unpublished American satire of the "genearchy" that overwhelmed the normally all-male Tuesday Club of Annapolis, in Alexander Hamilton, *The History of the Ancient and Honorable Tuesday Club,* 3 vols., ed.

Robert Micklus (Chapel Hill: University of North Carolina Press, 1990), 2:323–28, 334–36, 379–83.

51. Quotation: "The Character of her late Majesty," *NEWJ,* 9 May 1738 (from *Gentleman's Magazine,* December 1737). According to Stephen Taylor, "Caroline (1683–1737)," *ODNB* 10:202–7, Caroline was an adept political operator, but one would never know that from such tributes. See also, e.g., "An Extract ... concerning the illustrious Women, who had excell'd in polite literature," *AMHC* 2 (June 1745): 244–48, which mentions such learned queens as Margaret of Valois and Catherine of Aragon, but not as rulers. References to Queen Elizabeth are rare in colonial newspapers; *AHN,* accessed 18 July 2007, produced only nineteen hits, and most of those were brief. Two extended treatments, untitled essays signed "Z," in *Pennsylvania Gazette,* 8 April and 10 June 1736, celebrated her political skill but did not analogize from thence to conclude that other women were qualified to engage in politics.

52. "Of Ministers, and the Influence of the Fair Sex in the Government of States," *NYWJ,* 14 January 1751 (from "a late magazine," unidentified).

53. Untitled, unsigned essay headed "from the Craftsman, 21 July 1739," in *Boston Evening Post,* 15 October 1739. Another essay from 1739 made a similar point about clothing purchases; see Britannicus, "To the Ladies of Great-Britain," printed in ibid., 12 March 1738/9, and *Virginia Gazette,* 23 March 1738/9.

54. *A Serious and Earnest Address to the Gentry, Clergy, and the Other Inhabitants of the British Nation...* (Boston: Rogers & Fowle, 1746), 11, 12, 15. Originally published as [James Burgh,] *Britain's Remembrancer: or, the Danger Not Over...* (London: George Frier, 1746). See also a similar argument that does not, however, stress the patriotic and public goals of personal reformation as strongly: "The Power of Beauty, and the Influence the Fair Sex might have in reforming the Manners of the World," *AMHC* 2 (September 1745): 400–403.

55. The English Short Title Catalogue identifies seven London printings and one in Edinburgh through the end of the 1740s, along with two in Philadelphia, one in Williamsburg, one in New York, and one in Boston. Additional reprints followed in the 1750s on both sides of the Atlantic. Sophia Hume, *An Exhortation to the Inhabitants of the Province of South Carolina* (Philadelphia: William Bradford, 1748), 122–24, also included a lengthy excerpt from *Britain's Remembrancer* that focused on women's need to reform themselves and thus the nation.

56. As reported in Richard Peters to Thomas Penn, 17 November 1742, Richard Peters Letterbooks, 29:132, Historical Society of Pennsylvania, quoted in Wulf, *Not All Wives,* 194–95. Wright appears unique in assuming a role as a state actor at the time. See Frederick B. Tolles, "Wright, Susanna," in *NAM* 3:688–90.

57. When William Byrd returned to Virginia after a long stay in London, he recorded in his diary numerous conversations with men about politics, but only once did he even hint that a woman was included in those meetings; see Louis B. Wright and Marion Tinling, eds., *William Byrd of Virginia: The London Diary (1717–1721) and Other Writings* (New York: Oxford University Press, 1958), 371, 375–76, 454 (the woman), 477, and passim. See also a letter to Byrd in 1741 from an English female relative about women's participation in political conversations, "understand them or not" (Marion Tinling, ed., *The Correspondence of the Three William Byrds of Westover, Virginia, 1684–1776,* 2 vols. [Charlottesville: University Press of Virginia, 1977], 2:589. The Scots physician Alexander Hamilton, traveling in 1744, reported two political

conversations in which women participated; see Hamilton, *Gentleman's Progress: The Itinerarium of Dr. Alexander Hamilton, 1744,* ed. Carl Bridenbaugh (Chapel Hill: University of North Carolina Press, 1948), 5, 46.

58. King George's War (1739–48) was followed closely by the Seven Years' War (1754–63). On colonial literacy in general, see E. Jennifer Monaghan, *Learning to Read and Write in Colonial America* (Amherst: University of Massachusetts Press, 2005); and on letter writing, Konstantin Dierks, *In My Power: Letter Writing and Communications in Early America* (Philadelphia: University of Pennsylvania Press, 2009). See also Joel Perlmann and Dennis Shirley, "When Did New England Women Acquire Literacy?" *WMQ,* 3rd ser., 48 (1991): 50–67, and comment by Mary Beth Norton with reply by Perlmann, ibid., 639–48. On early American women's diaries, real and fake, see Norton, "Hetty Shepard, Dorothy Dudley, and Other Fictional Colonial Women I Have Come to Know Altogether Too Well," *Journal of Women's History* 10 (Autumn 1998): 141–54. A useful discussion of women's diaries is Brown, *Knowledge Is Power,* chap. 7.

59. See, e.g., Gelles, *Letters of Franks,* 51, 78; and *Letters and Papers of Colden* 3, in *NYHS Colls* 52 (1920): 277–78, 389, 401; ibid., 8, in *NYHS Colls* 67 (1934): 250, 255, 297, 307, 344. (The Colden correspondence consists primarily of letters from Cadwallader to Alice, rather than the reverse, but the contents show that he was regularly sending her newspapers, which he clearly expected her to read.) Eliza Lucas often included political and military news from South Carolina in letters to her father in Antigua; see Elise Pinckney, ed., *The Letterbook of Eliza Lucas Pinckney, 1739–1762* (Columbia: University of South Carolina Press, 1997 [orig. pub. 1972]), 9, 16, 22, 50, 54–57, 59.

60. Carol F. Karlsen and Laurie Crumpacker, eds., *The Journal of Esther Edwards Burr, 1754–1757* (New Haven, Conn.: Yale University Press, 1984), 60–61, 137, 140 (see 136–40 for the Braddock reports). Esther occasionally commented on politics; see ibid., 171. Abigail Dwight of Stockbridge, Massachusetts, followed the war news closely while her husband was serving in the army in 1756; see her letters to him in Sedgwick Papers II, Massachusetts Historical Society, Boston.

61. Gelles, *Letters of Franks,* 81, 109; Susan E. Klepp and Karin Wulf, eds., *The Diary of Hannah Callender Sansom, 1758–1788: Sense and Sensibility in the Age of the American Revolution* (Ithaca: Cornell University Press, 2010), 79; Pinckney, *Letterbook of Pinckney,* 128, 138, 155, and passim. Unusually, Pinckney sent political and military news to both men and women; women most often included such information in letters to men only. See also the letters to William Byrd III from his mother and estranged wife, which give war news but offer no opinions: Tinling, *Correspondence of the Byrds,* 2:629, 632, 679–80, 685.

62. Klepp and Wulf, *Diary of Sansom,* 77; Karlsen and Crumpacker, *Journal of Burr,* 178.

63. For rare examples of such analyses, see Pinckney, *Letterbook of Pinckney,* 89; Karlsen and Crumpacker, *Journal of Burr,* 96; and Gelles, *Letters of Franks,* 111.

64. Christian Barnes to Elizabeth Murray Smith, 20 November 1769, in *Letters of James Murray, Loyalist,* ed. Dorothy Forbes (Boston: privately printed, 1901), 122; Frances Tucker to St. George Tucker, 19 May 1772, Tucker-Coleman Papers, Earl Gregg Swem Library, College of William and Mary, Williamsburg, Va.; Mary Cranch to Isaac Smith Jr., 15 October 1774, in Lyman H. Butterfield et al., eds., *Adams Family Correspondence,* 4 vols. (Cambridge, Mass.: Harvard University Press, 1963), 1:171.

65. Abigail Adams to [unknown congressman], draft, c. January 1779, Butterfield et al., *Adams Family Correspondence,* 3:158. She may never have sent the letter. See also ibid., John to Abigail, 3:170, 183 (both February 1779), for his extended comments about why it would be viewed as "folly" for him to write to her about politics.

66. John Adams to Mercy Warren, 16 April 1776, in *Warren-Adams Letters…, 1743–1814,* in *Collections of the Massachusetts Historical Society* 72 (1917): 221.

Lady Chatham and Her Correspondents, 1740s–1760s

1. See Marie Peters, "Pitt, William, first earl of Chatham [Pitt the elder]," *ODNB* 44:452–70, esp., on Hester, 456–57; Leland J. Bellot, "Grenville, Richard, second Earl Temple," *ODNB* 23:739–42; and J. V. Beckett and Peter D. G. Thomas, "Grenville, George," *ODNB* 23:722–27. There is no biography in the *ODNB* of Hester Grenville Pitt. Information from these essays informs the discussion below.

2. These observations are based generally on correspondence from Hester Grenville, later Pitt, to George Grenville, from the late 1740s through the 1760s, in Stowe (Grenville) Papers, HEHL, HM 31550–576. The quotation is from a letter of 19 June 1760, HM 31564. Grenville's letters to the Pitts are in Chatham Papers, PRO 30/8, 34, TNA; the correspondence largely ceases in the 1760s.

3. William Stanhope Taylor and John Henry Pringle, eds., *Correspondence of William Pitt, Earl of Chatham,* 4 vols. (London: John Murray, 1838), 2:279 (Earl Temple to Hester Pitt); 1–9, 45, 54–55, 363–70 (William Pitt to Hester Pitt); 391–92 (Hester Pitt to William Pitt). See also letters to her from Richard and James Grenville, ibid., 192–94, 272–77, 281–83, 307–10, 414–15.

4. Earl Temple to Hester Pitt, 20, 24 January 1766, Chatham Papers, PRO 30/8, 62, ff. 111, 113.

5. Lady Chatham to Earl Temple, 22 July 1766, Grenville Papers, Add. MSS 42084, f. 112 BL; Earl Temple to Lady Chatham, 27 July 1766, Taylor and Pringle, *Correspondence of Pitt* 2:468–70 (draft in Add. MSS 42084, f. 116). For several awkward and prickly letters that passed between brother and sister in April–May 1768, see Grenville Papers, Add. MSS 42086, ff. 23–25, 32–33. In the last of these, 8 May, he told her, "The *proper* time for our meeting again is certainly not the present for many many reasons." The next letter from him to her in the Chatham Papers is dated 3 December 1768 (PRO 30/8, 62, f. 133). Finally, in February 1769, he again sent her a letter filled with both political news and statements of affection; see Taylor and Pringle, *Correspondence of Pitt,* 3:249–50.

6. Lady Chatham to her husband, n.d., PRO 30/8, 9, ff. 44, 209, 58. See also ibid., f. 88. For the petition on behalf of Wilkes, see HM 31583, Stowe Papers, HEHL. For examples of her acting as his secretary or surrogate, see Hester Pitt to Duke of Newcastle, five letters from February–March 1764, Newcastle Papers, Add. MSS 32596, BL; Lady Chatham to John Calcraft Sr., letters from November 1769 through April 1770, Calcraft Papers, Add. MSS 43771, BL, ff. 24, 28, 30, 34, 45 et seq. Volumes 3 and 4 of Taylor and Pringle, *Correspondence of Pitt,* contain numerous examples of her acting as his surrogate; see esp. 3:279 ff.

7. These letters are primarily in Chatham Papers, PRO 30/8; see vols. 5 (William to Hester), 7, 8, 9 (Hester to William). In addition, some letters that passed between them are printed in Taylor and Pringle, *Correspondence of Pitt,* vols. 2–4.

8. Quotations: Lady Chatham to Elizabeth Montagu, 21 May [1774], Montagu Papers, HEHL, MO 4131; Elizabeth Montagu to Lady Chatham, n.d. but 1770s, Chatham Papers, PRO 30/8, 50, ff. 81–82. See generally the letters in Montagu Papers, MO 4129–35; and in Chatham Papers, PRO 30/8, 50. On Montagu, a leader of the London bluestocking circle, see Barbara Brandon Schnorrenberg, "Montagu, Elizabeth," *ODNB* 38:720–25.

9. Hester Chatham to Earl Temple, 17 October 1777, Grenville Papers, Add. MSS 42087, f. 189.

5. Consolidating the Feminine Private

1. Why the young apprentice chose a female persona for his anonymous authorial debut is uncertain, but his brother James and associates often used feminine pseudonyms in satirical pieces; see n. 32, below, for such satirical *New-England Courant* essays.

2. *New-England Courant* (hereafter *NEC*), 2, 16 April 1722. The fourteen Silence Dogood papers are reprinted in Leonard W. Labaree et al., eds., *The Papers of Benjamin Franklin,* 39 vols. (New Haven, Conn.: Yale University Press, 1959–), 1:8–45. Michael Warner, *The Letters of the Republic: Publication and the Public Sphere in Eighteenth-Century America* (Cambridge, Mass.: Harvard University Press, 1990), 82–87, elides the implications of Silence's female persona in an otherwise insightful discussion. Franklin possibly modeled Silence on Mistress Sarah Kemble Knight, a similarly well educated, widowed household head, whom he would probably have known (or known of) in his Boston childhood. Silence's name has been interpreted as a sly riff on the sermons of the Reverend Cotton Mather, opposed by the *NEC* in the 1721 inoculation controversy.

3. Ioan Williams, ed., *The Criticism of Henry Fielding* (London: Routledge and Kegan Paul, 1971), 329. For a full discussion of this source, see chapter 4, n. 38. On rhetorical femininity, see Tedra Osell, "Tatling Women in the Public Sphere: Rhetorical Femininity and the English Essay Periodical," *Eighteenth-Century Studies* 38 (2005): 283–99.

4. *NEC,* 14, 28 May 1722. Ephraim Censorious could well have represented a restatement of objections to the subject of Silence's essay Franklin had heard in the print shop. An *NEC* predecessor for Silence was a nominal Rhode Island spinster who complained about younger women misbehaving in church, in ibid., 16 October 1721.

5. Of the fourteen essays, which appeared at intervals through 8 October 1722, three addressed ungendered subject matter and four others commented briefly on women. The essay criticizing female pride, which Ephraim requested, was published on 11 June.

6. Jenny Distaff first appeared in the tenth *Tatler* essay, and she reappeared periodically thereafter; see Donald F. Bond, ed., *The Tatler,* 3 vols. (Oxford: Clarendon Press, 1987), 1:87 et seq.

7. See primarily G. J. Barker-Benfield, *The Culture of Sensibility: Sex and Society in Eighteenth-Century Britain* (Chicago: University of Chicago Press, 1992); and Michael McKeon, *The Secret History of Domesticity: Public, Private, and the Division of Knowledge* (Baltimore: Johns Hopkins University Press, 2005).

8. For numerous seventeenth-century examples of ungendered meanings for *public* and *private,* see Mary Beth Norton, *Founding Mothers and Fathers: Gendered Power and the Forming of American Society* (New York: Alfred A. Knopf, 1996), 20–24 and passim (hereafter *FM&F*). For Addison and Steele's usage, see, for example, Bond, *Tatler,* 2:457; Donald F. Bond, ed., *The Spectator,* 5 vols. (Oxford: Clarendon Press, 1965), 1:73, 378. Two American examples: Speech of Governor William Burnet, 2 April 1729, in *New-England Weekly Journal* (hereafter *NEWJ*), 7 April 1729; J. Browne, "To the worshipful Mr. Thomas Bordley," *American Weekly Mercury* (hereafter *AWM*), 20 November 1721. See also John Brewer, "This, That and the Other: Public, Social and Private in the Seventeenth and Eighteenth Centuries," in *Shifting the Boundaries: Transformation of the Languages of Public and Private in the Eighteenth Century,* ed. Dario Castiglione and Lesley Sharpe (Exeter, U.K.: University of Exeter Press, 1995), 1–21.

9. Bond, *Spectator,* 3:271–72 (no. 342); Increase Mather, *A Discourse concerning the Death of the Righteous*...(Boston: B. Green, 1711), 18, 23–27 (quotations, 24, 25). Steele tended to use *domestic* as others would later use *private;* see Bond, *Spectator,* 3:32, 4:79. See also the analysis of Anne Hutchinson's failure to employ the concept *private* in the defense of her religious activities, in *FM&F,* 378–82.

10. Bond, *Spectator,* 1:348–49 (no. 81); and chapter 4, n. 14 of this book; [Joseph Breintnall,] "Busy-Body no. 17," *AWM,* 12 June 1729.

11. Quotations: Nathaniel Henchman, *A Holy and Useful Life*...(Boston: S. Kneeland, 1721), 14; Benjamin Colman, *A Holy and Useful Life*...(Boston: B. Green, 1715), 7; "Of Suitable Behaviour to Human Society," *New-York Gazette* (hereafter *NYG*), 11 August 1735. For the *Common Sense* essays: no. 32, reprinted in Williams, *Criticism of Fielding,* 330; no. 135, as reprinted in *New York Weekly Journal* (hereafter *NYWJ*), 22 September 1740. See, on these sources, chapter 4, nn. 38, 41.

12. Bond, *Tatler,* 2:444 (no. 172); 1:430 (no. 62). See also ibid., 1:473. By contrast, the Athenians had asserted that souls had no sex; see *Athenian Mercury* 5:3 (8 December 1691). On another occasion, Steele phrased sexual difference this way: "The Woman's Province is to be careful in her Oeconomy, and chast[e] in her Affection: The Man's, to be active in the Improvement of his Fortune" (Bond, *Tatler,* 1:368). Paradoxically, although Kathryn Shevelow, *Women and Print Culture: The Construction of Femininity in the Early Periodical* (London: Routledge, 1989), recognized that Addison and Steele offered "an early formulation" of "the equation between women's nature and domesticity, which figured the family as an area of private and feminine experience" (140), she employed the anachronistic language of *public* and *private* throughout her otherwise insightful discussion; see her chap. 4 (93–145).

13. Bond, *Spectator,* 2:8–11 (no. 128). See also ibid., 4:21–26 (nos. 433–34).

14. On such patterns, see Charles E. Clark, *The Public Prints: The Newspaper in Anglo-American Culture, 1665–1740* (New York: Oxford University Press, 1994), 141–64, 207–10, 259–65; and Ian K. Steele, *The English Atlantic, 1675–1740: An Exploration of Communication and Community* (New York: Oxford University Press, 1986), 132–68. Steele indicates that, on average, events were reported in the colonial press eighty-three days after they occurred in Europe (ibid., 158). Clark notes that local authors occasionally paid to have their works published in the newspapers. Among the items of English origin, articles taken from the *Gentleman's Magazine* (hereafter *GM*), *London Magazine,* and the mid-eighteenth-century *Universal Spectator* essay series seemed particularly popular with colonial editors.

15. Stephen Botein, "'Meer Mechanics' and an Open Press: The Business and Political Strategies of Colonial American Printers," *Perspectives in American History* 9 (1975): 127–225, focuses largely on political issues but usefully clarifies printers' motivations and gives circulation figures (see 149–50). For literacy information, see E. Jennifer Monaghan, *Learning to Read and Write in Colonial America* (Amherst: University of Massachusetts Press, 2005). The sorts of books available in Boston late in the seventeenth century are listed in the 1700 probate inventory of a Boston bookseller, printed in John Dunton, *Letters from New England* (Boston: Prince Society, 1867), 314–19.

16. Clark, *Public Prints,* 222, 249, 256. Clark, 249, cites the *New-England Weekly Journal* as the one early newspaper that appeared to recognize its partly female audience. David A. Copeland, *Colonial American Newspapers: Character and Content* (Newark: University of Delaware Press, 1997), chap. 6 and appendix 2, discusses the newspapers' lack of content involving women as subjects or presumed readers.

17. See Joel Perlmann and Dennis Shirley, "When Did New England Women Acquire Literacy?" *WMQ,* 3rd ser., 48 (1991): 50–67, with comment by Mary Beth Norton and reply by Perlmann, ibid., 639–48; see also Monaghan, *Learning to Read and Write.* The evidence suggests that American women's literacy expanded significantly no earlier than midcentury. Only two American magazines, one in 1745 and one in 1769, even ventured to publish before the 1770s. Both quickly failed. When Samuel Sewall courted several Boston widows in the 1720s, he took newspapers as gifts, thus implying that without a man in the house the women might not have had regular access to papers. See Richard D. Brown, *Knowledge Is Power: The Diffusion of Information in Early America, 1700–1865* (New York: Oxford University Press, 1989), 38.

18. Untitled, unsigned essay on the character of the fair sex, *NEWJ,* 24 March 1729.

19. *Reflections on Courtship and Marriage: in Two Letters to a Friend...*(Philadelphia: Benjamin Franklin, 1746), 2, 20, 31–33, and passim. The pamphlet, evidently of English origin, is of unknown authorship.

20. See, for instance, "Old Heathen Story," *Maryland Gazette* (hereafter *MG*), 11 March 1728/9, also printed in *Weekly Rehearsal* (hereafter *WR*), 22 May 1732, on the possible separate creation of men and women; and "Homespun Jack," *NEC,* 23 March 1724, expressing concerns about women wearing men's clothing; reprinted in *AWM,* 28 February 1738, from a 1737 issue of the *Boston Weekly Post-Boy* that seems to be no longer extant. On the latter topic, as in so many other regards, colonial writers were echoing the *Spectator;* see Bond, *Spectator,* 1:434–35, 4:28.

21. "Meanwell," untitled essay on patriotism, *NYG,* 15 April 1734; the 1737 essay: *GM* 7 (1737): 554 (see chapter 4, n. 38); *OED,* q.v. *oeconomy, economy.* See also references to both "private Life" and "private Family," in "The True Patriot," an article reprinted from a December 1732 British publication, in *WR,* 4 June 1733. The earliest colonial use of the phrase *private life* I have located is Civicus, "An Essay on Envy, Philosophical and Political," *AWM,* 31 August 1732, referring only to men. The earliest British use of *private life* in a familial context (found through an ECCO full-text search) appears to be J. Morgan, comp., *The New Political State of Great Britain...*(London: A. Campbell, 1730), 1:15. (Earlier British uses of the phrase employed *private* as a synonym for *secluded* or *nonpolitical.*)

22. *Common Sense* 135, 1 September 1739, as reprinted in *NYWJ,* 22 September 1740 (also see chapter 4, n. 41); [A Gentleman], *Man Superior to Woman*...(1739), as reprinted in *Beauty's Triumph*...(London: J. Robinson, 1751), 38.

23. "A Character," *American Magazine and Historical Chronicle* (hereafter *AMHC*) 2 (April 1745): 169. The parameters of *private life* were quite different when applied to men. An English essayist (in a piece reprinted in Boston in 1748, forwarded by a reader) defined a man's "general Character in private Life" as being "honest to his Tradesmen, kind to his Family, regular in his Conduct, not addicted to any notorious Vice, nor in Danger of growing necessitous by living at too much Expence." See "For an Elector," *Independent Advertiser,* 9 May 1748. A rare essay contending that women's household roles affected public welfare was published in the *Boston Evening Post* (hereafter *BEP*), 22 February 1742, submitted by a reader, but it was an excerpt from Richard Allestree's 1667 tract *The Causes of the Decay of Christian Piety,* and so it represented old-fashioned thinking at the time.

24. "U. Loverule," "Offences against Common Sense in the Ladies, particularly Wives," *South Carolina Gazette* (hereafter *SCG*), 27 June 1748. The only eighteenth-century women whose *public* role was recognized were the wives of the colonial governors William Burnet and Jonathan Belcher. See "An Elegy upon Mrs Burnett," *NYG,* 18 December 1727; *AWM,* 2 January 1728; *Boston Gazette* (hereafter *BG*), 15 January 1728; Burnet's husband had been governor of New York and New Jersey, then Massachusetts and Connecticut. Also see Thomas Prince, *Christ Abolishing Death*...(Boston: J. Draper, 1736), 39, a funeral sermon for Mary Belcher, whose husband was then governor of Massachusetts.

25. Quotations in this paragraph and the next two from "C.W." to Mr. [Andrew] Bradford, *AWM,* 15 April 1736; and an untitled article attributed to "forst. serm." [Thomas Forster's Sermons] in *Pennsylvania Gazette* (hereafter *PG*), 8 April 1736. The *PG* author once employed *mankind,* but in a phrase that clearly implied universal masculinity: "he esteems all Mankind as his Brethren."

26. Household expense management: *NEWJ,* 24 November–16 December 1728, passim. Courtship and marriage: e.g., *NEC,* 4 May 1724; *NYG,* 30 December 1734; *Virginia Gazette* (hereafter *VG*), 17 February 1737/8. Some of many misogynist satires: *PG,* 5 September 1734; *New-York Gazette, revived in the Weekly Post-Boy* (hereafter *NYGWPB*), 23 February 1747 [the same piece as in *PG,* adapted to New York)]; *New-York Weekly Post-Boy* (hereafter *NYWPB*), 13 August 1744.

27. For a brief but insightful discussion of the "cognitive dissonance" female writers would experience in such a context, see Warner, *Letters of the Republic,* 15–16. The fullest discussion of rhetorical femininity is Osell, "Tatling Women."

28. Quotations in this paragraph and the next are from "Martia" to the editor, *SCG,* 12 January 1731/2. Cf. other discussions of this exchange in Clark, *Public Prints,* 232–33; Elizabeth Cook, *Literary Influences in Colonial Newspapers, 1704–1750* (New York: Columbia University Press, 1912), 231–32, 234; and Cara Anzilotti, *In the Affairs of the World: Women, Patriarchy, and Power in Colonial South Carolina* (Westport, Conn.: Greenwood Press, 2002), 113.

29. "Rattle" to "Miss Martia's Papa," 22 January 1731/2, *SCG.*

30. Martia to the editor, 29 January 1731/2, ibid. Letters from nominal men in *SCG* continued the dialogue on reputations; see "Honestus," 29 January, and "ZX," 26 February. Letters that spring in *SCG* from nominal women focused on standard

topics: "Flotilla" (women's dress; 1 April); "Penelope Aspen" (gossip; 17 June); and "Laetitia" (beauty; 24 June).

31. Jenny Distaff provides a classic example of a rhetorical woman who never challenged such constraints; indeed, she told readers in July 1709, "you must expect the Advices you meet with in this Paper to be such, as more immediately and naturally fall under the Consideration of our Sex: History therefore written by a woman, you will easily imagine to consist of Love in all its Forms, both in the Abuse of, and Obedience to that Passion." (Bond, *Tatler,* 1:261 [no. 36]).

32. Clark, *Public Prints,* 231–39, has a brief section on women in the colonial press but fails to consider rhetorical femininity. Carla Mulford discusses the difficulties eighteenth-century women faced in trying to publish their work; see Mulford, ed., *Only for the Eye of a Friend: The Poems of Annis Boudinot Stockton* (Charlottesville: University Press of Virginia, 1995), 33–34. The *NEC* and its editor, James Franklin, were particularly notable for contrived satirical dialogues between pseudonymous men and "women"—often the same men. For example, "S.B." (a contributor named Gardner) complained in January 1721/2 of his "Scolding Wife," eliciting replies several weeks later from "Abigail Afterwit" (James Franklin), "Hortensia" (Gardner himself), and "Ann Careful" (Thomas Fleet). For the identification of the authors of these pieces, see Worthington Chauncey Ford, "Franklin's New England Courant," *Collections of the Massachusetts Historical Society* 57 (1923–24): 336–53, esp. 351–53.

33. See, for example, "An Extraordinary Petition to Parliament, from several Ladies of Quality," *SCG,* 28 July 1733 (from the *London Magazine*); petition from "Rachel Wishful" et al., ibid., 11 April 1743 (from the *Universal Spectator*); and "The Humble Petition of a Society of young women known by the Name of *The Petticoat Club ...,*" *NYGWPB,* 20 March 1749, reprinted in *MG,* 26 April 1749, and *SCG,* 22 May 1749. A reply from "A Batchelor" appeared in *New-York Evening Post,* 3 April 1749.

34. See, e.g., Dorothy Forecast, *NEC,* 25 November 1723; Mary Pensive, *NEWJ,* 5 February 1727/8; Mary Meanwell, *SCG,* 26 February 1731/2; and Hester Decent, *NYWJ,* 23 July 1739.

35. Husbands: *AWM,* 12 March 1730; *SCG,* 20 July 1747. Suitors: *NEC,* 19 March 1721/2, and *PG,* 26 June 1732 (the same letter, recycled by Benjamin Franklin); *SCG,* 2 November 1747, also in *MG,* 13 January 1748. Seducers: *NEWJ,* 25 March 1734; *AWM,* 25 November 1736, also in *NYWJ,* 6 December 1736. See also the poem by "Carolina," "On her Father having desir'd her to forbid all young Men the House," *SCG,* 3 August 1747.

36. "The Ladies Complaint," *VG,* 22 October 1736, and *SCG,* 15 August 1743; "Verses written by a young Lady, on Woman born to be controul'd," *SCG,* 21 November 1743; *AMHC* 1 (June 1744): 435; and *American Magazine* 2 (August 1769): 271–72. "The Ladies Complaint" was sung offstage during *The Generous Choice,* performed in London in 1700; the play followed two disguised women as they sought revenge against the man who had seduced them both. See Mr. [Francis] Manning, *The Generous Choice: A Comedy ...*(London: R. Wellington and A. Bettesworth, 1700), 5–6. The second poem, titled "Woman's Hard Fate," by "A Lady," appeared in *GM* 3 (July 1733): 371.

37. The first response poem is "Incog" to editor, *SCG,* 22 August 1743 (a poem that did not appear in *VG*); the author claimed it was "compos'd immediately upon

reading *The Ladies Complaint.*" The second is from *GM* 3 (July 1733): 371, and *SCG,* 11 November 1743.

38. "Deborah Sherman" to Mr. Whitefield, *BEP,* 21 January 1745 (reprinted in *SCG,* 18 March 1745); same to Mr. Fleet, *BEP,* 15 April 1745. On the *BEP,* Thomas Fleet, and the Sherman letters see Harry S. Stout, *The Divine Dramatist: George White-field and the Rise of Modern Evangelicalism* (Grand Rapids, Mich.: William B. Eerdmans, 1991), 187–88, 196–97, but some historians have erroneously cited the satires as genuine statements by a Whitefield follower. For a comment about Whitefield's appeal to women, see Mary Pringle Fenhagen, ed., "Letters and Will of Robert Pringle (1702–1776)," *South Carolina Historical Magazine* 50 (1949): 94. For two letters that used nominal women to make political points about local ordinances in New York, see "Deborah Careful" to Mr. Zenger, 2 September 1734, *NYWJ;* "Deborah Sl——e" to editor, 27 August 1744, *NYWPB.*

39. Thus when Sophia Hume, a Quaker public friend, published a religious tract in 1748, she began by observing that "a Woman's appearing on the Behalf of God and Religion" was "a novel and uncommon Occasion," and that only God's "Favour" had led her to undertake to appear "publickly in Print, or otherwise." She even remarked that she might be thought by readers to be "under some unaccountable Delusion, or affected with religious Madness." See Hume, *An Exhortation to the Inhabitants of the Province of South Carolina* (Philadelphia: William Bradford, 1748), 4.

40. "A General Review of Female Fashions Address'd to the Ladies," *AWM,* 25 November 1731, reprinted (untitled) in *WR,* 10 January, 1731/2; "Betty Pert" to editor, *WR,* 17 January 1731/2. See also the exchange between "I.F." and an unnamed woman in *NYWJ,* 26 June, 10 July 1749. A similar response to satires on women's dress in *Spectator* came from "Dorinda"; see Bond, *Spectator,* 3:161.

41. The first and last quotations in the paragraph come from an exchange published in *NYG,* 7, 13 June 1731 (the initial letter, "from an English paper," was first printed in *MG,* 20 October 1730); the other exchange is from *AWM,* 3, 17 July 1729. See also the attacks on tea as unhealthful, in *NEWJ,* 12, 19 July 1737 (to which no response was printed); and an exchange about the high cost of tea, *BEP,* 18, 25 August 1746.

42. "Generosa" to the editor, *AWM,* 5 January 1730/1, reprinted in *BG,* 15 February 1730/1. (I was unable to locate the essay to which she was responding.) "Generosa" was identified as Elizabeth Magawlay by David S. Shields; see his "The Wits and Poets of Pennsylvania: New Light on the Rise of Belles Lettres in Provincial Pennsylvania, 1720–1740," *Pennsylvania Magazine of History and Biography* 109 (1985): 100–102.

43. "Unpolish'd Thoughts" submitted to editor by H.C., *VG,* 20 May 1737, reprinted with some variations from *PG,* 8 October 1730. See a modern reprint in J. A. Leo Lemay, ed., *Benjamin Franklin: Writings* (New York: Library of America, 1987), 151–55 (not included in Labaree et al., *Papers of Franklin,* because Franklin's authorship was not confirmed at the time volume 1 was published).

44. "Andromache" to editor, 22 May, *VG,* 3 June 1737.

45. The untitled, unsigned essay was published in *AWM,* 17 September 1730. In diaries and letters, women railed about men's misogynistic comments: see, for example, Susan Klepp and Karin Wulf, eds., *The Diary of Hannah Callender Sansom: Sense and Sensibility in the Age of the American Revolution* (Ithaca: Cornell University

Press, 2010), 48, 56, 90; Carol F. Karlsen and Laurie Crumpacker, eds., *The Journal of Esther Edwards Burr, 1754–1757* (New Haven, Conn.: Yale University Press, 1984), 257. In 1756, Annis Boudinot replied in verse to "A Sarcasm against the ladies in a newspaper," but her poem was not published until 1805; see Mulford, *Only for the Eye of a Friend,* 74.

46. This paragraph and the next five summarize my reading of numerous books and articles on the architectural history of the seventeenth- and eighteenth-century American colonies. Few of these works discuss the gendered dimensions of housing design. Among the most important for my thinking have been the following: Richard L. Bushman, *The Refinement of America: Persons, Houses, Cities* (New York: Alfred A. Knopf, 1992), chap. 4; Edward A. Chappell, "Housing a Nation: The Transformation of Living Standards in Early America," in *Of Consuming Interests: The Style of Life in the Eighteenth Century,* ed. Cary Carson, Ronald Hoffman, and Peter J. Albert (Charlottesville: University Press of Virginia, 1994), 167–232; John E. Crowley, *The Invention of Comfort: Sensibilities and Design in Early Modern Britain and Early America* (Baltimore: Johns Hopkins University Press, 2001); Abbott Lowell Cummings, *The Framed Houses of Massachusetts Bay, 1625–1725* (Cambridge, Mass.: Harvard University Press, 1979), chap. 3 and appendix; Abbott Lowell Cummings, "Inside the Massachusetts House," in *Common Places: Readings in American Vernacular Architecture,* ed. Dell Upton and John Michael Vlach (Athens: University of Georgia Press, 1986), 219–39; Willie Graham, Carter L. Hudgins, Carl R. Lounsbury, Fraser D. Neiman, and James P. Whittenburg, "Adaptation and Innovation: Archaeological and Architectural Perspectives on the Seventeenth-Century Chesapeake," *WMQ,* 3rd ser., 64 (2007): 451–522; Bernard Herman, *Town House: Architecture and Material Life in the Early American City, 1780–1830* (Chapel Hill: University of North Carolina Press, 2005); James Horn, *Adapting to a New World: English Society in the Seventeenth-Century Chesapeake* (Chapel Hill: University of North Carolina Press, 1994), chap. 7; Jessica Kross, "Mansions, Men, Women, and the Creation of Multiple Publics in Eighteenth-Century North America," *Journal of Social History* (hereafter *JSH*) 33 (1999–2000): 385–408; McKeon, *Secret History of Domesticity,* chap. 5; Susan M. Stabile, *Memory's Daughters: The Material Culture of Remembrance in Eighteenth-Century America* (Ithaca: Cornell University Press, 2004), chap. 1; Robert Blair St. George, "'Set Thine House in Order': The Domestication of the Yeomanry in Seventeenth-Century New England," in *New England Begins: The Seventeenth Century,* 3 vols. (Boston: Museum of Fine Arts, 1982), 2:159–88; Kevin M. Sweeney, "Furniture and the Domestic Environment in Wethersfield, Connecticut, 1639–1800," in *Material Life in America, 1600–1860,* ed. Robert Blair St. George (Boston: Northeastern University Press, 1988), 261–90; Dell Upton, "Vernacular Domestic Architecture in Eighteenth-Century Virginia," in Upton and Vlach, *Common Places,* 315–35; and Mark R. Wenger, "The Central Passage in Virginia: Evolution of an Eighteenth-Century Living Space," in *Perspectives in Vernacular Architecture, II,* ed. Camille Wells (Columbia: University of Missouri Press, 1986), 137–49.

47. The 1798 direct tax lists show that most American houses remained small and poorly constructed in the late eighteenth century, with relatively few houses having differentiated spaces even then; see Carole Shammas, "The Housing Stock of the Early United States: Refinement Meets Migration," *WMQ,* 3rd ser., 64 (2007): 549–87. An example of a small dwelling, described by a witness as "a very good

House—better than common for that part of the Country," was a farmhouse near Albany owned by a loyalist couple. In testimony in 1785, the widow Mary Swords told the loyalist claims commission that her lost home had "two Rooms on a Floor besides 2 small Bed Rooms." See Audit Office (hereafter AO) 12/20, ff. 272–73, TNA.

48. See Bushman, *Refinement of America,* chap. 4; and Kross, "Mansions, Men, Women," on the development of specialized entertainment spaces.

49. For instance, see Elaine Forman Crane et al., eds., *The Diary of Elizabeth Drinker,* 3 vols. (Boston: Northeastern University Press, 1991), 1:xxxi, for telling observations on the flexible nature of sleeping arrangements in the Drinker household.

50. Mary Beth Norton, ed., " 'My Resting Reaping Times': Sarah Osborn's Defense of Her 'Unfeminine' Activities, 1767," *Signs: Journal of Women in Culture and Society* 2 (1976): 527.

51. See Stabile, *Memory's Daughters,* 24, 52, 92, on "closets" as small feminine spaces; and also Cummings, "Inside the Massachusetts House," 227. My thanks to Bernard Herman for a conversation on the subject of such closets. Cf. Kross, "Mansions, Men, Women," 396–401, which advances a different interpretation of tea tables. Cynthia Kierner, *Beyond the Household: Women's Place in the Early South, 1700–1835* (Ithaca: Cornell University Press, 1998), chap. 2, stresses the importance of dancing assemblies rather than tea tables as female-dominated sociable spaces.

52. Quotation: "Philopatriae" to editor, *BG,* 17 November 1747. On tea drinking in general, see David S. Shields, *Civil Tongues and Polite Letters in British America* (Chapel Hill: University of North Carolina Press, 1997), chap. 4, esp. 114; Shields, "Eighteenth-Century Literary Culture," in *The Colonial Book in the Atlantic World,* ed. Hugh Amory and David D. Hall (Chapel Hill: University of North Carolina Press, 2007), 460–61; and Beth Kowaleski-Wallace, "Tea, Gender, and Domesticity in Eighteenth-Century England," in Carla H. Hay and Syndy M. Conger, eds., *Studies in Eighteenth-Century Culture* 23 (1994): 131–45. In the cumulative index to Bond, *Spectator,* vol. 5, references to tea drinking, tea tables, and so forth occupy almost an entire column. The earliest reference to tea-drinking women I have found in the American newspapers is an essay by "Sisyphus" (Mr. Gardner) in *NEC,* 2 April 1722. Joseph Browne's letter to Thomas Bordley, printed in *AWM,* 20 November 1721, mentions a "Tea Table Report" about Bordley's wife but does not specify the sex of the tea-drinking gossipers, though presumably they were female. See, on tea's history, Alan Macfarlane and Iris Macfarlane, *The Empire of Tea: The Remarkable History of the Plant That Took over the World* (New York: Overlook Press, 2004); and Beatrice Hohenegger, *Liquid Jade: The Story of Tea from East to West* (New York: St. Martin's Press, 2006).

53. Ridris Roth, "Tea-Drinking in Eighteenth-Century America: Its Etiquette and Equipage," in St. George, *Material Life,* 439–62. Herman, *Town House,* 193, cites the inventory of a poor Baltimore artisan; among the family's listed possessions were a tea caddy and a tea tray (but no teapot or china cups). The exhibition catalog *Tea Drinking in the West* ([Nagoya, Japan:] Nagoya/Boston Museum of Fine Arts, 2001) illustrates tea dishes, pots, bowls, spoons, and other tea-related items.

54. Carole Shammas, *The Pre-industrial Consumer in England and America* (Oxford: Clarendon Press, 1990), 181–88, esp. 186; Shammas, "The Domestic Environment in Early Modern England and America," *JSH* 14 (1980): 14–17; Abbott Lowell Cummings, ed., *Rural Household Inventories: Establishing the Names, Uses and Furnishings of*

Rooms in the Colonial New England Home, 1675–1775 (Boston: Society for the Preservation of New England Antiquities, 1964), 115, 124, 147, 165, 191, 199 (for the earliest appearances of various tea-related items); Sweeney, "Furniture and the Domestic Environment," 261–90, esp. 274. But cf. on backcountry families in Virginia, Ann Smart Martin, *Buying into the World of Goods: Early Consumers in Backcountry Virginia* (Baltimore: Johns Hopkins University Press, 2008), 83–84, 124–27, suggesting that tea was not as popular there.

55. Quotations: Adolph B. Benson, ed. and trans., *Peter Kalm's Travels in North America*, 2 vols. (New York: Wilson-Erickson, 1937), 1:190; Katherine Hay to Sibyll Farnham, 23 June 1778, Hay Papers, Massachusetts Historical Society, Boston. For a gift of tea, see *Papers of the Lloyd Family of the Manor of Queens Village…, New-York Historical Society Collections* 59 (New York, 1926), 1:416 (also 439, for a reference to well-used teaspoons). For women's diaries noting tea drinking in Philadelphia, see Crane et al., *Diary of Drinker*; and Klepp and Wulf, *Diary of Sansom*. Both Elizabeth Drinker and Hannah Callender Sansom had tea in single-sex and mixed-sex groups.

56. In order, the sources describing these objects are AO 13/91, f. 3; AO 12/30, f. 358; AO 13/68, f. 261; AO 13/90, ff. 175–76; AO 13/126, f. 498; AO 13/80, f. 269; AO 13/79, f. 540; and AO 13/131, ff. 10–11.

57. Klepp and Wulf, *Sansom Diary*, 189; Cummings, *Rural Household Inventories*, esp. 169–71; Cummings, "Inside the Massachusetts House," 229.

58. Grace Galloway to Elizabeth Nickleson, 6 November 1753, HM 36845, Joseph Galloway Papers, HEHL. But "what is Much More disagreeable" even than the tea ritual with the women, she reported in the same letter, was that all her new husband's male friends called in the mornings for a week after the wedding to drink punch and to kiss her. "Nothing in Nature can be more Confounding then to be drag'd into the Company of 12 or 16 men in a Morning Just to be kiss'd & stared at" with no other woman present, Grace wrote, estimating that "Upwards of seventy Men" had kissed her that week. See also Herman, *Town House*, 73–75, on tea-drinking rituals; and his chapter on "the widow's dower" (155–91) on how the needs of sociability could affect a widow's share of her deceased husband's house. My thanks to Joseph Roach for the information about the need to pour tea slowly.

59. Catherine L. Courreye Blecki and Karin A. Wulf, eds., *Milcah Martha Moore's Book: A Commonplace Book from Revolutionary America* (University Park: Pennsylvania State University Press, 1997), 299. When drinking tea became politicized because of British tax policy in the 1770s, Griffitts lamented: "Why all their [revolutionaries'] Malice shewn to tea / So near, so dear—belov'd by me, / Reviving Draught, when I am dry—/ Tea I must have, or I shall dye." And to that poem her friend Susanna Wright added a note: "Alas! how could the wise & generous gent. who compos'd the Congress be so cruel to the whole female World, to debar them so totally of their favourite Potation?…I cannot for my Life see the propriety of making this innocent aliment the chief object of their Vengeance" (ibid., 247, 250).

60. Bond, *Spectator*, 1:21 (no. 4); "The Journal of a Modern Lady in a Letter to a Lady of Quality," *AWM*, 13 August 1730, identified as reprinted from "FOG's Weekly Journal." The one time a purported tea-table conversation (between two women, Lady Lurewell and Lady Loveless) was reproduced at length in the American press, it consisted not of scandal but of advice about how to deal with a husband who spent his time "Drinking, Gaming, and Whoring." See the dialogue "The Female

Council…at a Tea-Table Conference," printed seriatim in *Father Abraham's Alma-nack*…(Philadelphia: W. Dunlap, 1765–68), from August 1766 through March 1769, unpaginated. (Thanks to Karin Wulf for this reference.)

61. "The Advantages of a mutual Correspondence between the two Sexes," *SCG,* 6 December 1742 (identified as from *GM,* June 1742); "The Monitor No. 7," *VG,* 17 September 1736; "X," *NEWJ,* 4 December 1727; "Of Slander," printed in both *WR,* 12 February 1732/3, and *BG,* 24 September 1739 (identified as from the *Weekly Register*); "Tom Trueman" to editor, *Rhode-Island Gazette,* 18 October 1732. On rare occasions writers would blame men for such gossip too; thus "An Essay on Scandal and Evil-Speaking" remarked that *"if its fatal Streams* rise over the *Tea-Table,* the *Bottle* and *Bowl* have *their Share too* in the *Infection,"* and went on to decry men's penchant for slanderous talk. See *AMHC* 1 (December 1744): 670–77 (quotation, 670). See also, for example, the letter from "Philanthropos," *BG,* 17 February 1734/5.

62. "Anthony Afterwit" to editor, *PG,* 10 July 1732 (reprinted in Labaree et al., *Papers of Franklin,* 1:237–40); Carl Van Doren, ed., *The Letters of Benjamin Franklin and Jane Mecom* (Princeton, N.J.: Princeton University Press, 1950), 35.

63. "Alice Addertongue" to editor, *PG,* 12 September 1732 (reprinted in Labaree et al., *Papers of Franklin,* 1:243–48); "Patience Teacraft," "The Tea-Table," *PG,* 31 May 1733. Franklin claimed to have reprinted "The Tea-Table" from the *Rhode-Island Gazette,* but I have not located an issue that included the Teacraft essay. J. A. Leo Lemay attributed "Patience Teacraft" to James Franklin, then the publisher of that paper, and it was not included in *Papers of Franklin,* but the style seems to me unmistakable—very like Benjamin and unlike James's contributions to the *NEC.* When Benjamin, as "Janus," was editing *NEC* while his brother was in jail in Boston in 1723, a letter purportedly from his cousin, "Bridget Bisrous," attacked scandalous tea-table conversation. It is unclear whether Benjamin had a hand in drafting that critique (*NEC,* 19 August 1723).

64. "Penelope Aspen" to editor, *SCG,* 17 June 1732. "Penelope" was clearly familiar with Addison's negative views of women's conversation; see, e.g., Bond, *Spectator,* 1:67–68, 2:458–62, 499.

65. See, for example, Louis B. Wright and Marion Tinling, eds., *William Byrd of Virginia: The London Diary (1717–1721) and Other Writings* (New York: Oxford University Press, 1958), 399, 401, 403 (an unusual day when Byrd drank tea with another man and no women); Mabel L. Webber, ed., "Extracts from the Journal of Mrs. Ann Manigault, 1754–1781," *South Carolina Historical and Genealogical Magazine* 20 (1919): 59, 63.

66. Susan Stabile, "Salons and Power in the Era of Revolution: From Literary Coteries to Epistolary Enlightenment," in *Benjamin Franklin and Women,* ed. Larry E. Tise (University Park: Pennsylvania State University Press, 2000), 132–33; "To the Reformer of Manners: The Petition of Several of the young Tradesmen and Artificers…" published in both *AWM,* 29 May 1729, and *NYG,* 13 June 1731. See also Busy-Body no. 19, *AWM,* 26 June 1729, in which the Busy-Body (Joseph Breintnall) admitted being confused by the rapid repartee at a tea table he attended.

67. Alexander Hamilton, *The History of the Ancient and Honorable Tuesday Club,* 3 vols., ed. Robert Miklus (Chapel Hill: University of North Carolina Press, 1990), 3:130, 132.

68. Klepp and Wulf, *Sansom Diary*, 83, 48, 73, 81–82, 132, 128. Hannah herself directly encountered scandals when she tried to help a lone woman traveler to Philadelphia in February 1759, only to discover that the woman in question was in the midst of eloping to Long Island with an older husband (ibid., 90, 92, 95); and when her own maidservant was seduced and abandoned in 1769 (ibid., 238).

69. "Letter to a Lady on her Marriage," *NEWJ*, 15 February 1730/1 (with a second part published 1 March). Also reprinted in *AMHC* 3 (September 1746): 399–404, where it is identified as by Swift; and as an appendix to *Reflections on Courtship and Marriage*. Swift wrote this missive in 1727, directing it to an acquaintance, Deborah Rochefort. In the same letter Swift also told her that no matter how much she read she could never "arise in point of Learning to any great perfection."

70. Karlsen and Crumpacker, *Journal of Burr*, 257. Another eighteenth-century man who made this point was James Fordyce, *Sermons to Young Women*, 6th ed., 2 vols., (London: D. Payne, 1766), 1:78. He too was challenged, as one teenaged Philadelphian wrote to another, "How can my Fordyce say that there cant be friendship between Girls, if it is not true love and friendship, what is it I feel for thee—nothing less I am sure" (Peggy Emlen to Sally Logan, 4th day afternoon, 1768, in Margery P. M. Brown Collection, box 1, Historical Society of Pennsylvania).

71. Karlsen and Crumpacker, eds., *Journal of Burr*, 256.

72. Peggy Emlen to Sally Logan, 4th day afternoon, 1768, Margery P. M. Brown Collection, box 1; Anne Moore to Anne DeLancey, n.d. [early 1760s], "DeLancey Reminiscences," DeLancey Papers, Museum of the City of New York; Sarah Hanschurst to Sally Forbes, 1762, Sarah Hanschurst Letterbook, Library of Congress Manuscript Division; Christian Barnes to Elizabeth Smith, 26 May 1770, Christian Barnes Letterbook, ibid. See my *Liberty's Daughters: The Revolutionary Experience of American Women, 1750–1800* (Boston: Little, Brown, 1980; Ithaca: Cornell University Press, 1996), esp. 105–9, for more on such relationships. Mulford, *Only for the Eye of a Friend*, 5, stresses the importance of female friends for Annis Stockton.

73. Harriott Horry Ravenel, *Eliza Pinckney* (New York: Charles Scribner's Sons, 1896), 117; Elise Pinckney, ed., *The Letterbook of Eliza Lucas Pinckney, 1739–1762* (Columbia: University of South Carolina Press, 1997; orig. pub. 1972), 46; Karlsen and Crumpacker, *Journal of Burr*, 307.

Conclusion

1. *A True Copy of the Petition of the Gentle-women, & Trades-mens wives*...(London: J. Wright, 1642); *To the Right Honorable the high Court of Parliament: The Humble Petition of many hundreds of distressed Women, Trades-mens Wives, and Widdowes* (London: John Hammond, 1642), "The humble petition of many poore distressed women...," 1 February 1641/2, HO/PO/JO/10/1/115, Parliamentary Archives, Houses of Parliament, London. Later in the 1640s, female Levellers were more likely to refer to themselves as *women*, though they usually also mentioned husbands and families in the text of the petitions. See *To the Supream Authority of this Nation*...*The Humble Petition of divers well-affected Women*...(London: [no pub.,] 1649); *To the Supreme Authority of England*...*The Humble Petition of divers well-affected Women*...([London: no pub., 1649]). Rachel Weil makes a similar observation in *Political Passions: Gender, the Family and Political Argument in England, 1680–1714* (Manchester, U.K.: Manchester University Press, 1999), 4.

2. Hannah Woolley, *The Gentlewoman's Companion; or, A Guide to the Female Sec: containing Directions of Behaviour, in all Places, Companies, Relations, and Conditions, from their Childhood down to Old Age*...(London: A. Maxwell, 1673), title page; [Richard Allestree], *The Ladies Calling, in Two Parts* (Oxford: printed at the Theater, 1673); *The Ladies Library*, 3rd ed. (London: Jacob Tonson, 1722).

3. Cotton Mather, *Ornaments for the Daughters of Zion...which Directs the Female-Sex...in Every Age and State of their Life* (Boston: Bartholomew and Samuel Green, 1692); Harriott Horry Ravenel, *Eliza Pinckney* (New York: Charles Scribner's Sons, 1896), 115–17. A special issue of *South Carolina Historical Magazine*, 99 (July 1998), has three useful essays on Pinckney, clarifying some aspects of her personal biography.

4. Although it deals with a later time period, Denise Riley, *Am I That Name? Feminism and the Category of "Women" in History* (Minneapolis: University of Minnesota Press, 1988), addresses an issue similar to the one I am raising here. Misogynist texts of the *querelle des femmes* had of course long attacked *women,* and other texts had equally defended *women,* but my reference here is not to those stylized, formulaic debates but rather to quotidian practice, which, especially the usage of colonial women themselves, did not reflect the new phraseology consistently until the middle of the century.

5. Raymond A. Craig, *A Concordance to the Complete Works of Anne Bradstreet: A Special Edition of Studies in Puritan American Spirituality,* 2 vols. (Lewiston, N.Y.: Edwin Mellen Press, 2000). Bradstreet used *lady/ladies* 13 times, *male* once, *sex* in conjunction with *her* 5 times, and *gentleman* or *gentlewoman* not at all.

6. Benjamin Colman, *The Duty and Honour of Aged Women*...(Boston: B. Green, 1711), 11 (see also his "dedication" to the "Gentlewomen of Boston," who asked him to publish the sermon, i–iv); Laurel Thatcher Ulrich, "Vertuous Women Found: New England Ministerial Literature, 1668–1735," *American Quarterly* 28 (1976): 20–40. Cynthia Kierner, *Beyond the Household: Women's Place in the Early South, 1700–1835* (Ithaca: Cornell University Press, 1998), 41–42, in a very different context points to the 1730s as a time in which new public rituals revolving around women appeared in the South, suggesting a similar gendering process in that region.

7. Quotations in this paragraph and the next are from Benjamin Colman, *Reliquae Turellae, et Lachrymae Paternae*...(Boston: S. Kneeland and T. Green, 1735), 48, 60, 73, 75, 78. For a dated but still useful biographical study, see Clayton Harding Chapman, "Benjamin Colman's Daughters," *New England Quarterly* 26 (1953): 169–92. Ulrich points to another aspect of the same publication as a turning point—the terms used to describe Jane in an appended poem by a male admirer; see Ulrich, "Vertuous Women," 38. Later sermons continued the trend; see, for example, Charles Chauncy, *Joy, the Duty of Survivors, on the Death of Pious Friends and Relatives*...(Boston: S. Kneeland and T. Green, 1741), 19–23.

8. "Orinda" was the pseudonym used by Katherine Phillips, a much-admired poet who died in 1684. Jane and Ebenezer Turell were older than Eliza Lucas, yet displayed such gendered awareness earlier than she did. Boston had closer links to England than South Carolina, both because of the shorter sailing time across the Atlantic and the earlier and more numerous newspapers (the *South Carolina Gazette* was not founded until 1732, by which time Boston already had several weekly papers), which could help to explain the difference in language. Cara Anzilotti, *In the Affairs of the World: Women, Patriarchy, and Power in Colonial South Carolina* (Westport, Conn.: Greenwood Press, 2002), argues that gender did not become the crucial marker of

standing in that colony until the nineteenth century; see 1–12 (esp. 8) and 187–94 (esp. 188). (But see Eliza Pinckney's phraseology in the 1760s, quoted below.)

9. *Papers of the Lloyd Family of the Manor of Queens Village…Collections of the New-York Historical Society* 59 (hereafter *NYHS Colls*) (New York, 1926), 1:300, 301 (see 298–302 passim), 429, 430 (see also 428, 435, 2:590); Mary Lloyd, *Meditations on Divine Subjects: To which is Prefixed, an Account of her Life and Character, by E. Pemberton* (New York: J. Parker, 1750), 19, 4 (see also 7–33 passim). Mary Pemberton Lloyd was born in 1681, and her own religious meditations, printed, ibid., following 33, were ungendered, contrasting sharply with the rhetoric employed by the considerably younger Jane Turell, cited in n. 7, above.

10. The general observations about gendered patterns of correspondence are based on my reading of the family letters in *Letters and Papers of Cadwallader Colden, 9, NYHS Colls* 68 (1935), 1–184. A good brief introduction to this family is Brooke Hindle, "A Colonial Governor's Family: The Coldens of Coldengham," *New-York Historical Society Quarterly* 45 (1961): 233–50. Almost all the letters from the period in which women discussed political or military affairs (quoted in chapter 4) were addressed to men.

11. *Letters and Papers of Cadwallader Colden, 5, NYHS Colls* 54 (1921): 29, 203 (see also 37, 39, 217). For his quite different comments on the education of two young grandsons at about the same time, see ibid., 4, *NYHS Colls* 53 (1920): 339–40.

12. Elise Pinckney, ed., *The Letterbook of Eliza Lucas Pinckney* (Columbia: University of South Carolina Press, 1997; orig. pub. 1972), 184–85. See also other letters from the early 1760s that use "her sex" (178) and "my sex in general" (152). The contents of two letters from the 1740s with like locutions—"my own sex" (27) and "woman" (31)—are less sweeping in their application of the words. A comparison of the poetic works of two female Pennsylvanians transcribed in a commonplace book indicates a transition to more gendered language from Susanna Wright (b. 1697) to Hannah Griffits (b. 1727). Cf. Catherine L. Courreye Blecki and Karin A. Wulf, eds., *Milcah Martha Moore's Book: A Commonplace Book from Revolutionary America* (University Park: Pennsylvania State University Press, 1997), nos. 1–26 (Wright's poems) and nos. 30–47 (Griffits's poems).

13. Susan Klepp and Karin Wulf, eds., *The Diary of Hannah Callender Sansom: Sense and Sensibility in the Age of the American Revolution* (Ithaca: Cornell University Press, 2010), 55, 63, 69, 80, 192, 214. Hannah was avidly reading the *Spectator* and Addison's *Works* at the same time she was penning the 1758 entries; see ibid., 50, 74, 78, 81. For a discussion of self-reflective and gendered language used by women in the 1770s and 1780s and its implications, see Mary Beth Norton, *Liberty's Daughters: The Revolutionary Experience of American Women, 1750–1800* (Boston: Little, Brown, 1980; Ithaca: Cornell University Press, 1996), 111–24.

14. On the revolutionary disruptions and the Ladies Association, see Norton, *Liberty's Daughters,* chaps. 6, 7 (esp. 177–88). The Ladies Association organized in four states: Pennsylvania, New Jersey, Maryland, and Virginia.

15. This paragraph summarizes the argument in Rosemarie Zagarri, *Revolutionary Backlash: Women and Politics in the Early American Republic* (Philadelphia: University of Pennsylvania Press, 2007), chaps. 3–5, although she fails to note the parallel to Addison.

16. These developments may be traced in Linda K. Kerber, *Women of the Republic: Intellect and Ideology in Revolutionary America* (Chapel Hill: University of North Carolina Press, 1980); Norton, *Liberty's Daughters,* chaps. 8, 9; Jan Lewis, "The Republican Wife: Virtue and Seduction in the Early Republic," *WMQ,* 3rd ser., 44 (1987): 689–721; Anne Boylan, *The Origins of Women's Activism: New York and Boston, 1797–1840* (Chapel Hill: University of North Carolina Press, 2002); Elizabeth R. Varon, *We Mean to Be Counted: White Women and Politics in Antebellum Virginia* (Chapel Hill: University of North Carolina Press, 1998); Mary Hershberger, "Mobilizing Women, Anticipating Abolition: The Struggle against Indian Removal in the 1830s," *Journal of American History* 86 (1999): 15–40; Alisse Theodore Portnoy, "'Female Petitioners Can Lawfully Be Heard': Negotiating Female Decorum, United States Politics, and Political Agency, 1829–1831," *Journal of the Early Republic* 23 (2003): 573–610; Susan Zaeske, *Signatures of Citizenship: Petitioning, Antislavery, and Women's Political Identity* (Chapel Hill: University of North Carolina Press, 2003); and Judith Wellman, *The Road to Seneca Falls: Elizabeth Cady Stanton and the First Woman's Rights Convention* (Urbana: University of Illinois Press, 2004).

17. On the Duchess of Devonshire and other female political activists of the late eighteenth century in England, see Judith Lewis, "1784 and All That: Aristocratic Women and Electoral Politics," in *Women, Privilege, and Power: British Politics, 1750 to the Present,* ed. Amanda Vickery (Stanford, Calif.: Stanford University Press, 2001), 89–122; Susan Kingsley Kent, *Gender and Power in Britain, 1640–1990* (London: Routledge, 1999), 101–25, esp. 120; Linda Colley, *Britons: Forging the Nation, 1707–1837,* 2nd ed. (New Haven, Conn.: Yale University Press, 2005), 236–81, esp. 242–50; and esp. Elaine Chalus, *Elite Women in English Political Life, c. 1754–1790* (Oxford: Clarendon Press, 2005). Not all of these historians concur with my interpretation of reactions to the 1784 campaign.

❧ INDEX

abortion, 96
Adams, Abigail, 138–139
Adams, John, 138–139
Addison, Joseph: biography of, 112; and
 gender difference, 149; influence of, in
 America, 123, 126–127, 133, 138–139,
 153; influence of, in England, 140–143;
 popularity of, in America, 119; and pri-
 vate, 145–148; references to, in America,
 119, 161, 170; on women and politics,
 114–116, 118, 121. See also *Spectator;
 Tatler*
"Advice to a Lady" (Lyttelton), 126
"Advice to a Young Lady Lately Married,"
 6–7
Allestree, Richard, 87, 176
American Revolution, 180
American Weekly Mercury (Philadelphia),
 120, 160
Annapolis (Md.), 170
Anne (queen of England), 73–74, 110–111,
 180; John Dunton on, 100–103
anonymity: in *Athenian Mercury,* 78, 80, 83;
 of women's published letters, 88
Antigua, 176
Aristophanes, 44–45, 54
Assembly: of Virginia, 14–16
Astell, Mary, 77
Athenian Mercury, 76–77, 108, 111–112;
 female poets in, 87–88; female readers of,
 85–86, 89, 93, 95; gender difference in,
 96–97, 99; love and marriage in, 91–93;
 personal problems in, 80, 83, 85, 93–96;
 plan of, 78–82; success of, 80, 90. *See also*
 Dunton, John
Athenian Oracle, The, 90
Athenian Society, 80–82; illustration of, 84;
 women's letters to, 87–88

Bacon, Nathaniel, 30; biography of, 13;
 death of, 20; and Lady Frances Berkeley,

10, 13–14, 17–19; and Sir William
 Berkeley, 9–10, 13–14. *See also* Bacon's
 Rebellion
Bacon, Nathaniel Sr. (cousin of rebel), 13,
 17, 19, 28, 190n11, 195n43
Bacon, Thomas (father of rebel), 13, 17
Bacon's Rebellion, 14–16, 20–23, 27–28;
 high-status women and, 34–37. *See also*
 Bacon, Nathaniel
bastardy, 94–96
Beauty's Triumph, 132
Behn, Aphra, 87
Berkeley, Lady Frances: and Bacon's Rebellion, 10, 16; biography of, 10–13; and
 family property, 22, 29–31; and husband,
 13–14, 17–20, 22–28; insults commissioners, 23–27; and kin, 14; marriages of,
 11, 13, 33–34; and Nathaniel Bacon, 10,
 13–14, 17–19; opposes Herbert Jeffreys,
 31–33; portrait of, 12; and Sarah Drummond, 28–31; as state actor, 19–20, 22,
 31–34; and Thomas, Lord Culpeper, 33
Berkeley, Sir William: and aftermath of
 Bacon's Rebellion, 20–23, 32, 34; biography
 of, 11–13; and Herbert Jeffreys, 26–27;
 and Indian trade, 15; and investigative
 commissioners, 21–26; marriage of, 11, 13;
 and Nathaniel Bacon, 9–10, 13–14; and
 origins of Bacon's Rebellion, 15–16; and
 wife, 13–14, 17–20, 22–27; and William
 Drummond, 28
Berry, Sir John, 20, 28–29. *See also* commissioners, English
Beverley, Robert, 31
Bishops' Wars, 43
Blount, Sir Henry, 57–58
Board of Trade, 124
books, British. *See* publications, British
Boston (Mass.), 37–39, 105–107, 120–121,
 135; John Dunton in, 87
Boston Evening Post, 158